"Very few executives or board members look forward to the annual corporate clairvoyant ritual known as strategic planning, in no small part because of the unspoken recognition that 'our' crystal ball's vision of the future has no greater fidelity than the competition's glass sphere. Since luck has rarely proved to be a sustainable business model, there exists a desperate need for a system to implement that can manage the unmanageable: how do you commit resources now to service customers and markets that will emerge in a distant and inherently unpredictable future? Just as Raynor succeeded in unlocking the mysteries behind innovation in *The Innovator's Solution, The Strategy Paradox* provides an intelligent, robust, practical compass that the nontelepathic can use to navigate through the inevitable course corrections that will be required along the journey to success. Drawing upon extensive data from business, probability, mathematical and behavioral sciences, and graphically illustrating his thesis with real-world examples of both successes AND failures, Raynor beautifully explains how to create a portfolio of strategic options that will allow curative interventions as unforeseen circumstances and developments are inescapably encountered. . . . Raynor's approach to strategic planning is not only the best manual on the subject written to date, it is an essential survival tool."

—William Hunter, M.D., Founder, President,
and CEO, Angiotech Pharmaceuticals

"A rare and extremely valuable gem among countless 'also-ran' strategy texts. . . . Raynor provides managers a sophisticated, accessible, and highly usable approach weaving time, choice, uncertainty, and risk into a rich treasury of insights, highlighted by strategic flexibility, an intricate and powerful concept augmented by a practical toolkit that offers managers the possibility of true competitive advantage."

—Andy Boynton, Dean, The Wallace E. Carroll
School of Management, Boston College

"*The Strategy Paradox* is a most extraordinary business book: impeccably researched and argued, brutally honest and devoid of 'silver bullet' solutions to today's complex strategy problems. It has profound implications for business-strategy research, teaching, and practice and should be read by anyone interested in why some strategies succeed while other equally thoughtful strategies fail."

—Hugh Courtney, Distinguished Tyser Teaching Fellow,
University of Maryland, author of *20/20 Foresight:
Crafting Strategy in an Uncertain World*

THE

WHY COMMITTING TO SUCCESS

STRATEGY

LEADS TO FAILURE

PARADOX

(AND WHAT TO DO ABOUT IT)

MICHAEL E. RAYNOR

CURRENCY

DOUBLEDAY

NEW YORK LONDON TORONTO SYDNEY AUCKLAND

A CURRENCY BOOK
PUBLISHED BY DOUBLEDAY

Published in the United States by Doubleday, an imprint of The Doubleday Broadway
Publishing Group, a division of Random House, Inc., New York.
www.currencybooks.com

CURRENCY is a trademark of Random House, Inc., and DOUBLEDAY is a registered
trademark of Random House, Inc.

Book design by Tina Henderson

Library of Congress Cataloging-in-Publication Data
Raynor, Michael E.
The Strategy paradox : why committing to success leads to failure (and what to do
about it) / by Michael E. Raynor. — 1st ed.
p. cm.
1. Strategic planning. 2. Uncertainty. 3. Risk management. I. Title.

HD30.28.R384 2007
658.4'012—dc22

2006024888

ISBN: 978-0-385-51622-8

PRINTED IN THE UNITED STATES OF AMERICA

10 9 8 7 6 5 4 3 2

To the future . . . whatever it may be.

CONTENTS

ACKNOWLEDGMENTS

I have read several hundred business books in the course of writing this one, and I have always paused to read the Acknowledgments page, generally out of idle curiosity. Some of the books I read are seminal, cornerstone works; others are entirely overlooked, however worthwhile their contributions to the field. But regardless of their status or stature, there is one common denominator: most everyone who undertakes the intensely selfish endeavor of writing a book attempts to leave some mark on the primary tangible output of their intellectual odyssey that recognizes those who made that self-indulgence possible. For some reason, it is often easier to offer these sentiments publicly than in person.

In at least this one respect then, this book is the same as every other, famous or forgotten: as a gesture of thanks I am giving over the first couple of pages to those who supported and helped me. It is not much. It is not original. But it is heartfelt and genuine, and it is the best I can do.

I begin with my firm, Deloitte, which has provided me the context and opportunity over the last six years to develop these ideas through invaluable interactions with both clients and colleagues. I have been perhaps uniquely fortunate to find myself part of an organization that has gone out of its way to allow me to create a special kind of professional fulfillment.

Wes Neff at the Leigh Bureau has been a believer since before the beginning of this effort, seeing the possibility of something substantial in someone who got lucky. Roger Scholl at Currency/Doubleday has been similarly supportive; his patience and enthusiasm for these ideas have been more important than he realizes.

Johnson & Johnson, Alliant Energy, and BCE Inc. all feature prominently in this book, but only because of Dave Holveck and Ken Dobler at J&J, Erroll Davis (then CEO) and Flora Flygt (then director of corporate research and market planning), both formerly at Alliant Energy, and Peter

Nicholson, then Chief Strategy Officer at BCE. Being a consultant is the most rewarding when you have the chance to work for the most demanding clients who are tackling the most demanding challenges. They have all helped me and my colleagues learn what we never would have otherwise, and I shall be forever grateful for the opportunity to work with them.

Jim Wappler somehow found the time and energy to respond to my endless and always last-minute requests for some bizarre analysis of public company data or Compustat cross-tab. Jim can do things with Excel that are probably illegal in some states. He always offered his assistance enthusiastically and never failed to deliver more, and better, analysis than I asked for. Gaurav Singhal helped with similar data collection and analysis for the charts in Chapter 10. Susan Krauss in San Francisco and Khatija Mohammed in Toronto were unfailingly good natured and helpful in chasing down many half-remembered articles (. . . can you find something by someone . . . I think the title begins with "L" . . . it came out in the '80s . . . or maybe the '90s?).

In alphabetical order, Sandy Aird, Tom Barker, David Bushko, Mark Cotteleer, Richard Lee, Laura Martin, Phil Rosenzweig, and Bernard Tubiana all provided comments on various drafts of the manuscript, providing indispensable advice and serving as a sympathetic but critical audience as the ideas evolved.

Allen Morrison, in addition to filling that same role, provided the opportunity to develop these ideas with executive education program participants at IMD in Lausanne, Switzerland. The chance to hold these concepts up for scrutiny by several hundred senior managers from around the world was invaluable.

Stu Thornhill and Rod White at the Ivey Business School invited me to join in on some of their research into the relationship between strategy and performance. The resulting insights provide much of the conceptual and empirical foundations upon which this book stands, and I'm grateful for the privilege of this continuing collaboration.

Tom Eisenmann of the Harvard Business School was on my thesis committee when I was a doctoral student there. I did not lean on him as much now as I did then, but Tom has nevertheless contributed enormously to this project as well, and, although he does not know it (well, I assume he does now), a big part of finding the motivation to press on with this manuscript through winter's drear was his assurance that I wasn't wasting my time. I was willing to believe in these concepts to no small degree because Tom did.

A big part of what can make consulting personally as well as professionally gratifying are one's colleagues. Mumtaz Ahmed, Adriaan Davidse, and Howard Weinberg are, each in their own very different ways, gentlemen, scholars, and irreplaceable. I owe them all very different debts that must perforce go unpaid in kind. But gentlemen, my IOU is good, should you ever wish to call it.

Jim Goodfellow, another Deloitte colleague, contributed critically important insight very early on in the development of the ideas I have tried to give voice to in this book. His deep knowledge of boards forged the first link in the chain of reasoning connecting hierarchy, time, and uncertainty in ways that revealed to me what I believe to be a profound but long-overlooked truth. Without that inspiration this book would not exist in anything like its current form.

I single out Dwight Allen, also a colleague, for special mention. Dwight has played a role in the evolution and refinement of the concepts in this book that I can never completely acknowledge. He has made innumerable and invaluable contributions over the years in both theoretical development and client application. Over the last six months, Dwight has been indefatigable in reading through draft after draft, and his ability to see the text each time as if for the first time, to offer encouragement by identifying what is working and why, to highlight areas warranting improvement and to offer suggestions how, and to point out where I had inadvertently made things worse has been of inestimable worth. Everyone should be lucky enough to have a colleague like Dwight. I count myself among those few who have been.

I save for last those to whom I owe the most. My wife, Annabel, has kept our home running while I have been either chained to my desk upstairs or dealing with the inevitable indignities of air travel, all despite dealing with the inconveniences of a pregnancy that coincided with the really hard work of getting the manuscript through to production. (The new arrival is due in December.) Charlotte, our five-year-old daughter, sees none of my unusual professional existence as in any way unusual, for it is all she has known. And so, as only children can, she has helped me to keep it all in perspective while reminding me of what makes any of it worthwhile. I have no idea what her future holds, but she has already taught me that in life, unlike in business, it is the journey that matters most.

Mississauga, Ontario
October, 2006

THE STRATEGY PARADOX

CHAPTER ONE

WHAT STRATEGY PARADOX?

Most strategies are built on specific beliefs about the future. Unfortunately, the future is deeply unpredictable. Worse, the requirements of breakthrough success demand implementing strategy in ways that make it impossible to adapt should the future not turn out as expected. The result is the Strategy Paradox: *strategies with the greatest possibility of success also have the greatest possibility of failure. Resolving this paradox requires a new way of thinking about strategy and uncertainty.*

Here is a puzzling fact: the best-performing firms often have more in common with humiliated bankrupts than with companies that have managed merely to survive. In fact, the very traits we have come to identify as determinants of high achievement are also the ingredients of total collapse. And so it turns out that, behaviorally at least, the opposite of success is not failure, but mediocrity.

There is more at stake here than simply observing that accomplishing anything worthwhile requires at least making the attempt, while those who venture nothing can only ever avoid disappointment. Theodore Roosevelt, the twenty-sixth president of the United States, explained this much to us when he argued that the credit belongs to those actually "in the arena," whose faces are marred by "dust and sweat and blood."[1] His point was that victory demands valiant action, and that valiant action necessarily brings with it the risk of defeat.

In business, the kinship between these antipodes runs far deeper, to the nature of the actions one must take in order to prevail. Therein lies the strategy paradox: the same behaviors and characteristics that maximize a firm's probability of notable success also maximize its probability of total failure.

THE SIMILARITY OF OPPOSITES

Many opposites are not nearly as different as they first appear. For example, as Nobel Peace Prize winner Elie Wiesel observed, the opposite of love is not hate, but indifference; for at a minimum, to love or hate someone is to have intense emotions toward them.[2] We see how the similarities between love and hate often outweigh the differences when one is transformed into the other, a phenomenon that literature—from Gilgamesh to Shakespeare to Harlequin Romances—has exploited and explored for millennia.

The psychological proximity of love and hate is part of the hard-wiring of the human psyche. Dan Gilbert explains, in his book *Stumbling on Happiness*, that the same neurocircuitry and neurochemistry triggered in response to stressful events ("flight or fight") are also triggered in response to sexual arousal.[3] As a result, when we are stressed in the presence of a person we find sexually attractive, we have a tough time telling what we are responding to: are our passions inflamed (hate) because of a stressor, or are we aroused (love) because of the attractive person?

In the 1994 movie *Speed* starring Keanu Reeves and Sandra Bullock, Bullock's character, Annie Porter, appeals to this possible confusion when she notes, upon finding herself in the hero's arms after several near-death experiences, that "relationships that start under intense circumstances, they never last."

Call it an "emotional paradox": two very different dispositions—loving and hating—can have far more in common with each other than a seemingly intermediate state.

The strategy paradox is visible only when we can put under the microscope strategies whose only flaw was that they flopped. Chapter 2 explores two such strategies: Sony's Betamax VCR and its MiniDisc music player. In both cases, the company never set a foot wrong by the lights of how one is supposed to build a successful strategy: it understood its customers, identified viable market segments, developed cutting-edge products, executed flawlessly, and monitored and responded to its competitors' countermoves. Yet, in both cases, Sony came up short because the commitments the company had to make in the pursuit of greatness were undermined when the perfectly reasonable assumptions behind those commitments turned out to be wrong. Sony's failures were not a consequence of *bad* strategy, but of *great* strategy coupled with bad *luck*. Sony did everything necessary to maximize its chances of success, yet those same actions exposed it to the possibility of near-total defeat. In other words, when key uncertainties broke against it, Sony became a victim of the strategy paradox.

The purpose of this book is to describe how the strategy paradox can be resolved. In what follows, a new principle I call *Requisite Uncertainty* and a new management tool I call *Strategic Flexibility* provide a way for managers to implement the kinds of strategies that can deliver outstanding results while minimizing exposure to the vagaries of fate.

1.1 HIDDEN IN PLAIN SIGHT

Why is this the first you have heard of the strategy paradox? After all, there is no shortage of well-designed and well-executed studies offering useful insights into the defining characteristics of successful firms. Similarities to failed firms and the importance of luck have not featured prominently.

The reason most business research misses the strategy paradox is that few studies ever examine failure. In some cases, this is because pursuing the secrets of success seems more rewarding than picking through the wreckage of failure. In other cases, it is simply a flawed method: researchers embrace the idea that by studying winners they can discern their defining characteristics, forgetting that the factors differentiating winners from losers can be identified only by analyzing both. Finally, there is the reality that failures are often harder to document because failed companies are typically no longer available for study.

In light of these difficulties, researchers often compromise, comparing companies that have been very successful over ten or fifteen years (focal companies) with companies that have been less successful over that same time period (comparison companies). Some studies look for firms that have done very poorly over that time, and others look for comparison companies that have actually done pretty well—just not nearly as well as their focal companies. Either way, however, comparison companies have at least *survived* for the period in question, and over a ten-year period, mere survival is actually a pretty high bar.[4]

What this means is that most studies of the determinants of success have based their conclusions upon comparisons of the exceptional with the mediocre. Studies that systematically seek out successful companies will necessarily find those that in the past made the right commitments. And because the comparison companies are always firms that have performed less well, but not failed completely, they will tend to be firms that have avoided high-risk, high-return strategies. A review of more than thirty empirical studies, published in academic journals over the past twenty years, exploring the relationship between strategy and performance found none that had accounted for this bias.[5]

By examining primarily those companies that have guessed right and comparing them with those that have avoided guessing, what has been largely missed is the critical importance of managing uncertainty. The gallant charge and the cowardly retreat are not the only alternatives to catastrophic defeat. There is a way to boldly go, yet mitigate risk without compromising performance. Describing that solution is the promise of this book.

Accepting the strategy paradox forces us to accept mediocrity, giving up a chance at greatness as the price of our continued corporate existence. Resolving it will free us from a debilitating trade-off between risk and return and allow us to strive to be first without giving up the hope that we will last.

1.2 MUST COMMIT

The cause of the strategy paradox is as obvious as it is overlooked. A successful strategy allows an organization to create and capture value. To create value, a firm must connect with customers. For a firm to capture value, its strategy must be resistant to imitation by competitors. Satisfying customers in ways competitors cannot copy requires significant commitment to a particular strategy, that is, *strategic* commitments, to unique assets or to particular capabilities.

Commitments are a powerful determinant of success because they make a strategy difficult to imitate. To reduce strategic risk, many firms invest only in what has been shown to work. Since these latecomers wait while some firms—the lucky ones—make what happen to be the right commitments, lucky firms enjoy a period of relatively little competition: it takes time to replicate capabilities so painstakingly created. For example, new products snapped together from off-the-shelf components are usually easily imitated by competitors, while those based on proprietary technologies developed over years are far likelier to be the foundation of a durable franchise. The downside of commitment is that if you make what happen to be the wrong commitments, it can take a long time to undo them and make new ones.

The strategy paradox, then, arises from the collision of commitment and uncertainty. The most successful strategies are those based on commitments made today that are best aligned with tomorrow's circumstances. But no one knows what those circumstances will be, because the future is unpredictable. Should one have guessed wrong and committed to the wrong capabilities, it will be impossible to adapt—after all, a commitment that can be changed was not much of a commitment. As a result, success is very often a result of having made what *turned out to be* the right commitments (good luck), while failed strategies, which can be similar in many ways to successful ones, are based on what *turned out to be* the wrong commitments (bad luck). In other words, the strategy paradox is a consequence of the need to commit to a strategy despite the deep uncertainty surrounding which strategy to commit to. Call this *strategic* uncertainty.

New research detailed in Chapter 3 suggests that often the main factor separating success and failure is indeed luck. Firms that avoid strategic risk survive but do not prosper. Firms that accept strategic risk reap either great reward or utter ruin. For now, these seem to be the only alternatives to failure, and firms are forced to choose. There is no intrinsic merit in opting for greater returns over survival or vice versa; the problem is that firms must choose.

The Sony examples, referred to earlier, are not unique. The strategy paradox is more than a theoretical possibility or a curiosity; it is a general condition. As recounted in Chapter 3, an analysis of the competitive strategies of several thousand operating companies reveals that organizations pursuing the most commitment-intensive strategies generate the highest returns, but they also suffer the highest mortality rates. Seen in this light, Sony's failures were not a consequence of avoidable mistakes but the result of making commitments—the defining element of successful strategy—despite inescapable uncertainty. And when those uncertainties were resolved to Sony's detriment, it paid the price.

The strategy paradox rests on two premises: commitments cannot be adapted should predictions prove incorrect; and predictions are never reliably or verifiably correct. Are these premises true?

1.3 CAN'T ADAPT

For all we might think we know about how to make organizations agile, flexible, and adaptive, the data suggest strongly that, if anything, competitive advantage is eroding faster than ever. This acceleration is interpreted by some to mean that there is a greater need than ever for adaptable enterprises. Such an observation is entirely correct. Unfortunately, the acuteness of the need does not mean that it can be satisfied.

Most organizations exhibit some degree of adaptability. However, as explained in Chapter 4, adaptability is far less useful than we might like. Specifically, adaptability is viable only when the pace of organizational change matches the pace of environmental change. When the environment changes either faster or slower than the organization, adaptability is no longer sufficient. The bad news is that every organization will at some point face one or both of two types of mismatch between the two rates of change, and each can prove devastating.

Fast change leaves an organization's capabilities optimized for an environment that suddenly no longer exists. For example, when the price of oil rose 400 percent in a matter of weeks in the early 1970s, North American automakers found that the mainstay of their product lines—full-sized cars—

were singularly inappropriate to the new competitive conditions. Unfortunately, it took those same automakers years to design, manufacture, and market more fuel-efficient models, and they lost valuable market share to better-positioned competitors. (Ironically, the tide turned in their favor in the mid-1990s when cheap gas made SUVs all the rage; their good fortune began to evaporate once again in the face of high-priced petrol in the mid-2000s.)

Slow change prompts an organization to adapt to incremental changes in the environment around it, and because of these incremental adaptations, the company often fails to see the need for a more fundamental transformation. The auto sector's response to the current oil crisis may be subject to this slow change pathology. As oil prices have crept up, automakers have responded by extending the life of the internal combustion engine by dramatically increasing fuel economy and creating hybrid electric engines, among other technological advances. But the day may well come when, due either to the need to limit carbon emissions for environmental reasons or the inability of the general economy to absorb still further increases in oil prices, the internal combustion engine must be abandoned. Should that day arrive, companies that have been exploiting their adaptive capacity could well be overtaken by firms that are already aggressively pursuing alternative technologies intended to replace, rather than merely extend, a century-old technology.

Compounding the difficulties of responding to fast and slow change is the fact that most competitive environments are characterized by multiple rates of change, creating the impossible organizational task of changing at different rates at the same time.

As a result, adaptability cannot expect to resolve or even mitigate the strategy paradox.

1.4 CAN'T PREDICT

The first half of the paradox is commitment: companies cannot adapt their commitments should they turn out to be the wrong ones. Might we instead escape the paradox by predicting the future accurately enough to make consistently the right commitments in the first place?

This will not work for three reasons, which are explored in Chapter 5. First, no one can legitimately claim to have a meaningful ability to foresee the future in anything like the level of detail required to make consistently successful strategic commitments. Any such claims are illusory: with so many people predicting so many things, it is inevitable that someone is going to get something right occasionally. Since we cannot know who that someone is going to be, or what they are going to get right, the fact that some predictions turn out to be accurate is useless.

Second, predictions in the form of point estimates betray a fundamental misunderstanding of what the future actually is. The future is a range of possible outcomes, not a specific set of circumstances that will inevitably come to pass. A prediction of the future *as seen from the perspective of today* would have to describe each of the events that could happen and their associated probabilities. Unfortunately, there is no way to compare our probability-based description of the future with the true probabilities as they are today. For instance, if I say that there is a 10 percent chance of rain tomorrow, whether it rains tomorrow or not tells you nothing about the accuracy of my prediction, for either outcome is consistent with a 10 percent chance of rain.

One could, of course, note all those days for which I predicted a 10 percent chance of rain and then see if it rained on 10 percent of them. When it comes to weather forecasting, this is reasonable, but when it comes to strategic forecasting, the outcomes of interest are rarely repeated events. As a result, this kind of track record is impossible to establish. Consequently, we have no way of determining if someone can provide accurate, probability-based descriptions of the range of possible future events.

The third reason accurate prediction is impossible is the ubiquity of randomness. Randomness generally can be thought of as the absence of the kind of order that allows us to predict what comes next in a series. That is, we might be able to identify a pattern, but unless that pattern repeats in ways that allow us to foresee what follows, the series is ultimately random. It turns out that the systems we hope to understand and predict for the purposes of making strategic commitments are subject to two main sources of randomness.

First, most every economy is subject to exogenous shocks such as new technologies or regulatory regimes that create new competitors or upset long-standing equilibria. It is tempting to believe that we can overcome this problem by simply expanding the boundaries of our analysis. Unfortunately, once we begin expanding the scope of our model, we do not know when to stop. Before long we find ourselves compelled to build a "theory of everything" in order to predict anything.

Second, even if the dynamics of a particular system are predictable, competitive dynamics are highly sensitive to past commitments—what systems dynamics theorists call "initial conditions." What constitutes the initial conditions of a system is a judgment call, and getting it wrong makes any subsequent predictions highly suspect.

We can see these two sources of randomness at work in the evolution of

Toyota from its humble beginnings to a world-class auto manufacturer. The oil crisis of the mid-1970s was an exogenous shock that created a surge in demand in North America for smaller, fuel-efficient automobiles. Toyota made precisely these kinds of cars, and many customers who would not otherwise have purchased a Toyota were motivated to purchase one for the first time. Many were pleasantly surprised at the value Toyota offered, and stayed with the brand even as the pressure on gas prices receded. The oil shock was, in a sense, the lucky break Toyota needed to gain access to the mainstream of the U.S. auto market.

For General Motors to have predicted this shift in competitive fortunes, it would have had to focus not on its would-be competitor but on the geopolitics of the Middle East. GM would also have had to predict accurately the impact of that shock on consumer buying behavior, and that the "temporary" interest in Toyota would prove to have long-term implications.

Why was Toyota better positioned than other car companies, such as Ford or Chrysler, to steal a march on GM? Was Toyota blessed with a prescience or adaptability that allowed it to exploit events that others were blind to? Hardly: in Toyota's home market of Japan, gasoline had long been more expensive than in the United States, while economizing on space had long been a priority. These "initial conditions" are features of the Japanese market that can be attributed to geographical, political, and cultural traits that are centuries old. It is not as though Toyota had a "copy GM" strategy in the 1950s but changed course when it foresaw the oil crunch. Neither did Toyota adapt to the embargo when it occurred. Rather, as a consequence of home market pressures, the company since its birth had been committed to a strategy (small, fuel-efficient, inexpensive cars) that was eventually appropriate for the North American market for reasons few had foreseen. This takes nothing away from Toyota's success; as Louis Pasteur put it, "Fortune favors the prepared mind." But the corollary of this insight is that preparation without fortune—or worse, coupled with bad fortune—amounts to the wrong preparation.

In sum, prediction cannot resolve the paradox any more than adaptability can.

1.5 MANAGING STRATEGIC UNCERTAINTY

The strategy paradox is a consequence of the conflict between commitment and strategic uncertainty. The answer to the paradox lies in separating the management of each, charging some with the responsibility of delivering on the commitments the organization has already made, and others with the task of mitigating risk and providing exposure to promising opportunities.

The foundation for this division of labor is the traditional organizational hierarchy. As explained in Chapter 6, well-functioning hierarchies are defined by a clear separation between levels according to the time it takes for those at each level to know whether or not they have made the right decisions today. Most who work in large organizations have an intuition that this basis of organization is right. The CEO should be thinking about the long term, while divisional management (typically an operating division) is worried about the medium term, and in-the-trenches functional management has to deliver the goods.

In the short run, there is very little strategic uncertainty. We typically know (even if we cannot implement) the best way to create and capture value in the present. We cannot know how best to create and capture value ten or twenty years from now, and the range of strategies that might be optimal in the future only expands as we lengthen the time horizon under consideration. Consequently, there is a great deal of strategic uncertainty when considering the long run.

Senior management, because it is responsible for longer time horizons, should therefore focus its efforts on managing strategic uncertainty. Those lower down in the hierarchy, because they are responsible for shorter time horizons, should focus on delivering on the commitments already in place. This new organizing principle is called *Requisite Uncertainty*, because each level of the hierarchy is defined by its relationship to managing strategic uncertainty.

The implications of separating the management of uncertainty from the management of commitments are more far-reaching than it might seem. In the first place, Requisite Uncertainty provides a foundation for the widely held yet often violated belief that senior management should not be concerned with short-term results. There is very little that pulling on the strategy lever can do to improve this quarter's cash flow, and any CEO who is compelled to intervene frequently on issues that can affect current financial results is likely not able to pay enough attention to strategy.

Explicitly identifying strategic uncertainties and requiring that senior management attend to them might well be quite different from the more bottom-up risk-management processes many organizations have in place. Focused on important but shorter-term uncertainties such as the supply chain, the company's reputation, and so on, much of established risk-management practice overlooks the risk that the company has committed to the wrong strategy, and what to do about that.

Perhaps more controversially, applying the principles of Requisite Uncertainty implies that CEOs should not see their role in terms of making strategic choices—that is, commitments. Rather, they should focus on building "strategic options," that is, creating the ability to pursue alternative strategies that *could* be useful, depending on how key uncertainties are resolved. It implies also that the board should not concern itself so much with creating or reviewing the firm's strategy as with determining the most appropriate exposure to strategic risk and opportunity. Only by shifting the emphasis at the top of the hierarchy from making and executing strategy to managing strategic uncertainty can corporations hope to mitigate strategic risk while simultaneously creating strategic opportunities.

In Chapter 7, a case study of Vivendi Universal, a French media conglomerate, illustrates what happens when a CEO succumbs to the temptation of top-level, hands-on strategy making. Examinations of the diversified Canadian telecommunications company BCE Inc. and U.S. software company Microsoft highlight the benefits of an option-creating top management. In particular, the BCE and Microsoft cases show how corporations can manage strategic uncertainty in ways that investors cannot replicate.

However, it will be apparent from these examples that the success of an options-based corporate strategy has depended largely on the charisma, influence, and power of the CEO—it has required people such as Bill Gates to do this successfully. Not every company is led by such a titan. Consequently, we need an explicit, process-based description of how managers at all levels can contribute to managing strategic uncertainty in ways that mitigate risk and position a firm to capture emerging opportunities. This is the subject of Chapter 8, a case study of how Johnson & Johnson (J&J), the diversified U.S. pharmaceutical, medical devices, and consumer products company, has tackled this challenge.

J&J is breaking new ground in the management of strategic uncertainty. The company's operating divisions are not exclusively responsible for managing long-term strategic uncertainty. Rather, divisional leadership's primary role is to commit to a specific strategy, because making a commitment is the only way to create and capture value. But the range of strategies available to the operating divisions is a function of the opportunities created by the corporate office. In other words, because J&J's corporate level explicitly manages strategic uncertainty, J&J's operating divisions enjoy true *strategic flexibility*—a deliberate oxymoron that qualifies the irreversibility of strategic commitments without undermining their competitive power.

Operating divisions that manage their own long-term strategic uncertainty will most likely end up mediocre performers, avoiding high-risk bets to increase their odds of survival. In addition, since great performance demands relentless focus on a particular strategy, devoting resources—especially management time and attention—to creating options is typically beyond the capacity of an operating division. Consequently, Strategic Flexibility is not something a successful operating division can typically create for itself. Only by focusing the corporate office on the management of uncertainty can the overall corporation achieve high results (thanks to commitment-focused divisions) at lower risk (thanks to the uncertainty-focused corporate office).

Highlighted here is the profound difference between "growth" options and true *strategic* options. Often, companies will make a small investment in a new venture and see it as an "option" on future growth: if the venture takes off, then invest more in it; if it falters, let it wither, or perhaps even expedite its demise. Strategic options, however, enable established divisions to pursue fundamentally different strategies. A strategic option is an option on an element of an alternative strategy that might or might not be implemented, not simply an option on further investment in a new business that might or might not succeed.

Making the corporate office responsible for managing uncertainty is a significant break from much current thinking about the role of the corporate office. Most prescriptions on what a corporate office should do start with the premise that all competition takes place at the product market level—that is, in the domain of operating divisions.[6] This is true, but the conclusion that all corporate office activity must, therefore, be directed at improving the current competitiveness of operating divisions—by, for example, facilitating the capture of synergies—does not necessarily follow.

Drawing too direct a line between the actions of the corporate office and the performance of the operating divisions is an unhealthy side effect of our collective obsession with generating returns. The frameworks for developing competitive strategy that have emerged over the last thirty years have given us unparalleled insight into how companies can succeed. And competitive strategy remains enormously important, but it should be the preserve of divisional management. But just as there can be no left without a right, there is no return unaccompanied by uncertainty: operating divisions worry about competitive strategy to create and capture value; corporate strategy should be focused on the management of strategic uncertainty. Requisite Uncertainty delegates to corporate management responsibility for managing strategic risk and opportunity, leaving operating divisions to create and capture value. Strategic Flexibility is the corporate-level framework for managing strategic uncertainty through the creation of strategic options.

It would be a mistake to think that the distinction between corporate and competitive strategy, and hence Requisite Uncertainty, applies only to Fortune 500 corporations. Any organization with greater size and complexity than a sole-proprietor corner store—or even just the ambition to exceed that size and complexity—can benefit from thinking carefully about separating how to generate returns from how to manage uncertainty. If your organization has operating managers who report to still more senior managers, there is not simply the chance but the likelihood that there is an unhealthy overlap between the jobs each level thinks it is doing. In fact, the smaller the organization, the greater the temptation of senior management to involve itself in operating decisions, with the unfortunate consequence of leaving the management of uncertainty largely to chance.

1.6 THE TOOLKIT

J&J teaches us that strong results arise from driving individual operating divisions to pursue the kind of high-risk, high-return strategies that stand-alone divisions tend to avoid. Pushing divisions in this direction is done using a set of *constraints* defined by the corporate office. Resource constraints limit the time horizon a division can consider and the investment level it can support. Structural constraints restrict the operating scope of a division and enforce specific size parameters. And strategic constraints ensure that relentless attention is paid to particular customer groups and that the risk profile of a division remains within well-understood boundaries (typically enforcing a floor, not a ceiling).

Fighting the drift toward mediocrity is only half the battle: if J&J's corporate office did nothing more than drive its divisions to high-risk, high-reward strategic positions, overall corporate returns would likely show high variability and an average no better than any other portfolio of investments. What makes J&J special is that it goes beyond simply driving performance to actively managing risk *without undermining the operating divisions' focus on results.*

With divisions focused on generating returns, J&J manages uncertainty through a highly specialized organ of the corporate office that identifies the relevant strategic unknowns and devotes resources to creating the options needed to overcome them. Beyond simply "facilitating communication" or "investing in blue-sky opportunities," J&J is pioneering a new role for the corporate office, giving structure and repeatability to the insights and intuition that have traditionally been the preserve of a "heroic" CEO. The resulting framework, called Strategic Flexibility, has four phases:

Anticipate: build scenarios of the future
Formulate: create an optimal strategy for each of those futures
Accumulate: determine what strategic options are required
Operate: manage the portfolio of options

You might recognize here the silhouette of one or more established management tools—scenario-based planning, strategic planning, or real options, to name three of the more obvious ones. But Strategic Flexibility is not a pastiche of existing approaches. Integrating these tools and grounding them in a validated theory of organizational hierarchy creates something that is quite different from any of these tools on its own, or in mere combination with the others.[7]

Chapter 9 illustrates the first two phases using the case of Alliant Energy's mooted entry into the unregulated electricity-generating business. Alliant Energy is a $3.3 billion Wisconsin-based energy-utility holding company, and in 2002 the firm was considering whether to invest in nonregulated ("merchant") generating assets. Rather than commit heavily to a particular merchant generating strategy, the company considered a series of scenarios designed to capture the full range of possible futures over the relevant time horizon—about ten years. There is, of course, a well-developed body of work describing how to build scenarios; this case study describes which threads of that work are most relevant to the *Anticipate* phase of Strategic Flexibility.

With scenarios in place, the next step is to *Formulate* an optimal strategy for each scenario. Again, there is an established discipline of strategy formulation that can be relied upon to provide guidance for building a successful strategy given a set of competitive conditions.

In the context of Requisite Uncertainty, however, strategy formulation has very different objectives depending on one's relative focus on managing uncertainty or delivering on commitments. As illustrated in the Alliant Energy case study, the objective at the board and corporate level is to create strategic options. At the divisional level, where commitments to specific strategies have to be made, the key is to hedge the downside attendant to the chosen strategy. How this can be done effectively is demonstrated by SBC (now AT&T) in its response to increasing competition in consumer voice and data services, also explored in Chapter 9. Finally, at the functional management level, where the emphasis is exclusively on delivering on commitments, the key is to learn as efficiently as possible how to make the most of the commitments already in place. We see this kind of approach to strategy formulation in Chapter 9's final case study, Bell Canada's integration of its wireline and wireless telephony divisions.

With scenarios and strategies developed, the challenge now is to translate that analytical work into concrete action. The *Accumulate* and *Operate* phases are explored in the context of the M&A, joint venture, and partial equity stake investments that have been made in the financial services sector over the last ten years. Reinforcing the difference between simple growth options and true strategic options, examples from the investment banking and international finance sectors illustrate how the corporate office can create an ability for existing divisions to move in ways they could not if left to their own devices.

Accumulating the right portfolio of real options creates an investment strategy that mirrors the uncertain nature of the need for a particular asset. The key to realizing option value is to ensure that the investing company has the control required to *preserve* and *exercise* the option it has created. This is a delicate balancing act. If an option-generating investment is granted too much freedom, it can evolve in ways that make the ultimate exercise of the option impossible. Too little autonomy could undermine the viability of the option as a stand-alone investment, making it prohibitively costly to preserve or *abandon*.

Whether exercising or abandoning an option, there is a need for a healthy tension between divisional and corporate management when determining a course of action. Simple prescriptions of "top down" or "bottom up" belie the inevitable subtlety and nuance of corporate decision-making. Guiding principles for managing this tension are described in detail in Chapter 10, along with some observations on how to value a strategic option and how to ensure that the entire process is self-renewing.

This book is not the first to observe that the future is unpredictable and that strategy making must take uncertainty into account. What is new is that here uncertainty is not an afterthought, not something one considers after commitments have been made. Instead, uncertainty is placed at the core of decision making at the highest levels of the organization, for only in this way can we hope to address the paradox created by uncertainty.

In the context of Strategic Flexibility, scenarios are transformed from an adjunct to strategic planning into its foundation, for scenarios serve to define the key strategic uncertainties that a company faces (the Anticipate phase). Strategy development is no longer a determination of what commitments to make and is instead a process for identifying which risks a company will accept, hedge, or avoid (the Formulate phase). The Accumulate and Operate phases rely on the principles of Requisite Uncertainty, and make it possible for concrete investment decisions and ongoing strategic action at every level of the hierarchy to reflect the appropriate emphasis on commitment and uncertainty. The result is an integrated approach to creating greater value at lower risk. That is about as close as we can hope to come to getting something for nothing.

1.7 A NEW STRATEGIC CONVERSATION

I collaborated with Clayton Christensen on a book called *The Innovator's Solution*.[8] That book describes how organizations can create and sustain profitable growth. But there are no returns without risk, and I have come to think of the ideas in this book as the other side of the risk/return equation. As we seek value, what risks do we run, and how can we reduce those risks without abandoning our quest?

The strategy paradox is that the prerequisites of success are often the antecedents of failure. Faced with this painful trade-off between the returns to bold commitment and the risk of making the wrong commitment, most organizations forgo the possibility of glory for an existence bereft of greatness.

Not all business failures are a result of traits typically associated with success: incompetence, hubris, denial, and many other causes of catastrophe are decidedly not the stuff of victory.[9] But at least *some* failures *are* caused by a good strategy and solid execution. Only by understanding the strategy paradox's root cause can we build strategies that succeed deliberately, rather than only when fortune smiles upon us.

To mitigate the role of luck in success, we must expand our strategic conversation to include not merely the commitments required for success but also the uncertainties that will determine which commitments will succeed. We know a great deal about how to make and manage commitments. Our understanding of how to identify and manage uncertainties is far less well developed. As a result, expanding our strategic conversation in this way will require a new language and a new set of tools.

Requisite Uncertainty provides the foundation for separating the management of uncertainty from the management of commitment. The connection between hierarchical level, time horizon, and the degree of strategic uncertainty faced is the basis upon which responsibility for managing uncertainty is delegated primarily to the corporate office, while making and delivering on commitments falls mainly to the operating divisions.

This is only the first step: a better allocation of decision-making responsibilities is a necessary but not sufficient condition for resolving the strategy paradox. The rest of the answer lies in a new toolkit, Strategic Flexibility, which provides a step-by-step process for each level to address the uncertainties it faces and to deliver on its commitments. Combining these two concepts will further any organization's attempts to achieve the results it desires at a level of risk it can tolerate.

The strategy paradox has been largely ignored for too long, despite its ubiquity and its influence over the choices managers make. The goal of this book is to fuel the hope that although the future is uncertain, your fate does not have to be.

The strategy paradox arises from the need to commit in the face of unavoidable uncertainty. The solution to the paradox is to separate the management of commitments from the management of uncertainty. Since uncertainty increases with the time horizon under consideration, the basis for the allocation of decision making is the time horizon for which different levels of the hierarchy are responsible: the corporate office, responsible for the longest time horizon, must focus on managing uncertainty, while operating managers must focus on delivering on commitments. This is the principle of Requisite Uncertainty. A critically important tool in applying Requisite Uncertainty is Strategic Flexibility, a framework for identifying uncertainties and developing the options needed to mitigate risk or exploit opportunity.

---

1. Roosevelt made these points in a speech titled "Citizenship in a Republic," more commonly known as "The Man in the Arena." It was delivered at the Sorbonne in Paris on April 23, 1910. See http://www.theodore-roosevelt.com/trsorbonnespeech.html, accessed July 17, 2006.

2. See http://en.thinkexist.com/quotes/elie_wiesel/, accessed July 17, 2006.

3. Gilbert, Dan (2006), *Stumbling on Happiness,* New York: Alfred A. Knopf.

4. Four studies worth reading that make these kinds of comparisons are, in alphabetical order by first author's last name, Collins, James C., and Jerry I. Porras (1994), *Built to Last: Successful Habits of Visionary Companies,* New York: HarperBusiness; Collins, Jim (2001), *Good to Great: Why Some Companies Make the Leap . . . and Others Don't,* New York: HarperBusiness; Joyce, William, Nitin Nohria, and Bruce Roberson (2003), *What (Really) Works: The 4+2 Formula for Sustained Business Success,* New York: HarperBusiness; Marcus, Alfred A. (2006), *Big Winners and Big Losers: The 4 Secrets of Long-Term Business Success and Failure,* Upper Saddle River, NJ: Wharton School Publishing.

5. I am grateful to Terry Wang, a doctoral candidate at the Ivey Business School, for reviewing the relevant research.

6. See Porter, M. E. (1987), "From Corporate Strategy to Competitive Advantage," *Harvard Business Review,* Vol. 65, Iss. 3; and Goold, Michael, A. Campbell, and M. Alexander (1994), *Corporate Level Strategy,* New York: Wiley.

7. The specific application of these concepts was of course unique to Johnson & Johnson. The general structure of the four-phase Strategic Flexibility framework was born of research and consulting that had found prior expression in a number of publications:

Raynor, Michael E. (2001). "Strategic Flexibility in the Financial Services Industry: Creating Competitive Advantage out of Competitive Turbulence," Deloitte Research monograph, www.deloitte.com/research.

―――― (2001). "Managing Amid Uncertainty: New Thinking on How to Succeed in an Uncertain World," Deloitte Research monograph, www.deloitte.com/research.

―――― (2002). "Make Peace with Business Uncertainty." *Optimize*. August.

―――― (2002). "Strategic Flexibility: Charting a Path Through Uncertainty." *Convergence* magazine (South African Edition), Vol. 2(4).

―――― (2003). "Taking the Fork in the Road." *Strategy & Innovation*, Vol. 1(4), pp. 8–10.

―――― (2004). "Strategic Flexibility: Taking the Fork in the Road." *Competitive Intelligence*, Vol. 7(1), pp. 6–13.

Allen, Dwight L. Jr. and Michael E. Raynor (2004). "Preparing for a new global business environment: Divided and disorderly or integrated and harmonious?" *Journal of Business Strategy* Vol. 25(5), pp. 16–25.

Raynor, Michael E.and Ximena Leroux (2004). "Strategic Flexibility in the R&D Function." *Research and Technology Management*. Vol. 47(3), pp. 17–23.

8. Christensen, Clayton M., and Michael E. Raynor (2003), *The Innovator's Solution: Creating and Sustaining Successful Growth*, Boston: Harvard Business School Press.

9. A number of books have examined failure, among them Tuchman, Barbara (1985), *The March of Folly: From Troy to Vietnam*, New York: Ballantine Books; Schnaars, Stephen P. (1989), *Megamistakes: Forecasting and the Myth of Rapid Technological Change*, New York: Free Press; Bazerman, Max H., and Michael D. Watkins (2004), *Predictable Surprises: The Disasters You Should Have Seen Coming and How to Prevent Them*, Boston: Harvard Business School Press; Mittelstaedt, Robert E. (2005), *Will Your Next Mistake Be Fatal? Avoiding the Chain of Mistakes That Can Destroy Your Organization*, Upper Saddle River, NJ: Wharton School Publishing.

CHAPTER TWO

THE BEST-LAID PLANS

Success demands commitments to hard-to-copy, hard-to-reverse configurations of resources and capabilities that are aligned with the competitive conditions of a market. These commitments take time to bear fruit and so they must be based on beliefs about the future. These beliefs can turn out to be wrong. As a result, otherwise excellent strategies can fail simply because the conditions under which those commitments would have been appropriate did not materialize. Sony's attempts to create new consumer electronics formats—Betamax in video and MiniDisc in audio—illustrate how brilliantly conceived, carefully planned, and flawlessly implemented strategies can come to grief because of the antinomy of commitment and uncertainty.

Whatever the medium—be it music, movies, games, or, increasingly, literature—our gateway to the messages that capture, reflect, and create the meaning of our lives promises always to be an electronic gizmo of some description. Across audio, video, data, and text, installed and portable, the market for these devices is a $120-billion-a-year arena of winner-take-most (if not all) contests for supremacy.[1]

One of the great strategic blunders of the modern consumer electronics industry was Sony's Betamax video cassette recorder (VCR).[2] Sony created a mass market for the VCR when it introduced Betamax in 1975. For the next eighteen years, Sony offered consumers perhaps the best, most innovative product available, yet the format was a failure. Sony withdrew Betamax from the U.S. market in 1989, its market share a pitiful 0.3 percent, while Matsushita's VHS design dominated the market utterly.

A second strategic debacle is Sony's MiniDisc. Launched with great fanfare and promise in 1993, the device held out the possibility of translating Sony's stupefying success with the Walkman compact audiocassette players into the "disc age." Yet, despite heavy investment in the technology and associated content from its own record label, Sony was unable to gain any traction outside of Japan, and even there has been steadily losing ground since 2000 to "digital portables," e.g., MP3 players and Apple's iPod.

Why did Sony's Betamax and MiniDisc strategies fail? The company is, after all, hardly an example of sustained incompetence. From the transistor radio to the Walkman to PlayStation, Sony is as much an icon of success as anything else. Did they forget to follow their traditional recipe when cooking up Betamax and MiniDisc?

These failures are traditionally attributed to arrogance, a lack of foresight, and stubbornness. Critics claim that Sony did not work closely enough with other manufacturers, did not foresee the emergence of the video-rental market, did not collaborate with Hollywood studios, and refused to cut prices when the low end of the market, not the quality-obsessed videophiles, ended up determining who would ultimately succeed. In the zeitgeist of modern strategy, all of these errors were either avoidable or remediable at the time. What Sony teaches us, in the standard strategy curriculum, is that you must strive to understand your industry—even an entirely new one—and see far enough into the future to be able to make the right choices today. At the same time, you must find a way to build an organization that can adapt so that, should you have gotten it wrong in any material respects, you can bob and weave as required in response to any surprises that crop up.

Much of this analysis is polluted by hindsight. If we put ourselves in Sony's shoes and think about the choices Sony made from the perspective of when Sony made them, we learn a very different lesson. Sony made entirely reasonable commitments to strategies that had every chance of succeeding. Sony made those commitments because it felt they were necessary if great success was to be even a possibility. And the commitments it made were entirely reasonable given what was known when Sony felt it had to commit.

In other words, by the prescriptions of standard competitive strategy formulation, Sony was an exemplar of strategic analysis and implementation. The company's strategies failed not because they were bad strategies but because they were *great* strategies. Sony succumbed to the strategy paradox: in both the Betamax and MiniDisc cases, it committed when and how it did because that was the only way to achieve dominance. But it was also the best way to create the possibility of total failure. A detailed examination of these campaigns reveals that each initiative had all the ingredients of a successful competitive strategy. Unfortunately, each failed due to insufficient attention to the salient uncertainties that ultimately determined the outcome.

This explanation of the fates of Betamax and MiniDisc is not the strategic orthodoxy. The failures of the iconic Betamax and the undeservedly neglected MiniDisc are typically attributed to Sony's having made avoidable mistakes. Many believe that somehow Sony should have known better, or could have done something to respond as it became clear that their initial choices were fundamentally flawed. I disagree. I believe that in each case unforeseeable events derailed a strategy that any reasonable person would have given an excellent chance of succeeding and very little chance of failing as completely as it actually did. The disagreeable outcomes were not a consequence of bad strategic planning; they were a function of the nature of strategic planning itself.

As you read this chapter, ask yourself, "Is my strategy as carefully thought-out as Sony's was? Is it as consistent with my organization's core competence and culture? Is it as clearly positioned against specific customer segments and as powerfully differentiated from the competition? Have I learned from my past mistakes as effectively as Sony did?" Chances are that the answer to at least some of these questions will be "no," and many of you will conclude that even though Betamax and MiniDisc failed, Sony can still teach us a great deal about formulating and implementing a sound competitive strategy.[3]

Then ask yourself, "What assumptions are my strategies based on, and what reasons do I have to believe those assumptions will prove correct? Am I on firmer ground than was Sony? Am I any better at predicting what I need to do today in order to succeed tomorrow?" Again, my guess is that you will answer "no" to at least some of these questions. And if you have planned your strategies no better than Sony, and forecast the future no more accurately, what guarantee do you have that your results will be any more favorable, or are any less dependent on luck?

My hope is that when you finish this chapter you will have a new appreciation for (1) the inescapable reliance of traditional strategic plans on specific beliefs about the future; (2) how that need creates the strategy paradox, undermining the utility of such planning in guiding a company toward success with any reliability; (3) the degree to which the strategy paradox afflicts your organization's strategy.

2.1 YOU OUGHTA BE IN PICTURES

Masura Ibuka and Akio Morita founded Sony Corporation in 1946, focusing on audio electronics.[4] Expanding beyond audio, the company added video to the mix in the late 1960s as it sought to create a mass-market version of Ampex Corporation's video recorder for television broadcasting.[5]

Like many other companies working to extend Ampex's technology, however, Sony was unable to escape the design trade-offs between picture quality, price, convenience, and ease of use that kept the device beyond the reach of average consumers.

Undeterred by early failures, and in keeping with the company's traditions of technical excellence, Sony was the first to realize the breakthroughs that made a home-use video recorder possible, and was ready to go to market in 1970 with a recording technology that it felt would be widely adopted. Recognizing that a single format would increase customer acceptance, Sony sought to avoid a format war by cooperating with Matsushita, a much larger Japanese electronics firm that had been developing its own technology.[6] Matsushita proved unable to mass-produce Sony's initial design, and so allowing Matsushita to participate demanded several technical compromises, including wider tape, a larger cassette, and a bulkier housing. The resulting device, called the U-Matic, was too expensive and ungainly for home use, and found a market only with schools and other institutions.

Partly as a consequence of this delay, Palo Alto–based Cartridge Television, Inc. (CTI), was the first to offer a consumer-oriented VCR device, the Cartrivision.[7] Launched in 1972 with retail distribution primarily through Sears, the Cartrivision was sold as a TV/VCR bundle at first, to compensate for nonstandard video interfaces in commercially available televisions.

Designed as both a recording and movie-playing device, CTI lined up a deal with Columbia Pictures to make a small number of movies available, and ran the "Cartridge Rental Network" through a series of agreements with third-party retailers. The rental process was very involved. Rental shops carried no inventory due to the high cost of the tapes and the uncertainty of the market. Customers were therefore required to order a movie at a retail location. The retailer would then place an order with a distributor, who in turn would ship it to the retailer, from whom the customer could pick up the movie. In addition, Columbia stipulated that the cartridges be designed so that they could be rewound only by the distributor: if a customer wanted to see a movie at a theater multiple times, they had to buy multiple tickets, and the studio wanted to be sure that multiple home viewings would require multiple rentals.

With a 114-minute recording time, the Cartrivision fell just short of the two-hour bogey required for taping movies from broadcast television. Worse, as Christmas 1972 arrived, the entire stock of tapes, both blank and prerecorded, were found to have decayed in their warehouses. Plagued by technical glitches, an inability to kick-start the positive feedback between device sales and movie rentals due to an inconvenient retail channel, and impatient financial investors, Cartrivision went bankrupt by mid-1973, barely over a year after launch.[8]

It is difficult to know what Sony, or the industry generally, learned from CTI's failure. There was a lot wrong with it that could explain the disappointing results. The Cartrivision was relatively expensive, had low-quality video reproduction, offered limited and inconvenient movie viewing, required replacing one's television, and was technically unreliable. How would one know which of these to improve first, and by how much, in order to realize a more positive outcome? Nor do we know whether what Sony intended to launch in 1970 would have been better than the Cartrivision. If nothing else, however, it demonstrated that mass-market video technology was "in play," and that delay in introducing a new product was not costless: a more aggressive competitor might steal a march on hesitant rivals at any moment. Combining forces with Matsushita on the U-Matic format might well have motivated the quasi-commercial market to embrace video recording technology more quickly, but Sony's willingness to cooperate had cost it the chance to be the first to launch a consumer device.

Sony therefore had a choice to make: continue cooperating on the evolution of the U-Matic with Matsushita, or go its own way. Either path had material implications on the choices available to Sony in the future, a phenomenon known as "path dependency": what you do now affects what you can do later. If Sony pursued further cooperation, it would continue to be limited by Matsushita's inferior technical capabilities. If Sony chose to go it alone, it would have to make do with fewer resources and run the risk of a format war. Sony had contributed the lion's share of the technology to the U-Matic, and then it had been held back by Matsushita. Confident in its ability to create better products faster, and convinced that the best products would dominate the market—or at least be successful enough—Sony pursued VCR technology on its own under the Betamax brand.

Much to Sony's shock, Matsushita proved able to develop a VCR on its own, the VHS. Despite continuing technical advances by both companies, material trade-offs between cost and quality remained. Higher picture quality demanded more expensive parts and faster-moving tape, which served to increase costs and reduce recording times. Less expensive parts and slower-moving tapes resulted in less expensive machines and longer recording times, but lower-fidelity picture and sound.

These technical constraints precipitated Sony's next strategic choice: to focus on high quality or low cost. Matsushita had a long-standing tradition of driving down cost by optimizing its designs for manufacturability and exploiting economies of scale; it was a natural cost leader. Sony's historical emphasis on technical excellence gave it an edge on various dimensions of quality. In a manner that both reinforced and foreshadowed the company's commitment to product differentiation, Sony optimized high-fidelity recording and playback. Stung by the U-Matic experience, and in keeping with Morita's vision for the company—"Always lead, never follow"—Sony was also unwilling to make any design concessions to potential licensees. Since Matsushita could barely keep up with the manufacturing demands of Sony's designs, it will come as no surprise that Sony's intransigence on product quality severely limited the number of contract manufacturers it was able to enlist in support of the Betamax format.

The cumulative impact of these choices was that Sony was able to maintain its commitment to quality, but at the expense of manufacturing capacity, marketing budget, and distribution. Weighed against these disadvantages was the promise that in the event of Betamax's success, Sony would be able to scale up its own production organically and capture wholesale margins, which would exceed any licensing fees, while enjoying better pricing power due to lower levels of competition. In other words, Sony made a fundamental strategic bet: it pursued a product-differentiation strategy, with all the trade-offs that implied.

Matsushita's strategy was the mirror image of Sony's. Matsushita chose to back away from Betamax's level of performance on picture and sound and instead focus a higher proportion of R&D resources on manufacturability. This created two key performance differences between VHS and Betamax. First, the VHS was cheaper, and second, due to its larger cassette and slower tape speed, it had the two-hour recording capability required for taping movies broadcast on television.

In addition, because the VHS was easier to manufacture, Matsushita could license its technology more widely than could Sony. With more VHS makers investing in the format and more vigorous competition among those makers to improve the technology, Matsushita might have hoped that in time VHS would catch up to Betamax's performance levels. Furthermore, collectively the VHS makers could easily outspend Sony on marketing and advertising, and this, coupled with a more extensive distribution network, might have been seen as a way to compensate for any performance disadvantages. In other words, Matsushita made the opposite strategic bet, pursuing a cost-leadership strategy, with all the trade-offs that implied.

Betamax was released in 1974 as a bundle with a Sony Trinitron television, and was made available as a stand-alone device in 1975. Sony touted its invention as a way to time-shift broadcast television. Television and movie producers were profoundly concerned. Television advertising revenues were threatened because consumers would record programs and skip commercials. The movie business would collapse as customers abandoned theaters in favor of royalty-free bootlegged copies of movies. In an attempt to kill off the new device, Universal Pictures and Walt Disney Studios launched a class-action suit in November 1976 on behalf of their industry, seeking to have the machines declared illegal.[9] In 1976, almost two years after Sony's launch, VHS debuted with first-year sales of 110,000 units to Betamax's 1976 shipments of 175,000. Through 1977 Betamax continued to hold on to a slim lead, outselling VHS 56:44 while enjoying a 58:42 lead in installed base.

Consistent with Sony's strategy of differentiation, Betamax typically had a performance edge over VHS, albeit a small one, and usually was the first to introduce new features such as remote control, pause, and visible-picture scanning. With many more makers committed to VHS, however, any lead rarely lasted more than a few months before either Matsushita or one of its licensees was able to emulate Sony's innovation. For the same reason, although no single VHS maker matched Sony's product diversity, the total VHS line of VCRs available was invariably broader, covering a greater range of price, performance, and feature combinations.

Furthermore, since VHS devices were supported by a broad array of companies that competed not only with Sony but also with one another, VHS makers were soon found along the full spectrum of strategies: product differentiation, cost leadership, and many points in between. With customer preferences distributed along this continuum, VHS—if no single VHS maker—could appeal to a larger total number of consumers. By the late 1970s, it was clear that VHS would continue to close the gap and ultimately surpass Betamax in market share. All else equal, however, it was perfectly reasonable to assume that there would remain a segment of customers who preferred the performance characteristics unique to Betamax, and so Sony could well have hung on to a sizable and profitable niche. Since Sony produced nearly as many VCRs as Matsushita, the largest of the VHS makers, Sony's overall profitability would have been at least the same as that of any single VCR manufacturer, and quite likely higher since Betamax models were often premium priced.

All else is rarely equal. Seeing its market share erode as customers chose VHS's longer recording time over Betamax's superior video and audio reproduction, Sony introduced the BII version of Betamax in 1977 (and so the original format came to be called BI). The increased recording time compromised Betamax's video quality (although it was generally still better than similarly-priced VHS machines). Far more important was the incompatibility of the two versions of Betamax: tapes designed for BI could not be played on BII, and vice versa.

No doubt Sony managers felt that the incompatibility of BI and BII was not going to be a significant factor for consumers. Some BI owners might delay trading up to BII because changing formats would require them to own two machines in order to watch their library of BI recordings. The VCR market was young, however, and maintaining or expanding its market share of new purchases was surely more important to Sony than defending a young and small replacement market.

Unfortunately for Sony, 1977 was also the year that the video-rental market was reborn. Fox licensed fifty B-list feature films for distribution by a small entrepreneur. At that time the VCR market was split 50:50 between BI and VHS, since BII had just been introduced, so Fox made its movies available in the BI and VHS formats.

The BII proved far more popular than the BI, and since Sony's 1977 sales were almost two and a half times its cumulative sales since introduction in 1974, the BI was dropped in 1978, even though it was still close to 30 percent of Betamax's installed base. This left Betamax at a sudden and significant market share disadvantage in the eyes of the small video-rental shops that were sprouting up all over America. These space- and capital-constrained mom-and-pop storefronts had little or no interest in carrying two versions of Betamax; carrying it at all was enough to ask. Given BII's rapid ascendancy, they rationally chose to stock BII tapes. But since the introduction of BII and the licensing of movies for rent coincided, BII had not had time to establish significant market share. As a result, Betamax's effective share for the purposes of renting out movies was more like 33:66—a swing of 25 percent in a single year.

Betamax's market share continued to shrink in subsequent years, driven now by two forces. First, the larger range of VHS models appealed to a greater number of customers. Second, and ultimately far more important, there were increasingly strong network effects due to the availability of rental tapes: more VHS tapes available to rent, more VHS sales, more VHS tapes available to rent.[10] The explosive growth of the rental market—it doubled every year from 1982 to 1986, or a thirty-two-fold simple increase—drove Betamax to extinction in the U.S. market by 1989.

Sony's strategic bet was that the VCR would be used to time-shift television programming and that product quality would determine success. The company optimized its product for recording television shows with high-fidelity video and audio, and pioneered features that enhanced time shifting, such as visible picture scanning, which made it easier to skip over commercials. The nature of the technical trade-offs in video recording meant that these features could only be provided in a more expensive machine. Matsushita appealed to more cost-conscious consumers at the expense of inferior recording capabilities and other performance attributes.

FIGURE 2-1   **BETA AND VHS U.S. SALES FIGURES: 1975–1988**

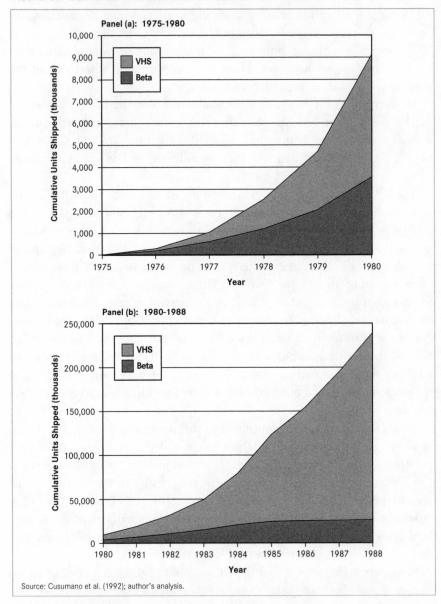

Source: Cusumano et al. (1992); author's analysis.

Through 1980, the battle between Betamax and VHS in the marketplace was essentially a fair fight. VHS overtook Betamax in annual production figures in 1978, and surpassed it in total installed base in 1979. In 1980, the cumulative market share split was 60:40 in VHS's favor—by no means an insurmountable disadvantage in most markets. What sealed Betamax's fate was the surprisingly strong network effect of the rental movie business, which amplified an otherwise unimportant market share lead in 1980, turning it into the basis of total market domination.

FOR ADULT AUDIENCES ONLY

One piece of the puzzle, notable by its absence in the published accounts I have found, is the role of pornographic video sales and rentals in the Beta/VHS battle. VCR technology made home movie-viewing a private affair. This was a boon to the adult entertainment industry, since it allowed consumers to avoid the social stigma of attending movie screenings in public theaters.

Anecdotal evidence suggests that Sony did not make production equipment and duplicating technology available to adult video producers, while Matsushita was much more accommodating. This difference in the addressable market might have been an important part of what allowed VHS to make up quickly the market-share lead enjoyed by Beta from 1976 to 1978. These same accounts reveal that Sony is similarly resisting making Blu-ray high-definition DVD technology available to the adult entertainment industry, while Toshiba's HD-DVD format is already widely available to producers.[11]

The role of adult video in determining the eventual victor in the battle between high-definition DVD formats is almost certain to be material: there is good evidence that pornographic content created an early and highly profitable market for DVDs, broadband Internet, and video on demand. But the VCR war was perhaps the precedent-setting case for establishing the role of adult entertainment in the adoption of new consumer electronic devices, and so it would have been difficult to say back in the late 1970s whether the availability of pornography on Beta was going to tip the scales. One can hardly fault Sony for not learning a lesson that had yet to be taught.

Sony made a short-run operational mistake by not designing a two-hour recording time into its original models. Some have pinned the failure of Betamax on this one misstep.[12] This is an overstatement, for it was an error Sony quickly corrected with the BII model: the VHS two-hour recording time advantage lasted only five months, from October of 1976 until March of 1977, with subsequent recording time advantages on either side similarly short-lived or of marginal competitive value.

What sank Betamax was the unforeseeable resolution of two key strategic uncertainties: (1) Would viewing rented movies at home drive adoption, or would time-shifting television programming be the "killer app"?; and (2) Would consumers opt for product quality or low price when choosing which VCR to buy? Sony's strategy was predicated on time shifting and high quality carrying the day. As it turned out, the right answer was home movie viewing and low price. Sony bet big—which is what you are supposed to do to be successful—but bet wrong.

Why did Sony not get it right? What prevented Sony from seeing how it should have positioned the technology? The conventional wisdom attributes the failure of Betamax to the preferential treatment the major Hollywood studios allegedly gave to VHS. By supposedly making their movies available in greater numbers for VHS, more consumers bought VHS than Betamax, which in turn made it more attractive for studios to release movies in VHS than in Betamax.[13] In other words, Betamax failed because Sony did not predict or respond to the network effects that determined which standard would prevail.

This explanation unfairly assumes that the data were unambiguous and that Sony made an unreasonable mistake in not responding to the video-rental market sooner and more vigorously. For example, there was a consensus by the late 1970s that home movie viewing was very likely going to become a significant business, even after the failed Cartrivision effort. Synergy between content and devices was hardly foreign to Sony, as the company has owned a record label since 1968, and the studio lawsuit would have made it tough to ignore the general sentiment that VCR technology had potential as a movie player.

However, despite general enthusiasm for the home movie sector, it remained unclear, even through the early 1980s, which technology would dominate home movie viewing. In late 1978, Philips, which had been squeezed out of the VCR market, teamed up with MCA to launch the Disco-Vision videodisc format. MCA, which at that time owned the largest catalog of films in the world, manufactured and distributed its movies for videodisc under its own label, and also secured deals with Paramount, Disney, and Warner Brothers for additional titles. In 1980, Pioneer launched its videodisc system, while RCA (a major U.S. licensee of the VHS format) and JVC (Matsushita's subsidiary) were slated to launch disc-based formats in 1981.[14]

Videodisc technology might seem quaint today—if it is remembered at all—but it was in many ways a precursor of today's fabulously successful DVD format. Although the players could not record broadcast television, they were less expensive than high-end VCRs and had much better audio and video. In addition, the movie studios were enthusiastic about videodisc. VCR tapes had to be recorded in "real time," that is, it took two hours to copy a two-hour tape, in massive "slave machine" operations. Worse, VCR tapes could be fairly easily copied by consumers. In contrast, the videodisc was "pressed," much like vinyl records, and was nearly impossible to copy due to the relative sophistication of the data tracks. This meant that individual movies could be sold for under $30, whereas VCR tapes cost up to $80.[15]

In addition, too heavy a reliance on the rental angle seemed unwise, given the challenges Cartrivision encountered establishing its rental distribution network. The lower price of videodiscs and resistance to piracy meant that, although a sound rental model existed (greatly aided by the superior longevity of videodiscs over VCR tapes), the studios were hedged: consumers could also buy, rather than merely rent, movies. A purchase model would be good news for studios, because it would greatly increase the number of discs the studios could sell, and it made the home movie business much like the music industry. As a result, it was not uncommon for industry observers to conclude that the VCR would become a niche product while videodiscs would be the mass-market device.[16]

With this in mind, consider the VCR market from Sony's perspective in 1978. Betamax and VHS were in a dead heat and there was no reason to think that anything in the foreseeable future would change that. The VCR-based movie-rental business had just gotten off the ground, and the only titles available were secondary movies from a relatively desperate Fox Studios (which, if its box-office fortunes were to turn around, might not release additional titles for rental). The last time someone tried to build a rental business it failed, even with studio support. At the same time, an alternative movie-playing technology was being launched by a major electronics manufacturer with an axe to grind (Philips) in collaboration with a major Hollywood studio (MCA). This alternative format had significant support from several other major Hollywood studios, some of which were suing Sony to have the Betamax declared illegal (the lawsuit, filed in late 1976, would not go to trial in District court until 1979). Consequently, Sony was wary of pushing the "home theater" aspects of Betamax, a reluctance echoed in the nonactivity of Matsushita on this front. Betamax's only advantage over the videodisc players was that it could record broadcast television, and its only advantage over VHS was that it could record broadcast signals better. Maintaining that performance lead required an unwavering commitment to innovation.

Under these circumstances, Sony's decision not to throw its weight behind the movie-rental business in 1978 was a prudent and perhaps even strategically astute move. If the major studios were suing Sony for enabling consumers to record broadcast transmissions, why think the studios would ever allow people to rent movies in a format that enabled piracy? Besides, the studios were lining up behind their own technology, which in addition to protecting their interests better was a superior movie-viewing system. Why would Sony antagonize such powerful adversaries? Instead, Sony could think of the market in terms of different machines for different purposes and focus on its competitive advantage. To the extent that a rental market ever did emerge, Sony would be at no significant disadvantage given the roughly equal market share for each standard. Thanks to Betamax's superiority over VHS in playback quality, Sony could have reasonably expected that at worst its share might erode slowly.

What surprised everyone was the speed with which the rental business emerged and the intensity of the resulting network effects on the market share of each format. Once the market tipped in the direction of VHS, its advantage was amplified throughout the value chain. By the early 1980s, companies that copied tapes for the rental stores were making drastic cutbacks in slave machines, installing VHS systems over Betamax at a 10:1 ratio. In almost no time, there was vastly more choice available in VHS and rental stores began dumping their Betamax inventory at $5/tape and stocking only VHS, even though Betamax had 25 percent of the installed base as late as 1984.[17] Movie studios, as much as they would have liked to have sold their movies twice—once in VHS and again in Betamax—soon followed and dramatically cut back the number of Betamax releases. Sony tried to support the availability of Betamax rental tapes with a direct-sales campaign and even established its own video label. By then, however, Sony was only delaying the inevitable.

If Sony could not have predicted what the right strategy was going to be, perhaps they could have adapted to the competitive context as it evolved. Assume that Sony drew a different conclusion from the early success of the video-rental market in 1977 and decided that success depended not on product quality but market share—which would have driven the availability of Betamax tapes, thus triggering an unstoppable positive feedback loop.[18] Given the observable success of low-cost, low-price VHS decks, this could have been most easily achieved by cutting the price of Betamax players. It has been estimated that had Sony cut its price in the 1978–1981 period, it would have driven VHS from the market by 1986, for all the same reasons that VHS ultimately proved victorious.[19]

This *ex post* solution assumes that Sony could have cut prices in the manner required to defend its early lead long enough to succeed. However, Sony's basic design decisions, made in the early 1970s in the wake of the U-Matic disappointments, were based on optimizing video and audio quality, not cost of manufacturing. Switching to a cost-leadership strategy even as early as 1978 would likely have meant the kind of redesigns that had stranded the BI, essentially forcing Sony to start over—not a move consistent with a push to increase market share. Besides, any shift in emphasis by Sony toward price-based competition would not be done in a vacuum. Matsushita and the VHS consortium had greater scale, greater cumulative volume, and had long emphasized cost control in their designs. Whatever cost reductions Sony might have been able to make, it is all but certain that Matsushita would have responded with even deeper cuts in cost and price. In short, Sony probably did not adapt because it *could not* adapt. The commitments it had to make in order to prosecute its chosen strategy precluded the kind of adaptation required, and those commitments were made on the basis of perfectly reasonable, if ultimately incorrect, beliefs about the future.

And so, as is often the case with conventional wisdom, a complex reality has been simplified at the expense of relevant, and illuminating, detail.[20] It was not necessarily arrogance that was behind Sony's decision to go it alone in the development of its VCR technology. Cooperating with Matsushita on the U-Matic meant not only sharing the market but also settling for a smaller market. Sony did not fail to notice the potential of the video-rental business, it simply concluded that the market would evolve slowly and was more likely to be dominated by videodisc systems than by the VCR. Studio support for VHS was the last domino to fall, not the first, and Sony responded as well as it could when it became clear what was happening. Finally, Sony did not ignore customer preferences when deciding to focus on picture quality over price in the face of consumer demand for a different set of trade-offs. Rather, the company likely had no other choice given the commitments it had made to a product-differentiation strategy at the design stage in the early 1970s.

Of course, one can make the case that the success of the VCR rental market had an enormous impact on VHS adoption, since that is what actually happened. My point is that when looking at the "future" (1985) from the point of view of the "past" (1977), alternative "histories" of the period are equally defensible. Sony made its commitments in the face of material strategic uncertainties, betting on TV time shifting and product quality. The company executed its strategy very well, overcoming a short-run operational error in order to extend recording time to two hours. In doing so, however, Sony found itself at a disadvantage in market share that mattered only because movie renting emerged at just the wrong time and became far more important than expected much more quickly than expected. Finally, Sony was unable to respond by cutting price, because the commitment to product differentiation made a timely and effective switch to cost leadership practically impossible.

Chalk up Betamax's demise to the strategy paradox. Sony created exactly the kind of strategy required to succeed, but in so doing, created the possibility of total failure. Had Sony bet right, Betamax would have been another line item on the company's long list of successes. In the event, Betamax was hobbled by relative consumer indifference to picture and sound quality, and the finishing blow was the unexpected ferocity of the network effects associated with movie rentals.

Just as Sony cannot be blamed for shortsightedness in its defeat, Matsushita can claim no credit for prescience in its victory. Considering the market in 1976, especially in light of the Cartrivision failure, it was entirely plausible that TV viewing and product quality would become the key drivers of success. Matsushita made the best machine it could, and that was a machine that was consistent with its historical strengths. And those turned out to be the right commitments to have made.

In other words, each company based its strategy on its own distinctive competencies and different assessments of what would lead to success in the long run.[21] Matsushita emerged victorious not because it made *better* choices but because it happened to have made, for reasons it could not have foreseen, what turned out to be the *right* choices. The critical strategic uncertainties favored Matsushita, not Sony. That is perfectly legitimate, of course; you still get to keep the money. But we call that "good luck," not "good strategy."

2.2 THE SOUND OF MUSIC

Sony's next three major initiatives in the consumer electronics business were the compact disc (CD), the digital audiotape (DAT), and the MiniDisc. These resulted in, respectively, total victory, crushing defeat, and a prolonged, zombielike existence that will certainly end in frustrating failure.

The most interesting of these examples is the MiniDisc, but to fully appreciate its significance, consider briefly the stories of the CD and DAT.

2.2.1 Compact Disc

The CD, launched in 1983, was developed by Sony and Philips.[22] This new technology provided a number of advantages over vinyl records, or LPs. The discs were more robust, smaller, and provided easy random access to individual tracks, often via remote control. Although the sound quality was inferior to that of LPs at first, for many users this was more than compensated for by these other advantages. Steady improvements in CD technology narrowed the sound quality gap to insignificance fairly quickly, eventually winning over all but the most exacting audiophiles.[23] With no format war to fight, and the technology required to make both the players and the pressing equipment licensed widely, the CD went from 1 million units sold in the United States in 1983 (vs. 210 million LPs) to parity with LPs by 1987, and never looked back.

The absence of a viable competitor to the CD was not the only factor contributing to the rapid rise and dominance of the format. Customers were so enamored of the CD that they were willing to pay a premium over vinyl. Since CDs were cheaper to make than LPs, the music industry's per-unit margins were much higher for CDs than for LPs. Even better, customers were not

FIGURE 2-2 **U.S. SALES OF VARIOUS PRE-RECORDED MUSIC MEDIA**

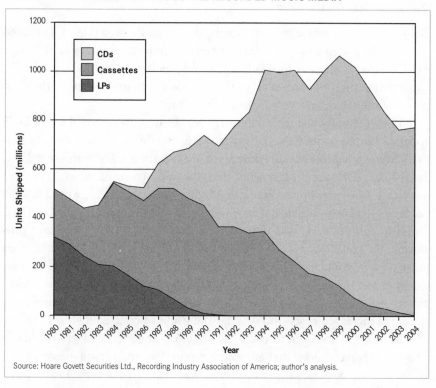

Source: Hoare Govett Securities Ltd., Recording Industry Association of America; author's analysis.

merely willing but keen to replace their music collections with CD versions of recordings they already owned, creating a booming business in re-releasing existing material. The result was that CDs proved a boon of unprecedented— and to date unequaled—magnitude to the record labels. The labels' support was therefore vigorous, and they aggressively released new content exclusively on CDs and actively eliminated vinyl as a format.[24]

This meant a brisk business in CD players of all types: home, car, portable, and personal systems were all in great demand.[25] Sony was only one of many makers, however, and it was always subject to price and feature pressure from competitors of every stripe. The company got its due in licensing royalties as one of the founding companies of CD technology, but the lion's share of the value created seems to have been captured by the music companies, not the product innovators.

As a result, although a great success as a product, the CD was less of a success as a business. A strategy based on collaboration and licensing was by no means a failure, but it managed to duck extreme success as well. Sony had avoided Betamax's fate, but the price had been the greatness that the company felt should define it.

2.2.2 Digital Audio Tape

Sony's follow-up music format was the digital audio tape (DAT), launched in 1987. Intended to replace the venerable compact audiocassette (CAC), DAT offered a number of CD-like features, including the display of track information, random access (even if it was slower than CDs due to the need to spool the tape), and very high-quality sound.

Not surprisingly, the record industry was vigorously opposed to the DAT format. Thanks to its CD-quality recording capability, home recordings on DAT were much closer substitutes for high-margin CDs than were CAC recordings. The same arguments that the industry used when trying to squelch CAC—that home piracy, in addition to being illegal, would kill the recording business—seemed if anything more relevant when applied to DAT. Even though the CAC was ultimately an unalloyed benefit for record producers, the truce that emerged remained an uneasy one.[26] If DAT had been successful, it would have extended the life of a recordable format, and worse, one that had thinner margins than CDs. Each new format also created additional distribution and inventory costs. Greater risk of piracy, thinner margins, and increased costs—no wonder the studios preferred disc to DAT.

The industry had been forced to accept CACs during the LP era because it was the only technology that allowed car, portable, and personal use, the last of these made possible largely by Sony's Walkman. By the early 1990s, however, thanks to the rise of auto, portable, and personal CD players, the CD was beginning to approach the functionality of the CAC, *sans* the recording capability, which to music industry executives was by no means a bad thing. The labels therefore refused to make any meaningful catalog of music available on DAT, which delayed the launch of the new format for years. Sony eventually broke the impasse by creating what is still known today as the Serial Copying Management System (SCMS). This technology permits the creation of a copy, but makes it impossible to "copy the copy."

As a consequence of the functional limitations and the uncertainty surrounding the technology's future, DAT player volumes remained very low: by 1990, Sony had sold a cumulative total of only 260,000 units. This meant that prices were quite high: over $1,000 for stand-alone decks and almost as much for portable players. With no prerecorded music to speak of, costly players, and expensive blank tapes, the personal-use DAT market never really got off the ground. The only demand that emerged was among amateur musicians and professional users making demo tapes who valued high-quality sound reproduction. Annual DAT player sales peaked in 1994 at just over 130,000 units, and Sony discontinued DAT in 2005 when monthly shipments fell below 100.[27]

Sony's DAT strategy in many ways emulated its approach to Betamax: a closed standard, sold on the basis of superior performance, and targeted—*de facto,* if not by design—at recording and copying applications. Had it been successful, it would have been fabulously successful. But as with Betamax, the requisite market conditions, even if plausible, never materialized.

2.2.3 MiniDisc

What could Sony have learned from the success of the CD and the failures of Betamax and DAT? That "copy only" is not enough to succeed; content is crucial to the success of a new format; early market share is critical in the event that positive feedback kicks in; and, in the U.S. market especially, convenience trumps sound quality as a spur to adoption.

Almost certainly with these expensive lessons in mind, in 1991 Sony announced its MiniDisc format, welcoming consumers to the "Disc Age." The technology was a direct competitor with Philips's Digital Compact Cassette (DCC), which Sony derided as "old fashioned."[28] Disks for the MiniDisc were smaller and more robust than CDs, which, despite advances in buffering technology, were still not entirely suitable for use during activities such as jogging. Better still, the MiniDisc could *record*. In sum, the MiniDisc replicated the functionality of the CAC in a higher-quality, more convenient form factor. Just as the CD has replaced LPs, the MiniDisc would replace the CAC, and the MiniDisc player would be the Walkman of the disc format.

Not only were consumers expected to love it, but the MiniDisc had a lot going for it on the supply side as well. Although incompatible with CD players, the discs were easy to manufacture in existing CD plants and enjoyed all the cost efficiencies of a pressed medium. In addition, having doubled down on the music business in 1988 with its purchase of CBS Records, renamed Sony Music Entertainment, Sony had become a major record label and so could ensure a meaningful supply of content upon launch. Understanding the importance of features other than sound quality, the MiniDisc's designers had compromised on fidelity, going with sophisticated, if "lossy," compression technology (so called because the compression software "lost" some of the underlying analog signal) to keep the discs and players small and rugged. Meeting these demands meant that the device was still expensive, at about $500. Blank discs were relatively cheap, though, at about $3 each, and prerecorded discs were no more expensive than CDs. Here was a device that combined the best of the CD with the best of the CAC.

But the MiniDisc failed. In 2000, almost ten years after launch, sales topped just 14 million units worldwide, 8 million of which were in the

FIGURE 2-3 **WORLDWIDE MINIDISC SALES: 1993–2004**

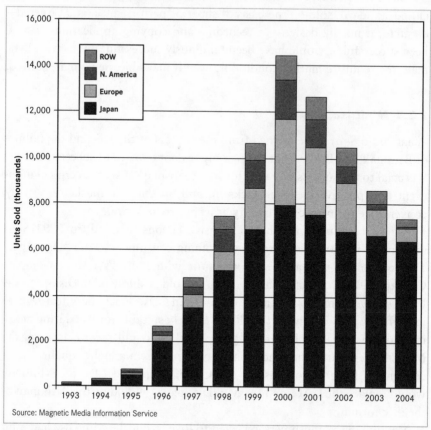

Source: Magnetic Media Information Service

Sony's MiniDisc was only a force in the Japanese market. Its weak showing in Europe and outright failure in the United States was a function of many interrelated factors. Perhaps one of the main differences between the Japanese and other markets was the higher penetration of personal computers and broadband Internet connections through the mid-1990s in North America and Europe. The incorporation of CD-R drives in PCs coupled with the ability to swap songs over broadband Internet connections created a recordable, disc-based medium that soon morphed into MP3 players, solving the portability problem at least as well as the MiniDisc could. MiniDisc's other advantage—being able to record live performances—was only a very small niche application in any market.

Japanese market. Cumulatively to 2004, there have been about 64 million MiniDiscs sold, compared with the 32 million Apple iPods sold in 2005 alone.

So what went wrong this time? Betamax was undone largely by a single, if powerful, mechanism: the rapid emergence of the video-rental business. In contrast, MD was ultimately quashed by a years-long confluence of several trends, few of which were discernible until it was too late to mount an effective response. Not only did everything that could go wrong for Sony actually go wrong, everything that went wrong *had* to go wrong in order to sink what was in fact a brilliantly conceived and executed strategy. In my view, it is a miracle that the MiniDisc did not succeed. To see why, we will have to follow several threads simultaneously, from the rise of the Internet, to the penetration of broadband networks, to the evolution of the personal computer (PC), to the development of the computer storage and software industries.[29]

Thanks to the success of CD players, the core laser technology used to read the discs had become very inexpensive, and by the late 1980s was a candidate for installation in personal computers. The data-storage capabilities of the CD, at 650 MB, vastly outstripped the floppy disk, giving rise to CD-ROM (Read-Only Memory) devices for reference books, such as encyclopedias, or games. Although these were not especially successful in the long run, the rapid proliferation of CD-ROM drives in the early 1990s made the CD the preferred medium for the distribution of prepackaged software: rather than twenty to thirty floppies to install the latest version of Microsoft Windows, a single CD would do the trick. As a result, compact disc technology was on two parallel tracks of technological evolution: the music business and the computer industry.

Once established as a data-access device, the attractiveness of recordable CD drives over floppies became obvious. There remained material challenges, but they were merely technical. CD-R (for "recordable") drives were available as early as 1988, but at a cost of $25,000. As is typical of such technologies, however, prices fell rapidly, more through innovation and learning than scale. By 1993, long before any commercially significant volumes had been reached, CD-R drives were $5,000, with the accompanying discs running about $30. The following year, prices were less than $1,000 and $7, respectively. In addition, CD drives installed in computers were exempt from SCMS restrictions, since that would have unreasonably limited the copies computer users could make of their own data.

Even at $1,000, CD-R drives were too expensive for the mass market, and so ZIP and JAZ drives from Iomega were briefly the dominant "beyond-the-floppy" storage devices. These drives were relatively inexpensive. However, because of their high mechanical content they were not on the kind of cost-reduction curve that CD-R technology was on, which had more electronic and optical components. In addition, Iomega discs were considerably more expensive than blank CDs on a per-megabyte basis.

Lacking a clearly dominant technology, the storage industry in the PC sector struggled through a few years of relative turmoil. In 1995 and 1996 it was not looking good for CD-R: adoption was slow and inventories were piling up. In response, producers began slashing prices, driving the cost of recordable discs to under $2. At that price, consumers realized that CDs had become the best data-storage deal around, for the discs were now so inexpensive that it more than compensated for the cost of the drives when compared to ZIP or JAZ systems. As a result, demand for CD-R drives exploded. With the increased volume came further cost reductions, putting the price of drives below $400 for the first time, which further fueled demand. Ironically, then, it was the spontaneous and widespread belief that CD-R technology was doomed that created the virtuous cycle that made it the most successful recording medium of all time.

Meanwhile, the Internet began its meteoric rise from thirty years of relative obscurity to mass-market consumer phenomenon. It started with the World Wide Web and Mosaic's Web browser, and accelerated rapidly with the birth of Netscape in 1994. The Web, coupled with the recently codified MPEG series of protocols for the digital compression of music files, enabled services such as the Internet Underground Music Archive (IUMA), first launched in 1993. IUMA's mission was to allow artists to connect directly with their audiences, circumventing the existing structure of the music industry. In the main, however, only artists who could not land a record deal went this route, and worse, without a way to burn the files retrieved from the Web to CDs, music purchased over the Web was captive on one's hard drive.

By 1997, like lovers fated to meet, music and the computer were united. Cheap CD-R drives and recordable blank CDs made it possible to rip, mix, and burn from CD to CD . . . to CD to CD, since there was no SCMS software in the way. The Web and MP3 had put innumerable music files on computer hard drives, all crying out to be liberated and played on any of the hundreds of millions of CD players worldwide.[30] The CD had become high quality, recordable, and infinitely duplicatable.

The conversion of the computer-based CD drive into a music player and recorder came just in time for component makers, for by the late 1990s the data-storage race had shifted gears. Hard-drive storage had become so cheap that tens of gigabytes were standard on most PCs, obviating the off-loading of files onto CD-based archives to "make space." In fact, it was the surfeit of hard-disc storage space that allowed people to keep music on their computers in the first place. The other bit-burning application, data backup, was being done over networks to central disc storage, or via inexpensive external hard drives. The only need for a small, convenient computer-storage device was porting data between computers, and flash drives, corporate networks, and the Internet had taken that over. As a result, the CD was no longer needed as a data-storage device. (The floppy, JAZ, and ZIP formats had all but disappeared.)

Then came peer-to-peer file sharing in the form of Napster in 1999, created by a seventeen-year-old Northeastern University undergraduate named Shawn Fanning. Napster was only successful thanks to another nail in MiniDisc's coffin, the proliferation of high-speed Internet connections. Without high-speed access, the download times for multi-megabyte music files would have kept peer-to-peer file sharing no more than a niche application. So where did "fast Internet" come from? You might think that something as significant as mass-market broadband was a deliberate strategic investment by cable and telecoms companies, but there is a case to be made that it was a welcome and unexpected side effect of competition in the cable TV market.

In 1994, GM's Hughes Electronics division launched DIRECTV, a satellite-based video distribution system, in collaboration with United States Satellite Broadcasting.[31] With 175 channels and an 18" dish, DIRECTV posed a serious competitive threat to the lower-capacity coaxial cable networks run by the cable companies. In response, the cable industry invested over $75 billion dollars in the mid-1990s, effecting what became known as the 750 MHz upgrade, which increased the bandwidth of many cable systems so that they could compete with satellite services providers.

Given the high fixed cost of trenching all that fiber, it is not surprising that many cable providers put in more capacity than they could immediately sell. One of the applications that emerged to make use of this surplus bandwidth was Internet access, since the cable companies could now provide much higher-speed service than the then-dominant dial-up connections provided by the phone companies. The success of cable-based Internet access forced the phone companies to invest in their own upgrades so that they could provide high-speed service as well using Digital Subscriber Loop (DSL) technology. The result was that within a few years hundreds of thousands of households in the U.S. had the kind of access speeds that had historically been the sole preserve of universities and government institutions.

Now all those songs stored on people's hard drives could be accessed by anyone with an Internet connection, mixed, ripped, and burned for free . . . but no longer exclusively to CDs. Instead, the rise of flash memory in the data-storage arena had given birth to flash-based MP3 players, the first of which was the Rio. Finally, after twenty years, music had been pried loose from the CD format. Music lovers were thrilled. Music companies were apoplectic.

It was content, then, that broke MiniDisc's back. Yet, oddly enough, it was Sony's recognition of the importance of content that hindered its ability to make the MiniDisc the *de facto* standard in the music business. Accepting the fact that a supply of prerecorded music was crucial to the success of the MiniDisc, Sony counted on its status as a major label to both jump-start the network effects of content availability and spur the rest of the industry to support the new format.

Those same interests, however, left Sony conflicted about just how easy copying should be on its new device. The MiniDisc had limited connectivity to computers, very slow CD copying, and respected the SCMS restrictions put in place during the struggles over DAT. All this made perfect sense at the time. There was no disc-based recording alternative in 1991 and Sony wanted to protect the interests of its own music business and to enlist the support of the rest of the industry.[32] As a result, by the time Sony began building into the MiniDisc the kinds of features needed to make it competitive with MP3 players, it was too late.[33] According to Ken Kutaragi, head of Sony Computer Entertainment (which created the phenomenally successful PlayStation), Sony was slow to respond because of concerns over copyright and the company's commitment to content/device synergy.[34]

But remember: Sony made this commitment only because a *failure* to make a similar commitment was felt to have been a contributing factor to the demise of Betamax. In the late 1970s and early 1980s, there was a real question about which technology would come to dominate the video-rental business: VCRs or videodiscs. Similarly, persistent uncertainty in the data-storage realm through 1996 continued to leave the playing field wide open. CDs had a clear connection to the music business, but in 1996 CDs were, if anything, the least likely storage technology to dominate. Despite a slow sales start for the MiniDisc, even as late as the mid-1990s there was little reason to think that the MiniDisc could not eventually gain momentum and become the music format of choice.

Neither was Sony blind to the possibility of online music distribution. Press releases announcing the MiniDisc in 1991 explicitly stated that Sony anticipated the day when customers would access their music over the Internet and burn the songs using the MiniDisc. Nor did Sony sacrifice convenience for performance, as it had with Betamax. To ensure that MiniDisc playing times could cope with even the longest albums yet remain compact, Sony sacrificed sound quality and invested in compression technology that allowed the MiniDisc to hold seventy-four minutes of music—more than enough for most CDs, and 25 percent more than the C-60 CAC tapes the MiniDisc was intended to replace. The players were robust and could deal with the shocks and abrupt movements of activities such as jogging, and so were vastly superior to portable CD players.

Other compromises, such as real-time recording (i.e., it took one minute to record a minute of music), hardly seemed compromises, since the perceived competition was the CAC, which suffered from the same limitation. As for the cost, Sony made the players as inexpensive as it could and actively solicited other manufacturers: by 1996, Sony accounted for only 41 percent of MiniDisc production, while Sharp produced 24 percent, Kenwood 20 percent, and JVC 7 percent.[35]

In short, just as with Betamax, Sony made entirely reasonable choices that simply *turned out* to be wrong, but that could not have been *predicted* to be wrong. Unlike Betamax, however, which was sunk by a single strategic uncertainty, the MiniDisc's living death was a result of a string of unfavorable resolutions to a number of uncertainties. Each of these was unlikely in its own right, and their collective probability must surely approach zero. Reflect for a moment on what Sony was up against:

1. Uncertainty in computer-storage technology:
   a. the rise of the CD as a data-storage device, despite the general failure of CD-ROM. Industry observers as late as 1996 gave CD-R little chance of ultimately succeeding.
   b. the oversupply of hard-disc storage space on most personal computers at just the right time so as not to undermine the push for cost-competitive CD-R technology
   c. the emergence of flash-based storage as a data-porting device, which gave rise to the MP3 player
2. Uncertainty in network infrastructure:
   a. the rapid penetration of broadband network access, made possible largely by the investment of the cable companies in upgrading their network to compete with satellite TV
   b. the advent of the Web
   c. the rise of Netscape, a small software start-up, as it stole a march on industry leviathan Microsoft in the Internet browser space, making the Internet a mass-market phenomenon after thirty years of relative inertia
3. Uncertainty in software:
   a. the general acceptance of MP3 compression protocols, when there was no real market or need for same
   b. the development of free peer-to-peer software for file swapping

Sony's commitments were reasonable ones, and its strategy was precisely the kind required to create and capture enormous value. Had the assumptions on which its commitments were made come to pass, the MiniDisc could have been an extravagant success and almost certainly have been no less than a viable consumer electronics product with perhaps a very bright future. There were no execution flaws, no bad breaks on the hardware or software side (as with Cartrivision or DAT), and no strategic offsides with

the record labels. Sony saw all the challenges it could reasonably have foreseen, and it faced up to them brilliantly.[36]

Instead, every critical uncertainty, none of which could have been foreseen, went against the company. The fundamental restructuring of the music
business around the computer and the Internet—a phenomenon that took
over a decade to emerge—left Sony strategically "stranded." By 2005, global
sales of MiniDisc players had fallen to 7 million units, almost 4.5 million of
which were in Japan. The same year, sales of "digital portables," that is,
storage-based rather than disc-based players, were almost 3.5 million units
in Japan, up from fewer than 130,000 four years earlier. Thanks to the strategy paradox, the MiniDisc is doomed.[37]

2.3 FIGHTING THE LAST WAR

Do you see your company reflected in Sony's experiences? Not the outcomes of these particular initiatives, of course, but the process: an inspiring
vision, customer focus, leading-edge technology, careful analysis, flawless
execution, adaptability . . . what more could you want?

Well, success, of course. But when a company can hit all the right notes
and still be off-key, there is something wrong with the instrument, not the
musician. Sony built and implemented its Betamax and MiniDisc strategies
the way one is supposed to . . . and failed. Sony managers *could* have come
to the right conclusions; the universe would have to be a malevolent place
indeed for success to be structurally impossible. The point is that at the time
Sony had to make its choices there was no way to tell definitively which
road was the right road, and there was nothing Sony could have done to
determine more accurately how to proceed. The existing tools of strategic
planning demand either prediction, which ignores uncertainty, or adaptability, which accepts it, because they have no meaningful mechanisms for
managing uncertainty.

Worse, because the future is perpetually unpredictable, no company
knows whether to learn from its defeats, replicate its successes, or remake
the rules entirely. Betamax failed because of the surprising nature of the
growth of the video rental market and the unexpectedly sudden defeat of
the videodisc format. The CD succeeded because the music business and
consumers loved the format: it had much better economics and was better
in all the ways that consumers wanted it to be better. DAT failed because of
the lack of content and pricey portable players.

Sony learned all these lessons very well when designing and launching
the MiniDisc. The company backed the device with its own content muscle
to avoid getting stranded by a lack of prerecorded music. It focused on cus-

FIGURE 2-4 **COMPARING STRATEGIC CHOICES: BETAMAX AND MINIDISC**

	Elements of Strategy			
	Customer use	Licensing	Features	Development of complements
Betamax	New: Time-shifting TV programs	Discouraged	Video and audio fidelity	Passive
MiniDisc	Established: portable music	Aggressively developed	Convenience	Active

Source: Author's analysis.

Sony cannot be accused of having repeated any putative "mistakes from the past" in launching MiniDisc. For each of four fundamental strategic choices that contributed to Betamax's demise, Sony made the opposite choice for MiniDisc. **Customer Use:** Betamax was attempting to create an entirely new market, while MiniDisc sought to build upon a market Sony understood well and dominated. **Licensing:** Betamax's technical complexity made it difficult for Sony to sign up licensees, a constraint Sony was willing to accept as the price of product leadership. With MiniDisc, Sony actively courted licensees to drive market acceptance. **Features:** Sony's engineers defined product quality for Betamax, but MiniDisc's features were dictated by the needs of customers. **Development of Complements:** Any consumer electronics device needs content. With Betamax, Sony found itself in a prolonged lawsuit over the TV time-shifting application, and allowed the video-rental business to evolve independently. But MiniDisc enjoyed the active support of Sony's music studio, one of the largest record labels in the world.

tomer needs for portability and ruggedness, and replicated an oft-cited source of success for both VHS and CDs by licensing its technology widely. Sony even waited before entering the U.S. market until the viability of the technology had been demonstrated in Japan, the world's second-largest music market. When the MiniDisc was a hit there, what other conclusion could you draw but that it was time to launch in America?

So what actually succeeded? Apple's iPod. Its characteristics? Initially, the iPod was a large, expensive device built around a closed hardware architecture and a proprietary software interface that had no particular support from any of the record labels. In other words, it was a strategy that should have failed—and indeed, it was a strategy many predicted would fail. But it did not. As it turned out, the key driver of adoption in the new music industry ecosystem was the ease with which people could acquire and manage their exploding libraries of digital music files. Apple, thanks to its history of hardware/software integration, was perfectly positioned to solve precisely that problem, and its success there allowed it to create iTunes, a terrifically successful online digital music store.

Was Apple insightful? Absolutely. Were they "foresightful"? No more than was Matsushita in emerging victorious in the VCR battle. Sony learned well the lessons of its previous wars. The problem is that the next war is always different from the last one, and it is almost never possible to tell just what those differences will be.

The failure of the MiniDisc in the United States should not, in my view, be attributed to a lack of strategic insight on Sony's part. As nearly as I can tell, Sony did everything it could have done to make the device a success. The MiniDisc failed because the landscape changed in unpredictable ways. The emergence and combined impact of the Internet and file-sharing software, advances in disk-drive technology, and the rise of flash-based MP3 players could not have been foreseen. Now that it has happened, we can certainly explain it, but understanding the past is very different from predicting the future.[38] Sony was not the victim of bad planning or lousy strategy or poor execution. Sony was done in by the strategy paradox. Again.

So what should Sony have done? The short answer, which will have to suffice for now, is that Sony focused too much on the pursuit of strategic success and not enough on the management of strategic uncertainty. How can companies manage strategic uncertainty in ways that mitigate the strategy paradox? In the next eight chapters, I will attempt to explain the concepts and tools required, and in Chapter 11 apply those tools to Sony's choices.

To begin that journey, consider the following question: why were Sony's commitments such that when they proved inappropriate the results were so disastrous? What is it about the kinds of commitments required for success that make potentially debilitating strategic uncertainties so difficult to avoid? In other words, why is there a strategy paradox in the first place? This is the subject of the next chapter.

Sony's strategies for Betamax and MiniDisc had all the elements of success, but neither succeeded. The cause of these failures was, simply put, bad luck: the strategic choices Sony made were perfectly reasonable; they just turned out to be wrong. The problem is that Sony focused too much on strategic success and not enough on strategic uncertainty.

---

1. Consumer Electronics Association: *CEA U.S. Sales and Forecasts*, January 2005.
2. Two other notable miscues were: (1) CBS's pioneering color television technology, introduced in 1951 but ultimately defeated by RCA's competing standard, which wasn't

introduced until 1954 (see http://inventors.about.com/library/inventors/blcolortelevi-sion.htm); and (2) the prolonged battle between 8-track tapes and compact audiocassettes (see http://www.recording-history.org/HTML/8track1.htm).

3. It is an interesting question whether or not the analysis of what follows is colored in any material way by the fact that Sony is a Japanese company. There is a school of thought that posits significant differences in business practices based on national cultural differences; see Hampden-Turner, Charles, and Fons Trompenaars (1994), *The Seven Cultures of Capitalism: Value Systems for Creating Wealth in the United States, Japan, Germany, France, Britain, Sweden, and the Netherlands,* London: Piatkus. I don't believe that the strategic issues explored here need be significantly qualified as a result of any putative uniquely Japanese traits.

4. Sony took its name from the Latin *sonus,* meaning sound. There is an apocryphal and erroneous urban legend that Morita was wandering the streets of the Big Apple recording the sounds of city life on his newly invented tape recorder and named his fledgling company using the acronym for "Sounds of New York."

5. This section is based on liberal borrowing and some synthesis of data and analysis from four sources: "Strategic Maneuvering and Mass-Market Dynamics: VHS over Beta" by Michael A. Cusumano, Yiorgos Mylondadis, and Richard S. Rosenbloom, *Business History Review,* Spring 1992; Ohashi, Hiroshi, "The Role of Network Externalities in the U.S. VCR Market in 1978–86" (May 2001), http://ssrn.com/abstract=291972; Wielage, Marc, and Rod Woodcock (1988), "The Rise and Fall of Beta," *Videofax,* Iss. 5., http://www.betainfoguide.com/RiseandFall.htm; and Rohlfs, Jeffrey H. (2001), *Bandwagon Effects in High-Technology Industries,* Cambridge, MA: MIT Press. These sources are not unanimous on all aspects of the data or their respective conclusions.

6. The salience of a standards war was doubtless a consequence of the consumer electronics industry's experience with the battle between 8-track cassette tapes and Compact Audio Cassette (CAC) tapes (indeed, CACs were "compact" in comparison to the 8-track standard). The 8-track was invented in 1964, and in 1965 was introduced as a custom option in Ford automobiles. Home players were introduced in 1966. The CAC had been invented in 1963 to record the spoken word and improved for music applications in 1966. Although the vinyl LP dominated home use due to its superior sound quality, there was no clear-cut victor in the portable music market for almost a decade, and the industry was saddled with supporting three commercial formats. The 8-track was not vanquished until the early 1980s, when it all but disappeared, largely as a result of the success of Sony's CAC-only Walkman.

7. For a history of the little-known Cartrivision, see http://www.angelfire.com/alt/cartrivision/, accessed February 1, 2006, or http://www.cedmagic.com/history/cartrivi-sion.html, accessed February 7, 2006. I'm grateful to Tom Eisenmann of the Harvard Business School for this additional nuance in the story.

8. To foreshadow a distinction that will become crucial later on in this chapter, Cartrivision was done in more by poor strategic choices and critical operational uncertainties than by fundamental strategic uncertainties. That is, their retail strategy was cumbersome, although it's unclear whether this was debilitating or merely constraining. Operationally, the deterioration of the tapes in their warehouses might well have been a crippling blow. The underlying strategy—that is, how they hoped to make money—actually turned out to be sound (recording TV programs and viewing prerecorded movies); they just couldn't pull it off.

9. The Federal District court that heard the case ruled in Sony's favor, only to be overturned by a U.S. Court of Appeals, which was then overruled by the U.S. Supreme Court in 1984, thereby establishing that the recording of television shows for private use was not copyright infringement. See the Museum of Broadcast Communications

Web site: http://www.museum.tv/archives/etv/B/htmlB/betamaxcase/betamaxcase.htm, accessed January 10, 2006. The MBC recommends referring also to Harris, Paul, "Supreme Court O.K.'s Home Taping: Approve 'Time Shifting' for Personal Use," *Variety* (Los Angeles), 18 June 1984; Lardner, James, "Annals of Law; The Betamax Case: Part 1," *The New Yorker* (New York), 6 April 1987; and Lardner, James, "Annals of Law; The Betamax Case: Part 2," *The New Yorker* (New York), 13 April 1987.

10. See "Network Effects and Platforms, Part I: Core Concepts" by Thomas R. Eisenmann, Harvard Business School note N9-806-055. Eisenmann's note does a very careful and thorough job of explaining the different types of network effects and the role of the constituent elements in a successful network. In this case, the video-rental business is a "two-sided" network business: the purchasers of the video player/recorders are one side of the network, video-rental operations and the movie studios are the other side. In this particular instance, each side of the network benefits from an expanding population of users on its own side and the other side: more consumers means more rental shops, which means more studios make movies available; more studios means more rental shops means renting is more attractive, which means more consumers.

During the first two years of the VCR market, when Betamax enjoyed a market share lead, network effects were in Betamax's favor, but they were weak, consisting only of the ability of users to share tapes they made themselves. Hollywood movies were unavailable in either format, for purchase or rental. Competition between the two formats turned on features, price, dealer support, and marketing—in short, all the "usual" components of product market competition.

11. Seitz, Patrick (2006), "High Def's Adult Situation Favors Toshiba," *Investor's Business Daily,* March 2.

12. Most recently, Lee Gomes in the *Wall Street Journal* (January 25, 2006) attributes Sony's ultimate failure entirely to the differences in recording times. Gomes's data seem to have been drawn from a draft of the Cusumano et al. paper cited above; the data I've used come from a reprint of the version that appeared in *Business History Review* (Spring 1992).

13. "Sony: Bad Strategy, or Bad Management?" *The Economist*, March 12, 2005, p. 12.

14. Sony entered the videodisc business itself, and along with Pioneer and other makers continued to produce pressings well into the 1990s. The installed base of videodisc players was estimated to be about 700,000 units worldwide in 1986 (vs. 155 million VCRs in the U.S. alone) and was projected to grow to 130 million by 1995. Although the videodisc business proved viable in Japan, other parts of Asia, and elsewhere, such projections proved overly optimistic. Source: *Magnetic Media Information Service* (henceforth *MMIS*), Vol. 9, Iss. 3 (April 1987).

15. A positive feedback loop was at work to drive the prices this high. The structurally higher cost of duplicating videocassettes meant that the consumer retail market was at first quite small. Consequently, the rental market emerged to spread that higher cost across many consumers. With a flourishing rental market, the studios could capture value only by charging very high prices for the tapes. And once they were charging very high prices for the tapes, they couldn't shift to a consumer market model: it is difficult to charge rental outlets $80 for a tape sold to consumers for $25; and if rental outlets can purchase their tapes at consumer market wholesale prices, they can drop rental fees low enough to undermine the consumer market. It is arguably because of this phenomenon that the consumer market for movies didn't really take off until the introduction of DVDs.

16. Londoner, David J., and Francine S. Blum (1981), *The VideoDisc Goes National,* Wertheim Research Department, January 2. This industry commentary expected VCR sales to peak in 1986 at 3 million units per year, while videodiscs were expected to reach

40 percent household penetration by 1990. In the event, VCRs sold over 150 million units in 1986 and the videodisc was never a factor in the U.S. market.

17. It's difficult to determine precisely why there was such a dramatic shift to VHS in the duplicating business, since these operations were presumably responding to downstream demand from rental stores. One hypothesis is that the rental stores, as small entrepreneurial operations, had limited capital to invest in inventory and limited space. Once the VHS market-share advantage reached a certain point, there would have been room for only a very small number of Betamax titles, and once the selection got small enough, it may well have made sense to discontinue Betamax altogether. After all, what's the point in carrying six Betamax titles alongside several hundred VHS format tapes?

18. Such a response would amount to making a very different commitment, especially if it meant selling at a loss in order to ensure sufficient market share. Expensive "racing behavior" can in fact be highly profitable, and the conditions under which racing is strategically prudent have been explored; see Eisenmann, Thomas R. (2002), "A Note on Racing to Acquire Customers," Harvard Business School publication N9-803-103.

19. See Ohashi (2001), op. cit.

20. What to include and what to leave out is always a judgment call based on the point one is trying to make. The danger is that one becomes too selective and leaves out important qualifying, or even falsifying, data in the interests of being compelling. For instance, in the version of the story I tell here, I leave out the fact that there were six competing VCR technologies, not just two. My belief is that this simplifies the story without distorting reality: the main rivalry in terms of market share was clearly between VHS and Betamax, even though the third runner, Philips, hung on for a decade.

21. This raises a fascinating problem around the definition of "core competence." Whether something is core or not is problematic enough; but let's assume that problem can be overcome: something is core if you're very, very good at it. Whether that capability is a competence or an incompetence, however, might well depend on factors far beyond your control. Sony's core skill was its design expertise; Matsushita's was its low-cost manufacturing. One turned out to be an incompetence, the other a competence, but not because of anything the firms themselves did. See Dougherty, Deborah (1995), "Managing Your Core Incompetencies for Corporate Venturing," *Entrepreneurship Theory and Practice,* Spring, pp. 113–35.

In addition, Sony's (and perhaps Matsushita's, but we'll never know) difficulty in adapting was similarly a function of the "core" nature of the capabilities under consideration. To be good at something requires commitment over time, and that same commitment makes it very difficult to change, and not just because it is difficult to abandon one set of commitments: even if abandonment comes easy, it still takes time to accumulate the expertise required to be sufficiently expert at new skills to be competitive. See Leonard-Barton, D. (1992), "Core Competences and Core Rigidities: A Paradox in Managing New Product Development," *Strategic Management Journal,* Vol. 13, pp. 111–25.

22. For a succinct description of the facts and strategic choices surrounding the development of the CD, see "Philips' Compact Disc Introduction" case series (A)-(C), HBS cases #9-792-035, #9-792-036, and #9-792-037, by Anita M. McGahan.

23. Many audiophiles insist that vinyl is a superior medium for the reproduction of sound, largely because it is analog—as are the sound waves created by speakers—rather than digital. However, for many users, any increased fidelity is more than overcome by the practical difficulty of keeping records free of scratches and dust.

24. Hoare Govett Securities, Ltd., "World Music Industry Report," March 1994.

25. Portable systems have their own speakers. Personal systems require headphones or earbuds.

26. The recording industry has long viewed devices that allow consumers to make copies of purchased recordings as a *bête noire*. Fair-use provisions that allow consumers to make copies of legally acquired recordings for their own private use make it difficult for the industry to have such technologies outlawed—although as the Betamax lawsuit demonstrated, that doesn't stop major players from trying.

The analog cassette was originally seen as a doomsday device that would in short order bankrupt the music companies. Its recording feature was important, of course, as it made possible the do-it-yourself "mix tape," which doomed the 8-track tape. (Eight-track sales peaked in 1974 and declined rapidly thereafter.)

Such recordings don't seem to have undermined album sales, and in fact, may well have spurred them: people knew that in buying an album with some well-liked tracks they could listen to them in a manner of their choosing. In addition, the analog cassette freed people from the LP's physical constraints, allowing auto, portable, and personal devices that were impossible with LPs. As a result, music companies profited handsomely by releasing most titles in prerecorded cassette format as well as LP: by 1980, cassette sales were two-thirds of LPs by unit volume.

The rise of the CD had little initial effect on cassette sales, which continued to grow through 1989, and as late as 1994 were still over 50 percent of CD sales by unit volume.

27. *MMIS* proprietary data. See http://mmislueck.com/ for details.

28. Most of the data on which this analysis is based is drawn from back issues of *Magnetic Media International Newsletter*. As a real-time account of industry observers' projections for technologies such as CD-R drives, it is free of the hindsight and survivor bias of historical accounts.

29. Philips's DCC format was developed in collaboration with Matsushita and never got off the ground, failing even more miserably than DAT. Sales peaked in 1995 at 220,000, and the format was discontinued in 1997, having sold a cumulative total of fewer than 550,000 players. DCC suffered from all the drawbacks that plagued DAT, and DCC players were even more expensive. Plus, blank tapes were buggy from the start, precluding DCC from a share of the amateur recording artist and studio market niches that DAT was able to create.

30. DIRECTV was not the first satellite system to launch. PrimeStar, owned by a consortium of cable companies, launched in 1991. With fewer channels and larger dishes, PrimeStar was unable to compete with DIRECTV or EchoStar's DISH Network, which went live in 1995.

31. The SCMS copy protections that developed through negotiations between Sony and the music industry, as part of the DAT agreements, were written into CDs as well, but were easily worked around via computer software.

32. There were limited efforts to make MD a data-storage device as well, essentially an attempt to work its way from music to storage, and back to music. There were certainly no deep technical challenges that precluded using it in this way. The problem was that Sony needed to negotiate interface protocols with the computer industry, something it proved ultimately unable to do.

33. These features included 32× recording speeds, high-density MD discs that store up to forty hours of music, much-improved connectivity with computers, and the ability to play MP3 files. Unfortunately for Sony, by 2001 Apple's iPod, which was based on disk-drive technology rather than flash memory, had 20GB of storage—enough to keep someone boppin' for a week or more.

34. "Proprietary Worries Delayed New Sony Products, Top Executive Admits," *Globe & Mail*, January 21, 2005, p. B12.

35. *Nikkei Weekly*, August 4, 1997, Vol. 35, No. 1785, p. 7.

36. Still more fascinating, since the MD was launched the same year as the DCC from Philips and Matsushita, Sony decided to hedge its operational risk in this format war: The firms cross-licensed MD and DCC technology to each other. This gave each an option on alternative technologies—but not, critically, on alternative *strategies*: both the cassette-based DCC and disc-based MD counted on the same underlying structure of the music business. The two technologies were simply different bundles of features and capabilities. See "Digital Compact Cassettes: Sound Wars," *The Economist,* May 16, 1992, Vol. 323, Iss. 7759, p. 89.

37. Unless it's not. After all, the point of these tales, and indeed of this book, is that the future is unpredictable. But its return from the dead seems highly unlikely. A dedicated set of niche users persists, enthralled by the MD's features and endlessly annoyed at the device's limitations (see Iver Peterson, "In a Nod to Niche Users, Sony Rethinks the MiniDisc," *New York Times,* June 17, 2004). This situation seems eerily redolent of the fate suffered by DAT.

Incidentally, the success of the iPod was hardly preordained, and seemed much less likely to succeed than the MiniDisc ever did. When first introduced, the iPod was derided as too expensive and wedded to yesterday's technology, as it is based on disk-drive storage rather than flash. (Or at least it was, until flash caught up to the iPod mini with 4GB of storage, at which point Apple seamlessly introduced the flash-based iPod Nano. High-capacity disk-drive-based iPods have moved on to video applications.)

38. That is why history and astrology are two different disciplines. That one is a credible field of investigation and the other is pseudoscience speaks volumes.

CHAPTER THREE

WHO DARES WINS . . . OR LOSES

The most profitable strategies are "extreme" strategies that commit companies to positions of either product differentiation or cost leadership. These extreme positions expose firms to a greater likelihood of bankruptcy by increasing the strategic risk they face. Consequently, the strategies likeliest to succeed are also likeliest to fail. That is the strategy paradox.

It is tempting to hope that Sony's misfortunes were a fluke, the sort of left-tail, six-sigma outcome that befalls only the very unlucky. The bad news is that Sony's fate illustrates a general condition. Well-established theory and the most recent empirical studies suggest strongly that the most successful strategies are built on unwavering commitments to specific courses of action: which products to make, what features to give them, which customers to sell them to, whether to make the best products or the cheapest, and so on. The stronger these commitments are, the greater the potential upside. At the same time, the strategies that have the best chances of succeeding brilliantly are also the ones most exposed to the most debilitating kind of strategic uncertainty. In other words, success awaits only if you have made the choices that future conditions happen to value; otherwise you fail.

The only way firms have found to avoid the risks attendant to extreme strategies is to avoid extreme strategies. This greatly reduces the possibility of achieving above-average returns, making the strategy paradox a form of the risk/return trade-off that has so long been a staple of financial theory and practice.

3.1 GOING TO EXTREMES

Among Michael Porter's many contributions to management thinking, in my view the most substantial and seminal is that all strategies can be thought of in terms of their position along a continuum between *product differentiation* and *cost leadership*.[1] These two dimensions define what amounts to "strategy space," and the state of technological understanding at a point in time defines the "production possibility frontier"; more prosaically, it limns the boundaries of what can be provided at what cost.

Porter's is not the only categorization scheme of this type.[2] For example, Treacy and Wiersema, in their 1995 book *The Discipline of Market Leaders,* identified three generic strategy types: *operational excellence, product leadership,* and *customer intimacy.* Going back to 1978, Miles and Snow proposed *defender, prospector,* and *analyzer* categories. James March, in a 1991 paper, suggested a dichotomy between *exploitation* and *exploration* strategies. There are many others.[3]

It turns out that these typologies, and others of like intent, have more similarities than differences.[4] Cost and efficiency are repeatedly identified as one type of generic strategy. That is, one can compete by providing a lower level of product performance, however defined, but at significantly lower prices. The labels are different, but the central elements of a *cost leadership* (Porter), *operational excellence* (Treacy and Wiersema), *exploitation* (March), or *defender* (Miles and Snow) strategy are cost, efficiency, reliability, and execution.

There is less similarity among the various approaches when it comes to the "other" dimension(s) of strategy. Nevertheless, the degree of convergence is remarkable: *product differentiation* (Porter), *product leadership/ customer intimacy* (Treacy and Wiersema), *exploration* (March), and *prospector/analyzer* (Miles and Snow) are all outwardly focused, with an emphasis on innovation, discovery, customers, or differences in product features or performance levels.

The reason for these similarities, I believe, is that each researcher is leveraging an underlying truth: resources are not limitless, and because time and space cannot be compressed, we live in a world of inescapable trade-offs.[5] Companies work constantly to push the production possibility frontier outward and have enjoyed remarkable success: customers get "more for less" today than they did yesterday in just about every product category. But at any given point in time, the frontier exists and it defines the current realm of the possible.

Choosing a strategy can therefore be thought of in terms of choosing a

THE MYTH OF THE HIGH-QUALITY, LOW-COST COMPETITOR

It is popular to claim that some companies have broken the trade-off between high quality and low cost, providing instead high quality *at* low cost. Toyota is commonly invoked as an example: the quality of its cars exceeds that of its competitors, yet it also has lower costs than those same competitors.

Toyota might well produce higher-quality cars at lower cost than its competitors, but this simply means that Toyota *defines* the production possibility frontier for automobile manufacture. The company's competitors have strategies that are "interior" positions—they have yet to reach the frontier.

The frontier is constantly moving outward, thanks to innovation. For example, there is a trade-off between power and fuel economy in the design of internal combustion engines. However, thanks to technological advancement, cars today have higher power and better gas mileage than they did fifty, twenty, or even five years ago.

Nevertheless, at any point in time, the state of the art is such that trade-offs must exist, if only because it is impossible to get something for nothing. This law is suspended for no one, not even Toyota. After all, even Toyota cannot produce Lexus quality for the cost of a Camry. The production possibility frontier is not merely an empirical fact; it is a logical necessity.

position on the production possibility frontier. The products or services a firm provides express the trade-offs they have chosen to accept between the various dimensions of performance and cost. Getting to the frontier is of course critical, but this simply means that a firm has mastered the existing state of the art in its industry. Strategy is something else altogether: it is about choosing where on the frontier you want to get *to*.

Many researchers assert that extreme or "pure" strategies at the edges of the frontier will generally lead to higher profitability than strategies in the middle, known as "hybrid" strategies.[6] Porter argues unambiguously for strategic purity:

> Becoming stuck in the middle is often a manifestation of a firm's unwillingness to make choices about how to compete. It tries for competitive advantage through every means and achieves none, because achieving different types of competitive advantage usually requires inconsistent actions.[7]

Others are less categorical in their conclusions but remain highly doubtful that hybrid strategies are likely to do even as well as pure strategies. No one argues that pure strategies should ever do worse than hybrids.

These assertions rest on the underlying trade-offs that motivated the strategic typologies in the first place. Recall that the production possibility frontier is simply a general statement of the fact that a firm cannot drive its costs down while simultaneously incorporating leading-edge, and hence highly expensive, components in order to achieve high levels of performance. Therefore, minimizing cost means accepting a lower level of performance on at least some dimension.

Consequently, a hybrid strategy is vulnerable to attack on either flank by competitors that have purer strategies.[8] A pure cost player should be able to underprice a hybrid competitor and lure away price-conscious shoppers, while discerning quality-conscious consumers will gravitate to players with a more nearly-pure differentiation strategy.[9]

Not only will companies with a hybrid strategy have a more difficult time keeping their customers, they will likely have higher costs due to increased complexity, which also makes it more difficult to make consistent choices.[10] For example, when managers of a company pursuing a pure strategy are faced with a choice, they know how to respond. If they are a product differentiator, they know to invest in the product. If they are a cost leader, they know to drive down the costs. In contrast, hybrid strategies require that managers walk a tightrope, sometimes choosing to reduce cost, at other times choosing to increase performance. The difficulty of making the right choice every time should not be underestimated, and the likely result is an aimless wandering along the edge of the production possibility frontier, confusing customers with respect to what they should expect from the company. Worse, the complexity will likely lead to frequent slips off the possibility frontier altogether, giving the competitive advantage to more focused competitors able to offer more for less.

We can see the downside of being stuck in the middle in an example from the retail industry. Sears, Roebuck & Co. began life as a catalog retailer in the late nineteenth century. Based on its success there, it expanded into store-based retail, and by the late 1920s the company was opening a new store every other business day. By 1931, store-based revenues exceeded those of the catalog business for the first time.

Much of the company's success came from anticipating correctly the impact of the automobile as a mass-market consumer good. The rise in car ownership led to greater customer mobility, which meant that store locations no longer had to be in urban centers where real estate was expensive. Cheaper land allowed bigger stores, which in turn allowed for a more extensive range of goods to be put on offer. Growing faster and more profitably than its downtown department store rivals, Sears's rise through the middle part of the twentieth century was largely a result of greater focus: it targeted the rising middle class while Marshall Field's and Macy's struggled to be all things to all people.

By the 1970s, however, the "rising middle class" was no longer an identifiable market segment. Retail concepts at the high and low end, in the form of Nordstrom and Wal-Mart respectively, began to find traction. These retailers were not "new entrants" by any means, but an increasingly stratified economic landscape had made the general retail market ever more fissiparous, and Sears found itself stuck in the middle.[11] As a result, since 1990 Sears's sales have been essentially flat, while Nordstrom and Wal-Mart have experienced strong growth.

In what promises to be a landmark study of the "pure vs. hybrid" hypothesis, Stewart Thornhill and Rod White of the Ivey Business School in London, Canada, have found a strong relationship between profitability and purity generally. Using a sample of more than 2,300 operating businesses across a wide range of manufacturing and services industries, they have concluded that the greater a firm's degree of strategic purity, the greater its profitability. The relationship holds at both the cost-leadership and product-differentiation ends of the spectrum.[12] In other words, strategy theory has had it right all along: the best strategies are the purest ones.

3.2 MONKEY SEE, MONKEY CAN'T DO

If firms occupying the extremes of the frontier enjoy superior profitability, why do other firms currently languishing in the middle not simply copy them, moving out to the edges as well and competing away the excess profits? How are these differences in profitability maintained?

Strategies are most successful when they have built up a position in the market that competitors cannot readily copy.[13] Those strategies that require *commitment over time* are the most difficult to emulate, for generally those strategies that take time to build will take time to duplicate.[14] It is not enough to choose a pure strategy: a firm must choose a pure strategy that can only be implemented successfully through long-term *commitment*, for only commitment ensures that you will create something resistant to opportunistic replication by competitors.

Formal academic research underlines the importance of commitment and attempts to define those circumstances under which commitment is critical. For example, "first-mover advantages" can confer real benefit.[15] Being first to ramp up production can allow a firm to exploit learning effects. Even just building production can dissuade would-be entrants through signaling. By acquiring key resources first, firms can preempt competitors. By acquiring customers and creating significant switching costs, firms can create difficult-to-overcome barriers to entry. As illustrated by the Betamax vs. VHS story, the existence of network effects (e.g., movie rentals) can often amplify this type of first-mover advantage.[16]

Strategies based on commitments are by definition very difficult to copy quickly. The subtleties of competitive advantage are too nuanced to be understood and emulated by competitors who are not willing to make the same kind of investment—in money and time—as a firm that has identified a profitable extreme position. Good strategies are not necessarily fragile, but they are intricate, with many interdependent, tightly linked components.[17] As a result, a company cannot shift quickly from its low-cost strategy to its competitor's product-differentiation strategy even if that is what the market favors.[18]

The notion of commitment in strategy also finds expression in the concept of "Big Hairy Audacious Goals."[19] BHAGs are explicit, nowhere-to-hide, psychological commitments to specific outcomes. Targets must be chosen with care and based on an understanding of a company's capabilities and constraints. Once chosen, the advice is unambiguous: march defiantly, yet humbly, forward and never look back. Committing in this way unleashes the drive and determination of the entire organization. The clarity of purpose that BHAGs bring can spur focused, consistent, highly effective action.

As with "hard" strategic commitments, BHAGs are resistant to mimicry. How could any company expect to galvanize its people around one compelling, long-term, burn-the-boats vision of the future, only to propose a new and different spine-tingling adventure that someone else has found to be attractive? You might get away with that once or twice, but repeatedly? A BHAG is a form of commitment, and commitments that change are not commitments.[20]

The implication, therefore, is that to maximize one's probability of success, the best strategy to pursue is an extreme, commitment-intensive one. This only makes one more sympathetic to Sony. In the Betamax and Mini-Disc cases, Sony's products not only defined the production possibility frontier, they also manifested as pure a product-differentiation strategy as one might imagine. Certainly, it would be difficult to claim that they were vulnerable to the kind of strategic "flanking" that has created such difficulty for Sears and other hybrid players. Furthermore, Sony's strategies were based on long-term commitments: the technologies Sony had mastered (video fidelity for Betamax; small size and physical robustness for MiniDisc) and the portfolio of assets it had amassed (especially Sony Music) were not easily copied.

As proof, one need only observe that no competing technology ever surpassed Sony's products on the dimensions of performance Sony sought to optimize. And as a BHAG, very little compares with "always lead, never follow." Had Sony's underlying strategic bets been the right ones, it would have been almost impossible for Matsushita or other electronics firms to follow suit—just as it was practically impossible for Sony to implement the low-cost and device/software strategies that ultimately prevailed in the Betamax and MiniDisc examples.

It is not a logical contradiction to say that high-commitment, extreme strategies on average yield higher returns, yet also acknowledge examples of such strategies that have failed. No one ever said that an "increased probability" of success means "guaranteed" success. So far, there is no paradox, just unexplained variance, an error term in our formula for competitive dominance.

The strategy paradox is revealed only when a critical research methods problem is tackled head-on. When measuring the performance of firms pursuing a given type of strategy, researchers can only measure the performance of firms that have not gone out of business. As a result, they see only the performance of the firms that survive—a phenomenon known as "survivor bias."[21] The observation that firms pursuing pure strategies enjoy higher average performance is necessarily based on the returns of only those firms that were not driven into bankruptcy. (You cannot observe the returns of a bankrupt company.) Pure firms do better, but we see only the returns of the pure firms that survived. If pure firms are driven from the field in disproportionate numbers, then the higher returns accruing to pure strategies come at the cost of a higher, but unobserved, risk of failure.[22]

Consequently, Sony is not evidence of the inappropriateness of commitments to pure strategies; it is evidence of how well such an approach works. Sony's commitment to pure strategies pays off, on average, consistent with strategic theory. The company has been able to make the right commitments often enough that it is around for its failures to be studied. It is when we take into account all those firms that bet so wrong they disappear that the strategy paradox comes into focus.

3.3 NO FREE LUNCH

In the finance arena, it is generally accepted that higher returns come at the price of higher risk.[23] Risk is generally decomposed into "systematic" and "unsystematic" risk. Systematic risk affects "the system," that is, the overall economy, and is generally unavoidable.[24] Investors can reduce the unsystematic, or "firm-specific," risk affecting the returns of their portfolios by holding shares in firms with uncorrelated returns.

In contrast, a critical and largely unspoken assumption behind the "pure strategies are better" argument is that pursuing pure strategies is essentially costless: the objective function is maximizing returns, pure strategies are more profitable than hybrid strategies, therefore pursue a pure strategy and eschew hybrid strategies. In fact, much of the thinking about strategy and risk concludes that risk and return are *inversely* correlated: better-performing firms have a lower risk of failure, and if pure strategies result in higher performance, then pure strategies should imply *lower* risk.

If pure strategies are such a great idea—delivering higher returns with lower risk—why do the vast majority of firms huddle in the middle of the production possibility frontier?[25] Part of the answer might simply be "because that is where the customers are." Arguments about "flanking" notwithstanding, is not the distribution of customer preferences across the differentiation-cost continuum an empirical question? Might there not be some markets where most customers prefer a middle-of-the-road trade-off between various dimensions of performance? Perhaps, but this possibility in no way speaks to the fact that profitability remains higher at the extremes. This means that companies *disproportionately* cluster in the middle, creating a level of competition for customers that drives down profits.[26] What kind of benightedness must afflict the general population of managers who appear so willing to accept nothing for something? Or do they know something that the rest of us do not?

What managers know, either intuitively or explicitly, is that return and risk in strategy are positively correlated. The causal link runs only one way. Higher returns imply higher risk, but not the other way around. That is, if a firm has high returns, it has typically achieved this at the cost of incurring great risk. However, merely incurring great risk does not lead to high returns: great risk, by definition, means that a firm has a greater probability of extreme success *and* a higher probability of extreme failure. The extreme strategies that increase the probability of success also increase one's probability of failure.

The rest of us have missed this because most of the work in this area suffers from a particularly acute form of survivor bias. Measures of risk have tended to rely almost exclusively on the volatility of cash flows or stock prices. Better-performing firms have tended to have smoother cash flows and researchers have interpreted this as equivalent to having lower risk. But volatility is not really of that much concern by itself. As long as the returns average out in the long run, financial markets should be indifferent to the shape of those returns over time. Cash-flow volatility is at best a proxy for a firm's underlying risk. The greater the amplitude of the fluctuations, the higher the probability that the firm will suffer a drop of sufficient magnitude that it defaults on its commitments and goes bankrupt.[27] A more direct measure of risk is therefore the probability of outright bankruptcy.

RISK AND RETURN IN STRATEGY RESEARCH

Various studies have found that higher levels of return on equity (ROE) are correlated with lower variance in ROE. Since variance in performance is often used as a measure of risk, this has led some to conclude that risk and return are inversely related.[28]

This finding has been explained using "prospect theory." Firms with high levels of performance do not rock the boat, taking an "if it ain't broke, don't fix it" approach in the hope of prolonging their strong performance. Because such firms do not try anything too different from what is already working well, high ROE causes low variance in ROE. Conversely, firms doing poorly attempt to remedy the situation by trying something new. Some firms figure it out, resulting in a recovery in their ROE levels, while others do not, resulting in high ROE variance for a population of low-performing firms.[29]

As suggested in the main text, volatility *per se* is not necessarily a bad thing. What matters, in the current context at least, is the probability of failure, as captured by the likelihood of bankruptcy, conditional upon pursuing a given strategy. Consequently, these studies are still tainted by the effects of survivor bias.

A larger question, of course, is how risk might meaningfully be measured prospectively rather than retrospectively. After all, risk is necessarily about the future, and there are no data about the future. As a result, the strategic risk that a firm faces (rather than the strategic risk that it has faced) is perhaps beyond measurement. Nevertheless, strategic risk is real and must be managed.

A recent study has examined precisely this, finding that operating companies pursuing higher-returning pure strategies suffer from a materially higher probability of bankruptcy compared to firms pursuing lower-performing hybrid strategies.[30] In other words, no doubt to the relief of the entire finance community, risk and return are correlated in strategy, just as in finance.

Take a moment to reflect on what this finding could mean. The unambiguous prescription for competitive success by the seminal and leading thinkers on competitive strategy is strategic purity, and it is the correct prescription. Pure strategies really are more profitable, even after controlling for industry, size, longevity, and all the other determinants of profitability that have so far been identified. So why are so many more firms pursuing a universally frowned-upon hybrid strategy? In the archetypal formulation, companies begin life with pure strategies. Successful companies ultimately exhaust the niches that valued their pure offers. Faced with the prospect of a low-growth but profitable existence, managers are lured by the siren-like call of larger markets. As they drift toward the middle, once-pure companies are forced to abandon the differentiation that defined their pure positions, and so their profits erode. In short, the prevalence of companies with hybrid strategic positions is seen as an unfortunate consequence of managers' pathological willingness to trade profitability for growth.

What has been ignored, however, is the mitigating role of risk in this equation. I do not recall reading anywhere in any of the leading studies any explicit or substantive warning that a pure strategic posture brings with it a higher mortality rate. The observation that pure firms earn higher returns, but also expire with greater frequency (again, controlling for size, age, industry, and a host of other factors) means that firms pursuing stuck-in-the-middle strategies are not necessarily victims of a growth fetish, but instead may well be making a perfectly rational trade-off between risk and return.

It is the collision of choice and strategic uncertainty that creates this trade-off. Imagine an industry in which there are three firms: one pursuing a pure product-differentiation strategy, one pursuing a pure cost-leadership strategy, and one pursuing a hybrid strategy. Customers who prefer a given firm's products are distributed equally. In order to remain in business, each firm must capture some minimum and equal number of customers, which is less than the average number available to them.[31]

Now assume that customer preferences change unpredictably over time. In this thought experiment, the first shift in preferences favors firms pursuing a strategy of cost leadership. This might happen if there were a general economic downturn and customers became generally more price sensitive. Under these conditions, the firm at the cost-leadership end of the strategy continuum will enjoy significantly higher profitability than firms located elsewhere, because it will end up with more customers above the minimum threshold required for survival. The firm pursuing the product-differentiation strategy will suffer much more than the firm in the middle of the strategic continuum, and so suffer a disproportionately higher risk of bankruptcy. A shift in customer preferences toward product leadership will result in a mirror-image outcome.

Such shifts constitute *strategic* uncertainty because the increased risk of failure is not a consequence of operational failings or the vagaries of financial markets. It is a consequence of having the wrong strategy. Pure firms enjoy a feast-or-famine existence, profiting mightily when customer tastes favor their strategies, and starving—often to death—when market preferences shift. When they fall on hard times, it is not necessarily a result of having executed their strategy poorly; they just have the "wrong strategy" for reasons that were unpredictable and uncontrollable. In short, pure firms are exposed to strategic uncertainty far more than are hybrid firms.

Take Apple, for instance. The California-based computer maker's history is well known and exhaustively documented.[32] The company rocketed to the Fortune 500 in the late 1970s in record time on the back of its fabulously successful Apple II and has repeatedly reinvented itself to become the darling of both consumers and investors, most recently with the iPod.

But the company has had its share of difficulties, too. Following the Apple II was the failed Lisa. The follow-up to the highly successful Macintosh and Mac Plus was the disastrous Newton. The company's terrifically successful iMac, an easy-to-use Internet-enabled personal computer, followed on the heels of the deservedly forgotten eWorld online service. And although the outcomes were radically different, all these products are perfectly consistent with Apple's strategy: make cool stuff that pushes the performance envelope by exploiting the integration of hardware and software design. It is a pure product-differentiation strategy, almost always soundly executed.[33]

The problem is that it does not always work. As the saying goes, a broken clock tells the right time twice a day. When consumers want what Apple knows how to make, the company seems unstoppable. When consumer preferences shift, Apple's fortunes fade. The company has made an underlying, fundamental strategic bet that is embodied in its hard assets, its capabilities, and in its sense of what the company is and what it stands for. That bet does not brook change, and that is what makes Apple both powerful and vulnerable. Apple's highs are hard to top; Apple's lows can be difficult to survive.

In general terms, in the extremes of strategy space only those firms that enjoyed the strongest results are likeliest to have the reserves necessary to survive until the next bout of good fortune. This periodic culling of the weak serves to increase the average performance level among firms with pure strategies, even as it increases the risk of bankruptcy for the overall population.

Both the Betamax and MiniDisc examples are consistent with this explanation. Sony chose specific kinds of product differentiation for each device. The company committed to the associated strategies, both exploiting and building the kinds of capabilities that come only with a significant investment of time and money. As a result, Sony had strategies that were both pure and difficult to imitate. The problem is that the market shifted in ways that left each product with too few customers to survive (in the case of Betamax) or thrive (in the case of MiniDisc). The markets could have sloshed back in Betamax's or MiniDisc's direction, but in both cases, no such happy event arrived in time to make a difference.

The more an organization pursues extreme profits, the more it must differentiate itself from its competition and the more it must make the kinds of strategic commitments that expose it to the ravages—and the rewards—of strategic uncertainty. It is strategic uncertainty that equilibrates risk and return as organizations create their strategies. Unfortunately, higher returns mean higher mortality. That is the essence of the strategy paradox.

3.4 OF MICE AND MEN

In "To a Mouse, Upon Turning Her Up in Her Nest with the Plough," Robbie Burns tells the tale of a mouse who, upon seeing the lush fields of summer turn brown and feeling the winds grow cold, invests mightily in the construction of a warm nest—a well-thought-out and -executed plan. The problem, of course, is that the farmer's plow turns up her nest, compromising her prospects for surviving the winter.

Strategy often has this character. It begins with a choice, is followed by commitment, and the outcome is decided for good or ill in large part through luck. Burns's mouse made a sound choice: to build a nest. She committed the resources required to make a good one. The outcome was poor for reasons she could not have imagined, let alone foreseen. Might it have been better to build in the forest, instead of in a field? Perhaps, but the forests bring their own set of risks. It was only after the fact that the field proved a bad choice. As Burns concludes:

> The best-laid schemes of mice and men
> Go oft awry
> And leave us nothing but grief and pain,
> For promised joy!

How much better off than the mouse are you? How many implicit assumptions are embedded in your strategy? How many unimaginable events could ruin your hopes for the future? What strategic uncertainties lie in wait around the next corner that will undo your best-laid plans?

Unable even to assess the risks they face, never mind address them, most firms choose to pursue "safe" strategies and forgo the kinds of returns that can be earned only through commitments to extreme positions. Is this strategic cowardice? It would be if environments were stable, controllable, or at least predictable. Strategic uncertainty would simply not exist if companies could choose the right strategy and stay there (a stable environment), shape the environment to their strategies (a controllable environment), or prepare themselves for a future they see coming (a predictable environment).

But none of these conditions holds, and so the trade-off between risk and return—between survival and riches—is not only theoretically sound but also empirically validated. Absent any meaningful way to manage strategic uncertainty, there appears to be an upper bound on the greatness we can achieve at any given level of risk. This boundary is defined by inescapable constraints on our abilities to adapt to, control, or foresee change. What are those constraints? The next two chapters address this question.

> *Extreme positions in strategic space create the highest levels of profitability but also create the highest levels of strategic risk and hence failure. That is the strategy paradox. The trade-off between risk and return appears inescapable, and most firms deal with that trade-off by accepting lower returns for a better chance of survival.*

---

1. For my money, these points are made most clearly in *Competitive Strategy*, New York: Free Press, 1980; and "What Is Strategy," *Harvard Business Review*, 1996. The other candidate for Michael Porter's "best idea" is the notion of characterizing industry attractiveness in terms of the net effect of "five forces" impinging on a firm's ability to extract profit: internal rivalry, the bargaining power of suppliers and customers, and the threat of new entrants or substitutes.

2. March, James G. (1991), "Exploration and Exploitation in Organizational Learning," *Organization Science*, Vol. 2, Iss. 1, pp. 71–87; Miles, Raymond E., and Charles C. Snow (1978), *Organizational Strategy, Structure and Process*, New York: McGraw-Hill Book Co.; Treacy, Michael, and Frank Wiersema (1995), *The Discipline of Market Leaders*, Reading, MA: Addison-Wesley. I am indebted to Stuart Thornhill and Rod White, both professors at the Richard Ivey School of Business in London, Canada, for their comparison of these typologies.

3. Most recently, see Moore, Geoffrey A. (2005), "Strategy and Your Stronger Hand," *Harvard Business Review*, Vol. 83, No. 12 (December). Moore describes a "complex systems" model designed to create customized solutions and recoup higher costs through higher prices, making up for low volume through a high-percentage margin, and a "volume operations" model designed to minimize cost and generate sufficient volume to compensate for a lower-percentage margin. Moore explains that these two models are difficult to reconcile within a single organizational structure. This seems fully consistent with product differentiation and cost leadership both in terms of the specifics of the concept and the theoretical implications of combining them.

4. Campbell-Hunt, C. (2000), "What Have We Learned About Generic Competitive Strategy? A Meta-Analysis," *Strategic Management Journal*, vol. 21, pp. 127–54.

5. At least, time and space cannot be compressed at speeds substantially slower than the speed of light. Such qualifications hardly seem necessary.

6. The most extreme positions—"pure" product differentiation or cost leadership— are archetypes; in reality, most firms will be somewhere on the curve, rather than on an intercept.

7. Porter, Michael E. (1985), *Competitive Advantage*, New York: The Free Press.

8. Chew, Bruce (2000), "The Geometry of Competition," The Monitor Company, http://www.monitor.com/cgi-bin/iowa/ideas/index.html?article=101, accessed January 16, 2006.

9. A more colloquial treatment of these ideas can be found in Silverstein, Michael J.,

with John Butman (2006), *Treasure Hunt: Inside the Mind of the New Consumer,* New York: Portfolio. Silverstein and Butman make the case that whereas in the past consumers tended to be somewhat consistent in their purchases—buying low-, middle-, or high-end merchandise almost all the time—today consumers are tending to mix up their purchases, skimping on many things in order to finance occasional splurges. This trend is amplifying the vulnerability of "stuck-in-the-middle" positions in every product market.

10. For an especially intriguing exploration of this phenomenon, see Miller, Danny, and Ming-Jer Chen (1996), "The Simplicity of Competitive Repertoires," *Strategic Management Journal,* Vol. 17. Miller and Chen find that firms with a less complex, but not less difficult to perform or imitate, set of processes underlying their competitive position outperform those depending on a highly complex set of activities. The argument is essentially that there's only so much management attention to go around, and the more complex your processes get, the harder it is to keep all the plates spinning. Hybrid strategies can be seen as more complex because they demand a finer-tuned balancing of a greater number of activities.

11. The increasingly bimodal nature of income distribution in the United States is often cited as the reason for the success of the high- and low-end retail concepts; that is, the viable "in-the-middle" strategy exemplified by Sears and other department store retailers, such as JCPenney, has been undermined only because there are no longer any customers "in the middle," not because of any necessary inferiority in their underlying strategy.

If this were all there was to the argument, however, we'd see continued success from mainstream department stores in economies that have remained more equitable in income distributions, such as Canada. Between 1971 and 1999, the overall "index of equality" in the United States has fallen from 0.36 to 0.16, with higher numbers indicating more nearly equal income distributions. Over the same time period in Canada, this same measure has gone up from 0.75 to 0.80. Yet the same "disappearing middle" in terms of retail concepts has emerged. For example, Eaton's, a century-plus-old family-owned department store retailer, held 50 percent of Canada's retail market in the 1950s, yet went bankrupt in 1999.

The business press saw in Eaton's demise a story of wealth and privilege on the part of the Eaton heirs that led them to take the business for granted (e.g., http://archives. radio-canada.ca/IDC-1-69-377-2341/life_society/eatons/clip9, accessed February 13, 2006). This might well be a proximate explanation—but it misses the larger picture, for Sears Canada, The Bay, and other "in-the-middle" retailers have similarly suffered at the hands of more focused competitors such as Wal-Mart on the low end and Holt Renfrew on the high end.

The moral seems to be that, shockingly, supply and demand are related: in the United States, income inequalities might well have led to the success of more focused retail concepts that had been simmering in the wings for decades, while in Canada markets proved as fissiparous as supply allowed. Which comes first is always an interesting question, but the end result seems always to be the same: focus pays.

12. Thornhill, Stewart, and Roderick E. White (2007), "Strategic Purity: A Multi-Industry Evaluation of Pure Versus Hybrid Business Strategies," forthcoming in the *Strategic Management Journal.* The method employed in this analysis is ingenious. Statistics Canada administers a survey annually to a stratified sample of Canadian companies. Part of the survey consists of questions regarding the relative emphasis the company places on different aspects of their operations: new-product development, R&D, cost reduction, and so on. Thornhill and White determine a ratio for each company that captures the balance between those efforts related to product differentiation versus cost leadership. Each company is then plotted in the resulting strategic space. This approach allows each company to

be characterized with respect to its competition, rather than with some idealized strategic archetype. This is crucial, since purity is necessarily a relative term.

Fascinatingly, and lending credence to the observation that the benefits of focus are not necessarily a function of income distribution, note that Thornhill and White's data come exclusively from the Canadian market.

13. Ghemawat, Pankaj (1991), *Commitment: The Dynamic of Strategy,* New York: The Free Press.

14. That is, if something takes me a long time to create, it is likelier that it will take you a long time to create it, too, *even after you've seen my solution.* Ghemawat seems to be talking about a "baking" phenomenon: as the saying goes, no matter how many people you put on the job, it still takes nine months to make a baby, and even after you've seen how I did it, you still can't do it any faster than I did. The alternative to "baking" is "learning," where one person first figures out, via long effort, patient trial, and expensive error, how to do something. In other words, if I've carefully watched you cross the stream, chances are I'll get across faster than you did and won't get nearly as wet, because thanks to you I now know where the stones are. Ghemawat includes an extensive discussion of the value of learning. But for learning to provide competitive advantage, it must confer the kind of insight that perforce can be gained only via experience, not mere observation, or else competitors will readily copy you.

15. See Lieberman, Marvin B., and David B. Montgomery (1988), "First-Mover Advantages," *Strategic Management Journal,* Vol. 9, pp. 41–58.

16. An alternative school of thought speaks of the "fast follower" model. As far as I know, there's been little evidence adduced to support the profitability of this approach. Part of the problem is definitional: when is someone "following fast" and when are they learning from someone else's mistakes to "get it right"? For example, was Apple a fast follower in the MP3 player business, or a leader? They were the first to get it right in a major way, but by no means the first to launch such a device. If fast follower means "wait and see what works, then copy that," there's little reason to think this will be profitable, since the fast follower will have little means of differentiation.

17. See, in particular, Porter's 1996 *Harvard Business Review* article "What Is Strategy?" in which he analyzes the many components of Southwest Airlines's strategy and their many interconnections.

18. See also Hammonds, Keith H., "Michael Porter's Big Ideas," *Fast Company,* Iss. 44, p. 150. Available at www.fastcompany.com/online/44/porter.html. Accessed January 10, 2006.

19. Collins, James C., and Jerry I. Porras (1994), *Build to Last: Successful Habits of Visionary Companies,* New York: HarperCollins; Collins, Jim (2001), *Good to Great: Why Some Companies Make the Leap . . . and Others Don't,* New York: HarperCollins.

20. See Sull, Donald L. (2003), "Managing by Commitments," *Harvard Business Review,* June.

21. Two recent books that explore the phenomenon of survivor bias are Pfeffer, Jeffrey, and Robert I. Sutton (2006), *Hard Facts, Dangerous Half-Truths, and Total Nonsense,* New York: McGraw-Hill; and Rosenzweig, Philip (2007), *The Halo Effect and Other Business Delusions: Why the Experts Are So Often Wrong and What Wise Managers Must Know,* New York: The Free Press.

22. Perhaps the most thorough and thoughtful treatment of the theoretical implications of how survivor bias colors the conclusions we draw about the relationship between strategy and success is Denrell, Jerker (2003), "Vicarious Learning, Undersampling of Failure, and the Myths of Management," *Organization Science,* Vol. 14, Iss. 3 (May–June), pp. 227–43.

Denrell's thought experiment posits firms that take great risk, and as a consequence enjoy either extremely high or extremely low levels of performance. Firms with extremely low levels of performance will be driven into bankruptcy. Denrell then shows that this kind of selection pressure results in an upward shift in the average performance of the remaining risky firms, which creates a spurious positive relationship between risk and return.

In what follows in the main text, the research I have done with Stewart Thornhill and Rod White shows that what Denrell posits as a theoretical possibility is an empirical fact. Building on the finding that pure strategies tend to have higher levels of performance, we then examine whether these firms pursuing pure strategies are likelier to go out of business; that is, are high-return strategies also high-risk strategies? It turns out that they are.

23. Sharpe, W. F. (1964), "Capital Asset Prices: A Theory of Market Equilibrium Under Conditions of Risk," *Journal of Finance*, Vol. 19, pp. 425–42.

24. It all depends on your unit of analysis. Systematic risk for the U.S. economy is diversifiable to some extent by investing in firms that operate in Europe or Asia, for example. To the extent that these economies' fortunes are uncorrelated, U.S.-level systematic risk can be diversified away. The vagaries of the global economy constitute truly unavoidable systematic risk.

25. Reitsperger, W. D., S. J. Daniel, S. B. Tallman, and W. G. Chismar (1993), "Product Quality and Cost Leadership: Compatible Strategies?" *Management International Review*, Vol. 33 (Special Issue), pp. 7–21. For a more managerially-oriented treatment of these same concepts, see Gottfredson, Mark, and Keith Aspinall (2005), "Innovation versus Complexity: What Is Too Much of a Good Thing?" *Harvard Business Review*, Vol. 83, Iss. 11.

26. The notion of strategic purity necessarily has an element of relativity: for any given distribution of firms in strategy space, only 5% can be in the most extreme 5%. However, the shape of that distribution is an empirical question. It could be uniform, with very nearly equal numbers of firms occupying all the occupied locations, or it could be multi-modal, with a number of high-density locations. It turns out that, as shown in Thornhill and White (2007) *op. cit.*, the distribution of firms in strategy space is highly peaked, with thin, long tails. As a result, that more firms do not move out to the edges of strategy space where returns are higher is a valid question. At a minimum, one could reasonably expect firms to distribute themselves along strategy space in a way that eliminates systematic differences in profitability. But they don't. And that's the issue.

27. Miller, K. D., and P. Bromiley (1990), "Strategic Risk and Corporate Performance: An Analysis of Alternative Risk Measures," *Academy of Management Journal*, Vol. 33, pp. 756–79.

28. Bowman, Edward H. (1980), "A Risk/Return Paradox for Strategic Management," *Sloan Management Review*, Vol. 21, Iss. 3 (Spring).

29. Bowman, Edward H. (1982), "Risk Seeking by Troubled Firms," *Sloan Management Review*, Vol. 23, Iss. 4 (Summer), and Fiegenbaum, Avi, and Howard Thomas (1988), "Attitudes Toward Risk and the Risk-Return Paradox: Prospect Theory Explanations," *Academy of Management Journal*, Vol. 31, No. 1 (March).

30. Thornhill, Stewart, Roderick E. White, and Michael E. Raynor (2005), "Strategic Purity and Firm Survival: Risk and Return Revisited," working paper, London, Canada: Richard Ivey School of Business, University of Western Ontario. Contact sthornhill@ivey.uwo.ca.

31. We could change the thought experiment to have firms occupying only those positions on the production possibility frontier that have in fact enough customers to

justify operations. We could further complicate matters by including multiple firms occupying the same position on the frontier where the numbers of customers preferring the particular product characteristics captured by a given location on the frontier would warrant it. These subtleties would greatly confuse the exposition of the argument without altering the results. Similarly, we could explicitly capture the possibility that product-leadership strategies have a lower customer threshold due to the likelihood that such firms enjoy higher margins and so require fewer customers to generate the profits needed to stay in business, while cost-leadership strategies might require more customers, since they will tend to count on lower per-unit margins but higher volumes. But who needs that headache, either?

32. A good history and overview of Apple's strategic twists and turns can be found in a series of Harvard Business School case studies. See "Apple Computer 1992," #9-792-081; "Reshaping Apple Computer's Destiny 1992 (abridged)," #9-300-002; "Apple Computer 1999," #9-799-108; "Apple Computer 2004," 9-904-460; and "Apple Computer 2005," #9-705-469.

33. See Hawn, Carleen (2004), "If He's So Smart . . . Steve Jobs, Apple, and the Limits of Innovation," *Fast Company*, Iss. 78 (January).

CHAPTER FOUR

THE LIMITS OF ADAPTABILITY

One possible response to strategic uncertainty is adaptability: changing one's strategy in accordance with the shifting demands of the market. Whatever its merits, adaptability works only when an organization can match its pace of change to that of the environment. Change that proceeds either faster or slower than the organization can respond creates insurmountable problems. In addition, fast and slow changes impinge on an organization simultaneously, and a company cannot adapt at different rates at the same time. Consequently, adaptation is limited in its applicability and is far from a sufficient response to the challenges posed by strategic uncertainty.

The dark side of commitment lies in the very real possibility of committing to the wrong things: creating products with the wrong characteristics or organizations with the wrong capabilities. Overcoming the risks of commitment has long been at least an implicit objective of managers, and perhaps the most recommended response is organizational adaptability.

An adaptable organization can change itself in important ways so that it remains attuned to the demands of the environment in which it competes. There is a vast literature that addresses how companies can maintain or reestablish the requisite fit through constant course correction. In other words, the adaptability school seeks to eliminate or at least reduce the role of commitment in successful strategy.

It is clear that people and organizations can adapt effectively. Consider, for example, Microsoft's oft-cited and well-regarded response to the rise of the Internet. In the mid-1990s, Microsoft's product suite was based on stand-alone personal computers with perhaps peripheral connections to company networks. As a result, Microsoft's strategy was built on the notion of islands of productivity. The rise of the Internet as a transforming technology in personal computing resulted in a remarkable transformation that served to "Internet-enable" many of Microsoft's key products: the islands in the archipelago had become *bone fide* nodes in a global network. Encapsulated in the now-famous mantra "embrace and extend," Microsoft did not fight the Internet or even resist it. In classic judo fashion, the company redirected the power of this new technology to its benefit.[1] Other companies can learn from this and create ways to be similarly adaptable, mitigating the risks of commitment without sacrificing competitive advantage.

However successful some companies have been at adapting to environmental change, it has long been recognized that the adaptive capacity of individuals, at least, is not without limits. In his seminal 1970 work *Future Shock*, Alvin Toffler concluded that tens, if not hundreds, of millions of people were about to be overwhelmed by change.[2] It was not merely change that was the problem, it was the nature of change. Its accelerating pace and increasing magnitude were unprecedented. The human psyche was unprepared and unable to cope, and the consequences promised to be catastrophic. In particular, Toffler cited the extreme pressure placed on individuals and families by businesses, which, in responding to the forces of change, had become a force of change in their own right. Companies were shuffling people from all levels of the hierarchy around the country or the globe, demanding that they continuously learn, unlearn, and relearn an ever-broadening scope of ever-faster-changing domain expertise. Toffler argued that it was simply going to be too much for many to handle.

These adaptive impulses are today the subject of a healthy research agenda. An assumption behind Toffler's argument is that companies can adapt to a rapidly changing environment. It was, after all, the adaptive behavior of companies that was to be a major contributor to future shock at the individual level. Concepts such as "logical incrementalism," "sense and respond," "emergent strategy," and "improvisation" all hold out the promise of enabling organizations to shift their strategic footing as circumstances require.[3]

Good thing, too. Over the last thirty-five years, the trends Toffler documented—and the demands they put on *organizations* to adapt—have, if anything, been amplified. Technological advances are subject to a positive feedback mechanism: better technology makes it possible to make even better technology. For example, faster microprocessors enable more powerful CAD-CAM software, which in turn leads to the creation of faster microprocessors. The shift to a knowledge-based economy is seen as enabling and rewarding the globalization of markets and supply chains, with enormous implications for the structure of labor markets.[4] Traditional barriers between manufacturing and service businesses, and between industries generally, are also increasingly in flux as companies seek competitive advantage through supply- or demand-side scope in response to increased pressure in their core businesses.[5]

(I make these claims circumspectly, for the rhetoric of change is often overblown. Each generation sees its world as particularly noteworthy with respect to the pace and magnitude of tumult it must face. The "good old days" are seen as a halcyon period of stability and tranquillity, while today is racked by tempestuous turmoil.[6])

Success stories capture the merits of adaptability. In light of the data, however, it would appear that at a minimum, firms have been largely unable to take this advice. A number of recent studies, taken together, suggest strongly that firms are less likely now to maintain a profitable position of market dominance than at any time in the past thirty years.[7]

The most telling of these studies, by Robert Wiggins and Timothy Ruefli, found that between 1974 and 1997 periods of superior performance shrank steadily. This is a critically important finding. It means that the best, most successful firms are less able than ever before to *stay* the best, most successful firms. In the context of the thought experiment in the previous chapter, this suggests strongly that markets are shifting more frequently and more severely, and that organizations have not become more adaptable to meet the increasing pace and magnitude of change. In other words, every strategic choice is subject to a greater-than-ever threat of strategic uncertainty. And so, whether or not *people* are in fact subject to the ravages of future shock is not something I have an opinion on, but I will suggest that *companies* are suffering from it, and their symptoms are only getting worse.

Whatever the general trend, research in the field is replete with examples and detailed case studies of organizations that have either recovered from or avoided catastrophe thanks to their ability to change in a timely and effective way. Surely organizational change is a viable response to environmental uncertainty.[8] Right?

Unfortunately, several studies have also demonstrated that the number of firms able to adapt to a changing environment, in a way that creates value over a long period of time, is vanishingly small. For example, Jim Collins's prescriptions in *Good to Great* are built on generalizations drawn from only eleven companies.[9] That is not Collins's fault; I am sure he would have loved to have had more data. There just are not that many companies that have managed to pull it off.

The paucity of long-lived successes in no way discredits the advice that organizational change researchers have to offer. The best of this work provides valuable, actionable guidance. The problem is much deeper. Organizational change is only a valid response to environmental change when the pace of change is the same for both.[10] As change accelerates, there is no choice but to increase organizational adaptability as well.[11]

This raises a number of significant problems. First, if the rate at which an organization can change falls beneath the upper bound of the pace of environmental change, then adaptability is necessarily an insufficient response. Second, an organization cannot possibly change at multiple rates simultaneously, yet will very likely face multiple environmental changes proceeding at different rates.

Adaptability, then, is a viable but limited response to a changing environment. Those limitations stem from the impossibility of adapting either to environmental change that proceeds faster than you can adapt (fast change), or change that proceeds more slowly than you are adapting to some other change (slow change). It is likely, therefore, that no matter how adaptable one might be, there is always something out there one cannot adapt to.

4.1 FAST CHANGE

Typically, an inability to adapt is defined as "inertia." This results when the relevant environment changes faster than can the organization.[12] Companies afflicted by fast change are not victims of bad management *per se*; rather, they find themselves designed for conditions that suddenly no longer exist. This kind of discontinuity is analogous to the environmental convulsions that led to the great Cretaceous extinction 65 million years ago. The "KT event" (so called because it marks the boundary between the Cretaceous and Tertiary epochs) is generally thought to be a meteor strike or strikes, the impact of which rapidly and dramatically altered the global environment, changing just about every ecosystem on the planet. Among the more notable casualties were the dinosaurs, a life-form that had dominated the planet for the previous 135 million years.

The saurians could not adapt because the mechanism of their adaptation—evolution via natural selection—permitted only very slow change compared to the rate of environmental change precipitated by the meteor's impact. This becomes obvious when we realize that no creature adapted to the immediate aftermath of the strike. Rather, the animals that endured had been, fortuitously, configured in ways that allowed them to survive for reasons having nothing to do with meteors or climate change. In particular, many more of the mammals survived than dinosaurs because the mammals had become homeothermic—that is, they had the ability to regulate their own body temperatures. Prior to the KT event, cold-blooded reptiles dominated but were at a disadvantage at night: when the sun went down, their metabolisms slowed considerably. To exploit that nocturnal niche, some reptiles became warm-blooded, which, along with other adaptations suited to foraging at night, turned them into what we call mammals. These creatures were much better able to tolerate the years-long "winter" resulting from the cloud of ash and debris raised by the meteor strike.[13]

An example of this kind of sudden and seemingly exogenous change in the business world is the meltdown suffered in the telecommunications equipment market in the wake of the popping of the "Tech Bubble" in 2001. As telecommunications service providers such as Verizon, WorldCom, AT&T, and Comcast rushed to build next-generation networks, growth in capital expenditure (capex) among these firms outstripped sales growth every year from 1993 to 2000. As a result, the equipment makers supplying the service providers enjoyed fantastic growth. Nortel Networks, for example, saw its revenue explode from $8 billion in 1993 to more than $30 billion by 2000. Informed observers hailed these firms as "stars of the Telecosm," the building blocks of the new age of broadband communications.[14]

FIGURE 4-1 **EXCESS CAPITAL EXPENDITURE AMONG TELECOMMUNICATIONS SERVICE PROVIDERS: 1991–2004**

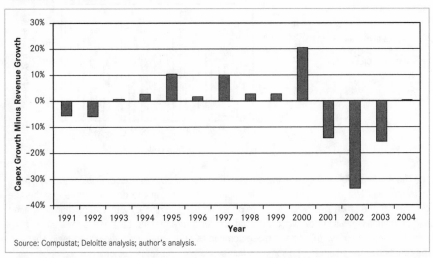

Source: Compustat; Deloitte analysis; author's analysis.

The bars indicate the difference between the growth rate in capital expenditure by telecommunications service providers (primarily telephone and cable companies) and growth in sales at the same firms. A negative number indicates that capex is growing more slowly than sales, while a positive number means capex is growing faster than sales. From 1993 to 2000, capex was growing faster than sales—clearly an untenable position. The so-called dot-com bubble was as much a "telecoms" bubble as anything else: the declines in capex from 2001 to 2003 were dramatic, driving many of the equipment supplier companies to the brink of disaster.

FIGURE 4-2 **REVENUE AND STOCK PRICE FLUCTUATIONS AMONG KEY TELECOMMUNICATIONS EQUIPMENT MAKERS: 1990–2004**

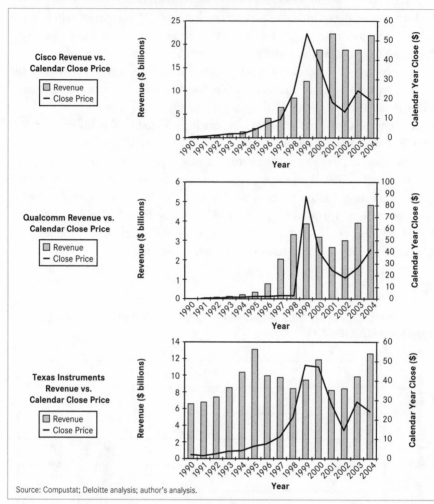

Source: Compustat; Deloitte analysis; author's analysis.

The three companies in the left-hand column (from top to bottom: Cisco, Qualcomm, and Texas Instruments) all enjoyed rapid stock price appreciation during the dot-com run-up of the late 1990s. With the crash in 2000, their share prices dropped significantly, indicating that the market had dramatically revised downward expectations for future growth. Each company's sales, however, recovered quickly. Yet none of these companies effected any significant strategic changes: they continued to sell largely the same products to largely the same customers.

The three companies in the right-hand column (from top to bottom: Nortel, JDS Uniphase, and Lucent) were similarly buoyed by the late-1990s bubble, and their revenues skyrocketed accordingly—driven largely by massive "excess" capital expenditure among their key customers, the telecommunications service providers. Their stock price plunges were more than simply a correction of inflated expectations; they were a reflection of the severe deterioration of the underlying economics of each company, something seen clearly in the significant drops in sales suffered by each firm.

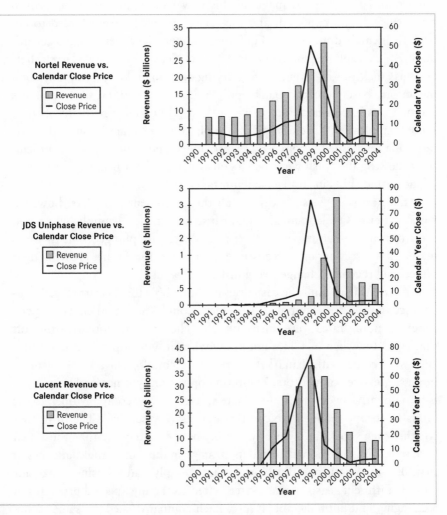

It is tempting to attribute the relative success and failure of these companies to the quality of their respective management teams. Almost certainly that played a role. But consider instead the possibility that each company was simply responding to the opportunities that presented themselves in the ways they were best able to respond. Those firms that survived relatively unscathed did so not because they were able to adapt effectively to changing circumstances; rather, their circumstances did not change much. Cisco's corporate clients kept spending on routers, Qualcomm's on mobile telecoms equipment, and TI's on chipsets. In contrast, Nortel, JDSU, and Lucent were beholden to the capex expenditure of a relatively small number of very large clients, and when they tightened their belts, no amount of organizational agility could replace tens of billions of dollars in revenue.

For reasons having little to do with foresight, some companies had developed strategies that allowed them to weather the storm, while some were adapted to conditions that changed far too quickly for them to respond effectively.

Then it all ended, and much faster than it had emerged. The new bit-burning applications that were to make all this new bandwidth profitable proved more elusive than expected, and the service providers were forced to cut back their capex dramatically. Equipment makers' revenues plunged accordingly. For example, beginning in 2001 Nortel Networks struggled to slash its costs as quickly as its revenues were drying up, and in the eyes of many commentators, barely escaped bankruptcy in 2002.[15] By 2005, the company's revenue was just over a third of its peak in 2000, and it had laid off over 70,000 employees. Lucent and JDS Uniphase were similarly hitched to the fates of a few large telecom services providers, and their respective difficulties following the crash were also a consequence of not being able to adapt to such rapid shifts in strategic circumstances.

It did not go quite so badly for all the equipment providers, however. Cisco Systems, Qualcomm, and Texas Instruments, for example, weathered the storm much better. Their stock prices certainly plunged, but this was merely a correction of unrealistic expectations for future growth; their underlying revenues changed very little.

It is tempting to fault the casualties of the bubble for their irrational exuberance. Surely the equipment providers could see that their customers' capex spending rates were unsustainable. The problem is that getting off that escalator when one does not know when it will stop is to run a different risk: ceding critical market share and technological advancement to more aggressive competitors. Exploiting opportunity is not pathological, it is a competitive necessity. Unfortunately, it leaves any company open to the kinds of abrupt change than can threaten its very survival. The firms that weather such shocks are typically not any better at adapting than those that succumb. Cisco no more changed its strategy in the face of the challenges of the 2001 recession than did Nortel. Cisco simply had a business that, for entirely different reasons, was better suited to the unexpected pressures of a changing and unpredictable future. Each company faced the same strategic uncertainty, but each had made fundamentally different strategic commitments and so enjoyed, or suffered, very different fates as a result.

There is a second type of fast change, one that has a much longer gestation period, even though it can seem extraordinarily abrupt. Consider, for example, the collision between European and South American civilizations in the sixteenth century. Each society had been developing along different trajectories for millennia, and each had evolved structures, value systems, and technologies that were appropriate to their respective environments. Transatlantic exploration by the Europeans, at first the Spanish, brought the two cultures into contact, followed rapidly by conflict.

The proximate cause of European domination of the New World was disease: the first explorers brought over highly contagious pathogens that were fatal to the indigenous population. The ultimate causes, however, are many. As Jared Diamond explains in *Guns, Germs, and Steel*, Eurasia enjoyed a largely consistent growing season since its east-west axis meant a large landmass spanned a relatively narrow range of latitudes. This meant that once a plant was domesticated, its use could spread rapidly. In addition, the luck of the draw left Eurasia with a population of domesticable animals for both food (chickens, pigs, goats, cattle) and farming (oxen, horses, dogs, cats). This allowed for the rapid development of large agrarian societies and extensive animal husbandry. Large numbers of people living in close contact with animals over a long period of time gives rise to some nasty bugs.[16] During the Middle Ages in Europe, that meant smallpox, to which Europeans (the ones who survived, at least) were immune.

In contrast, the north-south axis of North and South America meant that each region had different growing seasons, and so the development of agriculture across the entire landmass demanded the domestication of a large number of plants. Domesticating wild plants is very difficult, and so there was less agricultural surplus and less emphasis on animal husbandry— something that was further hampered by the lack of domesticable stock in the New World. Although the indigenous populations of North and South America made their own contributions to the repertoire of human disease (for example, syphilis and gonorrhea), it turned out that what the Europeans had to offer was not only more communicable but much deadlier.

The different configurations of the Eurasian and American landmasses were not the deciding factors in this tale; to posit a single cause does a disservice to the subtlety and comprehensiveness of Diamond's analysis. But certainly the underlying geography played a very important role, and explaining that means looking back hundreds of millions of years to the breakup of Pangaea, the supercontinent consisting of all the world's major landmasses. However long the fuse, the explosion was rapid and unambiguous: within an astonishingly short period of time the Spanish had conquered the Incas, establishing a pattern of deliberate and inadvertent genocide that remains, thankfully, unequaled.[17]

In business environments, this kind of "long fuse/big explosion" change often takes the form of "new-market disruption," a particular type of disruptive innovation.[18] In new-market disruptions, two different business models develop largely independently of each other. They focus on different customers with different needs, employ different technologies to serve those needs, and build different revenue models and cost structures in order to secure the profits necessary for survival and growth. Essentially, two different industries evolve separately.

These industries collide when the improvements in technology and process performance that characterize every industry happen to allow one of these sectors to serve the customers of the other. A disruption (in the technical sense) results when it turns out that the skills perfected by participants in one industry to meet the demands of their native environment have endowed them with a structural advantage over their new competitors. Clayton M. Christensen, in his 1997 work *The Innovator's Dilemma,* explains how four generations of disk-drive makers were disrupted by competitors born in entirely new markets. Each wave of disruption created new incumbents that were in turn disrupted in a manner almost identical to the process by which they had risen to dominance.

The first of five generations of disk drives in Christensen's recounting is the fourteen-inch-diameter Winchester drive. The dominant Winchester drive makers focused on increasing the storage capacity of their drives and reducing the cost per megabyte in order to appeal to the mainframe computer makers who were their customers. The next generation of disk drives was 8" in diameter, and companies competing in this space relied on smaller size and lower cost per drive to appeal to a new set of customers in the minicomputer business. As 8" drive makers competed against each other, they eventually were able to deliver storage capacity and per-megabyte costs that were competitive with the larger 14" drives, but with a smaller form factor, among other advantages. As a result, the 8" drive makers quickly dominated the industry, effectively "disrupting" the incumbents. Then came 5.25" drives in desktop computers, followed by 3.5" drives in laptops, and in each case the new form factor disrupted the incumbent.

It would be a mistake to attribute the success of disruptors to superior agility or adaptiveness. Compared to the pace of change within a given industry—say, the 5.25"-disc-drive industry—the pace of change in the 3.5"-disc-drive industry was not especially rapid or unpredictable. Each industry introduced new models at a similarly rapid pace and with similar rates and magnitudes of improvement. By the standards of any other sector, the leading companies in each industry were highly adaptive and able to cope with degrees and rates of change that would paralyze most firms. Once the two industries collided, however, the fuse had burned down to the powder keg and the inevitable explosion occurred. The winners were not decided on the basis of who adapted better. The survivors were those who happened to satisfy current needs best.

Fast change, then, cannot be addressed through adaptability. It is simply too . . . fast.

4.2 SLOW CHANGE

In addition to rapid changes in the environment, there are also very slow changes that often prove impossible to adapt to. Environmental issues, such as climate change, and social phenomena, such as shifting age or sex distribution in the population, can brew for decades, exerting gradual and cumulative pressures that ultimately become too much for existing structures to withstand. The final collapse might be sudden, but the change itself was slow, incremental, and visible from the start.

For example, in *Collapse*, a follow-up to *Guns, Germs, and Steel*, Jared Diamond explores the fate of the Greenland Norse.[19] Established by Erik the Red around 985 C.E., two main settlements on the southern tip of Greenland with a combined population of up to 5,000 survived for 450 years. They traded with Europe, built churches and a cathedral, irrigated their fields, adapted farming and animal husbandry techniques to their environment, and sourced critical supplies such as timber from as far away as what is now Labrador on the eastern coast of Canada. The Greenland settlements were a fully European, sophisticated, and highly interdependent society.

Sometime in the first half of the fifteenth century the last of the Greenland Norse died. The details of their miserable end remain a mystery, but they likely starved to death in Eastern Settlement, having hung on past the point when they might still have fled back to Europe. Remarkably, they refused to hunt or fish the abundant wildlife that sustained the Inuit, and so the Greenland Norse perished surrounded by food and other resources that could well have saved them.

How did they get into such a mess? Shrinking intervals between runs of colder-than-average winters and unusually short summers made it increasingly difficult to keep the herds of cows and sheep that their survival depended on. The same weather patterns that were making farming more challenging also made the North Atlantic trading routes with Norway stormier and more difficult to navigate. Consequently, the trading ships from Europe arrived less frequently. This made trade goods more expensive, as it restricted supply. Worse, by a stroke of bad luck, ivory, their most valuable export, went out of fashion in Europe. As a result, the Norse suffered an acute shortage of iron and other materials needed to build ships and mount expeditions to Labrador for timber. This forced them to use sod for building material and fuel, which undermined the quality of housing and degraded their pasturelands, further thinning their herds. As their economy weakened, their settlements were increasingly vulnerable to hostile indigenous populations, who had suffered centuries of antagonism at the hands of the historically more powerful settlers.[20]

This is hardly a complete explanation.[21] For present purposes, however, the most salient of Diamond's observations is that the Norse civilization failed in Greenland *because* the pace of change around them was so slow.

Over the course of centuries, the Greenland Norse had built an intricate social and economic structure that proved more successful and durable than any single settlement established by the Inuit. Their reliance on agriculture over hunting, their top-down political system, the central role of the Church, and trade with Europe had all served them very well for generations. As a result, when conditions began to sour, the Greenland Norse responded by innovating within the constraints of their existing systems and structures. They found ways to land just enough extra walrus each season, to bring back just that much more timber on each excursion westward, to eke just that much more hay from the outfield, and to gather just that much more milk from their herds. Because they could make these changes more rapidly than the rate at which various pressures were increasing, the Greenland Norse stayed ahead of the need for fundamental restructuring. They had no way of knowing how adverse their conditions would become, what the adaptive limits of their culture and technology were, or when these limits would be reached. Innovating within their system was a perfectly reasonable thing to do. In fact, it worked for a very long time precisely because they were able to outrun nearly imperceptible environmental change.

Eventually, however, the limits of their ingenuity were reached and the stresses placed on their society by the slowly changing environment overwhelmed them. As resources grew scarcer, the slack required for even small experiments completely disappeared and the pace of innovation slowed even as the need for it grew ever more acute. One drop at a time, the water behind the dam rose, and one sandbag at a time, the Greenland Norse reinforced it. Eventually, however, the dam burst, and when that happened, it was too late to dig a canal. In a classic paradox, during the good times there was no need for change, and by the time it was obvious that radical change was needed, there was no capacity to effect it.

In contrast, if everything had collapsed before their last seaworthy vessels had rotted, the outcome might have been very different. Even if the civilization collapsed, at least some, perhaps many, of its members might have survived if some had fled and sent help for those who remained. Instead, it was the slow erosion of their society over decades, if not centuries, that did them in. The glacial pace of change made the need for a more radical response nearly impossible to see, and ultimately impossible to implement.

In the business world, we see the challenges associated with slow change in the difficulties that large industrial corporations have had dealing with the end of underlying economic growth in their sectors of the economy.[22] As chronicled by Nitin Nohria, Davis Dyer, and Frederick Dalzell in *Changing Fortunes*, a fascinating study of the decline of the Fortune 100 from 1974 to 2000, the average annual growth rate of companies listed in the Fortune 100 in 1974 through 1999 was 1.6 percent, whereas profits grew at 2.4 percent. During this time, the overall economy grew much faster, driven by the rise of financial services, health care, high technology, and media and entertainment.

The large industrials initially responded, like the Greenland Norse, by redoubling their commitments to the solutions that had worked in the past. For example, just as the Greenlanders expanded the walrus hunt to compensate for declining terms of trade in ivory, industrial corporations intensified their diversification efforts, which had historically fueled profitable growth.

Were there any other options? The Greenland Norse could have, conceptually at least, adopted one of two alternative responses to the decline of their civilization. They might have taken a more conciliatory approach to the native peoples of what is now Newfoundland and Labrador in Canada and abandoned Greenland for a new, more hospitable location. Or they could have adopted the *modus vivendi* of the native Greenlanders, themselves Inuit immigrants from the Arctic Archipelago in what is now the Canadian territory of Nunavut. In the event, neither of these responses were open to them. Centuries of hostility had made relations between the Greenland Norse and the native peoples of Canada decidedly sour, and the mental and social reconstruction implied by the abandonment of their traditional lifestyle for that of the Greenland Inuit was simply too much.

The industrial corporation in America had eerily similar options. It could have attempted a metamorphosis into a "new economy" organization— essentially, a relocation to Labrador. Of the companies on the Fortune 100 list in 1974, only four attempted this, none with notable success. Monsanto exited industrial chemicals and became an agricultural biotechnology company; Westinghouse shifted from electrical equipment to media and entertainment; the Greyhound Corporation became Viad, shedding bus lines and meatpacking for trade-show support services; and AT&T shifted out of telecommunications equipment and computers, ultimately becoming part of SBC—which renamed itself AT&T.

Six of 1974's one hundred largest industrials pursued a combination strategy, analogous to adapting aspects of the Inuit hunter-gatherer lifestyle to a European culture. In ascending order of success, they are: GM, Ford, Kodak, Xerox, IBM, and General Electric.

Nine companies did what the Greenland Norse could not: innovate within their existing model to rekindle vitality. Among them are Johnson & Johnson, Coca-Cola, and 3M.

Finally, eighty-one of the companies in the 1974 Fortune 100 suffered a long, slow—albeit occasionally prosperous—decline. Unlike Greenland, which has no fundamental need for a Norse civilization on its southern tip, the economy is likely to require steel, cars, chemicals, and so forth in one form or another for some time to come. As a result, outright extinction for every industrial corporation is unlikely. But with that caveat, the vast majority of industrial firms studied by Nohria *et al.* have fared fundamentally no better than the Greenland Norse, and for all the same reasons.

Similar to the shifting weather patterns, declining economic prospects, and deteriorating living conditions experienced by the Greenland Norse, the secular shifts in the structure of the United States and global economies that undermined the relative importance and status of industrial corporations were neither sudden nor unnoticed. Theoretically, there is no question that many, and perhaps most, industrial corporations could have responded in a timely manner and reconfigured themselves appropriately. As corporations, they no more necessarily fell into decline than the Greenland Norse necessarily had to die.[23]

A second mechanism of slow change is found once again in disruptive innovation. Recall that new-market disruption stems from the evolution of a fundamentally different business model in a separate industry that eventually collides with incumbents who find themselves at an insurmountable disadvantage. The second type of disruption is "low-end disruption," and this plays out quite differently. Low-end disruptors find their foothold in the least attractive segments of an established industry. Faced with the challenge of earning all their profits from segments that are the least profitable to incumbent firms, these companies are forced to create entirely different business models offering very different price/performance trade-offs.

The creation of a viable low-end foothold might exert some slight pressure on the economics of successful incumbent firms, but, as often as not, an incentive to abandon the low end of an existing market is welcome. As Christensen explains, when integrated steel mills surrendered the reinforcement bar market to the lower-cost, lower-quality minimills, their economics improved because they could redeploy their production capacity to higher-margin products.

Minimill success in the lower-margin segments provided them with the resources and motivation needed to make better-quality steel while preserving their structural cost advantage. As a result, the minimills were able to move upmarket, carrying their lower cost structure into ever-higher grades of steel. Each time the minimills broke into a new tier of the market, the incumbent integrated mills stretched their existing model by increasing the quality of their steel in the tiers that remained exclusively theirs. Although this worked well at first, ultimately the integrated mills came under severe competitive pressure from the steadily advancing minimills. The change was slow—it took more than fifteen years for minimills to displace the integrated producers—and it was visible and indeed recognized from the very start. What made this slow change so insidious, however, was the ability of the incumbent steelmakers to respond effectively to incremental pressures for so long. By the time the need for thoroughgoing change was recognized, it was no longer possible.

4.3 LOOKING WHERE THE LIGHT IS BRIGHTEST

Adapting to environmental change can be a highly effective response. Like most managerial responses, however, it is most effective under specific circumstances. Adaptability works best when the pace of organizational change matches the pace of environmental change.[24] When these circumstances are not met, adaptability can become an instrument of an organization's destruction.

The mechanisms of fast change create shifts that no company can hope to adapt to. Exogenous shocks in the form of rapid and extensive deregulation have repeatedly created insurmountable challenges for many otherwise well-run organizations. That some companies in these sectors survive or thrive is generally not evidence of adaptability; it is evidence of good fortune.

New-market disruption, a mechanism of fast change, can brew for a long time, and often at a pace that is far slower than the pace of change within either of the industries involved. Each of the colliding industries is populated by companies engaged in vigorous but separate competition. Ultimately, in a manner rarely foreseen at the outset, the two industries intersect. The resulting clash between two radically different approaches to the same consumer need results in a rapid transformation of the underlying rules of the game, so rapid that incumbent businesses faced with a new-market disruption are uniformly unable to adapt in any meaningful way.

The mechanisms of slow change can take the form of secular shifts in the underlying structure of the economy, as befell the large industrial corporation. As the locus of wealth creation migrated from metal bending to mental bending, there was little competition between industrial companies and knowledge-based organizations in the traditional sense, but one sector became ascendant while the other went into decline. Even so, industrial organizations were able to preserve their status and performance for a long time despite the dawning realization that something important was happening.

A second mechanism of slow change, low-end disruption, is similarly obvious in its short-run specifics and equally insidious in its long-run implications. The ability to adapt successfully in the short run makes it impossible, ultimately, to adopt the kind of total transformation required to survive.

Finally, for any change a company chooses to adapt to, there will likely be additional environmental shocks or shifts that proceed either faster or slower. How can an organization's mechanisms of adaptability be attuned to such very different rates of change *at the same time*? In a world of trade-offs, this seems even theoretically impossible, never mind practically achievable.[25]

I hope to have established that organizational adaptability is not a cure-all as a response to environmental change. No company can hope to build an organization so nimble that it can adapt on the fly to seismic events such as market meltdowns, financial crises, or a complete rewriting of the competitive rules. When such changes have a long fuse, staying ahead of cumulative incremental changes often means that when the explosion finally comes, it creates equally debilitating upheaval. As for slow change, the gradual nature and visibility of the increasing pressures ironically make an ultimately successful adaptation almost impossible. We respond, logically enough, with incremental accommodations that serve us well in the short run, but which in the end merely paint us ever deeper into a corner.[26]

How much of a problem is this? How often does strategic uncertainty result in slow or fast change, rendering adaptation ineffective, and how often can organizations hope to succeed by matching environmental instability with organizational agility?

At one level, relative frequency is not important to you if you can already see either fast or slow change impinging on your organization: the rarity of any particular fatal disease is of no interest to you if you happen to have it. Even so, there is a case to be made that adaptability does not, and cannot, address a far broader range of strategic challenges than is generally recognized.

Well-run companies seem best able to adapt to changes precipitated by other, largely similar organizations. After all, Sony was not caught off guard in any strategically threatening way by Matsushita or Philips or Apple. It was the consumer shift to renting videocassettes and the emergence of the Web and Napster that sank Betamax and the MiniDisc, respectively. Competitors can certainly undermine your strategy, but competitive moves can often be parried by sufficiently adroit companies.

Unfortunately, strategic uncertainties often find their genesis far beyond the machinations of readily identified competitors. The industrial corporations were done in not by other industrial corporations but by the slow, inexorable shifts in the structure of the global economy wrought by technological, political, demographic, and a host of other forces. Humbled telecom equipment manufacturers were not bested by competitors any more than dinosaurs were bested by mammals. Rather, each simply fell victim to a new set of selection pressures that favored a different kind of animal. And disruptive innovation is a powerful force for economic change, manifesting itself as either fast change (new-market disruption) or slow change (low-end disruption).

In the end, the type of environmental change that adaptability can address may well be rather like the narrow band of visible light in the electromagnetic spectrum. From long, languorous reds to short, staccato blues, it gets almost all our attention, but it is a very small percentage of the total action: about 300 nanometers in a spectrum of wavelengths that runs from one ten-billionth of a meter to over a kilometer. Worse still, all those wavelengths we cannot see have proven enormously useful, such as X-rays and radio waves, and potentially highly dangerous, such as cosmic rays.

The moral is that what we can see most easily is not necessarily what we should look at most intensely. Like a man who drops his keys in the alley but looks for them under a streetlamp because the light is brighter there, a focus on organizational adaptability might well allow us to see a great many things—but not find what we are truly looking for.

Adaptation has its benefits and its place. We overestimate its applicability at our peril. Thanks to the pervasiveness of both slow and fast change, even the most highly adaptable organizations will require something more, and very different, if they are to cope with the demands of an unpredictable environment.

---

1. Rebello, Kathy (1996), "Inside Microsoft: The Untold Story of How the Internet Forced Bill Gates to Reverse Course," *Business Week*, July 15.

2. Toffler, Alvin (1970), *Future Shock*, New York: Random House.

3. The concepts mentioned are drawn from, among others, Quinn, James B. (1978), "Strategic Change: Logical Incrementalism," *Sloan Management Review* (Fall), pp. 7–21; Bradley, Stephen P., and Richard L. Nolan (1998), *Sense and Respond: Capturing Value in The Network Era*, Harvard Business School Press; Vivek Ranandivé (1999), *The Power of Now*, McGraw-Hill; Mintzberg, Henry, and James A. Waters (1982), "Tracking Strategy in an Entrepreneurial Firm," *Academy of Management Journal*, Vol. 25, Iss. 3; Brown, Shona L. and Kathleen M. Eisenhardt (1998), *Competing on the Edge: Strategy as Structured Chaos*, Boston: Harvard Business School Press; Crossan, Mary M., Roderick E. White, Henry W. Lane, and Leo Klus (1996), "The Improvising Organization: Where Planning Meets Opportunity," *Organizational Dynamics* (Spring).

The literature on organizational change is too extensive to even suggest where to begin. A recent compendium of current research and thinking on the topic is in Beer,

Michael, and Nitin Nohria, eds. (2000), *Breaking the Code of Change,* Boston, MA: Harvard Business School Press.

One of the more salient observations is that adaptability as a mechanism for coping with a fast-changing environment is limited by the extent to which an organization receives timely feedback on the appropriateness of the changes it pursues. In the absence of such feedback, it might be possible to change quickly in the face of any sudden discontinuity in the environment, but you won't know if your response was appropriate until such feedback arrives. Consequently, the pace of adaptation might well need to be *faster* than any environmental change, coping instead with the interval between unambiguous feedback from the environment with respect to your last change effort and the arrival of the next exogenous shock. See Eisenhardt, Kathleen M. (1989), "Making Fast Strategic Decisions in High-Velocity Environments," *Academy of Management Journal,* Vol. 32, No. 3.

In other words, assume an environmental shift requiring an adaptive response takes place at t(1). The organization realizes the need for such a response at t(2). The company requires until t(3) to implement a response, and it takes until t(4) to get feedback from the environment to know whether or not the response has been effective. Should some adjustments be required, the best the firm can hope for is to be actually *adapted* to (rather than simply adapting to) its new competitive context from t(4) until the next exogenous shock at t(5). On the other hand, should the second exogenous shock arrive in the interval between t(1) and t(4), the company will be continuously adapting and *never* be adapted to its environment and will instead spend all its efforts adapting to the changes that engulf it.

This last thought experiment reveals a significant conceptual flaw in much of the change-management literature. It is trendy to assert that competitive advantage stems not from a position in a market but instead from an ability to respond to change effectively (e.g., Volberda, Henk W. [1996], "Toward the Flexible Form: How to Remain Vital in Hypercompetitive Environments," *Organization Science,* Vol. 7, No. 5 [July–August]). This is false. Competitiveness can only come from superior positions in a market. Adaptability is simply a mechanism to concatenate competitive positions in order to extend an organization's life. The ability to change might well be a useful overlay that enables a company to enjoy a succession of advantaged positions in a market or markets over time, but the ability to change by itself confers nothing of any value.

None of these criticisms is meant to dismiss the value of adaptability. Rather, I am attempting merely to bound its applicability. My interpretation of the literature in this area is that the limits of change as an appropriate response to organizational turbulence have not been given their due. Establishing those limits empirically is beyond the scope of this book. But I hope to make a convincing argument that such limits exist and to establish at least anecdotally that these limits bind in meaningful ways on mainstream companies facing mainstream problems.

4. See Friedman, Thomas L. (2005), *The World Is Flat: A Brief History of the 21st Century,* for a popular account of these forces.

5. See Hitt, Michael A., Barbara W. Keats, and Samuel M. DeMarie (1998), "Navigating in the New Competitive Landscape: Building Strategic Flexibility and Competitive Advantage in the 21st Century," *Academy of Management Executive,* Vol. 12, Iss. 4 (November).

6. See Eccles, Robert G., and Nitin Nohria (1992), *Beyond the Hype: Rediscovering the Essence of Management,* Boston: Harvard Business School Press. See also Mintzberg, Henry (1994), *The Rise and Fall of Strategic Planning,* New York: The Free Press.

7. See Wiggins, R. R., and T. Ruefli (2005), "Schumpeter's Ghost: Is Hypercompeti-

tion Making the Best of Times Shorter?" *Strategic Management Journal,* Vol. 26, No. 10; Adrian Slywotsky (2004), "Exploring the Strategic Risk Frontier," *Strategy & Leadership,* Vol. 32, No. 6; Huyett, William I., and S. Patrick Viguerie (2005), "Extreme Competition," *McKinsey Quarterly,* No. 1.

8. An important but easily overemphasized piece of the puzzle is determining "unit of analysis" when speaking of organizational adaptability; that is, what is it that is doing the adaptation? Typically, researchers tend to focus on the "corporation" as defined by each company for itself. For example, studies of IBM's tribulations in the early 1990s look at IBM as a single entity, just as examinations of Microsoft's response to the rise of the Internet in the late 1990s treat Microsoft as an indivisible whole despite IBM's much higher degree of diversification.

If it is necessary to nail down specifically "what" does the adaptation, I think it's most helpful to look at it in terms of the smallest organizational unit that has an identifiable strategy: a particular product market focus, and a particular set of choices in place that define how that unit competes within that product market. This will typically be associated with the integrated financial reporting of results, i.e., its own profit-and-loss statement (P&L). Seen in this way, IBM didn't adapt, it launched new services businesses that exploited growth opportunities while elements of its hardware business withered. No single business adapted to change, and the appearance of adaptation is an artifact of the corporate form, not a manifestation of organizational agility. Microsoft, however, is in my view a much better example of adaptation because Microsoft was not nearly as diversified as IBM, and Microsoft competed in the same product markets in the wake of its reorientation around the Internet.

This nuance is important only to the extent that some of what is argued to be an example of organizational adaptability is actually a more subtle response mechanism that should be seen in terms of the challenges associated with creating new businesses within a larger corporate structure, not the challenges associated with renewing an existing business. I'm speaking specifically of the concept "ambidextrous organization," developed and elaborated over the last ten years by Michael Tushman and Charles O'Reilly (e.g., "Ambidextrous Organizations: Managed Evolutionary and Revolutionary Change," *Sloan Management Review,* Vol. 38, Iss. 4, 1996).

My reading of ambidexterity is that it requires a company to diversify in order to develop a new organization with a separate strategy within the existing corporate form, not in the interests of extending the life or renewing the competitive fortunes of an existing business, but rather to ensure that there is something new to replace the growth and profits of an inevitably stagnating core organization. The unspoken premise is that organizational adaptation within an established unit is essentially impossible, and that the true organizational challenge is to cope with the complexity that arises at the corporate level, where the conflicting needs of separate businesses pursuing different strategies must be reconciled.

9. I repeat here an observation from the notes to Chapter 1 of *The Innovator's Solution:* Chris Zook and James Allen found in their 2001 study *Profit from the Core* (Boston: Harvard Business School Press) that only 13 percent of their sample of 1,854 companies were able to grow consistently over a ten-year period. Richard Foster and Sarah Kaplan published a study that same year, *Creative Destruction* (New York: Currency/Doubleday), in which they followed 1,008 companies from 1962 to 1998. They learned that only 160, or about 16 percent of these firms, were able merely to survive this time frame, and concluded that the perennially outperforming company is a chimera, something that has never existed at all. Jim Collins also published his *Good to Great* (New York: HarperBusiness) in 2001, in which he examined a universe of 1,435

companies over thirty years (1965–1995). Collins found only 126, or about 9 percent, that had managed to outperform equity market averages for a decade or more. The Corporate Strategy Board's findings in *Stall Points* (Washington, D.C.: Corporate Strategy Board, 1988), which are summarized in detail in the text, show that 5 percent of companies in the Fortune 50 successfully maintained their growth, and another 4 percent were able to reignite some degree of growth after they had stalled. The studies all support our assertion that a 10 percent probability of succeeding in a quest for sustained growth is, if anything, a generous estimate.

More recently, *Big Winners and Big Losers,* published in 2006 (Upper Saddle River, NJ: Wharton School Publishing), concluded that 3 percent of all companies were able to outperform their industry averages for a decade.

10. Conner, Daryl (1993), *Managing at the Speed of Change,* Boston: Harvard Business School Press.

11. Conner, Daryl (1998), *Leading at the Edge of Chaos,* Boston: Harvard Business School Press. The corollary of this observation is that as the pace of change increases, so too must the pace at which the organization can change. See Das, T. K. (1995), "Managing Strategic Flexibility: Key to Effective Performance," *Journal of General Management,* Vol. 20, No. 3 (Spring).

12. See Hannan, Michael T., and John Freeman (1984), "Structural Inertia and Organizational Change," *American Sociological Review,* Vol. 49, pp. 149–64.

13. Another characteristic that proved important was the diversity of early mammalian teeth. The dinosaurs were so successful that they didn't need specialized teeth: they ate what their undifferentiated teeth allowed them to eat, which for the carnivorous species were largely other dinosaurs, and for the herbivores was typically a fairly narrow range of plants. The early mammals, as essentially scavengers, ended up evolving the four types of teeth we have to this day (molars, premolars, incisors, and bicuspids), which allowed for a wider range of herbivorous feeding patterns, and even the emergence of omnivores, which opened up still more food sources. In other words, exploiting the one ecological niche left by dinosaurs required a series of adaptations that collectively enabled what had become mammals to cross the KT boundary: they were warm-blooded and could eat most anything. See note 17 for sources.

14. Gilder, George (2000), *Telecosm: How Infinite Bandwidth Will Revolutionize Our World,* New York: The Free Press.

15. "Sales, profit could miss covenants: New report":[National Edition]; Ian Karleff. *National Post,* Don Mills, Ont.: July 5, 2002. p. FP1 / FRONT; "Analysts Ponder the Unthinkable: Nortel Investors Flee as Experts Utter the B Word. Bankruptcy Unlikely Soon, but Shareholders Would be Most Vulnerable":[Final Edition]; Bert Hill. *The Ottawa Citizen,* Ottawa, Ont.: Sept. 27, 2002. p. D1 / FRONT; "The Bankruptcy Run Isn't Slowing: High debt and low cash mean more candidates for 2003"; Michael Arndt in Chicago, with bureau reports. *BusinessWeek,* New York: Jan. 13, 2003. Iss. 3815, pp. 36–37.

16. This cycle has recently repeated. Increased wealth in China has driven up the demand for protein, leading to a rapid expansion of high-intensity, but often low-tech, chicken and pork farming. The peasants who work these farms often live in very close contact with their animals. Not surprisingly, China is suspected by some to have been the source of both SARS and the H5N1 strain of the avian flu.

17. We could just as well have looked at another example from natural history. The KT event cleared the decks for the mammals, which thrived and diversified quite remarkably over the subsequent 60 million years. In particular, the placental and marsupial mammals came to exploit similar ecological niches in different isolated continents. For example, there were mammalian big cats in North America, but marsupial versions in

Gwandanaland, the landmass consisting of present-day South America, Antarctica (which was then still tropical), and Australia. As it turned out, selection pressures in North America were such that the placental versions were better hunters—had bigger teeth, could run faster, and so on—and so when the Isthmus of Panama joined North and South America three million years ago, and the marsupials and placentals collided, the fight didn't last long, with most marsupials driven to extinction. Once again, long fuse, fast explosion. (Marsupials in Australia survived as that landmass broke off on its own before the placentals could invade. Unfortunately, in breaking away and drifting north, the climate dried out and the tropical forests that had supported such a diversity of marsupials disappeared. This is rather like the KT event in terms of the nature of the "fast change" it created.)

Incidentally, in another stroke of good luck, placentals are much better at raising young in cold environments, since their young develop to a much higher degree of maturity before being exposed to the environment. This was fortunate, because the joining of North and South America separated the Atlantic and Pacific currents, which meant that as the equatorial Atlantic current flowed north, it increased in salinity rather than mixing with the much larger Pacific, which had served to keep salinity levels rather more constant. Consequently, the warm Gulf Stream waters sank, thanks to the increased density resulting from their higher concentrations of dissolved minerals. This led to a dramatic cooling of the Northern Hemisphere and the onset of periodic ice ages. Marsupial mammals might well not have been able to survive these, and so if the South American marsupials had wiped out the North American placentals, they would have been driven out of their newly won territory by the advancing ice sheets. Who knows what would have arisen to fill the ecological niche created by the victorious but unable-to-occupy marsupials in this particular alternative history. If evolution teaches us anything, it is that nothing turned out as it did because it had to.

For a delightful exposition of these dynamics and contingencies, listen to "The Rise of the Mammals" on *In Our Time* on BBC Radio 4, available at www.bbc.co.uk/radio4/inourtime.

18. Christensen, Clayton M., and Michael E. Raynor (2003), *The Innovator's Solution: How to Create and Sustain Successful Growth,* Boston: Harvard Business School Press.

19. See Diamond, Jared (2005), *Collapse: How Societies Choose to Fail or Succeed,* New York: Viking.

20. This example illustrates the relative nature of fast and slow change. Change is fast or slow only in comparison to the relevant mechanism of adaptation. When the mechanism of adaptation is evolution, climate shifts of the sort captured in note 17 constitute fast change. When the mechanism of adaptation is technological advancement, as with the Greenland Norse, this sort of climate shift is an instance of slow change. (The KT meteor strike is fast change in either case.)

21. Diamond posits a five-point framework to explain the collapse of societies generally: environmental damage, climate change, hostile neighbors, friendly trade partners, and society's responses to its environmental problems.

22. See Nohria, Nitin, Davis Dyer, and Frederick Dalzell (2002), *Changing Fortunes: Remaking the Industrial Corporation,* New York: John Wiley & Sons, Inc. Nohria *et al.* provide an illuminating and insightful description and analysis of the secular shift in the importance of large industrial corporations since 1973 and the implications of this shift on strategy, structure, processes, and governance.

23. Additional examples of the difficulties created by slow change are in Bazerman, Max H., and Michael E. Watkins (2004), *Predictable Surprises: The Disasters You*

Should Have Seen Coming and How to Prevent Them, Boston: Harvard Business School Press. For example: the liabilities the airlines have to honor their frequent-flier miles. This problem was created slowly over decades, and the airlines have been able to adapt along the way by, for example, increasing the miles needed for various benefits. Nevertheless, the outstanding mileage balances continue to grow rapidly, creating an ever-greater liability. Bazerman and Watkins suggest that eventually the weight of this overhang will become too much to bear. This is one example of the challenges of slow change: the liability has grown so large precisely because the airlines have proven so adept at managing it.

Not all the examples given are instances of slow change, however. Others are purportedly "fragile" systems subject to catastrophic failure.

24. There are of course multiple approaches to making an organization adaptive, too, and presumably each of these is applied most effectively under circumstances that can be still more precisely defined. My point is only that circumstances can be defined where that class of responses known collectively as "adaptive" responses are most appropriate.

25. As far as I know, there is very little in the organizational change literature that identifies, let alone explores and attempts to resolve, this particular problem.

26. This discussion of fast and slow change is different from Bhaskar Chakravorti's delightful book *The Fast Pace of Slow Change* (2003), Boston: Harvard Business School Press. In his investigation of networked businesses, Chakravorti explains, in an evocative metaphor, how existing competitive equilibria must be carefully "unlocked" and rebuilt around a new equilibrium. The "fast pace" of the book's title captures the underlying pace of technological change and product innovation; the "slow change" is the often laborious and inefficient process of establishing a new status quo around that innovation. The kinds of competitive situations he focuses on are similar to those Sony faced with its Betamax and MiniDisc challenges. With Betamax, Sony was undone by the unexpectedly strong network effects of movie viewing on VCRs, and the MiniDisc got caught in the cross fire as the computer swallowed the music business. (Chakravorti examines the rise of peer-to-peer services such as Napster.)

Chakravorti's prescriptions for establishing new equilibria tend to employ the tools and methods of game theory in order to understand the motivations of the players. In this way, he says, it is possible to work with the local interests of the participants in a market in order to establish a particular desired new global optimum.

Without disagreeing with Chakravorti's insights, I'd suggest that often a powerful way to overcome the resistance to change evinced by established market structures is via new-market or low-end disruption. In each case, disruptive innovations create different products, different business models, and different value networks that evolve largely independently of established markets. When they have improved to the point that they provide a clearly superior alternative to the established market structure, once-reluctant participants are willing to shift quite rapidly. This is especially true for new-market disruption, since the innovation takes root by addressing a completely different set of customer needs, rather than merely "bottom-feeding" in an established market. It is for this reason that new-market disruption can create seemingly "fast change," even though the evolution of the innovation itself proceeded at a relatively "slow pace."

CHAPTER FIVE

THE LIMITS OF FORECASTING

Forecasting is a cornerstone of traditional strategic planning processes, and might be seen as a way to compensate for any limits to organizational adaptability. Unfortunately, it is impossible to forecast as accurately as is required for strategic planning or as is necessary to substitute for adaptability.

Adapting your strategy to environmental change is a great idea, but its application is necessarily limited. There are simply too many circumstances in which the pace of change in the environment is out of whack with the pace of change an organization can cope with. One way around this problem is to forecast the relevant change accurately enough and far enough in advance to begin altering your strategic footing on a timetable that accommodates the pace of change. By adding forecasting to whatever degree of adaptability you can manage, perhaps you can cope with uncertainty.

Alas, forecasting for the purposes of strategic planning, as it is typically practiced and employed, is fundamentally unable to serve the purposes to which it is typically put. This has significant implications for much of strategy-making, because strategies necessarily have assumptions about the future embedded in them. Planning of any type is future-oriented, and thinking about the future can only be done in terms of forecasts, predictions, assumptions, extrapolations, and so on. As a result, to claim that forecasting (in the context of strategic planning) is useless is tantamount to saying that much of strategic planning is not merely a waste of time, it is outright dangerous.

WHAT IS A FORECAST?

Dan Gilbert asserts that thinking about the future is a uniquely human trait.[1] He distinguishes between the kind of thinking about the future that goes into planning a birthday party, a seduction, or a new-product launch and what he calls "nexting"—the kind of moment-to-moment anticipation of the immediate future that raccoons engage in when they jump backward as the garbage can they are trying to tip over actually tips over.

I am willing to suggest that what Gilbert seems to posit as a dichotomy (nexting vs. *bone fide* thinking about the future) can usefully be thought of as a continuum, at least once one crosses the qualitative divide between the merely sentient and the truly self-aware. After all, stopping at a traffic light is based on a prediction: that to stop is safer and less likely to result in a traffic ticket than to continue. This is more than raccoonlike nexting, but it falls short of the kind of prediction that feeds into strategic plans—or seductions, for that matter.

Nassim Taleb distinguishes between "prophesying" and "forecasting."[2] He heaps scorn on the former because of its highly event-specific nature: calling who will win the World Series or guessing the price of oil next Tuesday. Forecasting, however, is entirely reasonable, provided it is wrapped in the appropriate probabilistic hedges. Much of what I have suggested here as the "right" way to think about the future attempts to respect Taleb's insights.

The kind of prediction and forecasting I take issue with falls into a "you-know-what-I-mean" category concerning variables of strategic moment that are forecast with a level of precision that makes strategic commitments possible—something probabilistic forecasts do not facilitate. These are predictions of the sort Sony no doubt made, if only implicitly, when, for example, committing to time shifting over movie viewing as the key application for Betamax, or to device/content synergy as a central pillar of MiniDisc's success. For now, I might have left myself without a word for the way one "should" think about the future, but this problem will be addressed in Chapter 9.

5.1 HOPE OVER EXPERIENCE

The need for accurate forecasting in strategy has long been accepted by the leading lights of the field. The author of a widely cited textbook on forecasting, Spyros Makridakis, noted in a 1990 publication:

> The ability to forecast accurately is central to effective planning strategies. If the forecasts turn out to be wrong, the real costs and opportunity costs . . . can be considerable. On the other hand, if they are correct they can provide a great deal of benefit—if the competitors have not followed similar planning strategies (as quoted in Mintzberg, 1994).

Similarly, Gary Hamel and C. K. Prahalad of "core competence" fame tell managers that knowing which competence to make core requires them to

> build the best possible assumption base about the future . . . Industry foresight gives a company the potential to get to the future first and stake out a leadership position . . . The trick is to see the future before it arrives (as quoted in Sherden, 1998).

Now, if the aspect of the future we needed to see were limited to variables such as the position of Neptune, strategic planning would be on solid ground. Our ability to predict planetary motion has been finely tuned and proven reliable. It is based on a theoretically sound understanding of cause and effect and has been empirically validated through repeated observation. But these are not the kinds of future facts on which strategic success turns. Instead, successful commitments must align with variables such as the general level of economic activity (is the economy in recession or is it expanding? by how much either way?), the pace and nature of technological innovation (will nanotechnology work?), the behavior of consumers (will they buy it and how will they use it?), and so on. In the absence of demonstrably reliable and sufficiently accurate predictions of these and many other variables, making commitments today that pay off only if they happen to fit with future circumstances demands not forecasting but necromancy.

Such prescience is in distressingly short supply. Winston Churchill, British prime minister during World War II and Nobel Prize winner in literature, summed up his views with "all prognosticators are bloody fools." To Churchill's vernacular add the equally pointed observations of Peter Drucker, the patron saint of management, who was, if anything, more damning, claiming that "forecasting is not a respectable human activity, and not worthwhile beyond the shortest periods."

Of course, mere assertion, even by sources as redoubtable as Sir Winston and Drucker, is not proof. William A. Sherden's *The Fortune Sellers* is, in my view, one of the best recent debunkings of forecasting. Rather than taking aim at disciplines that many dismiss because of their *prima facie* implausibility—such as astrology and fortune-telling—Sherden tackles respected fields: meteorology, economics, investing, technology assessment, demography, futurology, and organizational planning. In each case, he reviews the methods employed, the uses to which the predictions are put, and the accuracy of the field's leading practitioners. His conclusion is that only the weather forecast has improved, for we can now make specific plans concerning rain or shine about three days into the future. Sherden concludes:

The forecasting track records for all types of experts are universally poor . . . [forecasters] *routinely* fail to predict the major events that shape our world, or even the major turning points . . . whether it be the economy, stock market, weather, or new technologies (page 5).

Henry Mintzberg, in his book *The Rise and Fall of Strategic Planning,* reviews research on the accuracy of forecasts used as the basis of strategy formulation. He concludes that even the proponents of strategic planning cannot escape the fact that "long range forecasting (two years or longer) is notoriously inaccurate" (page 229, quoting Robin Hogarth). Extensive studies of the ability of stock analysts to forecast company earnings or public- or private-sector economists to forecast such critical variables as GDP— or even simply growth or recession—are similarly negative. For example, one study concluded that only 2 out of 60 recessions in a sample period across many different countries were forecast a year in advance, 40 remained undetected by April of the year of recession, and 25 percent of forecasts were still for positive growth in October of the recessionary year.[3]

But why tar all forecasters with the same brush? Just because forecasts are a waste of time "on average" does not necessarily imply that all forecasts are useless. Is it not possible that there are some forecasters with a track record of success? Might they know what they are doing?

Well, not really. The unfortunate fact is that track records alone are of no use when it comes to assessing forecasting ability.[4] The explanation often goes by the name of "monkeys at typewriters": if enough monkeys hammered away at typewriters for long enough, one of them would come up with the *Iliad*. Similarly, with so many prognosticators predicting so many different outcomes, it is all but inevitable that someone will come up with a run of accurate predictions. So if you know someone who has predicted anything with any consistency, it is important to determine the population that they have been drawn from. What looks like it should happen once or twice in the age of the universe might be nearer to a sure thing than you realize. Consequently, even several instances of seemingly notable accuracy are not remarkable at all: it was inevitable that someone get it right.[5]

What can make this difficult to accept is that the merits of a given forecaster depend on how *few* other monkeys were forecasting, not how *many*. Typically, when we want to demonstrate our prowess in some field, we want to be sure that we have competed against as many others as possible. Want to claim that you are the best 100-meter sprinter? Make sure that you have run against as many other sprinters as possible. If you have only ever raced against your little brother, claims of greatness will surely ring hollow.

Conversely, if there are 10^n monkeys typing for 10^n years and the *Iliad* emerges, no big deal. But if there were five monkeys in that room for five hours and one of them came up with even just "See Jane run," then, as Nassim Taleb puts it in *Fooled by Randomness,* you would like to meet that monkey. If you cannot limit, or do not know, the number of monkeys involved, then the only way to know if you have something special is by picking the poetic simian in advance—and you only get one try. (If you get repeated attempts, success reverts to a random event.) Similarly, when it comes to forecasters, it is not enough that someone get it right; we need to be able to say *who* will get it right *before* they perform their feat of soothsaying. Without being able to specify in advance who can see the future— that is, unless one can predict who will be the best predictor—*post hoc* claims of accuracy, the definition of a track record, are meaningless.[6]

In light of all this, if anything is worth remarking on in the forecasting field, it is that there are so few examples of visionary forecasters claiming an ability to predict something accurately. It would appear that for all the effort put into peering over the horizon, all we have to show for it is a record that is, if anything, collectively *worse* than pure luck.[7] That there remains a flourishing, multibillion-dollar market for predictions is, as Samuel Johnson observed of second marriages, a testament to the triumph of hope over experience.

5.2 THE FUTURE IS NOW

Some will dispute this conclusion. Unconvinced by the rules of randomness, they will point to forecasters who routinely get it right. Although I do not know of anyone who can predict anything of strategic relevance with the requisite accuracy, it is not a logical contradiction to assert that someone out there can call the forward LIBOR, or tell you which sector of the S&P will outperform this year, or even just win the office Super Bowl pool year after year. There is a problem with the claim that these people are accurate forecasters, however: it misunderstands the nature of the future, and ignores that to be able to determine how accurate a particular forecast has been, one must be able to compare a forecast of the future with the future.

Let me say that again. To determine the accuracy of a forecast, we must compare our forecast of the future *with the future,* not with the "future present" that eventually obtains. For example, it is not helpful to forecast the GDP of China in five years and then compare the number you pick with the actual GDP of China five years from now.[8] Rather, you have to compare your forecast of China's future GDP with what China's future GDP actually is *now.*

If this sounds like a distinction without a difference (or worse, irrelevant sophistry), please bear with me. What is the future, really? Is it "out there," waiting to be discovered? That is, is China's GDP in five years already determined, and we simply have to wait to find out what it is? Or rather, is there right now a particular probability for each of a broad range of possible GDP values? Of course, when five years from now gets here, the probabilities collapse: for every value that China's GDP is not, the probability of that value being China's GDP is 0, while for the one value that is China's GDP, the probability of that value being China's GDP is 1.

More generally, when viewed from the perspective of today, there is a probability of any given event occurring at any given point in the future. Summing across all events, all time horizons, and all probabilities, we can conceptualize a probability distribution function (PDF) for the future. This can be thought of as a "possibility space" of all events and their associated likelihoods for all time. If a given event happens or does not, its probability of happening collapses to 1 or 0.

More complex still, the probability of some events is contingent upon other preceding events. For instance, the probability of my winning next week's lottery depends upon my having a ticket for that lottery before the draw is made. When it turns out that I do not have a ticket, the probability of my winning (a future event) is zero. Other events are less certain. Every day that went by that I had not finished writing this book made it less likely that I would meet the publisher's deadline. But the probability of not meeting it did not fall to zero until the deadline had passed. Consequently, as events happen or do not, the probability density function for many future events also changes.

In other words, there is no specific future out there waiting to be discovered as time's arrow carries us toward it. Instead, there is a constantly shifting mass of probabilities, with events dropping in and out of the possibility space while new events enter. In contrast, forecasts, as generally used in strategic planning, tend to take the form of "next year's sales will be $100 million." This is nothing more than a guess. A guess that turns out to be correct is nothing more than a lucky guess.

Describing the future in this way is not prediction, or forecasting, as the terms are generally used. The exception, of course, is the weather forecast. We have all become used to the notion of "probability of precipitation" qualifications attached to calls for rain. Unfortunately, this honesty has not infiltrated much of standard business use. We rarely see these probabilities explicitly attached to forecasts such as sales projections. How often have you seen a business plan that states, *"there is a 50 percent chance* that next year's sales will be $100 million"? A set of such forecasts would meaningfully describe (worry about accuracy in a moment) the full possibility space for future sales: a 10 percent chance of sales of $150 million, a 1 percent chance of sales of $25 million, and so on.

An uncomfortable implication of adopting this way of describing the future is that we have no way of knowing whether the resulting PDFs are accurate or not. If someone says "there is a 30 percent chance that in five years China's GDP will be greater than that of the U.S.," how can we know if they got it right? We can determine whether or not China's GDP is greater than America's five years from now, but all that tells us is the probability distribution of the present five years from now: a likelihood of 1 for whatever China's GDP actually is, and 0 for all other values. What we want today is a description of the future, which is the probability *today* of all the circumstances that could obtain *tomorrow*. Guesses at specific values—even lucky ones—do not count because they are not descriptions of reality.

The bad news is that we cannot observe the true probability of future events. The universe is not a Las Vegas casino where the odds are known (even if unfavorable) and unchanging. With a coin toss or a roulette wheel we can set the theoretical odds (the coin has two faces, an American roulette wheel has thirty-seven slots) and observe repeated plays to determine that the game is fair. We do not so much predict the probabilities of given outcomes as establish them. When it comes to the kinds of events we typically want to predict, or at least specify probabilities for, we have no such insight into the underlying structure, nor do we have the luxury of repeated observations of similar events. Consequently, we have no way of finding out whether we are good at assessing the odds of any given event's occurring because we cannot compare our assessments with reality.

For example, how would one measure the accuracy of a prediction that there is a 15 percent chance that the stock market will go up tomorrow? As the hours tick away, the probability of the market going up or down changes as events transpire, up to the point that tomorrow comes and goes and the market went up or down, creating a probability of 1 or 0 that the market went up. But when the forecast was made, there was no way to determine its accuracy, because there is no way to compare the probability ascribed to the market's going up with the true probability of the market's going up. The fact that the market went up does not mean that, when assessed from the perspective of the day before, the probability of its going up was higher or lower than 15 percent. The only way to prove such a forecast wrong is if an event is given a probability of 0 and then it happens, or a probability of 1 and then it does not. For everything in between, outcomes say nothing about the accuracy of the probability-predicated forecast, and comparisons with what the future could actually hold are impossible. And since we cannot rerun the events from yesterday to today again, we cannot determine if that prediction would be right 15 percent of the time.[9]

As a result, descriptions of the future cannot be assessed for accuracy. Even if someone could correctly describe the PDF of the future, there is no way of knowing that they had done it. So, when it comes to track records, one should bear in mind the disclaimer that accompanies every mutual fund prospectus: past performance is not necessarily indicative of future returns. And when it comes to attempts to describe the future in a potentially useful way, one cannot even establish a track record. Demonstrably accurate predictions of what the future actually is simply do not exist.

5.3 UNCERTAINTY BOTH RANDOM AND DELIBERATE

To some extent, of course, our inability to see the future with any accuracy is a function of ignorance as much as the metaphysical nature of the problem. After all, a defining characteristic of human progress is our ever-increasing ability to understand, predict, and control our environment. Our lives today are what they are—for better and for worse, but on balance much for the better—because we understand much of how the world really works. Teasing apart underlying cause-and-effect relationships of interest has not only satisfied our curiosity, it has given us the power to predict the outcomes that matter and given us the ability to control, or at least influence and prepare for, those outcomes. The accuracy and reliability of the predictions made in different scientific disciplines vary, but almost every field can legitimately claim meaningful advances. As a consequence, much of what once appeared to be the province of the gods has been dragged into the realm of mortals. Our collective belief seems to be that anything still beyond our grasp is only temporarily so, and it will eventually fall under our dominion if we persevere in the belief that it shall.[10]

Such optimism is not baseless. But two facts put predicting accurately and usefully enough of the variables relevant to strategy-making permanently beyond our reach: randomness and free will.

In general usage, "random" typically means without apparent order or pattern.[11] There are some caveats, however: if the winning lottery numbers are 1, 2, 3, 4, 5, and 6, someone might conclude that these numbers are not random because there is a readily apparent order. These numbers, however, are in fact random because they are merely a sampling from a much longer series of numbers consisting of every week's combination of selected numbers. Seen in their proper context, the 1–6 series does not represent any underlying order because it provides no indication of what next week's numbers will be. So, when concluding that a process is random or not, we must be very careful that we understand the context of the sample of output before concluding that it tells us anything about what happens next.

In *A New Kind of Science,* Stephen Wolfram identifies three mechanisms of randomness. The first two are relevant for now:

1. Randomness injected into an otherwise orderly system from its external environment. Call these "exogenous shocks."

2. Randomness in initial conditions. A system might be orderly but highly sensitive to its starting position. If the starting position—the initial conditions—is anything less than orderly, a process of amplification transforms those inputs into random output. This is the domain of chaos theory.

If a system we hope to understand—say, wave motion or the success of a new product—has seemingly random outputs, it is often because it has experienced an exogenous shock. For example, a large boat might pass by, disturbing the wave patterns in unpredictable ways, or a competitor might unexpectedly launch its own similar, but better, product thanks to skills mastered in adjacent markets that had been irrelevant, and hence invisible, to incumbents (i.e., a new-market disruption).

This kind of randomness can be overcome by expanding the boundaries of the system studied. Changes in the system of waves or the market of interest were surprising because the boundaries of that system were not drawn broadly enough. Including the boat or the new entrant would have led to the right predictions. When randomness is a result of exogenous shocks, the remedy is to "endogenize the exogeneity."

But when do you stop expanding the boundaries? If you need to include the boat, perhaps you need to include other potential influences as well—from undersea rifts to faraway storms to the phase of the moon. Similarly for understanding market evolution: when do you stop including variables that might somehow affect the outcome? In other words, when randomness can be injected from the environment your only response is to include the environment in your system. That is a slippery slope, as soon a theory of everything is needed in order to have a theory of anything. Computational complexity will overwhelm you long before you have included everything you feel you should.

To illustrate, the fate of large industrial corporations might well appear obvious in hindsight, but only because we can work backward from effect to cause and so now know where to draw the boundaries of our analysis. We know that it is knowledge content that drives profit more than asset base and that this explains the structural decline in the significance of the steel industry versus health care. But in 1974, how could we have known that increasing the knowledge content of the steel industry was not a viable long-term solution? The answer is that we could not have, and so when thinking about the future of the steel industry we would have needed a comprehensive model of all economic activity, and any model with a 1:1 ratio with reality is no model at all.

Perhaps everything need not be included in the definition of a system in order to predict elements of the system. The effects of a storm thousands of miles away might well be dissipated sufficiently by the time they reach our shores that the storm has become essentially immaterial. Unfortunately, this does not hold true when working with a system that is highly sensitive to initial conditions—Wolfram's second mechanism of randomness.

Sensitivity to initial conditions is something chaos theorists study. Often captured in the metaphor of the "butterfly effect," the basic idea is that the flapping of a butterfly's wings in Brazil could cause a tornado in Texas. Chaotic systems might well be deeply understood, insofar as the laws that govern them can be described and have been proven to have high degrees of predictive power. However, the outputs of such systems are effectively random because of the deep impossibility of specifying precisely what the relevant initial conditions are.

This difficulty takes two forms. First, simply gathering sufficiently accurate and timely data is impossible. We cannot know the precise location and velocity of every particle at the same time and execute our computations fast enough to render useful predictions. In business environments, the reliability and timeliness of data are, practically speaking, equally challenging. To what extent do reported sales capture what has happened in the marketplace? Being "close" is not good enough when dealing with chaotic systems.

In Sony's case this was especially important, since the strength of the network effects that turned VHS's slight market-share lead in 1977 into total dominance was surprising and took effect quickly. More accurate and timelier data would not have allowed for accurate predictions of these effects for the same reason that expanding one's definition of "the system" would not have helped: one can never know *ex ante* what is timely and accurate enough.

Second, we do not know *ex ante* what constitutes "initial" when specifying "initial conditions." Is the butterfly flapping its wings the initial condition for the tornado in Texas? Perhaps the initial condition is the caterpillar in Caracas that the butterfly once was and the hurricane off Haiti that blew it to Brazil. When expanding the boundaries of a system to incorporate more of the environment, we do not know where to stop; when specifying initial conditions, we do not know where to start.

The inescapable conclusion, then, is that randomness—the lack of order or pattern—is a necessary component of every system we might want to understand and control. We are doomed to either draw our boundaries too narrowly, leaving ourselves open to an injection of randomness from the environment, or to underspecify the initial conditions that determine the ultimate outcome. Frequently, we are victims of both. Either way, it is uncertainty, not predictability, that best characterizes our future.

Wolfram's third mechanism is internally generated randomness, which he discovered through experiments in computational complexity. Wolfram found that simple systems can create random outcomes that are resistant to perturbations in initial conditions but nevertheless exhibit no pattern. He explains this in terms of the contributions that each element of a system can make to randomness. We can specify the environment and the initial conditions correctly and the system operates according to well-defined laws, but the output of the system depends on recursive computations—that is, on the internal features of the system, not merely its inputs and its rules.

This has the counterintuitive implication that the outputs of such systems are random but repeatable: if the system is set up in exactly the same way, the same output will result. But that output is genuinely random, insofar as it exhibits no discernible pattern, and nothing in the output tells you anything about what comes next. In other words, you can know the initial conditions and the rules that create the output but still not predict what comes next in a given system unless you run a simulation that operates on a 1:1 scale. You can do this with computer-generated automata, but predicting a market outcome by running a full-scale simulation is Pyrrhic victory at its most acute.

This mechanism is useful primarily as a metaphor rather than as a concrete explanation of why the future is necessarily unpredictable. In business, the analog to intrinsic randomness is that the players are humans with free will. This has two important effects on our ability to control, or even merely predict, how systems populated with such creatures will behave.

First, as demonstrated by Robert Lucas in the realm of macroeconomic policy, deliberate attempts to manipulate people's behavior provoke responses that often offset the intended effect.[12] Lucas's work, which earned him the Bank of Sweden Prize in honor of Alfred Nobel, shows that this interplay makes it very difficult for government policy to have any effect on an economy. For example, the central bank might observe that output is decreasing, and so increase the money supply in an attempt to stimulate the economy. People, observing this increase and understanding why the central bank is implementing it, respond by increasing their spending and so driving up inflation, nullifying the growth effects of any monetary stimulus. The net effect is no effect at all. On the other hand, unexpected shocks to the money supply—of the kind the central bank cannot implement due to the visibility of its actions—do in fact have an impact on the economy. In other words, monetary supply matters, but only when we cannot predict its movement.

Second, if others could predict what I would do under given circumstances, they might well be able to take advantage of that to my detriment. Therefore, it can often be in my best interests for others to not be able to predict my behavior. This can require that I behave in irrational and unpredictable ways on occasion, even if such actions might cost me in the short run.

For example, in the Ultimatum Game two players anonymously divide a surplus, say, $10, between them as follows. The "Proposer" proposes a division of the surplus. If the "Responder" accepts this division, then the surplus is divided accordingly. If the Responder rejects the proposal, each player receives nothing. The rational result is for the Proposer to propose a $9:$1 split and for the Responder to accept this. (For convenience, assume that the proposed division must be in increments of $1.) This maximizes the Proposer's benefit, and from the Responder's perspective, $1 is better than nothing. (The players are anonymous and the game is not repeated, so there is no obvious, immediate benefit in being "generous" or "fair.")

Such purportedly rational divisions almost never happen. Responders tend to reject "lowball" offers, preferring to deny the Proposer such a significant gain "at their expense." The generally accepted conclusion is that we are "punishing" those who behave unfairly and that the need to do this is so strong we will incur a cost to do it, even if we have no reasonable expectation of benefiting.

In repeated games it can be in our long-run interest to undermine our own short-term gains because it makes our bargaining position stronger in future negotiations. The licensing terms Sony offered Matsushita for Betamax can be seen as analogous to an Ultimatum Game. By accepting the technology on Sony's terms, Matsushita would have guaranteed itself a significant slice of the action at almost zero risk—akin to accepting a $1 offer. Instead, Matsushita rejected Sony's terms in favor of a necessarily far less certain future that depended on developing its own competitive technology and battling Sony in the marketplace.

We might want to claim that this is simply a different kind of rationality, not irrational behavior *per se*.[13] But even if it were irrational in its specifics, it created for both Sony and Matsushita a credible threat the next time around. Each company demonstrated that it is prepared to go it alone, and so when it comes to negotiating the next consortium deal, each side had better be willing to offer acceptable terms.

The larger point is that any company that is perfectly rational is perfectly predictable, and any company that is perfectly predictable is easily exploited when it is in a position of weakness. A judicious injection of "deliberate irrationality" into the mix can create enough uncertainty to prevent companies in disadvantaged positions from being exploited as thoroughly as they otherwise would be.

Finally, to the extent that moral reasoning—as opposed to simply economic gain—figures into human decisions, it is worth noting that even when the relevant moral codes can be specified, our behavior within those codes is highly variable and inconsistent. In the Ultimatum Game, sometimes $1 is accepted and sometimes $4 is rejected. If participants were punishing unfair proposals, why does this happen? Such dispersion within otherwise homogeneous populations presents a problem for those who would predict people's behaviors, for if our responses to something as fundamental as what is "fair" cannot be nailed down, who is to say what people will find compelling in a toothpaste?

The way one will respond to a given stimulus is not something people can predict, even of themselves.[14] Clearly, it is not our rational faculty that determines our behavior; apparently, it is not our moral faculty either.[15] The result is that human behavior is deeply, and irretrievably, unpredictable. And since business systems are populated by people, the systems themselves are subject to Wolfram's "internally generated" unpredictability—sometimes because we choose to be unpredictable for rational reasons, and sometimes because we simply cannot help ourselves.

5.4 FROM DILEMMA TO PARADOX

The tension between the need to make commitments and our general inability to predict the future has been identified and explored by other researchers.[16] The argument has generally been framed in terms of the *relative* advantage of commitment and the *relative* uncertainty of a given competitive context. Viewed in this way, different combinations of commitment and uncertainty demand different administrative systems in order to cope. When uncertainty and the benefits of commitment are low, a classic bureaucratic organizational response is entirely appropriate: the gears will grind out a perfectly reasonable solution to whatever challenges the organization faces. When either uncertainty or the benefits of commitment are high (and the complementary dimension is low), there is similarly a well-documented solution: "hustle" (i.e., highly adaptive organizations) for high-uncertainty/low-commitment environments, and "planning" (i.e., strategies based on accurate predictions) for low-uncertainty/high-commitment environments.

FIGURE 5-1 **THE STRATEGY DILEMMA**

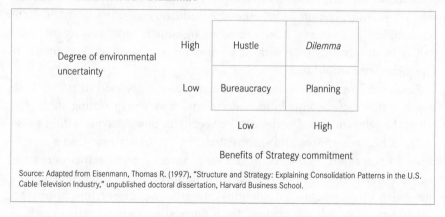

Source: Adapted from Eisenmann, Thomas R. (1997), "Structure and Strategy: Explaining Consolidation Patterns in the U.S. Cable Television Industry," unpublished doctoral dissertation, Harvard Business School.

It is only in high-commitment/high-uncertainty contexts that a form of strategy "dilemma" emerges as a result of a pincer between a need to commit despite an inability to predict. The implication is that few organizations need worry: most organizations can either predict (when commitment is valuable and uncertainty is low) or adapt (when uncertainty is high and commitment not necessary), while only the unlucky ones must deal with the contradictions of committing despite uncertainty.

This formulation does not go far enough. What constitutes a high level of commitment in one industry (say, retail) might well be immaterial in another (say, telecommunications), allowing us to array industries along the vertical axis. But differences *between* industries are not all that relevant when competition, by definition, takes place *within* industries: after all, department stores do not compete with phone companies. When looking at competition within industries, more of the right kinds of commitment is always better than less. Unfortunately, the more of a commitment one makes, the more one is exposed to whatever uncertainty there is—and neither adaptability nor forecasting can mitigate it.

What emerges is far more problematic, a conundrum that afflicts every organization: the strategy paradox. Success in business is relative, and so whatever the industry, firms that guess right and commit more vigorously to the strategy that fortune ultimately favors will defeat their competitors, but at the risk of catastrophe. That is why the strategies with the greatest probability of success necessarily imply the greatest probability of failure.

For some organizations, understanding this reality (even if only implicitly) results in a middle-ground, hybrid strategy that trades profitability for survival. For other companies, failing or refusing to accept this fact results in a strategy built on bravado and bluff. They commit boldly, based on what they believe to be exhaustive analysis and exciting BHAGs with their adaptive, learning, sense-and-respond organizations at the ready. But it does not work as often as the daredevils would like.

Neither can they overcome the strategy paradox by brute force. Holding doggedly to a belief in one's eventual ability to control, or at least predict, what matters does not change the fact that our inability to predict is fundamental and intrinsic to the nature of the systems within which we work. The limits of adaptability and forecasting constitute the "speed of light" in strategy: constraints that cannot be relaxed. It is just the way things are.[17]

So what do we do about it? Is it possible to at least mitigate the strategy paradox, achieving the possibility of greatness without necessarily risking one's doom? This book would end here if the answer were "no." However, we need not duck or dispel or defeat uncertainty to create viable strategies. The solution to the strategy paradox explained in subsequent chapters *embraces* uncertainty, putting what we do *not* know at the center of every decision every person in an organization makes. The broad outlines of this solution were sketched in Chapter 1. The next five chapters provide a more complete explanation, illustration, and road map for implementation.

> *Since business success is relative, greater levels of commitment to the ultimately correct strategy will always prevail over approaches based on adaptation. However, meaningfully accurate forecasting is impossible because track records are meaningless, the accuracy of predictions is impossible to assess, and events are subject to inevitable randomness. Therefore, great success is only ever possible if one accepts the risk of great failure. The strategy paradox therefore afflicts all firms equally. But there is a way out.*

---

1. Gilbert, Dan (2006), *Stumbling on Happiness*, New York: Alfred A. Knopf.

2. Taleb, Nassim N. (2005), *Fooled by Randomness: The Hidden Role of Chance in Life and the Markets*, New York: Random House.

3. See Loungani, Parkash (2001), "How Accurate Are Private Sector Forecasts? Cross-country Evidence from Consensus Forecasts of Output Growth," *International Journal of Forecasting*, Vol. 17, No. 3; Mozes, Haim A. (2003), "Accuracy, Usefulness and the Evaluation of Analysts' Forecasts," *International Journal of Forecasting*, Vol. 19, No. 3; Simos, Evangelos O. (2002), "International Economic Outlook: The World Economy in 2011," *The Journal of Business Forecasting Methods & Systems*, Vol. 21, No. 3 (Fall).

Perhaps most remarkable in the forecasting literature is the attention given to making forecasts credible and believable using methods other than creating accurate forecasts, e.g., Vanston, John H. (2003), "Better Forecasts, Better Plans, Better Results," *Research*

Technology Management, Vol. 46, No. 1 (January–February). The inference I draw from this is that the acceptability of forecasts is as much a social process as an empirical one, lending credence to Dwight D. Eisenhower's observation that "plans are nothing; planning is everything." To adopt this position is to abandon forecasting and strategic planning *per se,* for this aphorism has embedded in it the notion that the process of planning enhances an organization's adaptability, and adaptability is what matters. Furthermore, even if true, however finely tuned an organization's adaptive capacity, there are changes to which an organization can't adapt, as discussed in the previous chapter. Consequently, the process of building forecasts is either fruitless (because they are inaccurate) or limited in its applicability (because it enhances adaptability, which is limited in its applicability).

4. Taleb, Nassim N. (2005), *op. cit.*

5. According to Taleb, the probability of winning the New Jersey lottery twice is 1 in 17 trillion. Given how long the New Jersey state lottery has been in existence, this simply should not have happened yet. But it has. Curiously, however, this event isn't as rare as you might think when seen in its proper context: one of many highly improbable events, each with an inconceivably low probability of actually happening. In other words, two wins of the New Jersey lottery belongs to a population of such events, including multiple wins of every other lottery and every other imaginable freak coincidence—most of which have *not* yet happened. Summing across this entire class, it's been calculated that an unspecified piece of such astounding luck actually has a 1-in-30 chance of happening, making the double win of the New Jersey state lottery really rather run-of-the-mill.

6. A real-life example of this was recently reported in *New Scientist,* July 29, 2006. In "Famous Flying Ace Not Hotshot After All," the magazine summarizes the findings of researchers from the University of California at Los Angeles who studied the records of the German fighter pilots during World War I. Mikhail Simkin and Vwani Roychowdhury found that the overall ratio of victories to defeats for German airmen was such that a streak of eighty victories—such as the one that made Manfred von Richthofen, aka The Red Baron, famous—was bound to happen purely by chance.

7. Sherden notes that the general conclusion emerging from his synthesis of studies into forecast accuracy is that the "naïve" forecast—that is, that tomorrow will be just like today—generally beats any forecasting technique, no matter how sophisticated.

8. It's worth noting that forecasters' track records when making these kinds of forecasts is pretty poor. Peter Williamson recounts the results of a study done by *The Economist* magazine: in 1984, the publication asked four finance ministers, four chairmen of multinational companies, four Oxford economics students, and four London garbage collectors to generate ten-year forecasts on a number of key economic variables. In 1994, they tallied the results and found that company chairmen had managed a tie with the garbage collectors, with the finance ministers finishing last, even as the average prediction was more than 60 percent too high or too low. See William, Peter J. (1999), "Strategy as Options on the Future," *Sloan Management Review* (Spring).

9. It is true that someone who made a series of such predictions would have an accuracy rate simply by virtue of having made a series of predictions, but it would be of little use. It would say nothing about either the probability that this forecaster would be right next time ("past performance is not indicative of future returns . . .") or the accuracy of their assessments of the probabilities ascribed to a given outcome. There is a big difference between being right 15 percent of the time and correctly giving a 15 percent probability to a particular outcome.

10. I'm of two minds on this subject. In *The Innovator's Solution,* coauthored with Clayton M. Christensen, we held out the promise of understanding the seemingly random success of innovation using exactly this argument. For now, I'll hide behind the F.

Scott Fitzgerald observation that "the sign of a first-rate intelligence is the ability to hold two contradictory thoughts simultaneously and still retain the ability to function," and then affirm the consequent of that conditional.

11. For a very helpful discussion of randomness and its relationship to the very popular notion of chaos theory and complexity, see Wolfram, Stephen (2002), *A New Kind of Science,* Champaign, IL: Wolfram Media Inc., especially pp. 297–336 and pp. 532–60.

12. Lucas, Robert E. (1996), "Nobel Lecture: Monetary Neutrality," *Journal of Political Economy,* Vol. 104, No. 4.

13. Matsushita's choice not to accept Sony's terms is not perfectly analogous to an Ultimatum Game, because in an Ultimatum Game the Responder has no expectation of making up for the refused surplus via some other mechanism. Matsushita's choice could be framed simply in terms of expected value: They felt they'd do better on their own rather than accept Sony's terms. My point is that this calculation of expected value is based on assumptions about an uncertain and unpredictable future. Matsushita was choosing a higher return strategy at the cost of enduring higher uncertainty.

But the assumption of rationality cuts both ways: If Matsushita was being rational in rejecting Sony's offer, then the structure of Sony's offer must similarly be rational, and based on its assumptions about trade-offs between a single standard, higher volumes, and lower licensing fees versus the benefits of higher profits based on market dominance. Matsushita and Sony disagreed in these assessments, and that, as they say, is why we play the game.

The additional benefit to Matsushita is that by not cooperating in the face of aggressive licensing fees, the next time Sony has a neat product it wants to build a consortium around, it knows that Matsushita can credibly claim to be willing to walk away unless Sony offers reasonable terms. Precisely this kind of dynamic is playing out in the current rivalry between high-definition DVD standards.

14. Gilbert, Dan (2006), *op. cit.*

15. See Lawrence, Paul R., and Nitin Nohria (2002), *Driven: How Human Nature Shapes Our Choices,* San Francisco: Jossey-Bass. Human nature is posited to be a composite of four fundamental drives: to acquire, learn, protect, and belong. None of these is primary. Rather, they constantly compete for satiation, and in any given circumstance which will sway our choice is indeterminable. Morality is a form of rational overlay to help us manage these conflicts and establish some modicum of consistency over time, for although unpredictability can have strategic value, being predictable has its merits, too: without it, no one would know whether to trust you.

16. Eisenmann, Thomas R. (1997), "Structure and Strategy: Explaining Consolidation Patterns in the U.S. Cable Television Industry," unpublished doctoral dissertation, Harvard Business School.

17. That is, the speed of light could be something other than 299,792,458 m/s, but it's not; the universal gravitational constant could be something other than 6.6742 $\pm$ 0.001$\bullet$10^{-11} m^3 s^{-2} kg^{-1}, but it's not. Similarly, people could be perfectly rational wealth maximizers or perfectly moral beings, but fail on both counts, to the chagrin of economists and clergy.

CHAPTER SIX

IT'S ABOUT TIME

The strategy paradox arises from the need to make strategic commitments in the face of strategic uncertainty. Strategic uncertainty—which is different from operational or financial uncertainty—increases as one attempts to plan over longer time horizons. The traditional hierarchy provides a foundation for managing strategic uncertainty, because hierarchies function best when the levels within them are defined by the time horizons the managers at each level are responsible for. As a result, each level in a hierarchy copes with different degrees of strategic uncertainty. Lower levels have very little strategic latitude, focusing instead on delivering against past commitments, while higher levels manage strategic uncertainty more actively by mitigating strategic risk and positioning the firm to exploit future strategic opportunities. Midlevel managers in charge of operating divisions must translate the possibilities created by senior management into commitments that functional management must fulfill.

Structural problems require structural solutions. The strategy paradox is a structural problem: it is an inevitable consequence of the benefits of making the right commitments with the impossibility of knowing what the right commitments will be. Companies that hope to mitigate the risk/return trade-off that has long defined strategic decision-making cannot hope to achieve this within the confines of the existing commitment-based model.

If strategic uncertainty is the question, time is the answer. The longer the time horizon over which a strategy must play out, the greater the range of possible outcomes that must be considered and the less certain one can be of the probabilities associated with any given result.[1] The causal relationship between strategic uncertainty and time means that time is the most important dimension of any organizational structure.[2] Time is the axis around which every organizational structure should revolve, for it is time that determines the nature of the strategic uncertainty that must be addressed.

The notion that there is a distinction between the short and long terms, [...] to different hierarchical levels, is [...] otypically charged with "strate- [...]ts a company should enter, what [...]bilities it will need. Lower levels [...]," that is, short-term, challenges: [...] new advertising campaign, how [...]oblem, however, is that all these [...]entally the same way: in terms of [...] "right" choices. We have tended [...]s as harder than making the right [...]s been one of degree, not of kind. [...]he challenge of the strategy para- [...]mmitment in the formulation of [...]n. Instead, because the level of [...]ases with the time horizon under [...]must manage a different balance [...]ty and making or delivering on [...]today with the long term in mind [...]ay with the short term in mind; it [...]on. [...]d strategic uncertainty in this way [...] and responsibilities allocated to [...]scribed in this chapter is based on [...]ainty must be separate from the [...]y, when it comes to strategy, the [...]aging strategic uncertainty: miti- [...]re to strategic opportunity. This [...]O of an organization should not [...]rm performance of the organiza- tion, but instead occupy themselves with creating strategic options for the organization's operating divisions. The middle level—operating division leadership—must manage the uncertainty surrounding existing commitments and make the current strategy as robust as possible in the face of unpredictable events to which adaptation is impossible. Functional managers must focus nearly all their efforts on delivering on the commitments that have been made: there are no strategic choices to consider in the short term; instead, it is simply a question of playing the hand they have been dealt to maximum effect.

And so the commonsense statement that some managers look after the short term while others look after the long term implies the far less intuitive conclusion that a CEO should not make commitments and that functional management should not try to adapt. This chapter will make this connection and explore its practical implications.

6.1 THE PRINCIPLES OF STRUCTURE

Published in 1963, Alfred Chandler's *Strategy and Structure* gave rise to an aphorism that has informed practicing managers and organizational theorists ever since: structure follows strategy.[3] Chandler came to this conclusion based on his study of the organizational responses of DuPont, Standard Oil (New Jersey), General Motors, and Sears, Roebuck & Co. to the welcome stresses of profitable growth.

Each of these four large U.S. enterprises began, as most companies do, with a functional, or "U-form" (for "unitary"), organization: a hierarchy of management levels, with departments at each level defined by specific functions, such as marketing, production, research and development, finance, and so on. The executives in charge of the functions reported to the CEO.

Most organizations seek to grow, and there are essentially two ways to achieve this end: do more of what is being done (increasing scale), or do new things (increasing scope).[4] The former tends not to require any fundamental organizational changes, and so for some time each company grew naturally, and without significant growing pains, by increasing scale. Attracted by growth opportunities, or forced into new industries as a result of anti-trust action (as with Jersey Standard), each of the four began increasing its scope aggressively after 1910.

Growing by increasing scope proved enormously successful, and the four companies' U-form structures were soon unable to cope with the diversity of the markets they now served. Production departments could not deal with the large number of different products, the marketing departments could not cope with the increasingly diverse market segments, and R&D departments could not effectively manage basic research into the wide variety of radically different technologies each company now relied on. It was a classic case of "be careful what you wish for."

For example, between 1900 and 1910, DuPont grew by consolidating a variety of far-flung but generally similar operating businesses in each of high explosives (e.g., dynamite), black powder, and smokeless powder.[5]

Serving relatively homogeneous markets, the "most important dimension" of the company was the function—sales, finance, production, R&D, and so on—and each of these functions reported directly to the company's president. Increasing scope between 1910 and 1920 demanded the creation of multiple divisions within each function. An organization chart from the period shows a production department further divided into Explosives, Cellulose Products, Dyestuffs, and Paint and Chemicals. The sales department was still more fragmented, due to the perceived need to align specific sales activities with different markets.

The challenges of coordinating, say, the sales and manufacturing efforts associated with high explosives or, worse, the emerging markets of paint and chemicals eventually overwhelmed DuPont's generations-old U-form structure. And so by the mid-1920s, the company had reorganized around product groups, placing the production, sales, finance, and other functions associated with each class of products within its own division. Each division could then focus its efforts on the unique demands of the market it served. A corporate office was put in place to allocate resources—monetary, human, and otherwise—to the divisions based on appraisals of past performance and assessments of prospects for future success. The corporate-level departments were built around the functional expertise required to perform these resource-allocation and control tasks: finance, human resources, strategy, legal, and so on.

Jersey Standard, as a vertically integrated oil company, ultimately reorganized around different geographic regions to cope more effectively with the variegated supply-chain challenges in different areas of the United States. The Louisiana division, for example, sourced its crude domestically, while the Delaware division purchased its feedstock from overseas markets. For its part, Sears ultimately reorganized around its different retail concepts—primarily catalog and retail stores—after having tried to expand into store-based retail under the umbrella of its successful catalog operations. The fourth company in Chandler's quartet, General Motors, essentially mirrored DuPont's experience, but without an intervening period as a U-form. William Durant built GM by cobbling together a number of auto assemblers and auto parts makers. The result was a pastiche of diverse organizations with no centralized control or resource allocation. Alfred Sloan, aided by Pierre du Pont, a major investor in GM, put in place a corporate office and organized the company around specific products and brands, each focused on a different segment of the market as defined largely by price and quality: Chevrolet, Pontiac, Oldsmobile, Buick, Cadillac, and GMC. There were other divisions for defense contracting, diesel engine trains, and, briefly, airplanes.

These companies, each independently and for their own reasons, had created a new form of organizational structure: the M-form (for "multidivisional"). As a structural solution to a structural problem, this has been identified as one of the most significant management innovations of all time.[6] In general terms, the *strategy* of growth through diversification necessitated a change in *structure* in order to cope with the resulting complexity. Structure follows strategy because, as Chandler put it:

> Structure has been the design for integrating the enterprise's existing resources to current demand; strategy has been the plan for the allocation of resources to anticipated demand (1963, p. 383).

This general precept—that structure follows strategy—has become the managerial equivalent of the architectural principle that form follows function. Chandler uncovered part of the deep logic of organization design: that companies should organize around what matters most. That is, the most critical element of an organization's strategy is the best candidate for the basis of organizational departmentalization. For DuPont and GM, their growth strategies were based on product diversification, and so their divisions were organized around products. For Jersey Standard, differences in supply chain mattered most, and since these differences mapped, literally and metaphorically, to different regions, divisions were organized accordingly. And for Sears, growth demanded a diversity of retail concepts (e.g., catalog versus store-based) and each functionally complete division focused on a different one.

The notion that companies should organize around what matters most has been explored extensively by Jay Galbraith.[7] Galbraith explains that there are essentially five dimensions of corporate structure, and the most appropriate one for a given firm depends, as Chandler theorized, on the firm's strategic objectives. The five dimensions are function, product, market, geographic region, and process. Galbraith explains how companies can change their structures over time to reflect shifting strategic priorities. For example, over the course of more than a decade, Citibank evolved from country profit centers (a regional structure) to customer profit centers (a market-based structure). This change made sense because differences between customers had become more important than differences between regions.

Structure matters because it is a formal expression of a firm's strategic priorities. For Citibank, being organized around customers means having profit centers defined by customer segments. This in turn implies that when there is a trade-off to be made, the balance tips in favor of customer segments rather than in favor of a specific region or a product category. That is not to say that these other dimensions do not matter; it simply means that they are less important than the dominant dimension. In the end, something has to matter most.

Structure, as discussed so far, has been defined largely in terms of lateral differentiation: separating functions, regions, markets, products, or processes from one another. But within these divisions there exists in almost every organization of any size a vertical dimension of differentiation as well. This is hierarchy. How is this constructed, and what purpose does it serve?

This is a question worth asking explicitly, because hierarchy has taken more than its fair share of criticism. "Hierarchy" connotes having to seek approval from those with more authority but less information in a manner that invariably stifles creativity, extinguishes initiative, and creates unnecessary overhead and cost.

The most common defense of hierarchy holds that positions higher on the ladder serve as powerful integrating mechanisms that balance the centrifugal forces of differentiation unleashed by any particular departmental structure. In a functionally organized company, for instance, the R&D department deals with highly uncertain questions involving future technologies, whereas the production department is concerned with questions of efficiency and repeatability within a much more stable context. Despite the structural separation required by these intrinsic differences, there remains a manifest need for the two departments to work together—to be integrated—in order to ensure that the company's overall goals are met. For instance, all else equal, the R&D department should not be exploring technologies the production folks have no hope of mastering. One way to reconcile this tension is through a common boss: the general manager to whom the head of each department reports, through whom the requisite trade-offs are negotiated and implemented.[8]

Viewing hierarchy solely as an integrating mechanism does not do justice to hierarchy or integrating mechanisms. The tension between differentiation and integration was explored most famously by Paul Lawrence and Jay Lorsch in *Organization and Environment*.[9] They identify a number of integrating mechanisms, both formal and informal, that go beyond vertical hierarchy. In particular, they observe that the greater the differentiation between departments, the greater the technical knowledge needed to be a successful integrator. This typically implies that people from the middle of the hierarchy, not the "common boss" of the departments, are generally the most effective integrators. Galbraith, too, explores the need for integration, and he sees hierarchy as but one of at least five general types of integrating mechanisms.[10]

One of the hallmarks of progress in management has been the gradual development of circumstance-based theories. In the relatively early days of management research, that is, from about the turn of the nineteenth century until the 1960s, the quest was for a "single best way" to do everything: to organize, to grow, to innovate, and so on. With "contingency theory," Lawrence and Lorsch gave birth to what has become the current orthodoxy: that there is not a single best way to do anything, and that good theory must describe the circumstances under which particular tools or methods are useful.[11]

A theory of hierarchy might be an exception. Senior levels of a hierarchy are seen by many as not being exclusively, or even primarily, focused on integration. Rather, as Chandler points out, as the M-form emerged, the senior levels of the organization focused on long-term questions of organizational growth, while lower levels in the various departments concentrated on short-term operational issues. In his words, senior management is concerned with strategy and operating managers look after tactics. The only dimension of vertical differentiation Chandler observed is time; it is only horizontal differentiation that changes with a firm's strategic imperatives. Is time a "universal constant" of hierarchical structures? And if so, what does this mean for the management of strategic uncertainty?

6.2 HIERARCHY AND HORIZONS

For my money, the most undeservedly ignored management researcher of the modern era is Elliott Jaques (pronounced "Jacks").[12] The Canadian-born psychologist's work on the nature of hierarchy spans half a century and is based on extensive field data on how people behave at work and how they feel about their roles. His investigations of what people actually do when functioning within hierarchies revealed that, at every level, people had two bosses: their "boss" and their "real boss." The former was the person nominally responsible for their actions; the latter was the person from whom they could get a decision that mattered to their work. This "level skipping" went the other way as well, as those higher up in the hierarchy often found themselves having to go around their immediate subordinates in order to obtain relevant, timely information so that they could make the decisions required of them.[13]

Level skipping is a severe pathology in any hierarchy, for if the hierarchy is to have any substantive meaning it must serve as a decision-making chain of command. Violating the formal structure of the hierarchy means that the hierarchy itself is dysfunctional. Yet the phenomenon of level skipping is so common that most of us have come to conclude that it is an inevitable reality of organizational life.

As with many breakthroughs, Jaques's work began by questioning what the rest of us had accepted. In order to expose the underlying logic behind the recurrent phenomenon of level skipping, Jaques needed a way to distinguish between different jobs.[14] What is it that makes one job more demanding, complex, or "bigger" than another? Differences in skill sets are about the only observable characteristics, but they do not help: how do you compare the surgeon with the chief hospital administrator? The labor market might dictate salaries, but salary has no necessary correlation with appropriate hierarchical structure. In investment banking, for instance, traders often make far more than managers, while in Hollywood actors routinely take home more than directors.

Jaques hypothesized that time is the most important characteristic of any job:

> Any experienced manager, whatever his or her job, takes the great importance of time for granted. Things have to be done on time, planning is done about time, and organizing is done to achieve things in time. Sales efforts have to mesh with production capacity and programs; invoices and accounts have to be sent out and payments received on schedule; raw materials and other supplies have to be ordered and deliveries ensured to connect with production schedules; wages and sales have to be made out and paid at a precise hour; research investigations have to be completed on time or research budgets and programs will go haywire; and so on for every function in the organization. (1979, *op. cit.*)

Building on this premise, Jaques developed the idea that jobs could be defined in terms of time horizons. Sales directors might be responsible for this year's sales targets, while individual salespeople might worry about nothing beyond this quarter's results. The director of R&D might be worried about the evolution of basic technologies over a ten-year horizon, while bench scientists might be working on sub-problems that mature in three years. Every job certainly has other tasks associated with it that involve much shorter time horizons—filling out time sheets, submitting expenses, evaluating the performance of subordinates, preparing annual budgets, and so on—but each job is defined by the longest time horizon associated with any of the job's tasks.

To test these hypotheses, Jaques began by determining the time horizon associated with a given person's job and the time horizons associated with that person's "boss" and "real boss." In other words, he wanted to know the time horizon of the (person in the) position to whom one reports and the time horizon of the (person in the) position from whom one can get a useful decision. He found that everyone with a time horizon of less than three months treated the person with a time horizon of three months as their "real boss." Those with time horizons of between three months and a year went to those with a time horizon of a year for relevant decisions; and so on. Jaques identified temporally defined strata of decision making at two, five, ten, and twenty years, for a total of seven levels of hierarchy, no matter how complex the organization. Although known by several different names over the years, the generally accepted term for Jaques's theory has become "requisite organization," or RO.[15]

Level skipping arises because organizations are forced to break large groups of people into smaller subgroups in order to manage complexity, then create positions designed to integrate those subgroups. These integrating positions have a time horizon that is no different from that of the subgroups they coordinate. This "extra" layer of hierarchy is therefore a lateral mechanism, not a vertical one. Unfortunately, many companies often cannot distinguish between the two, and so this integrating role is often mistaken for a hierarchical one. It is not a pathology but a perfectly adaptive behavior for someone to skip over an integrating role (typically one's nominal boss) to get substantive decisions from the time-differentiated, and hence "true," hierarchical stratum above. In a mirror image, a person in the higher-stratum role often feels compelled to skip over the integrating role in order to inform appropriately the decisions they must make.

So, for example, a sales manager overseeing a group of salespeople is not likely to deal with a longer time horizon than the salespeople being managed. The sales manager is typically a lateral integrating role—a way for salespeople to communicate effectively and efficiently with, for example, production scheduling, in order to make trade-offs between making a sale by customizing an order and the production costs associated with such customization. This is not a time-horizon distinction, it is a "unit of analysis" distinction captured by different measures of performance: sales vs. profits. The true time-based hierarchical distinction often comes at least one level above the sales manager, say, the sales director, who is concerned with and measured on more than this year's sales.

In Jaques's view, these strata reflect quantum differences in decision making.[16] There is a discontinuous break in the complexity and difficulty of the decision making at each stratum in a well-functioning hierarchy. By way of analogy, water ranges from very cold to very hot between 0° and 100° Celsius, but ±1°C either side of that range there is a fundamental state change to ice or steam. Similarly, Jaques has found that, for example, the interval from 5 to 9½ years manifests material differences in the complexity of decision making, but these are differences merely of degree. In contrast, the difference from 9½ to 10 years is a difference in kind.

As support for this belief, Jaques points to evidence from "felt-fair" pay surveys, in which researchers test the correlation between various job attributes and the degree to which people feel they are fairly paid. For although, as suggested above, pay does not determine one's appropriate position in the hierarchy, proponents of RO hold that the greater skill required to cope with the complexity of longer time horizons is necessarily in shorter supply. This scarcity is reflected in the higher salaries that can be commanded by those with the skills to perform effectively at each level.

The labor market, like any other market, can be inefficient, resulting either in over- or underpay. People can see through these distortions when reflecting on their own pay, and have an intuitive sense of what constitutes fair pay to them given their job's demands. Of the variables tested, time horizon has had, in many studies spanning more than twenty years, the highest correlation with feeling fairly paid, at 0.86. Other potential candidates: "know-how" came in at 0.45, "job impact" at 0.34, "freedom to act" at 0.25, and "seniority" at 0.05. Even more impressive, the relationship between time horizon and felt-fair pay is consistent over time when corrected for inflation, suggesting that not only are the time quanta that define job strata immutable, so are the relative felt-fair pay differentials associated with those strata.

Our understanding of lateral structure—that is, the dimensions around which departments in an organization should be created—is quite well-developed. As captured by Galbraith, the basic principle is to organize around whatever needs to be most tightly integrated in order to compete successfully: functions, geographic regions, products, customers, or processes are the most likely dimensions. Others might emerge. Lawrence and Lorsch teach us that these divisions serve to differentiate parts of the organization from one another, and that this differentiation is critical to success—in fact, such differentiation is the point of creating departments in the first place. But there is a need simultaneously to integrate these divisions in the interests of collective effort. And so, integrating roles are required, their nature and complexity determined by the nature of the integration.

RO provides an often-neglected complement to these much-studied contingencies of organization structure: a basis for understanding the hierarchy, or the vertical dimension.[17] Whereas the basis of lateral divisions is highly contingent and evolving, Jaques's work suggests strongly that the time basis of hierarchical divisions is much more stable. As initially suggested by Chandler, and intuitively understood by most practicing managers, the more senior levels of the hierarchy are defined by the longer time horizons over which their decisions play out. Capturing these differences in terms as plastic as "strategic" and "tactical," however, creates more problems than it solves. RO gives a formal, theory-based expression to these intuitions based on careful and extensive empirical testing.[18]

For all its intuitive pull and empirical substantiation, why has RO not become more mainstream, either in management research or practice? Some of those who have devoted much of their professional lives to the study and application of RO attribute the disconnect to the sociology of ideas and to the personalities of Jaques and Wilfred Brown, the CEO of the Glacier Metal Company, where Jaques's initial research was conducted. One commentator notes:

> Neither Jaques nor Brown felt the work of most management academics held scientific validity, so they simply ignored it and did not cite it. In turn, management academics did not cite Jaques and Brown. The net impact has been the isolation of this theory from the main dialogue on management and organizations. This has tended to keep awareness of the theory low.[19]

Perhaps there is another piece to the puzzle. For all the power of RO, it remains, as nearly as I can tell, essentially descriptive and predictive. That is, it describes how hierarchies function and predicts certain elements of an effective hierarchy, such as relative pay differentials. What it seems to lack is a prescriptive element, one that describes how people functioning at a given stratum can function better.[20] In addition, although RO provides a way to think about what separates hierarchical strata, the complementary question—what brings them together?—remains relatively unexplored. Lawrence and Lorsch pointed out that structure must both differentiate and integrate. Divisions based on Galbraith's dimensions and associated integrating roles do so laterally. Hierarchies, it would seem, must do the same vertically. RO differentiates the strata on the basis of time horizons to ensure clear lines of accountability, but on what basis are the strata integrated so that the rolling three-month windows at the bottom of the pyramid cumulate to the twenty-year plan devised at the top?

6.3 REQUISITE UNCERTAINTY

So far I have begged the questions of why longer time horizons imply greater complexity and why the nature of that complexity is a sound basis for establishing hierarchical strata. After all, the number of subordinates one has surely implies greater job complexity, yet Jaques dismisses this as a foundation for hierarchical structure. However, RO merely establishes empirically that time horizons are connected with felt-fair pay; there is no causal explanation of why that should be the case. I think the theoretical foundation of this finding lies in a connection between uncertainty and time horizons—specifically, between *strategic* uncertainty and time horizons.

Many uncertainties can compromise an organization's performance, but not all of them are strategic. For example, a key supplier might fail to deliver critical inputs to a just-in-time production process, but a firm with a highly interdependent supply chain left gasping for air because of wildcat strikes at an upstream facility does not need to change its strategy; it needs to diversify its supplier base.[21] Similarly, quality lapses might threaten valuable brand equity built up over years, a rogue employee might evade established control mechanisms, putting the entire company at risk, the vagaries of financial markets might create unexpected exposures to currency or interest rate fluctuations, and so on.[22]

Each of these uncertainties can be debilitating, even cataclysmic, but they are essentially operational or financial in nature. They are not strategic, because the tools required to manage them are not the instruments of strategic change.[23] Bad strategies might make you more vulnerable to these sorts of twists of fate, but good strategies by no means protect you from them.[24] And similarly, having operational and financial uncertainty under control does nothing—*nothing*—to protect you from strategic uncertainty.

Strategic uncertainty is a *bone fide* class of uncertainty that must be addressed with a particular set of tools.[25] Only if an uncertainty has implications for the basic elements of how a company creates and captures value is it *strategic*. In other words, strategic uncertainties bear on the long-term commitments a company has made to achieve a given position on a particular production possibility frontier.

The uncertainties that undid Sony's Betamax and MiniDisc efforts were strategic because they concerned underlying structural changes in the industries in which Sony competed. It was strategic uncertainty that unseated each succeeding generation of disk drive maker and overthrew the integrated steelmakers in Christensen's study. It was strategic uncertainty that left better than eight out of ten large industrial corporations in Nohria's study unable to cope with the tectonic shifts in the locus of wealth creation in the modern economy. None of these companies would have fared any differently in the long run had they better executed those things to which they had committed themselves. They did not need to be better; they needed to be different.

The reason they could not be different quickly enough and in the right sorts of ways is that these companies had true strategies: specific sets of capabilities that were resistant to rapid imitation by competitors, but as a result difficult to change. The commitments that make success possible necessarily constrain an organization's latitude for action in the short run—that is why commitment-based strategy and organizational adaptability are conflicting objectives. Strategies can change only in the relatively long run. If they could change quickly, then adaptability would be a more broadly applicable response to environmental turbulence.

Circumstances might get resolved for or against you in the short run, thanks to the forces of fast change, but this simply reveals whether you made the right or wrong choices in the past. Raising your gaze to the horizon makes strategic choice a possibility, but the deep unpredictability of the future creates material uncertainty regarding which commitments to make. It is therefore only in the context of longer time horizons that strategic uncertainty exists.

And so we are left with one of life's little ironies: the longer your time horizon, the greater your range of choices for action, but the less certain you can be of what precisely to do. In contrast, the shorter your time horizon, the more certain you are of the right course of action, but it is less likely that you will be able to pursue it.

The role of time horizons in defining the responsibilities of each level in the hierarchy can now be understood in terms of strategic uncertainty. Strategic uncertainty is minimal in the short run: the underlying structures of markets and technologies simply cannot change that quickly. It is only over longer periods of time that strategic uncertainty bears on managerial decision-making. Jaques showed that grappling with the challenges of longer time horizons is justly the province of senior management. Consequently, senior managers must face up to the fullest flower of strategic uncertainty. As we work our way down the hierarchy, the need to manage strategic uncertainty wanes because truly strategic responses are simply no longer possible. Instead, the responsibility shifts to delivering on the commitments already in place. The responsibilities attached to each level of the hierarchy are determined by the balance between managing uncertainty and managing commitments. These responsibilities do not necessarily imply more difficult decisions, but they certainly imply fundamentally different ones.

It bears noting that all types of uncertainty increase with the time horizon under consideration. The exogenous shocks that might disrupt a supply chain are likelier to happen sometime in the next ten years than in the next ten days for the same reasons that, all else equal, it is likelier to rain sometime in the next ten days than in the next ten minutes. Inflation or currency-rate fluctuations are similarly subject to wider swings over longer time periods than shorter ones.

At the same time, operational and financial uncertainties are subject to greater swings in the short term, and they are not open to nearly such significant variation in the long term as are strategic uncertainties. For example, interest and exchange rates can fluctuate quite widely in the short term but are subject to self-correcting mechanisms that limit the extent of their fluctuations in the very long term. Empirically, the range over which these factors have fluctuated has been falling steadily for decades. Going back several hundred years, swings in the growth rate of most developed economies have dropped from on the order of regular shifts of 20 to 30 percent to ranges in the single digits.[26] In contrast, strategic uncertainties only increase, without limit, as time horizons lengthen. Largely thanks to constantly changing technologies and relentless innovation, the nature of the economic activity that will prove profitable in the future gets only more uncertain the farther forward we look.

In other words, the differences in the nature of the operational and financial uncertainties faced by different levels of the hierarchy are differences of degree, and they increase only marginally as one moves up the chain of command. Managing operational and financial uncertainty is everyone's job, and much of the risk-management field is dedicated to developing the tools and processes required to do this effectively.

Managing strategic uncertainty, however, is not everyone's job. Strategic uncertainty increases monotonically as time horizons are extended. Time horizons uniquely define the strategic uncertainty to be considered, and so those responsible for the longest time horizons—the board of directors and corporate management—must address the most profound questions, including what does the company need to look like ten or twenty years into the future in order to be successful? Of course, predicting this with any precision is impossible, and so corporate-level investments should reflect this unpredictability: tentative, easy-to-reverse explorations of new markets, technologies, and business models are the kinds of bets corporate managers should place. Such investments do not constitute "making strategy," however, precisely because they are not commitments of the kind that hold out, on their own, any possibility of competitive success. The intent is not to decide *how* to succeed, but to ensure that some element of the corporation is *positioned* to succeed regardless of what the future holds.

It falls to the middle of the hierarchy—operating division leadership—to choose from among the strategic options made available to it by the corporate level. This is where the choices that constitute competitive strategies are made. At this level, managers consider risks attendant to the chosen strategy only to the extent that particularly critical assumptions might prove wrong. These risks are managed by hedging key elements, but all in the service of making a particular strategy as successful as possible no matter what. Finally, functional managers should not worry much at all about strategic uncertainty, but do the best they can to make good on the promises others have made, sometimes years before.

The organizational design challenge is to allocate responsibility for managing uncertainty and delivering on commitments. Since the defining element of each level's responsibilities is the degree of strategic uncertainty it must manage, I call this model *Requisite Uncertainty*, in homage to Jaques's seminal work.

The idea that a company must cope with today's pressures while positioning itself to capitalize on tomorrow's opportunities is not a recent insight. The problem is that much of this advice seeks to enable individual managers at all levels to deal with their own short-term/long-term conflicts. For example, one carefully articulated formulation argues that every level of the hierarchy must function on three time horizons (time horizons 1, 2 and 3, or short, medium, and long) simultaneously.[27] Corporate executives

FIGURE 6-1 **REQUISITE UNCERTAINTY**

Organizational Level	Time Horizon		Strategic Balance
	Absolute	*Relative*	
Board	10 years to ∞	20	*Uncertainty*
Corporate	5–10 years	10	
Operating Division	2–5 years	5	
Function	3 mos.–1 year	1	*Commitment*

Source: Adapted from Jaques (1979); author's analysis.

The "operating division" in this diagram captures what would be in Lawrence and Lorsch terms the primary dimension of structural differentiation. As described by Galbraith, the operating division is the product, customer, process, or region around which the organization is built. The functions (e.g., marketing, finance, production, etc.) all report to the general manager who heads up the relevant operating division. Each operating division general manager reports to the corporate office. Other structural elements, such as a corporate marketing organization to whom the operating division marketing executives might report, are horizontal integrating mechanisms, and so are not captured here.

The "absolute" time-defined strata are taken from Jaques's work. The "relative" time horizons are suggested to account for the possibility that the degree of strategic uncertainty captured in a given time horizon might well be increasing, or might vary by industry. Different circumstances might therefore require hierarchies based on different temporal quanta.

should concern themselves with the operating success of today's businesses while also allocating resources to businesses that are small today but have the potential to become tomorrow's growth engines. Managers of each division must similarly cope with the implications of all three horizons on the business they are responsible for, just as each product within each business must also wrestle with short-, medium-, and long-term issues.

Bombardier, the Canadian aerospace manufacturer, is cited as an example. At the time of the original study, the company had six divisions: Transportation (train, subway, and other railcars), Motorized consumer products (snowmobiles, personal watercraft, etc.), Aerospace (commercial and corporate jets), Capital (financing), Services, and International expansion. The Transportation, Motorized consumer products, and Aerospace divisions constituted the short term (horizon 1) for the corporate office, the Capital business fell into the medium term (horizon 2), and Services and International were long-term (horizon 3) initiatives. Within the Aerospace division, the short term was occupied by product-development issues in each of its two divisions, Commercial and Corporate aircraft. The medium term was defined by opportunities in fractional jet ownership (compared to the business model of sales and leasing). The long term consisted of promising opportunities in global chartering. Finally, within each of the Commercial and Corporate aircraft operating divisions there were short-, medium-, and long-term considerations defined by the relevant product-development issues. Presumably, we could keep going, drilling all the way down to design engineers, sales executives, and product schedulers.

This model is essentially fractal in nature: the degree of complexity remains the same at every level, as each level must define and manage its own three time horizons. This is an extreme example of the general tendency among conventional approaches to this problem to accept that at least one level of the hierarchy must deal with the duality of short- and long-term considerations. At least one—and in this model, all—managers must somehow either develop, or be blessed with, a combination of mental agility and powerful enough analytical frameworks to operate in multiple time horizons at once. In other words, they must both deliver on their existing commitments and position the organization for future success. There is no attempt to separate the management of uncertainty from delivering on commitments.

It turns out that the skills required to operate in multiple time horizons simultaneously are in terribly short supply; at best, 5 percent of the population is able to clear this cognitive hurdle.[28] Building a model of management that requires such skills as a matter of course is optimistic enough, never mind a model that requires essentially every manager at every level to have that kind of intellectual and emotional capacity. Such an approach does not resolve the strategy paradox—it replicates it.

Requisite Uncertainty sees the challenges faced at each level of Bombardier's hierarchy very differently.[29] Starting at the bottom, product-development initiatives within the Commercial and Corporate Aircraft divisions suffer from no strategic uncertainty. The people managing these initiatives are not really dealing with different time horizons, just different time "periods." In other words, their planning must take into account how long it takes to design a new airframe. There is material operational uncertainty associated with undertaking, but very little strategic latitude.

Moving up a level, to the Aerospace group, management is well and truly committed to a strategy: the manufacture of airframes.[30] But there are material uncertainties surrounding how best to pursue that strategy. For example, beyond selling aircraft, fractional jet ownership and global chartering are alternative business models that might define the industry's future. These opportunities have been around for decades, and one would hope that Aerospace management would have been exploring them for some time. By setting up an exploratory sales force devoted to these markets, the company could come to a better understanding of the implications of these new markets on the design and development of airframes. In this way, should they prove to be significant growth opportunities, Aerospace management would be able to shift the objectives of the product-design groups below them as necessary.

Finally, at the corporate level, questions concerning international expansion into China or exploiting synergies between financing and manufacturing activities speak to longer time horizons and so open up a high degree of strategic uncertainty. The corporate office should therefore allocate resources to small initiatives in these areas, with an eye to changing the commitments on which subordinate levels of the hierarchy will ultimately have to deliver.

By the lights of Requisite Uncertainty, product-design groups deal with material operating uncertainty, but no strategic uncertainty, over a time horizon of eight years. Operating divisions implement specific strategies, but with an eye to key contingencies and uncertainties that pose material risk or present genuine opportunity. Corporate management takes the relevant long view for each of its divisions and considers how best to reconfigure divisional assets to ensure continued growth and profitability.[31]

Consider a more general example. Salespeople are likely charged with making this period's targets—measured perhaps daily, weekly, monthly, or quarterly. Many uncertain factors affect the sales force's ability to achieve its targets: a competitor cuts price, a key customer declares bankruptcy, a piece of legislation changes the rules of the game, and so on. There is little the sales force, or the organization in general, for that matter, can do to adapt its *strategy* to these kinds of changes. The products, customers, channels—in short, the underlying strategy of the organization—simply cannot change fast enough. The responsibility of the sales force is to run the play that has been called. This layer of the hierarchy has no choice but to operate within the constraints of past commitments made by higher-ups.

The very top of the hierarchy is defined by the opposite extreme. Rather than delivering on commitments, the corporate layer should be thinking about risk and opportunity. This means deciding which markets to explore, which contingencies to prepare for, and which risks to avoid, hedge, accept, or seek. With the longest time horizon, the degrees of strategic uncertainty are greatest, and so making commitments is a fool's errand.

The middle layer is stuck with perhaps the most challenging decisions. No corporation can succeed without eventually committing to a course of action. Yet any commitment necessarily entails risk. Divisional leadership, then, must make a bet on a specific strategy, at the same time taking steps to mitigate the downside should key assumptions prove wrong.

In other words, under Requisite Uncertainty, a well-functioning hierarchy is *differentiated* by the degree of *strategic* uncertainty addressed at each level and *integrated* through a cascading series of strategic commitments as those uncertainties are resolved.[32]

None of this should be interpreted to mean that people at each level have nothing to contribute to those working at other levels in the organization. Top management might well have insight and experience that can be of use to those dealing with short-run operational issues. Salespeople, who are among those closest to the marketplace, will likely be well positioned to pick up the weak signals that suggest a long-term strategic challenge is brewing. And crisis management can often require everyone's full attention. But just because the salespeople have their ears closest to the ground does not mean they should be crafting ten-year contingencies. Similarly, the technical expertise of senior managers does not mean that they should be making operating decisions. The challenge is to determine how best to ensure that each level makes the relevant contributions to every other level.

Connecting the various levels of the hierarchy in this way is consistent with how strategy actually gets made in most organizations. There is a forty-year tradition in management research, known as the "resource allocation process" model, that has laid bare how decisions tend to crystallize in larger companies. The notion of the CEO and the senior management team working out the strategy, then issuing marching orders to the rest of the company, is a realistic archetype for very few firms.

Rather, the corporate office has tended to set specific targets for growth or profitability or other measures of success, known collectively as the *corporate context*. Functional management recognizes gaps in the organization's ability to meet those targets. Perhaps quality is too low, or production capacity is insufficient, or critical capabilities are needed. Having identified the problem, functional managers then *define* the types of investment required to solve it and meet the demands of the corporate context. Divisional managers work the middle ground, giving *impetus* to specific projects that they feel will best meet the targets set at the corporate level.[33]

Requisite Uncertainty extends the definition of corporate context, demanding that corporate management not only set performance targets but also define the strategic uncertainty that the other layers of the organization must manage. It is therefore no great departure from established models or practice to suggest that top management does not make strategy; in reality, it rarely has. Instead, Requisite Uncertainty provides an explicit principle upon which to base the management of both sides of the strategy coin: commitment and uncertainty.

The simple fact is that no one can do everything. The division of labor— that is, activities designed to generate returns—happens *horizontally* across most organizations, with units oriented around functions, processes, customers, geographic regions, and so on. Requisite Uncertainty divides a different kind of labor—the activities designed to manage strategic uncertainty—*vertically* through an organization, with layers of the hierarchy oriented around the relevant time horizons.

6.4 THE ROLE OF THE BOARD OF DIRECTORS

The discussion so far has focused exclusively on the challenges facing managers. It is worth asking what is the role of the board of directors in a company operating according to the principles of Requisite Uncertainty.

Most commentators frame questions of corporate governance in terms of agency theory. In one formulation, managers enrich themselves at the expense of essentially everyone else, gaming equity-linked compensation packages by artificially, and sometimes fraudulently, inflating the value of their companies.[34] In another version, dominant shareholders exploit their control positions to extract value from a company via questionable and sometimes illegal transactions with other companies they also own or control.[35] Either way, the objective of good governance is to build control systems that thwart such self-dealing.

Fortunately, there are well-known substantive measures that can reduce the frequency and severity of internal control lapses. In the case of Enron, for example, the board failed to detect and put a stop to unethical and illegal practices by members of the senior management team. The corrective measures required are at least conceptually straightforward and often consistent with generally accepted, if not legally mandated, best practices.[36] They include: separating the chairman and the CEO positions; ensuring a significant majority of independent directors on the board and committees with independent directors in chairmanship roles (e.g., the compensation and audit committees); holding meetings of independent directors without management present; board-level review of the corporation's strategy and other significant decisions (e.g., acquisitions); and so on. Such measures by no means guarantee that there will be no control failures, but there is compelling evidence that these and other related practices will be rewarded with increased returns to shareholders.[37]

At many other companies, on the other hand, the board's failure was far more subtle and difficult to pin down. Take, for example, Vivendi (discussed at length in the next chapter). Vivendi was pushed to the brink of bankruptcy as a consequence of the fallout from CEO Jean-Marie Messier's ultimately failed attempt to create a global media conglomerate. Much of the *post hoc* criticism smacks of hindsight bias. For example, the board is accused of failing to stop Messier from "overpaying" for acquisitions. But no one knew that Vivendi had paid too much until the strategy had failed!

Board-level remedies for these kinds of lapses in strategic judgment typically focus on decision-making processes.[38] There is a general consensus that directors do not and cannot know as much as management about the company, the industry, or the relevant strategic challenges. Nevertheless, most informed observers feel that either the CEO should "make better use" of the board, or the board should be actively involved in strategic planning. At a minimum, this requires that directors engage the executive team, challenging key assumptions about the strategy, and contribute their insights and expertise.

This is all surely excellent advice. It is clear that better decision-making processes lead to better decisions.[39] However, better decision making does not remove or even mitigate the challenges posed by unpredictability and the limits of corporate adaptability. Open and frank discussions between the board and management about what to commit to do not suspend the strategy paradox.

Consider, for example, corporate boards in the United Kingdom, where for decades the chairman and CEO roles have routinely been separated, as opposed to the United States, where combining the roles is still the norm (although this is changing). In the United Kingdom, the chairman tends to be far more involved in the development of strategy than are independent board members of U.S. firms. The most observable consequence of this is that there is now one more qualified, experienced, and motivated person assisting the CEO in setting strategy.

There is no reason to think this is bad. However, there is no evidence that British firms create better strategies or are any less vulnerable to strategic uncertainty as a result. In fact, the heavy involvement of an otherwise independent board member in strategy formulation can often lead to a form of "co-opting" or "groupthink," ironically undermining the independent review of strategic plans that the board is typically thought to provide.[40] The challenge posed by the strategy paradox is not an agency problem, because the strategy paradox is not a consequence of either criminality or decision-making bias. Resolving the strategy paradox means wrestling more effectively with the inescapable reality of an unpredictable and potentially radically changing future.

Under Requisite Uncertainty, the board grapples with the longest time horizon of all: the "going concern" assumption behind every healthy corporation. Practically speaking, the board does not address specific time frames but can legitimately be said to be looking to the performance and survival of the firm *ad infinitum*; after all, the board's fiduciary responsibilities generally run to the shareholders *and the corporation*.[41] Consequently, it is legitimately—and perhaps primarily—the board's role to consider carefully the trade-offs between risk and return implied by any strategy that management might propose, with an eye to both shareholder returns and the corporation's survival.

CUI BONO?

The question of to whom the board owes its fiduciary duty is at times a contentious issue. The debate is typically framed in terms of a tension between the interests of shareholders and stakeholders.[42] Shareholders supply capital to the corporation and stakeholders are, depending on the theorist, employees, suppliers, customers, governments, society at large, the environment . . . the list goes on.

Shareholder theory holds that the corporation's "objective function" is, or should be, the maximization of shareholder wealth. In seeking to maximize shareholder wealth, the corporation must obey the law, and it is through the law that other stakeholders can seek to secure their interests.

Stakeholder theory (or Corporate Social Responsibility theory) argues that the corporation's responsibility is to all parties that it affects.[43] On this view, the corporation is a moral actor and so should not seek to maximize the welfare of a single stakeholder (shareholder) to the detriment of others. The brighter lines of legal constraint are not sufficient to enable civil society: as individuals we all operate within boundaries defined by occasionally blurry moral codes and ethical customs, and corporations are no different.[44]

The courts have been deliberately ambiguous on the matter.[45] Many landmark business cases are heard and decided in Delaware's Chancery court, where rulings in corporate disputes can be seen as an attempt to balance competing interests using notions of "fairness" rather than law.[46] The seemingly conflicted nature of the Court's rulings—finding sometimes for shareholders and sometimes for stakeholders—might be a reflection of the fact that corporations are legal fictions, created and tolerated by society because their existence, presumably, serves social ends. As a result, no party ever always comes first.

A third, and often overlooked, school of thought known as Contractarianism suggests that the corporation simply contracts with various constituencies for the inputs required to survive.[47] One interpretation of this theory is that the corporation is not a mechanism for the enrichment of shareholders—or anyone else, for that matter. Instead, every corporation seeks its own survival and growth, and pays whatever it must to those it must in order to achieve those ends. Shareholders must be given a competitive return, employees must be paid competitive wages, and customers must be provided with competitive products. In this context, government's job is to ensure that each of these markets functions fairly and efficiently: no "greenmail," no "poison pills," no "union busting," no "unsafe" products.[48]

Whether the corporation serves first shareholders, stakeholders, or itself, it must still manage strategic uncertainty. However, the resources devoted to the management of strategic uncertainty will depend on which theory motivates the board's decisions. Shareholders are typically highly diversified and highly liquid, and so need relatively less assistance managing risk than do, say, employees who are perforce much less diversified and less liquid. A corporation seeking first its own survival will manage strategic uncertainty to the extent required to persist, but because strategic change can often require significant asset reallocation, likely not as aggressively as prescribed by stakeholder theory, which places a higher value on the preferences of employees, communities, and other affected parties.

When management prepares a strategy, the board's necessary involvement is not to engage the substance of that strategy—for example, should a given acquisition go through or not, should a new market be entered or not, should a new product be developed or not. Such participation might very well be helpful, and best practice suggests that management should take advantage of the board as much as possible. But the board does not have privileged insight into what the right commitments will be.[49] Instead, it is the board's role to determine whether all the relevant strategic uncertainties have been identified, to insist that ways of managing that uncertainty have been developed, and to make sure that the associated costs of managing that uncertainty are acceptable.

The board then has four alternatives in assessing management's strategy:

1. It could conclude that management needs to *seek* greater uncertainty in order to generate additional opportunities. Management might well have built a strategy that drifts toward the middle of its industry's strategic space, sacrificing returns in exchange for a greater possibility of survival. Since part of the board's fiduciary responsibility is to shareholders, and serving shareholders typically implies generating higher economic returns, there can be sound reasons for the board to insist that management pursue a more uncertain strategy.

2. It can *accept* whatever uncertainties are implied by management's strategy: not all risks can be mitigated, not all opportunities pursued. The informed acceptance of uncertainty is a valid business decision.

3. It could choose to *avoid* a given uncertainty. For example, entering a particular market might offer enormous opportunity, but at commensurate strategic risk. If the board deems that level of risk too high, and unmanageable at acceptable cost, then the board can simply instruct that the market not be entered. This decision would not be based on an assessment of the suitability of the strategy itself—that is, management might well have crafted the best possible way to enter this particular market, and the strategy is expected to generate acceptable returns. The issue is the risk incurred by seeking those returns.

4. Finally, and most powerfully, the board can insist that management *manage* the uncertainty. That is, the board could require management to develop a way to mitigate the strategic risk while still preserving the ability to exploit the associated strategic opportunity.

By responding to strategic uncertainty with one or (more likely) a combination of the above (seeking, accepting, avoiding, or managing), the board determines the company's overall exposure to strategic risks and opportunities. It is then management's role to create the exposure that the board has deemed appropriate.

This distinction is critical. The expectation should always be that "management knows more" and so although the board can offer advice, it might be ill-advised to overrule management's strategic choices. Similarly, the board might not know as much about the strategic uncertainties facing the corporation as management does or how best to address those uncertainties. But, unlike substantive questions of strategy, the issue here is not knowledge; it is fiduciary responsibility. Every compensation scheme has frailties, and equity-based compensation skews the risk preferences of high-level managers.[50] In a world where managers are responding to high-powered incentives based on grants of stock or stock options, there is an asymmetry of risk between the corporation's various stakeholders (shareholders, employees, etc.) and management. Management will tend to have a bias toward far riskier investments than others, not as a consequence of malice or deceit, but because that is what the compensation system typically rewards. Conversely, long-term career managers more interested in the stability of their tenure and personal empire-building may well need to be directed to generate greater corporate exposure to promising opportunities. Either way, what is required is a countervailing force to management's structurally induced preferences, and for standard agency reasons this force must be separate from and senior to the CEO. That can only be the board.

The board cannot decide what the company's strategy should be. However, the board is uniquely positioned to determine how much exposure to risk and opportunity the corporation should have. That is, the board determines the risk/return profile of the firm. This is materially different from helping management make better strategy. Instead, Requisite Uncertainty calls upon the board to define the parameters of risk and opportunity within which management must function.

How a board might evaluate a CEO's performance is profoundly affected by this principle. CEO tenure has been dropping steadily for more than a decade, and companies are increasingly turning "outside" to find new CEOs, seemingly with the expectation that new blood will generate a rapid improvement in corporate performance.[51] How can we square the reality that CEOs seem to have five-year terms with the prescription that the CEO is responsible for managing long-term uncertainties?

The ability of the CEO to have a positive impact on short-term operating results is surely quite limited. We often either credit or blame CEOs for short-term results, but this often makes no more sense than the praise or pillory received by politicians who have the good luck or misfortune to take office just as an expansion or recession hits. Of course, the decisions CEOs make matter a lot, and if they make the wrong decisions they can certainly destroy a lot of value in a very short time (as will be shown in the next chapter). But, thanks to entropy, creation and destruction are not symmetrical processes. Creating and implementing the right strategy necessarily takes time.

Evaluating and rewarding a CEO based on stock-price movements is consistent with Requisite Uncertainty, since, after all, stock price captures the present value of the future. There are three problems with this, however. First, there is the problem of separating signal from noise. Markets move in mysterious ways, and sorting out random fluctuations from *bone fide* responses to specific actions is extraordinarily difficult.[52] CEOs would be hard-pressed for all but the most momentous decisions to know whether the market approves or not of the course of action being followed. Second, because the market *reacts*, that is, judges the merits of a decision after it has been made, how is the CEO to know how to *act* in the first place? Third, stockholders will have a different risk/return preference than the corporation, valuing the survival of the corporation less highly than the corporation itself might. Even if it were possible to follow the "lead" of the market, doing so would amount to just as much an abdication of the board's responsibilities to the corporation as would turning over executive decision-making authority to union leaders or government regulators.

As a result, the board must assess the CEO's performance based in large part on its subjective assessment of how well the chief executive has positioned the firm to cope with future uncertainties.[53] One need not wait ten years to see if the CEO made the right decisions, because the corporation's risk/return profile over a ten-year time horizon can be described and evaluated today. Whether a CEO's tenure is fifteen years or five, the board is in a position to pass judgment on how the CEO's actions bear on the firm's stance *today* with respect to the uncertainties that define *tomorrow*.

Applying these principles is not a straightforward matter. In the next chapter, we see what happens to three companies that, respectively, ignore these prescriptions, adopt them by half-measures, and embrace them.

> *Hierarchies should be structured around time, with higher levels focused on longer time horizons. Strategic uncertainty increases with time. Therefore, the higher the hierarchical level, the greater should be the emphasis on the management of uncertainty. Consequently, the board's role is to determine the corporation's overall exposure to strategic uncertainty. Senior management must then develop mechanisms for hedging the relevant strategic risks and ensuring that the relevant strategic opportunities remain viable. Operating division management must commit to a specific strategy but work to avoid catastrophic outcomes should key assumptions prove invalid. Functional management is charged with delivering short-term results.*

---

1. Some believe the opposite: predicting the short-run future is impossible, but long-run forecasts stand a much better chance of being correct (e.g., Davis, Ian, and Elizabeth Stephenson [2006], "Ten Trends to Watch in 2006," *The McKinsey Quarterly* [January]). Such claims typically rest on changing the criteria for successful prediction. For example,

reliably forecasting China's GDP for the next quarter is impossible, for reasons we've explored. In contrast, it is asserted that forecasting China's GDP will grow over the long term seems a safe bet.

Let's put on hold for the moment whether or not such a statement is in fact true; after all, one can easily make the argument for declines in China's GDP over the next, say, five years based on energy shortages, political turmoil, trade imbalances with the United States, and so on. For now, consider only that the precision demanded of the two forecasts is very different: the long-range prediction is granted much wider latitude in terms of outcome and time horizon. In other words, claims of superior prescience over the longer term trade on comparing point predictions over a specific time period with broad directions over an unspecified time period. There's no way to control for these differences when attempting to compare accuracy. As a result, I'm forced to conclude that such claims are unfalsifiable and hence essentially empty.

In contrast, the argument for a greater range of uncertainties associated with the longer term is based on fundamental facts of the universe. The speed of light determines the time required for one event to affect another. That is, if something happens more than one light-year away from me, that event can have no effect on me for at least a year. That event lies beyond my one-year "event horizon." As I look farther into the future, a greater number of events falls within my event horizon, increasing the combinations and permutations of possible interactions between events, which in turn creates a greater range of possible outcomes, making my uncertainty concomitantly greater.

On a more human scale, it takes time for events in one place to transmit their impacts fully: an increase in the money supply works its way through to inflation and consumer demand slowly, and in the time it takes for that to happen, other events can occur that can skew the anticipated impact of such a perturbation on any given equilibrium. Similarly for any attempt we might make to influence or prepare for the longer term: the longer our time frame, the broader our event horizon, and hence the more unpredictable the end state becomes.

2. There are of course material uncertainties of other types—specifically, operational and financial uncertainties—which must be identified and managed. These can manifest themselves in the very short run, and although they increase over time, they are also self-correcting, and so increase within limits. For example, your supply chain might be vulnerable to the bankruptcy of a supplier. But considering this uncertainty over the long term does not typically lead to the conclusion that one needs to prepare for the possibility that all of one's suppliers might go bankrupt, for just as the odds of a supplier going bankrupt increase with time, the odds of new suppliers emerging also increase with time. Similarly, the range over which, say, interest rates might fluctuate in the next year is not much greater than their likely range over the next five years, since other macroeconomic variables, such as exchange rates and trade flows, serve as counterweights to extreme values.

3. Chandler, Jr., Alfred D. (1963), *Strategy and Structure: Chapters in the History of the American Industrial Enterprise,* Cambridge, MA: MIT Press. Subsequent work has demonstrated that structure drives strategy at least as much as the other way around, but for reasons and in ways that are very different from the mechanisms by which strategy leads structure. More on this anon.

4. Exploring the trade-offs between scale and scope is a monumental task, one which Chandler took up in *Scale and Scope: The Dynamics of Industrial Capitalism,* Cambridge, MA: The Belknap Press of Harvard University Press, 1990.

5. This and following paragraphs summarizing the evolutionary paths that led to the emergence of the M-form simply rehearse the arguments made by Chandler (1963).

6. Hamel, Gary (2006), "The Why, What, and How of Management Innovation," *Harvard Business Review*, Vol. 84, No. 2 (February), pp. 72–84.

7. Galbraith, Jay (2002), *Designing Organizations: An Executive Guide to Strategy, Structure, and Process (New and Revised)*, San Francisco: Josey-Bass.

8. In *The Modern Firm: Organizational Design for Performance and Growth* (2004, Oxford University Press), John Roberts explains hierarchies exclusively in terms of the integrating role a given level of the hierarchy plays for the levels below it.

9. Lawrence, Paul R., and Jay W. Lorsch (1967, 1986), *Organization and Environment,* Boston, MA: Harvard Business School Press.

10. As recapitulated in *Designing Organizations* (Galbraith, *op. cit.*), these are (i) voluntary and informal groups, (ii) E-coordination, (iii) Formal groups, (iv) Integrator, (v) Matrix organization. Of these, (iii)–(v) make the most explicit use of hierarchical position.

11. This idea has been developed most fully by Clayton Christensen in a series of publications. See, in particular, "Why Hard-Nosed Executives Should Care About Management Theory," *Harvard Business Review,* Vol. 81, No. 9 (September), with Michael E. Raynor, and "Anomaly-Seeking Research: Thirty Years of Theory Development in Resource Allocation Theory," in *From Resource Allocation to Strategy*, Joseph L. Bower and Clark G. Gilbert, eds. (2005), New York: Oxford University Press.

12. Jaques is not unknown to management scholars, and many of his books remain in print, so he is by no means obscure: at http://www.canadiancentre.com/ejbiblio/ejbiblio.htm (accessed February 2, 2006), you can find a fully annotated bibliography and guidance through the 3,500 books and 300 peer-reviewed journal articles supporting Jaques's findings. See also http://www.requisite.org/main.html (accessed February 2, 2006) for a compendium of research and related materials that explore Jaques's ideas.

Despite this substantial body of work, to give you some sense of relative visibility, a Google search for his name results in 466 hits; "Alfred D. Chandler, Jr." gets 37,100; while Peter Drucker and W. Edwards Deming, two management theorists of similar vintage, generate 1.96 million and 313,000 hits, respectively. As a doctoral student at the Harvard Business School, I was never assigned even a paper by Jaques, and in looking through syllabi of other doctoral programs, I've never seen his work assigned.

Perhaps the most accessible exposition of Jaques's theories is his article "In Praise of Hierarchy," *Harvard Business Review*, 1990 (January–February). The most complete is likely *A General Theory of Bureaucracy,* New York: Halstead Press (1976).

13. This reality is likely what gives rise to the aphorism "Senior management is always two levels above you."

14. Jaques addresses this question succinctly in "Taking Time Seriously in Evaluating Jobs," *Harvard Business Review,* 1979 (September–October).

15. Jaques, Elliot (1999), *Requisite Organization,* Arlington, VA: Cason Hall & Co.

16. I use the term "quantum" in its strictest sense. In quantum physics, a quantum is not merely a discrete, indivisible quantity, it is the smallest possible quantity. For Jaques, the strata he identifies are indeed quanta: the smallest possible differences in time horizon that have organizational meaning. In general usage, the term "quantum" typically refers to a large change (e.g., "quantum leap"), much to the dismay of high-energy particle physicists everywhere.

17. A recent exploration of the hierarchy is Harold J. Leavitt's *Top Down: Why Hierarchies Are Here to Stay and How to Manage Them More Efficiently,* Boston: Harvard Business School Press, 2005. Leavitt explains hierarchies largely in terms of a "necessary evil" that must be "humanized." In contrast, Jaques sees hierarchies as highly effective organizational forms. Many of Leavitt's criticisms of hierarchies seem to stem from his observations on the inadequacies of hierarchy as a mechanism of horizontal integration,

and on these terms his objections are well-founded. What Jaques adds to Leavitt's critique is a positive argument for the hierarchical structure: that hierarchies create a division of labor with respect to specific kinds of decision making, rather than the largely discredited view of hierarchy as a supervisory mechanism by which the more competent ensure that the less competent do as they're told.

18. In terms of Christensen's description of theory building (see note 11, *supra*), the phenomenon of interest that Jaques describes is "level skipping" in a hierarchy. He categorizes these levels in terms of their associated time horizons. He develops a theory of cause and effect in terms of the strata he identifies, and tests the predictions of that theory using felt-fair pay surveys. As nearly as I can tell, research in the RO field has tended to replicate and refine Jaques's theory, which is important and useful work. But it is not enough to advance the theory. Greater emphasis on anomaly-seeking research would help extend and elaborate RO in ways that might help it gain the visibility and acceptance that it could well deserve.

19. Ken Craddock, unpublished annotated bibliography of RO and related research. See note 12, *supra*. Craddock further explains that companies using RO see it as such a competitive advantage that they refuse to acknowledge it. Such claims are, of course, difficult to verify.

20. I make this claim tentatively and with due circumspection. One can't read everything on anything, and Craddock's annotated bibliography runs to more than 500 pages.

21. See, for example, Billington, Corey, Blake Johnson, and Alex Triantis (2002), "A Real Options Perspective on Supply Chain Management in High Technology," *Journal of Applied Corporate Finance,* Vol. 15, No. 2 (Summer); or Sheffi, Yossi, and James B. Rice, Jr. (2005), "A Supply Chain View of the Resilient Enterprise," *MITSloan Management Review* (Fall). I dispatch supply-chain uncertainties with a wave of the hand out of respect for the magnitude, complexity, and importance of the issue, not to be dismissive. The topic is simply so large that I would do it disrespect to even begin to peel back the covers.

22. For instance:

Supplier uncertainty: In March 2000, a fire shut down a Philips semiconductor plant in New Mexico, which in turn disrupted cellular phone production at Nokia and Ericsson. Nokia had a more diverse supply chain and had contingency plans for such a disruption, while Ericsson did not, allowing Nokia to weather the storm much more effectively, stealing market share from its Nordic rival—not thanks to better strategy, but thanks to the superior management of an operational risk. See Latour, Almar (2001), "A Blaze in Albuquerque Sets Off Major Crisis for Cell-Phone Giants," *Wall Street Journal,* January 29, 2001, A-1, as recounted in Schoemaker, Paul J. (2002), *Profiting from Uncertainty: Strategies for Succeeding No Matter What the Future Brings,* New York: The Free Press.

Brand uncertainty: In 1994, Intel's Pentium chip was found by its customers to have a flaw in its floating point unit (FPU). Intel knew about the flaw, but it was not exceptional: it was the kind of bug that invariably creeps into any semiconductor, and so the company proceeded as usual. The company's successful branding campaign around "Intel Inside," however, had elevated the company to a standard-bearer for quality and reliability, and so the rules had been changed—by Intel! The fallout cost the company nearly half a billion dollars. Intel had run afoul of executing a particular element of its own strategy of connecting directly with customers due to an operational risk; the strategy itself remains valid and a critical component of the company's continued success. See Grove, Andrew S. (1996), *Only the Paranoid Survive: How to Exploit the Crisis Points that Challenge Every Company,* New York: Doubleday.

Rogue employee: In February 1995, Barings Bank, the 200-year-old bank that had financed Britain's Napoleonic Wars, was bankrupted by Nick Leeson, a twenty-eight-year-old Singapore-based trader. Leeson had been speculating heavily on the Japanese stock market using highly leveraged derivatives, and when the tide turned against him he fraudulently masked his losses, hoping for a lucky break. The subterfuge caught up with him before his luck returned. The bank went under and Leeson got six years in prison. The strategy of an investment bank trading on its own account is certainly risky, but it's not a bad strategy, at least if judged by its widespread use. Barings simply failed to manage the operational risk created by this component of its strategy. See Rawnsley, Judith H., and Nicholas W. Leeson (1995), *Total Risk: Nick Leeson and the Fall of Barings Bank,* Toronto: HarperCollins Canada.

Currency uncertainty: Mexico-based Cemex is second only to France's Lafarge in the cement and ready-mix concrete industry. In the mid-1990s, the industry was consolidating globally, and to remain competitive Cemex moved aggressively, but prudently, to acquire relevant assets and diversify its revenue base outside of Mexico. This required taking out significant U.S. dollar-denominated loans at a time when about half of Cemex's revenues were still denominated in Mexican pesos. As a result, the company was caught in the cross fire of the 1994–1995 peso crisis, in which the Mexican currency's value fell by more than 40 percent. Cemex's share price was punished (along with the broader Mexican equity market) and the firm's debt was downgraded by various ratings agencies. The company was essentially the victim of an underlying financial risk rather than any misplaced strategic bets or operational missteps. Indeed, thanks to the soundness of the underlying strategy and the firm's ability to execute that strategy effectively, the company's financing partners were willing to provide the requisite bridge facilities, and Cemex emerged largely unscathed. See "Cemex: Half of Firm's Revenues from Outside Mexico," Dow Jones Newswire, January 27, 1995.

23. Grouping uncertainties into strategic, operational, and financial categories seems to be the most parsimonious classification system. See *Disarming the Value Killers: A Risk Management Study,* Deloitte Research, 2005, http://www.deloitte.com/dtt/cda/doc/content/DTT_DR_VKillers_Feb05.pdf, accessed February 20, 2006.

24. See, for example, Hyman, Michael (2005), *New Ways for Managing Global Financial Risks: The Next Generation,* New York: Wiley; or Merton, Robert C. (2005), "You Have More Capital Than You Think," *Harvard Business Review,* Vol. 83, No. 11 (November). I feel the same way about financial risk as I do about operational risk—perhaps even more so!

25. The Joint Committee on Corporate Governance classifies risks as strategic, operational, leadership, partnership, and reputation; see *Beyond Compliance: Building a Governance Culture,* Canadian Institute of Chartered Accountants (CICA), Canadian Venture Exchange (CDNX), and Toronto Stock Exchange (TSE). Other groups have additionally identified interdependence, regulatory, legal, environmental, brand risk, distribution risk, regulatory risk, human resources risk, and so on almost ad infinitum; see DeLoach, James, and Nick Temple (2000), *Enterprise-Wide Risk Management: Strategies for Linking Risk & Opportunity,* Financial Times Management.

Such extravagance in categorization misses the point of creating categories in the first place. A good classification scheme allows managers to determine the circumstances they are in so they can employ the most appropriate tools to solve a given problem. This means that uncertainties should be classified according to the tools used to manage them. For useful early work that seeks to categorize risks in this way, see Slywotzky, Adrian J., and John Drzik (2005), "Countering the Biggest Risk of All," *Harvard Business Review,* Vol. 83, No. 4 (April).

26. See in particular Tobin, James (1992), *Asset Accumulation and Economic Activity,* Chicago: University of Chicago Press; Zarnowitz, Victor (1992), *Business Cycles: Theory, History, Indicators, and Forecasting,* Chicago: University of Chicago Press; and Glasner, David (1997), *Business Cycles and Depressions: An Encyclopedia,* New York: Garland Publishing. The peak-to-trough amplitude of business cycles has been decreasing for some time, with a particularly strong dampening in the wake of the Second World War. This has been a consequence of the reinforcing effects of the countercyclical fiscal and monetary policies of governments and the shift to services in the economy, which are much less subject to swings in consumption: you can delay purchasing a new car or refrigerator for another year far more easily than you can delay purchasing the health care you need.

27. Baghai, Mehdad, Stephen Coley, and David White (2000), *The Alchemy of Growth,* London: Basic Books.

28. See Forsythe, G. B., S. A. Snook, P. Lewis, and P. Bartone (2002), "Making Sense of Officership: Developing a Professional Identity for 21st Century Army Officers," *Future of the Army Profession,* L. J. Matthews, ed. (2002), New York: McGraw-Hill Publishing, pp. 357–78; and Bartone, P., G. B. Forsythe, S. A. Snook, R. C. Bullis, and P. Lewis (2001), "Leader Development at the U.S. Military Academy, West Point: New Directions in Programs, Theory and Research," a paper presented at biennial meeting of the Inter-University Seminar on Armed Forces and Society (October 2001), Baltimore, MD. In the nonmilitary context, see Kegan, Robert (1994), *In Over Our Heads,* Cambridge, MA: Harvard University Press.

For a synthesis of these views and their implications for the prevalence of leaders with the ability to cope with paradox, see Putz, Michael, and Michael E. Raynor (2005), "Integral Leadership: Overcoming the Paradox of Growth" (unpublished). This paper is available from the author at mraynor@deloitte.com.

29. These suggestions are based solely on the recounting of Bombardier's actions in Baghai et al. (2000), *op. cit.* Bombardier may or may not have considered or be pursuing any or all of these initiatives.

30. To describe this strategy fully would require a specification of Bombardier's position on the airframe industry's production possibility frontier. Bombardier is in many ways a disruptor of the larger airframe makers, Boeing and Airbus. A full description of their strategy is, however, beyond the scope of this section.

31. It is possible to see the "Horizons" framework as consistent with Requisite Uncertainty. The questions that fall to each level appear to me to manifest different levels of strategic uncertainty. In addition, "Horizons" does not seem to make or imply quantitative claims regarding how long each time horizon is, nor if the time horizons are consistent across levels of the hierarchy or across divisions. This is important because, as noted in the text accompanying Figure 6-1, strategic uncertainties might emerge far more slowly in Aerospace than in Services or Capital. Consequently, corporate executives might be looking out fifteen years for Aerospace but only five years for each of the other two.

In suggesting this potential consistency, I fear I am taking too many liberties with their work. My sense is that Baghai *et al.* see their framework as truly fractal and consider the level of strategic complexity to be similar across all levels.

32. In *20/20 Foresight: Crafting Strategy in an Uncertain World* (2001), Harvard Business School Press, Hugh Courtney identifies four levels of uncertainty: (1) a "clear enough" future that allows for specific plans, (2) "alternate futures" that requires only discrete alternatives to be defined, (3) a "range of futures" best captured through scenarios, and (4) "true ambiguity," where even defining boundaries is impractical. Each type of uncertainty requires a different set of tools to be effectively managed. Courtney

notes that longer time horizons can lead to higher levels of uncertainty. Part of what I think the current discussion adds to Courtney's insights is the connection between strategic uncertainty, time horizons, and hierarchical levels. Level 1 uncertainty ("clear enough") is the domain of the lower levels of the hierarchy, where execution is the name of the game. Moving up through the hierarchy lengthens the relevant time horizon, increasing the strategic uncertainty to be addressed. As a result, the tools Courtney identifies—scenario-based planning and real options in particular—have different applications, depending on which level in the hierarchy is using them.

33. The seminal work in this field is Bower, Joseph L. (1970), *Managing the Resource Allocation Process,* Division of Research, Harvard Business School.

34. Byrne, John A., "How to Fix Corporate Governance," *BusinessWeek,* May 6, 2002; "Designed by Committee," *The Economist,* June 15, 2002.

35. Coffee, Jr., John C. (2005), "A Theory of Corporate Scandals: Why the U.S. and Europe Differ," *Oxford Review of Economic Policy,* Vol. 21, Iss. 2 (Summer). Coffee suggests that one sees more managerial-driven fraud in the United States and more shareholder-driven fraud in Europe.

36. Banks, Eric (2004), *Corporate Governance: Financial Responsibility, Controls and Ethics,* New York: Palgrave.

37. It has been noted elsewhere that Enron's board manifested many of the structural characteristics typically identified as "best practices," resulting in an appropriate call for the board of directors to be sure to actually *do* the right thing as well as be configured in a manner that makes it *possible* to do the right thing. See Lorsch, Jay W., and Colin B. Carter (2004), *Back to the Drawing Board,* Boston, MA: Harvard Business School Press.

Even so, structural characteristics do seem to matter; see Millstein, Ira M., and Paul W. MacAvoy (1998), "The Active Board of Directors and Performance of the Large Publicly Traded Corporation," *Columbia Law Review,* Vol. 98. Millstein and MacAvoy find that companies graded "A+" by CalPERS for board independence and rated "high" by the authors for board activism earned significantly higher economic returns over the 1991–1995 period. It is difficult to conclude from this study, however, whether the improved performance was a consequence of reduced slack in firms with allegedly better governance (that is, thanks merely to better control) or better strategy.

38. Charan, Ram (1998), *Boards at Work: How Corporate Boards Create Competitive Advantage,* San Francisco: Jossey-Bass; Conger, Jay A., Edward E. Lawler III, and David L. Finegold (2001), *Corporate Boards: New Strategies for Adding Value at the Top,* San Francisco: Jossey-Bass; Carter, Colin B., and Jay W. Lorsch (2004), *op. cit.*

39. Roberto, Michael A. (2005), *Why Great Leaders Don't Take Yes for an Answer,* Upper Saddle River, NJ: Wharton School Publishing.

40. Zelleke, Andargachew Shifferaw (2003), *Freedom and Constraint: The Design of Governance and Leadership Structures in British and American Firms,* unpublished doctoral dissertation, Boston: Harvard Business School.

41. Bork, Paul (2005), "Fiduciary Duties of a Director of a Delaware Corporation," Foley Hoag LLP, Boston, MA. Available at http://www.fhe.com/files/tbl_s5084FileUpload/FileName5632/67/fiduciaryDuties-bork102805.pdf; accessed April 26, 2006.

42. See featured debates on the topic in the *Mid-American Journal of Business* (2003), Vol. 18, Iss. 1, and *Organization Science* (2004), Vol. 15, No. 3.

43. See Zenisek, Thomas J. (1979), "Corporate Social Responsibility: A Conceptualization Based on Organizational Literature," *Academy of Management Review* (July); Moser, Martin R. (1986), "A Framework for Analyzing Corporate Social Responsibility," *Journal of Business Ethics,* Vol. 5, Iss. 1 (February); Moir, Lance (2001), "What Do

We Mean by Corporate Social Responsibility," *Corporate Governance,* Vol. 1, Iss. 2; Carriga, Elisabet, and Domènec Melé (2004), "Corporate Social Responsibility Theories: Mapping the Territory," *Journal of Business Ethics,* Vol. 53, pp. 51–71.

44. In a famous defense of shareholder theory, Milton Friedman argued that the maximization of shareholder value must be pursued "while conforming to the basic rules of the society, both those embodied in law *and those embodied in ethical custom*" (emphasis added). This is a slippery slope. Permitting a corporation to view moral codes or generous interpretations of the "spirit of the law" as constraints turns the corporation into a moral actor, and shareholder theory rapidly becomes, in practice, indistinguishable from stakeholder theory.

45. Allen, William T. (1997), "Inherent Tensions in the Governance of U.S. Public Corporations: The Uses of Ambiguity in Fiduciary Law," Conference on Corporate Governance, Max-Planck-Institut, Hamburg. Available at http://ssrn.com/sol3/papers. cfm?abstract_id=10565, accessed December 20, 2004; Allen, William T. (1993), "Our Schizophrenic Conception of the Business Corporation," *Cardozo Law Review,* Vol. 261, Iss. 14. Allen's opinions are worth taking seriously: he was the Chancellor of the Delaware Chancery Court, the most important corporate court in the United States, from 1985 to 1997.

46. Rawls, John (1975), *A Theory of Justice,* Boston: Harvard University Press.

47. Bradley, Michael, Cindy A. Schipani, Anant K. Sundaram, and James P. Walsh (2000), "The Purposes and Accountability of the Corporation in Contemporary Society: Corporate Governance at a Crossroads," *Law and Contemporary Problems,* Vol. 62, No. 3. A variant of this view is found in Bainbridge, Stephen M. (2002), "Director Primacy: The Means and Ends of Corporate Governance," UCLA School of Law research paper no. 02-06.

48. I use "scare quotes" for these terms because each is intended to capture the moral opprobrium attached to their conventional uses. Whether or not the facts in a specific case constitute such behavior is a matter to be decided by the courts.

49. Consider, for instance, an example reported by Rob Norton in *Corporate Board Member* ("Your Tricky New Role in Strategy," March–April 2005). Norton recounts that the Becton Dickinson board reviewed an acquisition proposed by the CEO of the medical supplies company. The target was a firm that manufactured diagnostic devices for a particular disease. Some board members felt that there was a strong possibility that a vaccine would soon be launched for that same disease, largely obviating the target's products. On the basis of the board's misgivings, the acquisition was scuttled. A vaccine did ultimately emerge, justifying the board's concerns.

If one of the board members knew something that management didn't about the relevant research, or if management had failed to do its homework, this is not a cause for celebrating the board; it is cause for indicting management. Given the same information, if management endorses a strategy and the board disagrees, there is no reason to think that the board will guess right with any greater frequency than management.

50. Bebchuk, Lucian, and Jesse Fried (2004), *Pay Without Performance: The Unfulfilled Promise of Executive Compensation,* Cambridge, MA: Harvard University Press. Managers granted options that have value only when the stock price increases above a certain level will necessarily be motivated to make higher-risk, higher-return choices in order to drive their options into the money. This is not pathological behavior; it is what options-based incentive schemes are designed to do (see Kerr, S. [1975], "On the Folly of Rewarding 'A' While Hoping for 'B,'" *Academy of Management Journal,* Vol. 18, Iss. 4). In light of this, the repricing of options to reward managers even though performance

targets that once seemed reasonable come to appear out of reach is both unconscionable, because it retroactively changes the rules of the game, and entirely reasonable, because it mitigates what might otherwise manifest itself as reckless risk-taking.

51. Khurana, Rakesh (2002), *Searching for a Corporate Savior: The Irrational Quest for Charismatic CEOs,* Princeton, NJ: Princeton University Press.

52. The research method known as the "event study" attempts to infer market reaction from specific company events, such as a merger announcement, by teasing out common cause from special cause variation in stock prices. It is very difficult to see significant effects in even such landmark actions as mergers, and the conclusions are far from uncontroversial.

A big part of the problem might well be that even if a board were able to determine that the market responded favorably to a CEO's decisions in the past, it would not therefore be able to conclude that they had a good CEO on their hands. In the paperback second edition of *Fooled by Randomness,* Nassim Taleb explains that repetition is the key to assessing whether one has any meaningful skill. Yet the higher one goes in the hierarchy, the less repetitive the tasks are that one must perform, and hence the more difficult it is to determine whether or not one has demonstrated skill, for which one should be rewarded, or simply been lucky. He calls this the "inverse skills problem." It's such an illuminating observation that it's too bad it's in a postscript to the book.

That is not to say, of course, that CEOs have no impact on a firm's performance. Recent research suggests that the CEO accounts for approximately 15% of the variance in a firm's returns to shareholders, about the same as accounted for by industry. See Mayo, Anthony J., and Nitin Nohria (2005), *In Their Time: The Great Business Leaders of the Twentieth Century,* Boston: Harvard Business School Press. The problem is we don't know how CEOs have this impact.

53. The question of what motivates the board and how the board is monitored is a fascinating one: *quies custodiet ipsos custodes* (who will watch the watchers)? The "agency problem" remains unresolved, in my view, and no system is perfect; they can all be gamed. In this formulation, the board is essentially a trustee operating in the interests of the corporation, because society has mandated that corporations should do so in order to maximize social welfare. Directors should be paid well for their services, but those services must be informed by a sense of duty and professionalism. When those virtues are lacking, the corporation will be vulnerable to self-serving behavior. But this is no different from the situation today.

CHAPTER SEVEN

MAKING CHOICES VERSUS CREATING OPTIONS

Vivendi under Jean-Marie Messier pursued a commitment-based strategy and was nearly bankrupted when the assumptions on which that strategy was based proved false. BCE's senior management built a diversified portfolio of partial equity stakes that created a strategically flexible corporation, but lacked the formalized processes required to implement this approach for its most significant strategic bet, with disastrous results. Microsoft, thanks largely to the very nearly unique power and influence Bill Gates enjoyed during his tenure as CEO, was able to pursue an options-based strategy far more consistently, and so manage strategic uncertainty far more effectively.

The need to manage strategic uncertainty can be seen in sharp relief in how three firms have grappled with the challenges created by "convergence," the collision of telecommunications, media, and technology. Beginning in the early 1990s, there was a dawning realization that digital technologies might revolutionize much of the modern economy.[1] Everyone was sure that everything would change, but there was no consensus on how, when, or to what effect. The diversity of opinion was remarkable, as evidenced by the proliferation of frameworks for understanding "new media."[2]

Each individual piece of the new puzzle had long dealt with its own characteristic uncertainties. Telecoms companies had coped with regulatory unpredictability. Media companies addressed the inevitable hit-or-miss nature of entertainment products. Technology companies were attuned to the challenges of rapidly changing technologies. But convergence created an entirely new set of strategic uncertainties. What was going to converge with what, and who would profit from the coming transformation? Would distribution

UNCERTAINTIES IN TELECOMMUNICATIONS, MEDIA, AND TECHNOLOGY

In the telecommunications space, critical uncertainties remained salient and unresolved through much of the 1990s, particularly with respect to the relative merits of the phone companies' and cable companies' technological infrastructures.[3]

Media companies had long worked with a "blockbuster" economic model thanks to the unpredictable nature of whether a given media property would be a bust, counted among the walking wounded, or a huge hit.[4] More recently, the traditional opportunities for economies of scale and scope in large media companies have been called into question thanks to new digitally based forms of distribution and consumption. Specifically, these changes create the possibility for a shift from blockbusters to "long-tail" businesses, in which content of limited mass appeal can nevertheless become very profitable.[5] The impact of the long-tail phenomenon on traditional media companies is uncertain. Some believe that it could be of significant benefit, while others see the value accruing to the providers of search technology such as Google.[6]

Finally, technology companies find themselves competing in the consumer electronics space as never before, struggling to deal with fundamentally different technology cycles and consumer requirements. By way of example, how many people have a five-year-old television in their house? Now how many have a five-year-old computer? How many people would tolerate a television as reliable as a computer? These industries appear to have radically different production possibility frontiers, and so they require very different strategies to succeed. What sort of mash-up emerges from the collision of high-tech and consumer electronics—never mind adding media and telecommunications to the mix—remains to be seen.

(e.g., telephone companies) and content (e.g., media companies) vertically integrate? Would new "aggregator" roles (e.g., Web portals) emerge and capture most of the value? How would the underlying architectures (e.g., the PC and the Internet) evolve, who would control their evolution, and what influence would key players have?[7] Convergence pressured an entire population of large companies to act despite not knowing just what to do.

The three case studies in this chapter illustrate three different responses to the strategic uncertainty precipitated by convergence. First, the rise and fall of Jean-Marie Messier and France's would-be media titan Vivendi Universal provides a salutary tale of what happens when the CEO is bent on making commitments that pay off only under the most heroic assumptions of predictive prowess. Messier essentially accepted the strategy paradox, hoped he could beat the odds, and made bold commitments in the face of massive uncertainty.

The case of CEO Jean Monty and Montreal-based telecommunications conglomerate BCE Inc. is a useful foil. On the surface, Monty seems to have suffered a similar, if less dramatic, fate, retiring under a cloud as a consequence of a major commitment gone wrong. What Monty did not get credit for was the fact that in BCE's mainstream telecoms business he had succeeded in exploring a variety of opportunities while hedging significant strategic risk. BCE therefore provides a powerful example of a very different approach to corporate strategy, one more nearly consistent with the prescriptions of Requisite Uncertainty. In the end, however, Monty was unable to escape shareholder and other pressures, and so at best temporarily eluded the strategy paradox.

The third panel in the triptych is Microsoft, which has successfully navigated a highly uncertain and commitment-intensive industry for three decades. The company has managed this feat largely through a separation of generating options and making commitments in ways that accepted and embraced the uncertainty implied by ever-longer time horizons at each level of the organization. In short, it is a full-blooded example of how Requisite Uncertainty generates higher returns at lower risk. By achieving persistent and significant success despite the uncertainty it faced, Microsoft can claim to be one of the few that have resolved the strategy paradox . . . for now.

7.1 VIVENDI: THE PARADOX ACCEPTED

In July 2002, Vivendi Universal (Vivendi), then one of France's twenty largest companies and the second-largest media conglomerate in the world, came within ten days of filing for bankruptcy. Under severe pressure from his board, Jean-Marie Messier, the forty-four-year-old chairman and chief executive, resigned and was replaced by Jean-René Fourtou, the sixty-two-year-old semiretired vice chairman of Aventis, a pharmaceutical giant. Fourtou had little latitude given the company's precarious cash position, and so promptly sold off most of the media properties that Messier had acquired over the previous four years, often receiving far less than their purchase prices. Vivendi shareholders lost more than €100 billion in equity value as a result of the company's failed media strategy.[8]

The details of Vivendi's implosion make a splendid yarn; it would be difficult for such a rapid and complete disaster to be anything other than dramatic. As fascinating as the personalities, politics, and backroom machinations might be, Messier's mistake was not making the wrong strategic choices. As we shall see, few felt Messier's choices were ill-advised when he made them, and it is only with the benefit of hindsight that Messier's foresight is found wanting. Instead, Messier's downfall lay in his seeming belief that his role was to make strategic choices at all. In other words, Messier, as the most senior corporate manager, focused his attention on making and managing commitments, and as a result there was little attention given to coping with the many and significant uncertainties that colored Vivendi's chosen strategic landscape.

When Messier became CEO of what was then called *Compaigne Général des Eaux* (*CGE* or, in a loose but convenient translation, General Water) in 1994, he took over a money-losing, haphazardly diversified utility company. The outgoing chief executive and chairman, Guy Dejouany, had spent his twenty years as chief executive pursuing growth by investing the predictable and beneficent cash flows of the company's 120-year-old water utilities business in real estate, construction, health care, telecommunications, and various other sectors. Revenues increased by an order of magnitude between 1976 and 1994, but at the expense of overall profitability: the company experienced a net loss of Fr3.5 billion in 1995—the first since its founding by Imperial decree in 1853 under Napoleon III. Real estate values had collapsed, debt levels had increased sharply, and the share price was stagnant. CGE lacked both satisfactory operating results and a compelling strategic direction.

Messier quickly proved to be an effective operating manager. He created a formal organization chart, centralized capital allocation in the corporate office, and divested some of the company's 2,700-plus operating subsidiaries. He reorganized what remained into three groups: Utilities, which were large and profitable; Telecommunications and Media, which had growth potential and needed capital; and Construction and Property, which Messier wanted to dispose of quickly but could not due to the illiquidity and size of the asset base.

The results were encouraging. CGE went from a loss of €562 million in 1995 to net incomes of almost €300 million in 1996, €822 million in 1997, and €1.1 billion in 1998. The capital markets responded accordingly, dealing shareholders annual returns of 35 percent, 32 percent, and an impressive 51 percent in those three years.

Messier's ambitions for the company went beyond a simple restructuring, however. He was determined to remake CGE into a global champion of the digital age. To feed Cegetel, the company's fast-growing mobile telephony subsidiary, in 1997 Messier reluctantly diluted CGE's ownership position to 44 percent in order to secure capital from British Telecom and Germany's Mannesmann. The continuing twenty-year run of profits at Canal Plus, CGE's pay-TV service, was used to finance the acquisition of NetHold, beating out U.S.-based DIRECTV. The winning bid valued NetHold's subscribers at an unprecedented $1,600 each, and financing the deal would consume Canal Plus's free cash flow for years to come. Messier then added a 55 percent stake in AOL France (terms undisclosed) and acquired the two-thirds of Havas, France's largest media group, that CGE did not already own for approximately $6 billion. This gave Messier an enviable position in European publishing, and, thanks to Havas's stake in Canal Plus, made CGE the controlling shareholder of that business as well. When the May 1998 annual board meeting approved renaming the venerable company "Vivendi"—from the Latin "to live"—it provided symbolic but important affirmation that CGE was committed to a new strategic path.

As Messier saw it, he had chosen that new path from a limited menu. Focusing on the water utilities business, however profitable it might be, did not offer sufficiently compelling growth opportunities. The future lay with the Communications and Media group, and the future seemed to be arriving quickly. European mobile operators were tying up all around him, and Cegetel was ill-positioned to be a player. Vivendi was not in a position to acquire other mobile operators such as Orange, E Plus, or KPN, and buying UMTS ("3G") mobile licenses failed the most basic financial projections. If anything, Vivendi had become a possible takeover target, to be broken apart for its cash flow (in Utilities) and its growing and soon-to-be profitable Cegetel division.

The strategic choices available to Messier crystallized in the fall of 1999. UK-based Vodafone, the largest mobile operator in the world, made a run at Mannesmann, a German conglomerate with a portfolio defined by the #2 mobile services provider in Germany (behind Deutsche Telekom's T-Mobile). Vodafone's offer violated the consensual traditions that governed Germany's market for corporate control. This at least partly explains why Messier found Mannesmann's CEO, Klaus Esser, open to a Cegetel/Mannesmann merger that would preserve both Mannesmann's and Vivendi's independence. Mobile operations would be headquartered in Germany under Esser, while the media and Internet assets would be managed by Messier out of Paris, and the two would be co-CEOs of the combined entity. The Utilities business, which Messier had grouped into an operating company called Vivendi Environnement (VE), would issue its own equity, with Vivendi retaining control.

The deal began to founder over questions of control and price. Mannesmann's shares were driven up as a result of Vodafone's hostile bid, which made a merger of equals increasingly difficult for Esser to swallow. Chris Gent, Vodafone's CEO, exploited this rift in the mooted Franco-German alliance and enticed Messier with a better deal: if Gent acquired Mannesmann, he would give Messier the 15 percent of Cegetel Mannesmann owned (giving Vivendi control of Cegetel), his word that Vodafone would not launch a hostile bid on Cegetel, and an Internet alliance that would ultimately take shape as "Vizzavi" (i.e., *vis-à-vis* from the French for "face-to-face").

In late 1999, this deal seemed a second-best, fall-back position. Why pass up a chance to participate in the consolidation of European mobile telecoms in exchange for a gamble on mobile Internet? But when the merger between AOL and Time Warner became public in early January 2000, the Vizzavi venture suddenly had a credibility it had previously lacked. Mannesmann's offer became the weaker of the two, characterized as a defensive, subscale move that relegated Messier's Internet half of the equation to second fiddle. The creation of AOL Time Warner was the impetus that emboldened Messier to commit the company to the Internet and new media.

At the time, the company had only Canal Plus and a smattering of other minor media properties, but there was good reason to think that could change dramatically and quickly. In the fall of 1999, Edgar Bronfman, Jr., CEO of Seagram's, had begun looking for buyers of Universal Studios. Canal Plus could not afford it. NewsCorp. did not want to afford it. Bertelsmann did not like the risk. Sony was still figuring out the role of content in its portfolio. Disney would likely have found the culture clash more trouble than it was worth. But Messier and Bronfman got on famously, and that personal connection was the foundation of Messier's $44 billion acquisition of Seagram's, an acquisition that made Vivendi a player in the content world.

In the wake of the Seagram's deal Vivendi renamed itself again, becoming Vivendi Universal (VU). In a series of transactions over the next two years, Messier would spend more than $20 billion, picking up the rest of Canal Plus, Houghton Mifflin (a Boston-based publisher), and USA Networks (a cable channel operator and TV production company headed by the legendary Barry Diller). Numerous other investments were made, including substantial stakes in NewsCorp.'s U.K. satellite broadcaster BSkyB, U.S. satellite TV company Echostar, and a host of Internet properties, including Uproar, MP3.com, and Scoot Europe.

Despite the Cegetel and Canal Plus assets, Messier's strategy was not built on vertical integration between content and distribution. He wanted to create a new kind of media conglomerate. Traditional media companies created value in essentially one of two ways. First, by leveraging a successful property in one medium in other media: a successful movie becomes the foundation for TV shows, soundtrack sales, Broadway shows, books, and so on. Second, leveraging a successful property in a given medium to make other content in that same medium more successful: control over scheduling and programming allows media companies to generate exposure for otherwise overlooked content that can compete with alternative offerings but cannot find an audience without an initial major "draw."[9]

Attempting to enter the media industry on its own terms would have been enormously difficult. But Messier's explicit premise was that the Internet would change everything—and fast. Convergence among technologies, especially the Internet and wireless communications, made possible new business models that he felt gave Vivendi a chance to break in, to acquire the pieces and assemble a new and different media company model, one based on relationships with consumers rather than merely selling content to them, or selling them to advertisers.

The merger between AOL and Time Warner in early 2000 lent credence to this model. Seen at the time as the union of "new" and "old" media, Messier viewed the deal as a harbinger of the new age and as representative of the kind of bold action needed to capitalize on the incipient secular industry change. Messier wanted VU to be in the vanguard with AOL/TW, while other media groups just did not "get it."[10] Disney, Sony, and Viacom in particular were relying on content-only models and would be left behind. Rupert Murdoch's NewsCorp. was a hybrid between the relationship model and the content-driven model, while Thomas Middelhoff at Bertelsmann "got it" but was constrained by his board from acting aggressively on that understanding.

Messier saw little danger of getting ahead of the new economy. In his view, the threat was that he would not act quickly or decisively enough. The perceived need to move quickly had practical implications. For example, Vizzavi burned through its €1.65 billion in start-up funding with impressive alacrity. No one knew precisely what "killer app" would justify the huge acquisition premiums and enormous debt VU took on to finance its deals, but perhaps there did not need to be one silver bullet. Instead, it would be a host of innovations, big and small. Universal Music would put Vizzavi software on every one of the 300 million CDs it sold each year, making Vizzavi a computer-based as well as a mobile-based Internet portal overnight. Movie trailers and music clips would be broadcast to mobile subscribers all over Europe to announce new releases and spur demand with targeted promotions. Messier knew there were risks; he simply believed they would be overcome.

Alas, they were not. By early 2002, the wheels were starting to come off the bus. The stock market crash that began in 2000, induced by the dot-com meltdown, hammered VU stock, making a variety of acquisition covenants horribly burdensome. The flotation of VE stock was an unexpected disaster, leaving the company without the expected lump sums required to retire debt, even though the sale meant that VU had relinquished a significant share of the cash flows from VE that had been used for debt service. Synergies within VU—that is, the payoff from a relationship-based media company—proved elusive, and cash flows at the various media properties did not jump as expected.

Problems compounded: international expansion at Canal Plus was prov-

ing disastrous, goodwill write-downs topped €13.5 billion, and debt bal-
looned from a forecasted €8.5 billion in 2001 to €14.6 billion for VU and
another €14.3 billion for VE. The company would report a loss of €13.6
billion in 2001, the largest one-year loss in French corporate history. VU's
debt was becoming unserviceable, which resulted in threatened downgrades
by the ratings agencies, increasing VU's interest rates and hence debt-service
obligations—the first turn of a death spiral.

On July 1, 2002, Messier resigned, beating the board to the punch. With
ironic symmetry, the erstwhile CGE was, once again, a haphazardly diversified, money-losing conglomerate. Even the stock price, at just under €25,
was the same as when Messier had become CEO in 1994. Fourtou was
installed as the new CEO, and he proceeded to dismantle the VU empire,
hanging on to only those media assets that poor market conditions ren-
dered essentially illiquid.

Messier admits that he pushed the company a "little" too far and a "little"
too fast. Writing in 2002, Messier held to his belief that the major acquisitions—acquisitions that ultimately created the debt load that caused VU's
near-collapse—were all justifiable and necessary. Perhaps some partial stakes
in African telecom companies or the odd dot-com acquisition were a bit premature, but the cornerstone deals were an essential part of the vision. To have
passed them by would have been not to pursue the strategy. Messier attributes
his inability to create a new-age media empire largely to speculators and unjustified pressure from creditors. His position is that VU could have succeeded
but for these undeserved attacks, which precluded the company from making
the acquisitions it needed to get it over the top. Success, rather like tomorrow,
was always just a deal away. Edgar Bronfman, Jr., had a different take: "We
were ahead of our time, way ahead. And that's the same as being wrong."

Given the leitmotif of this book, it would hardly be appropriate to fault
Messier for having guessed wrong about the timing and nature of the convergence between the Internet and media. General market sentiment, which
turned so disastrously against Messier and VU in general, was, in
1999–2000, far more ebullient than anyone at VU dared hope. For example, the day before the announcement of the Vizzavi joint venture with
Vodafone, Messier predicted that in five years the portal would be worth
€5–10 billion. Market analysts pegged the venture's worth at €20 billion the
day of the news release. As it turned out, they were both wrong: Vizzavi,
despite its rich funding, failed to crack the top ten mobile portals even in
France, and by 2002 was thought to be essentially worthless.

In the end, it did not really take much to derail VU's grand plan. The
recession in the real economy in 2001–2002 was one of the lightest on
record, and the significant decline in the stock market had been made up in

the S&P within four years. The Nasdaq, even without recovering its late-twentieth-century froth (arguably a good thing), has still delivered returns of more than 11 percent annually since 1994, suggesting that the late-nineties run-up truly was an aberration. Other media companies continue to enjoy their historical levels of profitability, although the markets remain wary of the ability of many established players to adapt to threats from New Economy successes such as Google.[11] In contrast, Vivendi's commitments held the promise of great success, but when everything didn't go exactly as planned, the company's bold moves precipitated its near-collapse. Rather than sinking in a once-in-a-century storm, VU almost capsized in a mild squall because the company had been rigged for only smooth sailing.

7.2 BCE: THE PARADOX ELUDED

The convergence of technology, media, and telecommunications that so inspired Messier was both a once-in-a-lifetime opportunity and a potentially mortal threat to an Old Economy telco. New technologies and services might whet a nearly insatiable consumer appetite for bandwidth, but with that came the specter of cable and Internet-based voice services, not to mention the genuinely disruptive threat of replacing traditional wireline service with wireless phones.[12] Addressing these and many other related questions meant facing up to a strategic challenge of the first order: what businesses should a telecoms company be in? What capabilities did it need to compete, and more pressingly, what resources would it need to control in order to be able to compete in the future? When would the seemingly imminent technological and regulatory changes manifest themselves in ways that required a decisive and committed change of direction?

The challenges associated with these uncertainties were intensified by the seemingly irreducible magnitude of investments required to remain a viable player in almost any sector of the industry. Acquiring or building assets such as a viable wireless business or new video services, or restructuring long-established organizations around new value propositions (e.g., service bundles), are all typically some combination of difficult, time-consuming, and expensive. Yet the competitive environment seemed to demand moving quickly, and so waiting out the storm before choosing a tack did not seem a viable choice.

Many incumbent telecoms firms responded with significant commitments that almost universally failed to live up to expectations. In the United Kingdom, France, and Germany, mainstream telecoms companies ended up paying enormous fees for "third-generation" wireless licenses, believing that the additional bandwidth would prove its worth by enabling advanced services via wireless access to the Internet.[13] In the United States, AT&T invested billions in cable systems and wireless networks in an attempt to control what were thought to be the strategically critical thoroughfares on the emerging-but-still-nebulous information superhighway.[14] In both cases, the result was the destruction of significant shareholder wealth as these big-dollar commitments failed to generate the anticipated returns.

Enthusiasm for all things converged did not stop at the forty-ninth parallel. Beginning in the mid-1990s, Canada's largest telecoms company, BCE Inc., found itself grappling with profound questions of corporate scope as it considered investments in wireless telephony, media, e-commerce, computer and network systems integration, and more. The company's response to these challenges was not only a break with its own past, but a step forward—albeit an inadvertent one—in the evolution of corporate strategy.

BCE was founded as the Bell Telephone Company of Canada, formed by an Act of the Canadian parliament in 1880.[15] The company's first wave of diversification began over a century later, when in 1983 CEO Jean de Grandpré restructured the company, creating "Bell Canada Enterprises" (BCE). BCE was designed initially as a holding company so that management could pursue growth opportunities beyond the limits defined by the original Act. Only Bell Canada, the division responsible for the legacy phone company operations, continued to be bound by those obligations.

Freed of its legislative constraints, the company sought growth, regardless of where it could be found. Between 1983 and 1990, BCE launched a wireless telephony business and acquired full ownership of an oil and gas pipelines company, a trust company, a real-estate developer, and a commercial printer. The corporate office was simply a central bank, redirecting the rich cash flows of the phone business to other initiatives.

Perhaps not surprisingly, given the track record of this kind of diversification, poor results and pressure from investors led Raymond Cyr (who succeeded de Grandpré as CEO in 1988) to shed all of these assets, save the wireless telephony business, between 1990 and 1993.

Between 1995 and 2001, BCE embarked on a second, very different wave of diversification. Rather than commit to full ownership stakes in companies thought to hold valuable growth prospects, the company took a series of tentative and incremental steps in the form of partial stakes in a number of different companies. These investments were not seen simply as self-contained growth vehicles; rather, their value lay largely in their potential role in either protecting or growing the core telecommunications business. These initial equity positions allowed BCE to explore the viability of such synergies yet withhold the significant additional investment required to realize them until it was clear that the expected value could in fact be captured.

To see the uniqueness of BCE's approach in sharpest relief, contrast how BCE handled two specific growth opportunities—wireless telephony and network integration services—with the approach taken by other telecoms conglomerates.[16]

BCE launched BCE Mobile (Mobile) in 1984 as part of the BCE's first diversification push. At the time, it was a wholly owned subsidiary for the simple reason that wireless telecommunications was a brand-new industry and entering via acquisition was not possible. BCE could have provided the capital necessary to underwrite the network rollout and customer-acquisition costs associated with the rapid uptake of services, but Bell Canada (Bell), BCE's largest operating division, had a very different risk/return profile from Mobile's. Consequently, in 1987 BCE sold 35 percent of the company to outside shareholders in order to allow Mobile to grow while protecting Bell's dividend. Mobile's public float had the added benefit of providing powerful motivation to its executive team.

In the ensuing decade, Bell and Mobile operated entirely independently of each other, and with good reason: the wireless and wireline businesses had different technological infrastructures, different cost models, different market and competitive dynamics, and were in very different places in their respective life cycles. By selling off only a portion of Mobile's equity, however, BCE avoided having to choose between the two industries without compromising its position in either one.

By the late 1990s, technological and market convergence had significantly eroded the differences that had mandated their separation a decade earlier. Wireless services had become a mass-market offering, much like wireline services. In addition, rapidly falling costs and prices coupled with continued technological improvements meant that the long-anticipated "wireless substitution" was at last becoming a reality. Finally, both Bell and Mobile were facing increasing competition in their own markets, and each was therefore looking for ways to defend its existing position as well as grow.

These changes in industry dynamics created new opportunities for cooperation between Bell and Mobile. Each could offer the other a key complementary service that could contribute to its own competitive health. From the corporate perspective, fostering collaboration between the two divisions provided a way to cope with the potential of the disappearance of distinct wireline and wireless markets and to transition the company to a more solutions-focused structure.

One of the first opportunities for synergy was in retail distribution. Up until 1999, Bell maintained a chain of Teleboutiques, retail locations that sold only Bell products: branded phone equipment, telecommunications services, and so on. A chain of Phone Centers served the same purpose for

Mobile. The integration opportunity was to develop a single retail presence that would sell the full suite of BCE's communications services.

However, as an independent company with minority shareholders, Mobile's participation could only be secured through an extensive negotiating process designed to ensure that minority shareholders' interests were protected. It was not enough that the overall impact of combining retailing strategies would be strongly positive: that benefit needed to be allocated back to Mobile and to Bell in precisely specified and legally binding terms.

This proved enormously difficult to accomplish. The boards of both companies had to approve any deals, and fiduciary responsibilities demanded that each party have explicit agreements regarding what the benefits of cooperation would be. The uncertainties surrounding what they were attempting to accomplish precluded the necessary level of formalization. Although BCE, Bell, and Mobile executives were convinced of the value of the synergies, it was structurally all but impossible to take any substantive action.

In order to be able to pursue this and other opportunities, BCE bought back the outstanding equity in Mobile for C$1.6 billion, a 31 percent premium to Mobile's market price one month prior to the deal. The company was renamed Bell Mobility (Mobility) and made an operating subsidiary of Bell.

Taking full ownership of Mobile obviated the protracted and generally fruitless negotiations that focused on allocating wealth rather than creating it. With common ownership, interests were now much better aligned, and the division of benefits was a managerial decision, not a fiduciary responsibility. This greatly facilitated more rapid and decisive action, turning what had once been board-level decisions about how best to allocate value into managerial decisions about how best to create it.[17]

This newfound strategic and operational freedom allowed Bell to pursue a number of synergies. It reduced network infrastructure costs, combined retail distribution, and introduced bundled products such as Simply One, which integrated mobile and wireline services. These initiatives were only possible thanks to BCE's full ownership of both operating companies. In short, the buyback was precipitated by a belief on the part of senior BCE executives that the "time was right" to exploit synergies between wireless and wireline services. The opportunity to act on that belief would have been lost to BCE had it divested itself fully of the wireless business in 1987. Yet maintaining full control and having to fund the expansion of Mobility in the intervening decade would have chewed up valuable capital and left BCE exposed to the very real strategic risk that synergies would not emerge. The company's chosen path successfully managed the *risk* that the wireless and wireline businesses remained separate while enabling BCE to capitalize on the *opportunity* created by their ultimate convergence.

If this seems like such a reasonable and rational approach that it borders on the unremarkable, then ask yourself why BCE was nearly unique among incumbent telecoms companies in adopting it. Consider how the development of a wireless division played out among American telecoms companies. As part of the terms of breakup of the Bell System in 1984, AT&T's licenses for mobile telephony services passed to the newly formed regional phone companies.[18] There were sharp differences in the assumptions these companies made with respect to how best to pursue the mobile telephony business.[19] For example, BellSouth saw cellular as a growth opportunity and sought to keep prices low in order to drive adoption. In contrast, USWest treated cellular as a high-margin, low-volume niche and looked instead for growth in multimedia applications. As a result, despite very similar starting points and underlying market opportunities, ten years after launch, BellSouth had more than 1.5 million subscribers to USWest's 600,000. USWest ultimately exited the industry, selling its wireless assets to AirTouch.

Similar stories could be told for each of the seven RBOCs born of AT&T's dissolution. Initial assumptions about the market colored each company's expectations, which in turn drove the commitments they made. Those commitments compounded over time in classic "snowball" fashion, making it practically impossible for any of these wireless companies to change course once the "right" approach became clear. They all guessed, with varying degrees of accuracy, and their respective results reflect that. Unlike BCE, none of them was able to structure an approach that both mitigated risk and made it possible to seize the opportunity that ultimately emerged. Some pursued the opportunity and accepted the risk; that it paid off does not change the fact that they took a material risk.[20] Others avoided the risk at the cost of shutting themselves out of the opportunity. That they suffered for their choice does not change the fact that they incurred materially less risk.[21]

BCE is all the more remarkable because the Mobility example was not an isolated case. Beginning in the mid-1990s, many telcos found that their marquee customers were looking for service providers who could integrate IT systems with communications and data networks. In response, many telcos began to create an in-house IT consulting capability. In the United States, acquisition was the preferred route. For example, MCI acquired SHL Systemhouse in 1995, Sprint acquired Paranet in 1997, and SBC (now AT&T) acquired Sterling Commerce in 2000. In Europe, the organic route was more popular, as shown by the birth of British Telecom's Syntegra, Telecom Italia's Finsiel, and Deutsche Telekom's T-Systems, among others.

At first, BCE was no different. Bell followed the organic path, launching Bell Sygma. This changed in 1995 when Bell created a distribution alliance with Canadian IT consulting firm CGI and, as part of the deal, acquired just shy of 20 percent of the firm. Seeking to avoid duplication of effort and to create greater scale, then-CEO Jean Monty engineered a merger of Bell Sygma and CGI, giving BCE a 42 percent ownership position in CGI. BCE now had a much larger and more capable IT consulting capability, but at the cost of full control, something all the other telcos that had entered this space enjoyed.

If the nature and extent of the integration opportunities had been clear, such partial ownership might have been a significant constraint: as the Mobility case shows, taking advantage of synergies can require full control. However, as with wireless/wireline integration, it was unclear precisely how networking services and IT consulting were going to complement each other. Where other telcos either committed to the opportunity or avoided it completely, BCE had the kind of access required to determine whether or not material opportunities for integration would emerge while preserving capital and avoiding any debilitating constraints on CGI's growth.

As it turned out, unlike the Mobility experience, no significant synergies emerged for Bell or any other major telco. By the early 2000s, most had abandoned their efforts to integrate network management and IT consulting services and had either sold off (typically at a substantial loss) or written down their investments. BCE, in contrast, was able to extricate itself from CGI far more gracefully. IT consulting is not a bad business to be in, but it has not turned out to be a powerful strategic complement to network management capabilities. As a result, CGI continued to grow, in large part through acquisitions using its own stock as currency. BCE chose not to invest in those acquisitions, and by 2003, BCE's stake in CGI had fallen to 29.9 percent. In 2006, after CGI's share price had recovered from the tech-stock collapse of 2001, BCE sold the last of its CGI equity for C$1.1 billion.

It is important to note that in both cases—wireless and IT consulting services—BCE was no better or worse at finding integration opportunities than its competitors. Its advantage was that by structuring its investments as partial equity stakes and then managing those investments appropriately, BCE was able to gain a window on an emerging market and position itself to act as the relevant uncertainties were resolved. The company mitigated the risk of commitment without forgoing a nascent opportunity through inaction.

These examples illustrate a way of reconciling the need to act when considerable uncertainty surrounds what to do. In the case of wireless, BCE was able to remain connected to its wireless division even as that division grew in ways and at a pace that was beyond what BCE could have supported had it retained full ownership. As opportunities for integration came into focus, BCE was able to acquire the control it needed to exploit emerging synergies. The U.S. RBOCs either bet right on cellular, as in the case of BellSouth, or they bet wrong, as in the case of USWest; either way, they were locked into the commitments they had made.

In contrast, meaningful synergies between IT consulting and network services never materialized. Everyone who bet on this particular growth opportunity was simply wrong. However, BCE's approach gave the company exposure to what *could have* turned out to be a valuable growth opportunity, but in a way that made it possible to change course relatively painlessly when it turned out to be a dead end.

In more general terms, BCE provides a groundbreaking example of the application of "real options" to corporate strategy. Its investments conferred the right, but not the obligation, to invest further in order to pursue a particular growth strategy. This created valuable flexibility—*strategic* flexibility—in the face of an uncertain future. Both options (Mobility and CGI) were created by the corporate office, but either exercised or abandoned—that is, turned into commitments—by the operating divisions. This is entirely consistent with the prescriptions of Requisite Uncertainty: the corporate office manages strategic uncertainty by creating options; the operating divisions choose concrete strategies by making commitments. Subsequent chapters will have a great deal more to say about real options on strategy, but the topic is worth a preliminary discussion here.

Financial options give the contract holder the right, but not the obligation, to acquire a specified asset at a specified price within a specified period. So, for example, if you hold a call option on Acme Corp. stock with a strike price of $10 and a exercise period of three months, then you have the right to buy Acme Corp. stock at $10 anytime within the next three months (if it is an American option; a European option would give you the right to buy the stock only at the end of three months). Option contracts cost less than the stocks on which they are written, and so they require less commitment than buying a given stock outright, yet generate exposure to the "upside." Options thus offer a lower-commitment way to pursue significant investment returns.[22] A real option applies to a real asset, as opposed to a financial asset, and although real options have the same conceptual structure, they tend to lack the precisely specified parameters that characterize most financial options.[23]

BCE held real options on wireless/wireline integration and IT consulting/network integration thanks to its partial ownership positions in Bell Mobility and CGI. If BCE had done nothing, it would have run the risk of missing out on valuable growth opportunities. At the same time, full ownership would have entailed a level of investment that almost surely would have demanded the vigorous pursuit of integration: the acquisition premium required for full control can only ever be justified by a belief in the existence of synergies.[24] For example, companies that acquired or built full-scale IT consulting arms were effectively committed to a synergy-based strategy.

BCE's solution was to create a window onto these opportunities yet avoid acquisition premiums by taking only partial equity stakes. As a result, it was able either to exercise the option (Mobility) or to walk away from its investment when synergies did not materialize (CGI). In other words, other telcos "bought the stock," whereas BCE "bought the option."

Finally, a big part of why a real options-based corporate strategy can be so powerful for companies in situations similar to BCE's is that none of the individual organizations in BCE's portfolio could have adapted in real time to the uncertainties each faced, and for all the reasons explored in Chapter 3. Wireline/wireless integration is an example of "slow change." The implications for the late 1990s of what was happening in the mid-1980s were impossible to see. For fifteen years, wireless evolved in a parallel universe, having at most only modest impact on Bell's business. As a result, Bell was able to continue on its charted course, making the kinds of incremental short-run adaptations to its wireline operations that kept the company on an even keel.

Without viable options on integration, when it became clear that integrating wireless and wireline services and infrastructure offered a competitive advantage, Bell would have been faced with an all-at-once radical change, likely involving the acquisition of a totally unrelated wireless player. This kind of strategic reorientation has a very low chance of success.[25] Instead, BCE's ownership position in Mobile provided a running start that allowed Bell to make the kind of progress that has preserved its market lead.

The IT consulting industry is a good illustration of "fast change." Rapid technological and marketplace changes created the possibility of a new kind of integration between IT systems and telecommunications networks. Bell would have been incapable of effecting immediate change in response to these perceived opportunities. Had it committed quickly to the pursuit of such integration, changing course quickly, as it became clear that synergies were not as valuable as at first anticipated, would be even more difficult. Because CGI was an independent company, letting it go its own way did not reflect poorly on Bell management. But if Sygma, as a fully owned subsidiary of Bell, had been unable to find ways to capture synergies, it would have been a black mark on Bell's management—and so Bell's management might well have pursued those synergies far past the point when abandoning the quest would have been the most rational course.

If BCE under Jean Monty did so much right, why have I said that the strategy paradox was merely eluded rather than resolved? There are two reasons. First, BCE's corporate strategy was not built explicitly on the management of strategic uncertainty through the creation of real options. Often, BCE's partial equity stakes, which were so crucial to the optionlike structure of their investments, were motivated by capital-constraint considerations and the reluctance of the entrepreneurs with whom they dealt to give up control of their firms.

Second, to put a caveat on an aphorism from Chapter 2, it is not *always* okay to do the right thing for the wrong reason. The generally inadvertent nature of BCE's option-driven corporate strategy made it very difficult for Monty to explain the value of what BCE had created. In early 2001, for example, Monty gave an interview in which he acknowledged that BCE was trading at a discount to the imputed value of its stand-alone businesses. He then stated that if the company's various convergence initiatives did not begin to deliver the incremental cash flows required to create significant new shareholder value, he would consider selling off at least some of BCE's portfolio.[26]

What could be more reasonable? Monty had created a basket of assets that hedged very real strategic risk to the large and valuable mainstream telecommunications company.[27] If, as happened with CGI, these options turned out not to be worth exercising, he could abandon them. But such statements were not well received by the investment community. Most institutional investors did not see the value of hedging the underlying strategic risk that Bell faced. All they saw was the investment made in seemingly unrelated assets and the returns required to make those investments pay off. In the words of one analyst commenting on Monty's apparently less-than-wholehearted endorsement of the company's convergence-based strategy, "that's a hell of a thing to say when you consider the billions of dollars invested in the past few years."[28] In fact, takeover specialists had begun circling BCE by late 2000, estimating the conglomerate's holding company discount at up to 35 percent.[29]

In response to his critics, the day after his thoughtful observations on the uncertainty surrounding convergence, Monty adamantly professed the company's commitment to making convergence a reality and delivering the kinds of services only an integrated telecommunications firm could provide. "No one should doubt our conviction that we are on the right path," he said.[30]

Monty's ambivalence toward building corporate strategy on real options and his belief in the merits of commitment despite uncertainty are most evident in BCE's investment in Teleglobe. This Montreal-based company had held a government-mandated monopoly on overseas voice calls originating in Canada.[31] Privatized in 1987, Charles Sirois, a serial entrepreneur in

Canada's telecommunications industry, felt the company was significantly underperforming. So he parlayed a 20 percent minority stake into effective control and had himself installed as CEO in 1992. In 1998, he surrendered Teleglobe's Canadian monopoly on overseas traffic in exchange for access to international markets, especially the United States. He then set about spending more than C$5 billion connecting 160 cities worldwide with fiber-optic cable. It was a bet other companies, such as Global Crossing and 360 Networks, were willing to make as well. The general belief was that the appetite for bandwidth would be insatiable and the only risk was leaving money on the table by not building enough capacity.

BCE had a 23 percent stake in the company, a position that allowed it to back Sirois's quest for control of the company in 1992. In early 2000, even as Teleglobe was issuing earnings warnings, Monty announced that BCE would acquire the rest of the company in a stock, cash, and debt deal ultimately valued at C$7.4 billion, more than 10 percent of BCE's total market capitalization. This was big money. Recall: the buy-back of Mobility was C$1.6 billion for an established and growing business with revenues of C$840 million, while the investment in CGI that created the option consisted largely of folding its own operations into a similarly established enterprise. In both cases, the option BCE took was on integration with Bell; the businesses themselves were going concerns. In contrast, Teleglobe was a huge, all-in bet on an evolving business model in an uncertain market.

Once in full control of the company, it became clear that BCE had purchased a pig in a poke. The initial 23 percent stake had not provided the opportunities for lower-risk exploration that a true option would have. The revenue projections that had appeared to justify the acquisition proved significantly overstated. Teleglobe was carrying assets on its books at values orders of magnitude over their true value. One such asset, Excel Communications, had been purchased by Teleglobe for $3.5 billion, yet was sold back to the original owners for $225 million while BCE got to keep Excel's $1.3 billion in debt.

Despite efforts to staunch the flow of red ink, such as slashing capital expenditures, Teleglobe was unable even to service its debt. BCE found itself siphoning off free cash flow from Bell to keep the sinking ship afloat. In 2002, BCE stopped servicing Teleglobe's debt, Teleglobe declared bankruptcy, and BCE wrote off the entire investment. Although BCE never suffered anything like the kind of near-death experience Vivendi had, as a direct result of the fallout, Monty resigned at only fifty-four, the Teleglobe debacle a blight on an otherwise brilliant career.

It is tempting to claim that if BCE had done its homework more carefully, it would not have done the Teleglobe deal at all. Perhaps. But this is just another way of saying that if things had not gone wrong they would have gone right. The irony is that for all the strategic risk BCE faced and managed so well, the one big bet Monty made in the face of material risk was the one that undid him. BCE avoided a Vivendi-like fate of being dismantled at fire-sale prices just to meet its bond payments. But Monty's career still ended prematurely and he was excoriated in the Canadian press, blamed for destroying over a third of BCE's market value because he had not seen the future more clearly.[32]

This is the wrong criticism, for the same reason it is wrong to fault Messier for not seeing the future of media more clearly: no one can know what the future will hold. Messier's mistake was pursuing nothing but commitments. Monty's mistake was not understanding the power of the options-based strategy he had stumbled into and sticking with it as he continued to plumb the uncertainties of his industry.

7.3 MICROSOFT: THE PARADOX RESOLVED

Given Microsoft's now decades-long dominance of the computer operating system market, one can be forgiven for concluding that the company's founder and chairman, and CEO from the company's inception until 2000, William H. Gates III, had a knack for seeing what lies on the road ahead. This would appear to be a plausible claim. From the BASIC complier for the MITS Altair (the world's first *bone fide* personal computer) to .Net (the application platform for Web-based applications), the company seems to have followed a single-minded strategy: make Microsoft products the platform for personal and corporate computing.[33]

As a general explanation of why Microsoft has been so successful for so long, this is almost certainly correct. But it is also incomplete, for it overlooks the uncertainty that surrounded which platform would succeed.[34] An alternative hypothesis is that Microsoft's success is attributable primarily to a corporate-level strategy based on real options and managing strategic uncertainty. Unlike Vivendi, which committed to becoming a specific kind of new-age media company, Microsoft has long pursued multiple initiatives in parallel, committing to Windows—the source of its current success—only once the relevant uncertainties had been largely resolved. And, unlike BCE, Microsoft appears to have a deliberate and purposeful understanding of the merits of this approach, for it continues to explore different strategies, resisting the temptation to make large, irreversible bets until the fog occluding the future has lifted.

Eric Beinhocker of the Corporate Executive Board explains Microsoft's multipronged approach by describing the company's booth at the 1988 installment of Comdex, the largest of the annual trade shows for the computer industry.[35] According to Beinhocker, other major players used their booths to describe coherent, purposeful strategies premised on their well-articulated visions of the future. Apple had its graphical user interface (GUI) systems on display. Sun, Xerox, and AT&T had created a graphical version of Unix, while Hewlett-Packard, Digital Equipment Corporation, Apollo, and Siemens Nix-dorf had allied to launch the Open Systems Foundation. Perhaps most significantly, IBM, long Microsoft's partner in the development of DOS, had thrown much of its consumer software muscle behind OS/2, it own version of a GUI-based operating system that aimed to be compatible with DOS, as powerful as Unix, and as easy to use as Apple's OS. Each was an attack on Microsoft's DOS-based dominance of the IBM PC architecture.

Microsoft's booth, on the other hand, was more "Middle Eastern bazaar" than twentieth-century trade show, replacing the "glorious vision" with a buffet of seemingly unrelated products. Windows 2.0, the company's attempt at a GUI, was available to preview. Windows 1.0 had been nearly unanimously panned, but Microsoft clearly felt that abandoning the project after only one try would have been premature. DOS 4.0 was out, offering new levels of functionality and performance on a platform that, despite its success, was clearly showing its age and would soon be eclipsed by . . . something or other. Microsoft was a codeveloper of OS/2 with IBM, and so that, too, was on display, along with the latest versions of Word and Excel for Macintosh, where Microsoft was an applications leader despite its distant second place to WordPerfect and Lotus in the DOS world. To top it all off, there was even a corner devoted to SCO Unix, an operating system Microsoft was distributing and would take a major stake in only a few months later. In other words, Microsoft's mix included its current business (DOS), the next generation of that business (Windows), and a slice of every other company's attempt to unseat both (OS/2, Macintosh, and Unix). In Beinhocker's words, it did not make sense to ask, "What was Microsoft's strategy?"; the right question was "What were Microsoft's *strategies?*"

As we now know, Windows was the winning bet. There also turned out to be significant synergies between the Windows OS and Microsoft's GUI-based word-processing and spreadsheet applications, originally developed for the Macintosh, that took shape in the Microsoft Office applications suite. But in 1988, there was no way of knowing that would be the outcome. It seems reasonable to suggest that neither Gates nor anyone else in senior decision-making positions knew this would be the case; why else devote precious and scarce resources to so many seemingly disparate initiatives? Microsoft might have been confused about which bet to make, but that was perfectly reasonable. In the face of that confusion, it created a series of options, each designed to deal with the demands of different possible market outcomes. Each option would be exercised only as it became clear that additional commitment was justified by commensurately lower risk. Those that were geared to the needs of a future that never arrived—like OS/2—were eventually abandoned.

In the middle 1990s, just as Microsoft might have been tempted to declare victory in the OS and applications world, new threats and opportunities emerged. As at Vivendi and BCE, the rise of the Internet and World Wide Web and the convergence of technology, media, and telecommunications promised to undermine the source of Microsoft's historical success. In computers, Microsoft's home ground, the Web was to become the platform, while open-source software such as Linux was felt by some to have a performance profile better adapted to the needs of distributed computing. Other devices, particularly the television and the mobile phone, were poised to become new growth opportunities for interactive content, possibly leaving firms such as Nokia, the leading mobile phone maker, and Sony, the consumer electronics giant, better positioned than Microsoft to dominate the new space.

Microsoft responded by leaping on its horse and galloping off in all directions. Between 1994 and 2005, the company made more than 200 acquisitions or investments in other companies across just about every segment of the telecommunications, media, and technology sector. Some of the more notable deals exhibit all the characteristics of an options-driven corporate strategy on the different platforms that might have, or still might, emerge. Whether online, mobile, new media or old, Microsoft is hedging its bets more aggressively than ever.

Take the $30 million joint venture Microsoft launched in 1995 with Dreamworks SKG. Christened Dreamworks Interactive, the venture's mandate was to develop games and CD-ROMs for the PC, giving Microsoft a window onto this market and a chance to establish its development tools as a platform for the new medium. This was consistent with the company's existing strategy (be the platform of choice) while recognizing the uncertainty surrounding *which* platform would succeed. Microsoft had created an option on a potentially valuable strategy. As it turned out, PC games and CD-ROMs never really took off (for reasons discussed briefly in Chapter 2) and Electronic Arts bought Dreamworks Interactive in 2000 for an undisclosed sum. The option never came into the money, and Microsoft abandoned it.[36]

Seemingly convinced that gaming could still have a significant role to play in defining the next computing platform (or the next or the next . . . you get the idea), Microsoft has invested approximately $4 billion developing and launching the Xbox game console. Having eclipsed perennial second fiddle Nintendo in 2005, Microsoft no doubt hoped that Xbox's successor, Xbox 360, would eat into Sony PlayStation's 70 percent market share. Continued devotion to the sector can be seen as a growth opportunity in its own right, for the gaming market is a $13-billion-per-year industry. The strategic option value stems from the fact that gaming consoles have eclipsed personal computers in some aspects of computing power and become multimedia centers and online access points. As a result, game consoles could become a significant platform technology that might one day collide with Microsoft's bread-and-butter computer software business.[37]

Windows CE (for "consumer electronics") is an operating system designed for mobile phones, personal digital assistants (PDAs), and other "smart" devices. As with the gaming sector, mobile and handheld devices are more than simply a large market on their own; they could ultimately converge with the personal computer industry, eclipsing the PC as the cornerstone device for personal information access and management. As a result, one way of looking at Microsoft's dedication to this sector is in option terms: at some point, the consumer electronics and personal computer industries will collide, and having a significant presence in both will position Microsoft to dominate the resulting converged space.[38]

Another fascinating convergence play is Microsoft's $220 million investment in MSNBC and its affiliated Web site, MSNBC.com. Operated by NBC, MSNBC was the first cable news channel to compete directly with CNN. The explicit intent was to explore any emerging synergies between cable television and online news. The channel has struggled, however, unable to achieve what Fox News has since done: unseat CNN as the cable news ratings leader. Consequently, Microsoft sold majority control back to NBC while retaining its 50 percent ownership in MSNBC, which has established a leading position in online news.[39]

Microsoft did not abandon this option entirely, partly because of its success morphing MSN, the company's online division, into a successful suite of online businesses consisting of search, news, e-mail, and other services. In 2005, the division earned $405 million in operating profit on $2.3 billion in revenue; 2006 results show revenues flat and operating losses of $77 million. Whatever one might think of those numbers, MSN gives Microsoft a presence in the online world and creates the opportunity to explore strategic opportunities, thereby hedging the risk that the locus of value creation and capture might migrate off the desktop and into cyberspace. Although the original intent of the MSNBC effort was to explore the convergence of old media and new, MSNBC could yet become an important part of MSN's arsenal, converging new media with even newer media.

Finally, consider Microsoft's $5 billion investment in cable television provider AT&T/MediaOne in 1999. This stake and others (e.g., $1 billion in Cox in 1997 and a stake in TimeWarner's Road Runner broadband service) bought Microsoft the right to explore the viability of the television set-top box as yet another possible platform for new services.[40]

Many of these investments might smell an awful lot like strategic commitments: how can $4 billion on Xbox, $6+ billion on cable, and over $10 billion invested in MSN over the years, legitimately be seen as merely options? Two qualifications are necessary. First, Microsoft earns more than $12 billion of net income on $40 billion in annual revenue, and as of year end 2005 had almost $38 billion in cash on hand. When protecting and extending that kind of a franchise, even the average $2 billion a year invested in MSN is a cost-effective strategic insurance policy.

Second, many of Microsoft's option-like investments are profitable. They are not as profitable as the core business (few businesses are), and so under normal circumstances they would not get funded until every opportunity to grow the core operations had been exhausted. Consequently, these options cost Microsoft only the foregone avenues of growth that might have been more profitable still.

Of late, Microsoft's many and varied efforts have been even less coherent than the company's 1988 Comdex booth. The desire to be "the platform" is still apparent, but on which devices and how? Not even Microsoft can say for sure. Its strength is accepting that it does not know what the future will hold and avoiding commitments in favor of a portfolio of real options that position it to succeed regardless of how the relevant uncertainties are resolved.

7.4 HEDGING THE UNHEDGABLE

Any firm attempting to manage strategic uncertainty using the kinds of real options described above will find itself with a diversified portfolio of operating companies. BCE and Microsoft ended up with not only a highly heterogeneous group of businesses but also wide variety in the level of control they enjoyed. Equity stakes ranged from the low single digits (e.g., Microsoft's 5 percent in AT&T) to near-total ownership (e.g., BCE's 65 percent stake in BCE Mobile).

Some might argue that anything that requires a firm to diversify is necessarily bad. There is, after all, an abundance of evidence strongly suggesting that diversified firms perform worse than firms that "stick to their knitting."[41] It would be a mistake, though, to conclude that diversification destroys value. The critical distinction is between the *average* level of performance for the firm as a whole and the *marginal* performance of each additional line of business into which a firm enters. If diversification efforts lower the performance of the firm overall, but the performance of each new business venture is still above the firm's average cost of capital, then diversification will *create* value. Empirical investigations have shown that many firms tend to diversify more or less in this manner.[42]

There are also important differences among diversified firms. Some firms diversify in order to leverage their powerful control mechanisms and to wring the best possible performance out of each operating division. The divisions themselves have little in common; it is the bilateral relationship between each division and the corporate office that creates value. This is *unrelated* diversification.

Diversification in the form of *vertical integration* creates value in a very different way. The operating divisions of vertically integrated firms have explicit supply-chain connections with one another. The corporate office creates value by facilitating exchanges between these divisions that would otherwise have to take place in relatively inefficient product markets.

Finally, the corporate office creates value through *related* diversification by enabling operating divisions to capture synergies by sharing critical resources, both tangible and intangible. Everything from common distribution channels to patents to brands can form the basis of related diversification. (See Appendix A: "How Diversification Can Create Value," for more detail.)

Within this framework, what are we to make of the kind of real options-based diversification we see at Microsoft and BCE? Is Microsoft's Xbox game console vertically integrated, related, or unrelated to the company's core computer operating system and applications business? What about MSN? Or the ownership stake in cable operators? In BCE's case, it is hard to argue that CGI was related to the core telecommunications business: CGI was divested because no material synergies emerged. And BCE Mobile was not related in practice when BCE owned 65 percent of it, since the inability to capture synergies between the two divisions is what prompted BCE to acquire the firm outright: only then could BCE integrate the renamed Bell Mobility with the wireline operations of Bell Canada.

What Microsoft and BCE illustrate is an obvious truth that is typically overlooked. A firm's diversification profile—whether unrelated, vertically integrated, or related—is not a function of the operating divisions within its portfolio; it is a function of the relationships among those divisions and between each division and the corporate office. A firm's diversification strategy can therefore change as a result of changes in the relationships between *existing* divisions. These changes are implemented by managers but can be precipitated by shifting competitive contexts that create synergies where none existed, or nullifying synergies that were once critical. Therefore, diversification should sometimes be understood *dynamically*: a firm can transform itself from an unrelated to a related diversifier *without altering* its portfolio. In fact, Microsoft and BCE diversified as they did hoping that such changes would occur. It is unlikely that Microsoft acquired part of a cable company because it wanted to be in the cable television business. A more reasonable assumption is that the company is hoping that material synergies between cable technology and some or all of online services, consumer devices, and software will emerge, giving Microsoft the opportunity to exercise the option that its initial investment has created.

Similarly, BCE did not get into the IT consulting business because synergies existed. Instead, BCE was hoping that technological and market shifts would *create* the opportunity to leverage key resources or vertically integrate at some point in the future. Only when such changes occurred would BCE be justified in exercising the option created by its initial stake in CGI. Microsoft and BCE pursued what was initially *unrelated* diversification, hoping that market evolution would allow them to become *related* or *vertically integrated* diversifiers. Their diversification profiles were not attempts to create or capture value in the present. Rather, the companies were positioning themselves to create and capture value in the future through related or vertically integrated strategies—*without* committing to them.

Could a company delay its diversification initiatives until the nature of the synergies to be captured had become clear? Perhaps, but there is no free lunch: waiting forces a company to accept the risk that the most valuable partners will be tied up in other deals, or will command large control premiums since the value to be captured will be evident to all. Outright acquisitions have long been shown to enrich selling shareholders far more than acquiring shareholders.[43] Firms often overpay because they buy either when they do not know enough about what value there is to create and capture (e.g., many of Messier's ill-fated purchases at Vivendi), or because they wait until they, and everyone else, knows exactly what is at stake. Acquisitions with significant and generally acknowledged strategic value tend to leave very little value for the acquirer.[44]

Diversification that creates real options on the pursuit of new strategies is referred to as "strategic diversification." Strategic diversification creates value for shareholders because it positions a firm to pursue new strategic opportunities more effectively and at lower cost than outright acquisition. To be sure, strategic diversification creates a portfolio of real options, all of which come at some cost, and not all of which are exercised; some will inevitably expire out of the money. Nevertheless, the portfolio of real options created through strategic diversification reduces the strategic risk a firm faces and increases the universe of strategic opportunities it can pursue. To the extent that the firm balances the cost of real options with their risk-mitigating and opportunity-enhancing value (a topic explored in Chapter 10), shareholders will enjoy a higher risk-adjusted return than firms that do not engage in strategic diversification.

This kind of diversification is especially valuable when industry boundaries are shifting due to technological, regulatory, or market uncertainties. Under these circumstances, the suite of assets required to compete effectively are rarely housed within a single firm. For example, the strategic opportunity created by the convergence of wireline and wireless services is not available to stand-alone wireline and wireless companies. Consequently, an investor holding equity in more focused wireline and wireless players would be exposed to the strategic risk that wireline/wireless integration will reshape the sector. BCE, however, was positioned to exploit this same opportunity because it had diversified in the appropriate way. BCE faced lower strategic risk and enjoyed greater strategic opportunity than any portfolio of focused firms that an investor might assemble.[45]

The kind of strategic risk used in Chapter 3 to illustrate the strategy paradox was a cartoon: the wholesale shift of market preferences from cost-leadership to product-differentiation strategies. Financial investors can diversify away this sort of risk by assembling a portfolio that includes a number of companies pursuing extreme strategies at either end of the strategy spectrum. Recalling the retailing example, a financial investor might simply buy shares in several discount retailers (e.g., Wal-Mart and Target) and several high-end retailers (e.g., Nordstrom and Neiman Marcus). Diversification *within* strategy types hedges operational risk, while diversification *across* strategy types hedges strategic risk. There is no good reason for a firm to have a portfolio of operating divisions pursuing different strategies, since this simply hedges strategic risk in precisely the same way that investors would.

Nevertheless, there is a role for firms to manage the more complex strategic uncertainty created by shifting industry boundaries. No portfolio of independent firms can create the kinds of real options needed to allow large, sophisticated enterprises to respond in a timely way to the forces reshaping their markets. Strategic diversification is not a "portfolio play," and it is not the stereotype of a diversified firm with a sunglasses division and an umbrella division hoping to make money no matter the weather. In fact, strategic diversification is unlike vertical integration, unrelated, and related diversification because it is not about creating value directly. Strategic diversification is about the other side of the value equation—uncertainty. Strategic diversification allows firms to lower their strategic risks while increasing their strategic opportunities.

7.5 MERE MORTALS NEED NOT APPLY

These case studies are intended to provide some texture for the preceding discussion of hierarchy and time horizons. They focus on the role of the corporate level, largely as a counterweight to the broadly circulated view that senior management's primary role is to make commitments. They illustrate what I have proposed in earlier chapters: that the highest levels of the hierarchy should be focused on managing strategic uncertainty. The strategic uncertainty implied by the time horizon that defines senior management's responsibilities swamps any ability to peer meaningfully into the future, and so their emphasis should be on creating options, not making choices.

But how should those charged with managing the "options" feel about their lot in life? For example, how should Serge Godin, the CEO of CGI when it was BCE's option on IT consulting, have viewed his responsibilities? From Jean Monty's perspective, CGI was an option. But to Serge Godin, CGI was a commitment: his job was to make CGI as successful as he could. Now, within that context there will be uncertainties, and so someone in Godin's position might well have viewed different market opportunities or different business models based on, for instance, contingent payments tied to clients' productivity increases, as options. He could have been expected to have set people in charge of each of these initiatives in order to create and explore those options. However, in the spirit of cascading commitments, the people charged with each of these opportunities would need to see them as commitments to deliver on.

Similarly at Microsoft: MSNBC was an option to both NBC and Microsoft on the convergence of cable television news and the Internet. If those who ran the channel and its affiliated Web site saw the venture as "just an option," they might not have taken quite as seriously the critical decisions they had to make: which advertisers to pursue, what content to run, and so on. Down another level, those charged with selling advertising to specific industries, or with producing particular sorts of content, need to see their initiatives not as options but as commitments to be honored, their tasks worthy of every ounce of creativity they can muster.

At the top of the pyramid, then, the board and corporate office grapple with the profound strategic uncertainties that could shape or reshape an industry's evolution, then create options on the kinds of assets required to survive and succeed in these very different possible futures.

Those managing the operating divisions, be they part of the existing mainstream (e.g., Microsoft's OS division or BCE's Bell Canada telephone company) or options on new strategies (e.g., Microsoft's mobile phone initiatives or BCE's IT consulting division), are responsible for making their businesses as successful as they can. They must work within narrower boundaries and explore fully and vigorously the viability of the domain entrusted to them. Only then can the corporate level determine the value of the option their business represents. This might well require making a variety of forays into different areas within their boundaries, each foray an option designed to manage the uncertainty they face.

And finally, those squaring off against the close-up realities of customers and competitors—the "hunting parties," if you will—can serve the greater good only if they do everything within their power to succeed, within the context defined for them. Each level serves to mitigate strategic uncertainty only by treating its responsibilities as unshakable commitments, and innovating aggressively within the boundaries set for them in order to make good on those commitments.

The rough outlines of this approach can be found in earlier frameworks developed to cope with uncertainty. For example, some have suggested that in turbulent environments the appropriate role of senior management is to articulate a "guiding philosophy," or "strategic intent," as a way to tell the firm "where to look for opportunities" without overspecifying what those opportunities should be. Such organizations need to be extremely flat, with individual, highly focused units within a diversified corporation seeking out and exploiting evanescent chances to seize fleeting competitive advantage.[46]

There are at least two limitations to this approach. First, as discussed above, if diversification is merely a mechanism to cover different and unrelated bets, it need not be done under the umbrella of a single corporate owner. Shareholders can diversify that kind of unsystematic risk far more efficiently themselves. Corporate diversification makes sense to shareholders only if it either captures synergies or creates options on synergies that investors cannot replicate.

In a corporation where the onus for all innovation is on operating divisions, synergies will generally be missed because the operating divisions will be hamstrung by the organizational constraints that define their mandate. For example, in BCE's case, exploiting synergies between Mobile (wireless) and Bell (wireline) was so difficult as to be practically impossible even though both organizations were exploring opportunities for cooperation. They could not get it done because the ownership structure created fiduciary responsibilities for each organization to its own shareholders and other constituencies. Only because the corporate office intervened and acquired Mobile outright were the constraints binding both organizations relaxed and the capture of valuable synergies made possible.

A second problem is that individual divisions will necessarily be constrained from exploring opportunities that are "too big" for them to handle. Again, BCE's example is instructive. When Bell created Bell Sygma, Bell's first attempt at building an IT consulting capability, it had to be done within the constraints of Bell's operating and investment budget. Given the demands of the IT consulting market, Sygma was forced to look for partners in order to achieve the scale it needed to be successful. This is what led Bell to take a 20 percent stake in CGI. The company did not take a more significant position because doing so was beyond its capability. At the same time, running its own IT consulting arm while contributing to the success of a larger, better-established competitor was counterproductive. Only a material intervention from the corporate office could remedy the situation. Folding Sygma into CGI was not something Bell could have done, because that was beyond its strategic boundaries. Yet it was the best course of action, for it created a more powerful IT consulting capability while also giving BCE a level of control and insight into the industry that created an option on future opportunities for integration.

Other scholars, most notably Tom Eisenmann of the Harvard Business School, observe that the most effective response to these constraints so far has been the imposition of a top-down, resource-allocation process. That is, rather than settle for setting strategic intent and letting the divisions figure out where the real opportunities lie, deliberate, substantive interventions by senior management are required to drive strategy in the right direction. In fact, the classic "hands-off" corporate office is not only unable to address this kind of strategic uncertainty, it is demonstrably dysfunctional and can undermine not just the profits of an individual division but of the corporation as a whole.[47] By definition, if a division is facing strategic uncertainty, then it is the boundaries that define each division that are subject to the kind of unpredictable change to which they cannot adapt. Only thunderbolts from Mount Olympus in the form of a corporate-driven reconfiguration of divisional assets can overcome the entirely necessary constraints that define divisional priorities.

For all its merits, there remains one significant drawback to this approach: very few managers seem able to pull it off. The media companies Eisenmann studied that were best able to cope with turbulent environments were all led by dominant shareholders who saw themselves as principals: Sumner Redstone at Viacom, Rupert Murdoch at NewsCorp., John Malone at TCI. In fact, one of Eisenmann's more startling discoveries was that "agent managers"—that is, CEOs of large, complex organizations—tend to flee turbulent environments, while owner-operators are prone to double down.[48]

The reason, Eisenmann explains, is that generally, corporate executives in diversified companies lack the detailed industry knowledge required to make the right choices regarding when and how to act. Messier, for example, had not grown up in the media sector, and so he was well-advised to leave the specifics of running individual businesses to those who understood them best—the managers of the various operating divisions. Eisenmann's theory implies that this left Vivendi unable to exploit any emerging synergies because each division was structurally unable to see beyond its own interests. In addition, agent managers are subject to capital market pressures that dominant shareholders typically are not. As a result, agents tend not to be able to bide their time, acting only when they feel it is appropriate. For example, investor pressure forced Monty to set specific deadlines on when his convergence strategy would be successful. The Teleglobe disaster was playing out even as the two years Monty had given himself to deliver on convergence was drawing to a close, and he had nothing to show for it.

In light of these constraints, is it any wonder that, of these three case studies, the most effective at implementing an options-based corporate strategy was Microsoft, led by its founder and dominant shareholder, Bill Gates? Gates has the in-depth knowledge needed to identify those avenues worthy of exploration, as well as the industry savvy necessary to determine when and how to exercise any of the options so created. Messier, in contrast, necessarily had to rely on divisional managers to determine how best to run each of the businesses he acquired. BCE's Monty certainly had the requisite industry knowledge, having spent his career leading major organizations in everything from phone service to equipment manufacturing, but he was still on the hook to shareholders. Gates, in contrast, had the level of personal control required to avoid speaking in specific terms about when and how the company's many and varied initiatives might pay off.[49] In fact, Gates has long made it a point to describe the company's various non-PC investments as experiments, and despite their price tags, as essentially immaterial to the overall company.[50] Monty could never have gotten away with describing CGI as an "experiment," even though that is what it was.

Given the difficulty associated with managing strategic uncertainty, is it possible for anyone other than "special cases" like Bill Gates to adopt these principles? How can mere mortals functioning in the context of a more traditional agent-managed organization learn from him? In the next chapter, Johnson & Johnson, one of the most successful and most admired companies in the history of American business, provides in outline a template for answering these questions.

For a company to take strategic uncertainty seriously, it must avoid making commitments in the face of uncertainty and instead create strategic options that can be exercised or abandoned depending on how those uncertainties are faced. Only in this way can a firm hope to deal effectively with an environment that changes unpredictably. Implementing such an approach requires knowing which options to take, how much to invest in them, how to manage the options over time, and when and how to exercise or abandon them. Doing this successfully requires a corporate office that is able to direct and guide the actions of operating divisions.

---

1. See, for example, Negroponte, Nicholas (1995), *Being Digital*, New York: Vintage Books; and Tapscott, Don (1997), *The Digital Economy*, Toronto: McGraw-Hill.

2. I did a review of twelve such frameworks published between 1988 and 1996 as part of my doctoral studies. Some of the differences in categorization were superficial: categories such as "transport," "distribution," "conduit," "networks," and "transmission" tended to capture a similar core of telecommunications, cable, and satellite companies. This is unsurprising: the banks and consultancies that published these frameworks needed to differentiate themselves from their competitors, and it's not good practice to adopt someone else's nomenclature unless you have to.

Beyond these high-level similarities, however, there were profound differences in the various assessments of which companies would be affected by convergence, the numbers of categories required to capture relevant differences, and how best to take advantage of the expected coming change. For examples of such frameworks see Hagel, John, and Thomas R. Eisenmann (1994), "Navigating the Multimedia Landscape," *The McKinsey Quarterly*, No. 3; and Yoffie, David B. (1997), "CHESS and Competing in the Age of Digital Convergence," Chapter 1 in *Competing in the Age of the Digital Convergence*, David B. Yoffie (ed.), Harvard Business School Press.

3. "Pipe War,"*McKinsey Quarterly*, 2001, No. 1.

4. Garvin, David A. (1980), "Mergers and Competition in Book Publishing," *The Antitrust Bulletin* (Summer), and (1981), "Blockbusters: The Economics of Mass Entertainment," *Journal of Cultural Economics*, Vol. 5, No. 1 (June).

5. See Anand, Bharat N. (2005), "Making Sense of Media Conglomerates," Harvard Business School note N9-704-466, July 11, 2005, for a discussion of the traditional scale and scope model. The seminal work on the "long tail" promises to be Anderson, Chris, (2006), *The Long Tail: Why the Future of Business Is Selling Less of More*, New York: Hyperion.

6. Martin, Laura (2005), "The 'Long Tail' Drives Entertainment Industry Growth," Soleil Media Monthly Equity Research.

7. A great deal of effort has gone into trying to determine how the locus of profitability shifts and how best to capture that profit as industries evolve. Raynor and Christensen (2001, *Integrate to Innovate: The Determinants of Success in Developing and Deploying New Services in the Communications Industry*, Deloitte Research Monograph, www.

deloitte.com/research) suggest that in each industry, at a point in time, there is a "basis of competition," and that whichever component in an industry's value chain contributes most to improvements in that basis of competition will capture most of the profits. Recent work by Marco Iansiti and Roy Levien (2004, *The Keystone Advantage: What the New Dynamics of Business Ecosystems Mean for Strategy, Innovation, and Sustainability*, Harvard Business School Press) takes a slightly different but not antithetical approach, exploring the more sophisticated notion of business "ecosystems" and the ways in which companies can contribute to the creation and capture of value within an evolving value "web." As I suggested, these efforts are worthwhile and must continue. If we ever get it exactly right, and can in fact predict how future competitive battles will unfold, the strategy paradox will become irrelevant. But I wouldn't hold my breath.

8. The details of the Vivendi Universal story recounted here are compiled from, in order of their publication: Messier, Jean-Marie (2000), *j6m.com: Faut-il Avoir Peur de la Nouvelle Économie?* (j6m.com: Must We Fear the New Economy?), Paris: Hachette Littératures; Burgelman, Robert B. (2001), "Vivendi Universal," Stanford Business School Case SM-96; Emmanuel, William (2002), *Le Maître des Illusions: L'Ascension et la Chute de Jean-Marie Messier* (The Master of Illusions: The Rise and Fall of Jean-Marie Messier), Paris: Economica; Messier, Jean-Marie, and Yves Messarovitch (2002), *Mon Vrai Journal* (My True Diary), Paris: Balland; Montgomery, Cynthia A. (2003), "Vivendi (A) and (B): Revitalizing a French Conglomerate," Harvard Business School Case 9-799-019 and 9-703-418; Johnson, Jo, and Martine Orange (2003), *The Man Who Tried to Buy the World: Jean-Marie Messier and Vivendi Universal,* New York: Portfolio; Khurana, Rakesh, Vincent Dessain, and Daniela Beyersdorfer (2005), "Messier's Reign at Vivendi Universal," Harvard Business School Case 9-405-063.

9. See Anand, Bharat N. (2005), *op. cit.* Anand does a particularly good job of documenting how hits can create a valuable slipstream for other content using the example of the Indian television market. Zee TV, the dominant channel, had thirty-five of the top fifty shows. Star TV, Zee's main competitor, poured significant resources into finding a hit. Zee TV, convinced that their success neither depended upon nor could be threatened by one or two programs, turned to low-budget programs as a way to cut costs and increase profits. In July 2000, Star finally found its hit, and within a month that one program had reversed the two companies' relative fortunes, with Star claiming forty-two of the top fifty shows—even though the only real programming change was the introduction of their one new hit and scheduling existing programming around it. What this demonstrates is that while genuine hits are rare and unpredictable, most content is "good enough" to warrant consumers' attention. The challenge is to get that attention, which is what "tent pole" content is able to do.

10. The AOL/Time Warner merger has been famously troubled and ruthlessly attacked by both commentators and investors. Tremendous shareholder wealth has evaporated, and, according to some, cannot be recaptured in the company's current form: in early 2006, Carl Icahn attempted to gain control of the company in order to break it up, undoing not only the AOL merger but also earlier mergers into cable systems and other media. Icahn and Time Warner (the "AOL" was dropped from the name in 2003) reached an agreement in February 2006 that turned on cost cutting, stock buybacks, and corporate governance changes (see http://www.msnbc.msn.com/id/11415485/, accessed March 6, 2006).

The main reason Time Warner was spared Vivendi's fate is that Time Warner's misstep was financed without the kind of debt exposure Vivendi was saddled with. As a result, when AOL's value collapsed and the anticipated synergies didn't emerge, stockholders suffered, but the company was never in danger of going bankrupt. CEO Jerry

Levin stepped down in 2002, as did COO Bob Pittman, and Steve Case resigned from the board in 2005.

Popular accounts decrying the deal point to hubris, greed, stock mania, culture clash, and so on as the source of current difficulties. Some suggest that the key players should have known it wasn't going to work, pointing to public questioning of the sagacity of the deal up to a year prior to the merger announcement. As ever, though, for every article in 1999 suggesting the end was near, there were at least two arguing that a new era was about to dawn. The issue isn't whether or not someone predicted disaster, because someone always does. The mistake was not in making *this* commitment. My position is that, when considering strategic uncertainty, the problem is making commitments at all. See Klein, Alec (2004), *Stealing Time: Steve Case, Jerry Levin, and the Collapse of AOL Time Warner,* New York: Simon & Schuster; Munk, Nina (2004), *Fools Rush In: Steve Case, Jerry Levin, and the Unmaking of AOL Time Warner,* New York: HarperBusiness; Swisher, Kara (2003), *There Must Be a Pony in There Somewhere: The AOL Time Warner Debacle and the Quest for the Digital Future,* New York: Three Rivers Press.

11. See Martin, Laura (2006), "Short Positions as Sentiment Indicators: Which Media Industries Are In and Out of Favor," *Soleil,* February 16.

12. For a more detailed exploration of the general strategic uncertainties facing the telecommunications industry, see Raynor, Michael E. (2001), *Strategic Flexibility in the Communications Industry: Coping with Uncertainty in a World of Billion-Dollar Bets,* Deloitte Research monograph (www.deloittte.com/research/strategicflexibility). A discussion of the disruptive potential of wireless telecommunications technology can be found in Raynor, Michael E. (2005), *The Hundred-Year Storm: Wireless Disruption in Telecommunications,* Deloitte Research monograph (http://www.deloitte.com/dtt/research).

13. Binmore, Ken, and Paul Klemperer (2002), "The Biggest Auction Ever: The Sale of the British 3G Telecom Licenses," *The Economic Journal,* Vol. 112 (March), pp. C74–C96; and Wray, Rick (2001), "Wireless Remorse," *The Industry Standard*, April 27.

14. See Ackman, Dan, "AT&T and the Selling of St. Michael," *Forbes.com,* September 28, 2001 (http://www.forbes.com/2001/09/28/0928topnews.html), accessed March 6, 2006.

15. See Surtees, Lawrence (1992), *Pa Bell: A. Jean de Grandpré and the Meteoric Rise of Bell Canada Enterprises,* Toronto: Random House, for a more detailed history of Bell and BCE.

16. For a fuller treatment of BCE and its innovations in corporate strategy, see Raynor, Michael E. (2005), "Strategic Flexibility: Corporate-Level Real Options as a Response to Uncertainty in the Pursuit of Strategic Integration," in *From Resource Allocation to Strategy,* Joseph L. Bower, and Clark G. Gilbert, eds., Oxford: Oxford University Press, Chapter 14. The approach described here looks at only two strategic opportunities (wireless and network integration services). The book chapter cited provides additional examples in e-commerce and satellite television.

17. Randy Reynolds, formerly CEO of Mobile and President of Mobility in 1999, explains:

. . . one of the governance issues we had [when pursuing synergies] before [the buyback] was if you took a 10% cut across the top for all those bundled services, who takes the cut? And where [are] the provision economies that make the bundle more profitable to us? And when you've got minority shareholders in individual companies, that's a somewhat tricky decision.

As a combined entity, it's still tricky, but now it's only a battle between Guy Marier, John Sheridan, and me over who gets what slice of the revenue. But for the shareholder it doesn't matter any more. So it's a relatively unimportant decision, one that can get made in an afternoon between the three of us, instead of having to get made through the development of business plans, me cranking up my machinery, them doing the same, it going to both boards, and all that run-around. Now, if we think it makes sense for the overall company, we can go ahead and act. That's the benefit.

18. The seven "Baby Bells" were Ameritech, Bell Atlantic, BellSouth, NYNEX, Pacific Telesis, Southwestern Bell, and USWest. The companies were created with the explicit intent of making them roughly equal in assets and revenues. The similarities among the companies, including, and perhaps especially, their common culture and history, make them a remarkable setting for analyzing the emergence of differences between firms. The landscape has of course changed considerably since then, as Bell Atlantic and NYNEX are now Verizon, while BellSouth, Southwestern Bell, Pacific Telesis, and Ameritech are AT&T, and USWest was acquired by Qwest.

19. The definitive study of the evolution of the wireless telephony industry in the United States is Noda, Tomoyoshi (1996), *Intraorganizational Strategy Process and the Evolution of Intra-Industry Firm Diversity: A Comparative Study of Wireless Communications Business Development in the Seven Bell Regional Holding Companies,* unpublished doctoral dissertation, Harvard Business School. A subset of Noda's findings appears in Noda, Tomo, and Joseph L. Bower (1996), "Strategy Making as a Process of Iterated Resource Allocation," *Strategic Management Journal,* Vol. 17 (Summer), pp. 159–93.

20. When it comes to measuring organizational performance, especially for the purposes of executive compensation, the risk incurred in the pursuit of any given level of return is almost universally ignored. We can use *beta* as a *post hoc* measure of a firm's historical unsystematic risk, but we do not routinely or systematically include *ex ante* estimates of risk in our strategic decision-making. See Buehler, Kevin S., and Gunnar Pritsch (2003), "Running with Risk," *The McKinsey Quarterly,* No. 4. Often, this is because we lack a generally accepted method for measuring the risk, especially the downside risk, either *ex ante* or *ex post,* associated with binary outcomes. See Miller, Kent D., and Jeffrey J. Reuer (1996), "Measuring Organizational Downside Risk," *Strategic Management Journal,* Vol. 17, No. 9.

21. Perhaps the most similar structure among the RBOCs was the 50/50 joint venture between BellSouth and SBC when they merged their wireless divisions to create Cingular. The problem with that structure is that there was no efficient take-out or exit strategy for either party because their interests could be expected to be identical: if mobile became a vital part of a landline telco's portfolio, each would want to buy out the other, and if the expected synergies did not emerge, each would want to sell.

22. Options are often seen as very risky financial instruments due to their highly constrained time element. A stock in a going-concern company might well fall, but absent bankruptcy, the possibility of a recovery remains. A call option that expires becomes worthless. As a result, a stock purchased at $50 that falls to $30 is only a 40 percent loss if one sells. A call option on that same stock purchased for $5 with a strike price of $55 that expires before the stock ever reaches $55 (that is, that expires "out of the money") has a value of $0, for an irrevocable loss of 100 percent. On the upside, should the stock rise to $60, the option holder has realized a gain of 100 percent: they purchase the stock at $55 thanks to their call option, then sell it at $60, the prevailing price, for a gain of $5, while the option contract itself cost only $5. The purchaser of the stock realizes a gain of only 20 percent, since they net $10 on an investment of $50. The risk and leverage aspects of real options can be quite different from that of financial options, something that will be explored in subsequent chapters.

23. There is an extensive literature on real options, and Chapter 10 will place the current framework within this larger context. For now, note only that the idea of new business ventures having "option value" has been around for over twenty years. See Kester, Carl W. (1984), "Today's Options for Tomorrow's Growth," *Harvard Business Review,* Vol. 62, No. 2 (March–April).

My take on the field is that although the notion of option value is well-developed, the implications for how to create, manage, communicate, and realize the value of those options are generally overlooked. It is by connecting hierarchy, time horizons, strategic uncertainty, and real options that I hope to be able to define the roles of each level in an organization so that it is possible to more systematically and hence effectively realize the value of real options and related concepts (such as scenario-based planning).

24. Sirower, Mark L. (1997), *The Synergy Trap,* New York: The Free Press.

25. See Nguyen, Huy Quy (1998), *Anatomy of a Radical Change,* unpublished doctoral dissertation, McGill University Faculty of Management, for an examination of the mechanisms and success rates of incremental and radical changes in a large telecommunications company. Nguyen concludes that "modest-in-scope" changes have about an 85 percent success rate, while "major" initiatives have a 20 percent success rate.

26. Waters, Richard and Scott Morrison, "Splitting Up BCE Future Option, Monty Says: Two-year Evaluation: Chairman Not Happy with Early Returns on Converged Services," *National Post,* April 2, 2001.

27. In addition to the risks from wireless/wireline integration and IT consulting, there was the threat of integrated video and high-speed Internet services offered by cable providers, as well as opportunities in e-commerce and media. BCE's portfolio of options hedged these threats through the company's ExpressVu satellite TV joint venture and the 65 percent ownership stake BCE held in BCE Emergis, an e-commerce enablement company, as well as its joint venture in television broadcasting and newspapers, Bell Globe-Media.

28. Mark Quigley of Yankee Group, quoted in the same *National Post* article cited in n26.

29. Rubin, Sandra, "Takeover specialists eye BCE," *National Post,* November 27, 2000. Such estimates were certainly extremely aggressive. For instance, the value of Bell was estimated using the $3,000 per local access line that local loop carriers were getting in the U.S. market, which had begun to consolidate. However, as the dominant player in the Canadian market, Bell was not a valuable addition to incumbents seeking economies of scale. It was the entrenched incumbent subject to significant competitive pressure and strategic risk.

30. Reguly, Eric, "The Convergence Revolution Can Wait, But Can Investors?" *The Globe & Mail,* April 7, 2001.

31. The details of the Teleglobe story recounted here are taken from Yakabuski, Konrad, "The End of an Aura," *Report on Business* magazine, July 2002.

32. It is worth noting that, in a manner very different from what happened at Vivendi, when Monty offered his resignation to BCE's board, it at first refused to accept it. In fact, they tried four separate times to convince him to reconsider and stay. Despite the fallout from Teleglobe, Monty still had enormous credibility inside BCE; it was in the eyes of the investment community that he had lost some of his luster. Recall also that the Teleglobe write-down happened in a particularly toxic environment for CEOs as the Enron, WorldCom, Global Crossing, Tyco, and other high-profile examples of chief executive malfeasance were very much in the news. Although there was never any suggestion that Monty or anyone else at BCE was involved in any improprieties, several commentators observed that "the Street" needed a scapegoat. See Van Praet, Nicolas,

"Mr. Decisive Walks: Monty 'Has Become the Scapegoat' for BCE's Board," *The Montreal Gazette,* April 25, 2002.

33. The sources of Microsoft's success are explored at length in Iansiti, Marco, and Roy Levien (2004), *The Keystone Advantage: What the New Dynamics of Business Ecosystems Mean for Strategy, Innovation, and Sustainability,* Boston: Harvard Business School Press. Iansiti and Levien explain that Microsoft is the "keystone" of its "ecosystem" and that the company's investment in supporting developers—the people who write the applications that we use every day—is what drives the success of Microsoft's operating systems and server platforms.

The "keystone" metaphor in Iansiti's and Levien's book comes from biology, which identifies "keystone species": species in an ecosystem whose health is crucial to the health of an entire ecosystem. The example Iansiti and Levien use to illustrate the term is the Pacific coast sea otter, a "keystone predator" that serves to keep the sea urchin population in check. When the sea otter population declined in the late nineteenth century as a result of the fur trade, the sea urchin population exploded, which dramatically reduced the kelp forests, since sea urchins and kelp compete for the same resources. The diversity and density of many fish populations that live in kelp forests then also went into decline. When the sea otter population rebounded, the sea urchin population was dramatically reduced, the kelp forests recovered, the fish returned, and the health of the ecosystem was restored.

The provenance of the term "keystone" is architectural: an arch is built by placing shaped stones on a scaffolding, ascending from each wall up to the apex. At the apex, a key-shaped stone (the "keystone") is the last stone put in place, completing the arch and allowing the weight of the stones in the arch, as well as any roof above it, to be transferred to the outer walls. If the keystone is removed, the entire arch collapses.

I've chosen to speak of Microsoft's platform-based strategy in terms of a "cornerstone" because the company's application development platforms are put in place "first" in order to create a new ecosystem around new protocols. In architecture, the cornerstone is the first stone put in place that provides a point of reference for the construction of the rest of a building. With BASIC, DOS, Windows, .Net, and so on, Microsoft has successfully done essentially the same thing: put in place the first element of an ecosystem that then grew up around what they had created. Removing either a keystone or a cornerstone leads to the collapse of any edifice, but for very different reasons. With the former, the arch collapses because it can no longer support its own weight; with the latter, the building collapses because its support has been removed.

34. The strategic risk Microsoft faces is exacerbated by the success of its existing Windows platform. The company's strategy of ensuring backward compatibility and its now decades-long dominance of the personal computer operating system market means that innovation is becoming increasingly difficult. The need to test thousands of peripherals and third-party software, as well as work with hundreds of PC makers, imposes a burden on Microsoft that less dominant players, such as Apple, simply don't bear. Microsoft's Windows strategy of compatibility has been a big part of its success, but that same strategy has created a very real risk that the company will be unable to innovate as quickly or effectively as rivals pursuing a different strategy. As a result, and as ever, the source of past success is increasingly a binding constraint on future change. See Lohr, Steven, and John Markoff (2006), "Windows Is So Slow, but Why?" *New York Times,* March 27.

35. Beinhocker, Eric D. (1999), "Robust Adaptive Strategies," *Sloan Management Review* (Spring).

36. Smith, Sean (2005), "Dreamworks Sale: Why the Dream Didn't Work," *Newsweek,* December 19; company reports.

37. *The Economist,* "Way Beyond the PC," November 26, 2005; company reports.

38. *The Economist,* "The Fight for Digital Dominance," November 21, 2002; company reports.

39. *The Economist,* "Citizen Gates," November 23, 1996; company reports.

40. In addition to the sources already cited, see Moeller, Michael (1999), "Who Do You Want to Buy Today?," *BusinessWeek,* June 7; "On to the Living Room," *Business-Week,* January 21, 2002.

41. Typically, researchers have looked at relationships between a firm's diversification profile and performance from an agency theory perspective, positing that diversification is a natural but pathological result of a desire on the part of firm management to grow. The sometimes explicit assumption is that diversification depresses a firm's otherwise acceptable performance. See Rumelt, R. P. (1982), "Diversification Strategy and Profitability," *Strategic Management Journal,* Vol. 3, pp. 359–69; Porter, Michael E. (1987), "From Competitive Advantage to Corporate Strategy," *Harvard Business Review,* Vol. 65, No. 3; Berger, P. G., and E. Ofek (1995), "Diversification's Effect on Firm Value," *Journal of Financial Economics,* Vol. 37, pp. 39–65.

Recent work has questioned this causality, exploring the possibility that firms diversify when they are performing poorly in an attempt to find new growth opportunities. In other words, although it is true that diversified firms underperform focused analogs, it is the diversification that is the effect and the poor performance the cause. This explanation of diversification is more closely aligned with the assumptions of prospect theory, that is, that we do things we wouldn't normally do in order to escape unpleasant circumstances. When the environment is pleasant enough, we tend to try and not rock the boat. This line of investigation has been pursued in Kampa, Jose Manuel, and Simi Kedia (2002), "Explaining the Diversification Discount," *The Journal of Finance* 57(4), and Villalonga, Belen (2004), "Does Diversification Cause the Diversification Discount?" *Financial Management,* 3(2).

As Henry David Thoreau put it: "It's not what you look at, it's what you see."

42. Montgomery, C. A., and B. Wernerfelt (1988), "Diversification, Ricardian Rents, and Tobin's q," *RAND Journal of Economics,* 19(4), pp. 623–32.

43. Sirower, Mark (1997), *The Synergy Trap: How Companies Lose the Acquisition Game,* New York: The Free Press.

44. There are of course implementation risks as well. An acquisition that seems reasonably priced at first can become expensive *ex post* if integration expenses have been underestimated.

45. See Raynor, Michael E. (2002), "Diversification as Real Options and the Implications on Firm-Specific Risk and Performance," *The Engineering Economist,* Vol. 47(4).

46. Chakravarthy, Bala (1997), "A New Strategy Framework for Coping with Turbulence," *Sloan Management Review* (Winter).

47. The debate is best framed by works such as Goold, Michael, and Alexander Campbell (1998), "Desperately Seeking Synergy," *Harvard Business Review* (September–October), and Eisenmann, Thomas R., and Joseph L. Bower (1999), "The Entrepreneurial M-form: Strategic Integration in Global Media Firms," *Organization Science* (Special Issue on Cultural Industries). Goold and Campbell argue strongly for the divisions to take the lead in the identification and pursuit of any synergies. The role of the corporate office is only to be sure that the "internal market" for integration is transpar-

ent and well-functioning. Intervention by corporate masters distorts the division-specific incentives that are required to keep each division running well. Eisenmann and Bower note that it is only when the benefits and mechanisms of cooperation are structurally unclear that exploiting synergies within a single corporate structure is required. If the corporate office can make such integration opportunities sufficiently clear to fully autonomous divisions that they can exploit them on their own, why have a diversified corporation at all? Their case evidence on this is compelling. See Eisenmann (1999), *Tele-Communications, Inc. (A): Cascading Miracles,* Harvard Business School case 899-215, and Eisenmann and Bower (1996), *Viacom Inc.: Carpe Diem,* Harvard Business School case 9-396-250.

48. Eisenmann, T. R. (1997), "Structure and Strategy: Explaining Consolidation Patterns in the U.S. Cable Television Industry," unpublished doctoral dissertation, Harvard Business School; ———. (2000), "The U.S. Cable Television Industry, 1948–1995: Managerial Capitalism in Eclipse," *Business History Review,* Vol. 74, pp. 1–40; ———. (2002), "The Effects of CEO Equity Ownership and Firm Diversification on Risk Taking," *Strategic Management Journal,* Vol. 23, pp. 513–34; ———. (1998), "Diversification and Risk Taking in the U.S. Cable Television Industry," Harvard Business School working paper 99-003.

In this series of publications, Eisenmann describes how cable systems that operated as divisions of diversified companies were divested by the conglomerates that owned them and consolidated by a small number of owner-operators and entrepreneurs. This shift in ownership was accompanied by a shift in the perceived uncertainty surrounding the future of the industry precipitated by technological changes that created new competitors such as satellite and telephone companies, as well as the need to invest heavily in the provision of new services, such as high-speed data and video on demand. Intriguingly, this perceived shift in strategic uncertainty did not manifest itself in greater variance in cable companies' cash flows: that would have been the result of short-run operational uncertainty, and the industry faced comparatively little of that when these ownership changes were taking place in the early 1990s.

Eisenmann, then, found that exit rates for agent-managed firms increased with higher levels of uncertainty. Other researchers have found that the converse is true for entrepreneurs: entry rates fall as the uncertainty within a sector rises; see O'Brien, Jonathan P., Timothy B. Folta, and Douglas R. Johnson (2003), "A Real Options Perspective on Entrepreneurial Activity in the Face of Uncertainty," *Managerial & Decision Economics,* Vol. 24, Iss. 8 (December). Consequently, that the cable systems sold off by diversified firms were acquired by existing players, rather than by new entrants, is a general phenomenon and not idiosyncratic to the cable sector.

49. It's worth considering whether the latitude granted Microsoft is a function of the firm's healthy profit margins and tens of billions of dollars of cash. Such a response merely backs up the question: why would shareholders allow the company to sit on such enormous relatively unproductive assets? The answer is the same: because Gates had the personal control and decades-long track record that only a founder-CEO can have. Of course, it's possible to be over-insured as well, and over the last several years Microsoft has been paying out larger dividends and buying back shares as a means of returning some of this cash to shareholders.

50. "Microsoft and 21st Century Media," *Wired,* June 1996.

CHAPTER EIGHT

STRATEGIC FLEXIBILITY

Every operating division functions within constraints: there is only so much money it can spend, so long it can wait for a payoff, certain types of customers it can serve, so much risk it can take. These constraints make possible the focus required for success, but they also make it very difficult for a division to manage strategic uncertainty effectively. Johnson & Johnson (J&J) has found a way to preserve the benefits of constraints while using its corporate venture capital arm to transcend those constraints and manage the strategic uncertainty faced by the operating divisions in ways the divisions cannot. This has allowed J&J to mitigate the strategy paradox.

Dave Holveck had a problem.

Upon being appointed President of Johnson & Johnson's (J&J) corporate venture capital arm, Johnson & Johnson Development Corporation (JJDC), Holveck found himself with a portfolio of more than $400 million. In conjunction with J&J's Corporate Office of Science and Technology (COSAT), led by Ted Torphy, Holveck's charge was to ensure that J&J's 200-plus operating companies (OpCos) were connected in the right ways to the emerging technologies that could shape their competitive futures. JJDC could point to a number of significant successes over its thirty-three-year history, including the early-stage investments in what became the Ethicon Endo-Surgery, Vistakon, and LifeScan divisions. But as he assumed his new position in early 2004, Holveck felt that JJDC was in danger of slipping into strategic irrelevance.

J&J's highly decentralized structure had led the various OpCos—for all the right reasons—to focus on the markets and technology platforms that were critical to their individual businesses. As a consequence, when JJDC found technologies that it thought could serve as a foundation for significant growth, there was no way to give these new opportunities an organizational home—short of creating a new OpCo, which was often not an appropriate response.[1] All that remained was a traditional venture capital liquidity event, and even when profitable, this was not an acceptable solution. Typically, JJDC's investments were too small to move the needle for even a $500 million OpCo, let alone the $50+ billion J&J mothership, and J&J investors who wanted a venture capital play could make those investments on their own.

As a result, JJDC had begun to make almost exclusively small, incremental investments designed to further the objectives of the OpCos. But this created its own problems. For example, the sponsors of projects that had been rejected by the OpCos often approached JJDC for funding. They claimed that their initiatives were worth backing but had fallen off the table at the OpCo level for any number of reasons. Consequently, the internally generated deal flow that came JJDC's way was subject to classic adverse selection: the good opportunities got funded by the OpCos and the dregs were sent to JJDC for what was, from the OpCos' perspective, free money.

Into the mix add some fundamental shifts in the nature of competition in life sciences (an omnibus term for pharmaceuticals, biotechnology, medical devices, health care delivery services, and so on). The regulatory environment in the United States and many other countries had shifted from a nearly exclusive focus on safety to include a need to prove enhanced efficacy in order to secure approvals. In other words, it was no longer good enough merely to "do no harm"; new devices and drugs often now had to demonstrate that they "did good" or, even more exigently, that they "did better" than existing treatments. Clearing this additional hurdle is far more expensive, and it began to strain OpCo resources, limiting their ability to innovate.

Whom J&J viewed as its primary customer was also changing. Historically, physicians had been the key decision-makers, and so J&J had worked diligently to demonstrate the superiority of its solutions to doctors. Due to cost-containment considerations and increased consumer awareness, however, the customer was becoming just as likely to be a hospital group, insurer, or consumer, depending on the circumstances. Finally, technology was being developed far more quickly and within a global context, in ways that promised entirely new platforms of innovation rather than simply the development of individual drugs or devices. For example, stem-cell research, gene therapy, proteomics, and nanotechnology all touch many different therapeutic areas. Each is too big, too expensive, and too far-reaching in its implications to be left to the resources, expertise, and interests of a single

OpCo, yet each could well redefine the rules of the game for just about every market J&J competes in.

In short, in order to explore and develop future growth platforms, JJDC needed to invest in ways the OpCos could not, yet if it did invest in initiatives beyond the purview of the OpCos, there was no way to take its discoveries to market. On the other hand, even if JJDC aligned its investments with the strategic priorities of the OpCos, anything that looked interesting should either stay with that OpCo or not be done at all: if the OpCos did not want it, how would JJDC ever hand it back? It was a classic catch-22.

Dave Holveck had a problem.

8.1 THE FREEDOM OF CONSTRAINTS

J&J is a paragon of corporate virtue, however you define it. It was one of only eighteen companies featured in *Built to Last* as an exemplar of the management practices required to grow and prosper over the long term.[2] It routinely appears on the *Fortune* list of most admired companies. Fueled by a century of rapidly advancing medical science and the willingness of consumers and governments around the world to spend an increasing share of their total wealth on the fruits of the resulting innovation, J&J masterfully parlayed a buoyant but highly competitive industry into one of the longest runs of growth and profits ever achieved by any corporation.

A big part of the company's success has been its nearly unique ability to acquire or launch new OpCos in order to pursue specific market opportunities. To ensure that J&J as a whole understands its technologies and its customers, each OpCo has historically been highly specialized, focusing on a specific and limited set of products and customers. OpCos have tended to be broken up not because they get too big but because they get too diverse. A corollary of this focus has been a considered and principled self-sufficiency and autonomy for the OpCos, with only very gradual and circumspect integration.

For example, in the 1980s J&J had thirteen separate operating companies, each with its own distribution infrastructure, selling to hospitals. Hospitals, in an attempt to cut costs, were consolidating into hospital groups or at least purchasing consortia, centralizing their purchasing decisions. Companies such as American Hospital Supply Corporation (AHS) had enjoyed enormous growth and profitability by creating a "one-stop" supplier to face off against the newly centralized purchasing operations.

J&J was aware of this shift and was able, ultimately, through the creation of J&J Hospital Services, to respond appropriately. But the timeliness and efficiency of the company's response were limited by its principles of decentralization and divisional autonomy.[3] This is a trade-off that J&J accepted.

The importance of decentralization and OpCo autonomy merely underscored the nature of Holveck's problem. JJDC is a specific example of the general phenomenon of "corporate venture capital" (CVC).[4] Most commentators see CVC as serving a growth imperative: a large, established corporation invests in a small start-up either to increase the returns earned in the core business or to create entirely new growth engines.[5] In general, the ability of corporations to generate new growth using CVC is highly suspect. Few companies have ever built "new leg" businesses, although on average CVC is, if anything, more successful than traditional VC when investing in businesses close to the core.[6]

How could JJDC make a difference when seventeen of Johnson & Johnson's nineteen major OpCos qualified for the Fortune 1000? In a company where anything that undermined OpCo autonomy and independence was viewed with deep suspicion, investing "close to the core," that is, investing in ventures that were aligned with any given OpCo's strategic priorities, would very likely have been redundant and would have violated a key J&J operating principle. Yet moving farther away from the core would have undermined JJDC's probability of success.

Holveck found his answer by examining the other side of the autonomy coin. J&J was highly decentralized, but there were still meaningful constraints; success demanded it. For instance, *resource* constraints limited the time and money an OpCo could devote to any given initiative, so that no single OpCo carried the fortunes of the entire firm and each OpCo was focused on delivering results. *Structural* constraints limited the scale and scope of OpCo operations, keeping complexity manageable. *Strategic* constraints kept every OpCo focused on its markets and its customers.

Collectively, these constraints defined the ambit of each OpCo. But just as they channeled and focused OpCo energies, they also limited the opportunities that any OpCo, and hence J&J as a whole, could explore. In a munificent environment, when science is marching rapidly forward and customers welcome each new innovation, the costs of these limitations are minimal. But as the capital intensity of life sciences has skyrocketed, the willingness of markets to absorb the concomitant price increases has waned. Consequently, new opportunities increasingly lay beyond the boundaries that have historically defined the OpCos.

Removing these constraints was not a viable response. No business can escape all resource, structural, and strategic constraints because no business can function without them. Try to imagine a company with unlimited time and money, no scope or scale boundary conditions, that could serve every possible customer and could take every conceivable risk. Constraints are what define an operating company; they are the cell walls of a living organism without which the vital essence would bleed away.

Attempting to loosen these constraints so that the OpCos might adapt to an uncertain future as it arrived would have failed, for the reasons rehearsed at length in Chapter 4 ("The Limits of Adaptability"). To those reasons add the fact that any operating company with constraints sufficiently lax that it could adapt to a broad range of strategic challenges would be amorphous to the point that it could not compete effectively in the present. Selection pressures in competitive markets are sufficiently strong that any operating company that lacks focus is weeded out pretty quickly. In other words, the limits to adaptation are in part a consequence of the binding nature of resource, structural, and strategic constraints.

Finally, to reconfigure these constraints so that new opportunities could be captured by existing OpCos would have demanded that one predict precisely *where* beyond the existing boundaries new opportunities were going to fall. This is impossible, because, as discussed in Chapter 5, the future cannot be foretold. Worse, any new structure—any particular reconfiguration of these constraints—would still suffer the same limitations: there would always be something valuable just beyond the new boundary conditions. Instead, J&J needed a way to manage the strategic uncertainty facing the company as a whole—something that was clearly beyond any possible configuration of OpCo constraints.

J&J wisely avoided Vivendi-like big bets, yet lacked the owner-manager structure of Microsoft, but still hoped to avoid BCE's fate, precipitated by managing strategic uncertainty without a formal process. Holveck felt that JJDC could move beyond the traditional conceptualization of CVC and become the organ of the corporate office that managed strategic uncertainty. Achieving this goal meant Holveck would first have to understand both the benefits and the drawbacks of the constraints that limited each OpCo's actions. Second, he would have to figure out how to compensate for those constraints without undermining their effectiveness. Finally, he would need an explicit framework for communicating his objectives throughout the organization and coordinating the action of thousands of people across hundreds of divisions.

8.1.1 Resource Constraints

What any organization can achieve is in large part a function of three key resources: money, time, and people. When it came to people, the OpCos competed in the internal and external labor markets largely unfettered. Few people were "off-limits," and the internal protocols for recruiting people from other J&J divisions ensured merely transparency and civility; they did not limit who could do what. Time and money were different matters.

Money OpCos had to get their operating budgets approved by the corporate office. These budgets set the resources allocated to each division and the financial returns the OpCo was responsible for generating with those resources. The principle of decentralization dictated that, once secured, the OpCos had considerable freedom in deciding how to allocate their budgets in order to secure their current and future performance.

There was one critical exception. Each OpCo was subject to a cap on what it could invest in R&D in any given year. That limit varied by division to reflect the structural characteristics of the different industries in which OpCos competed. The limits permitted only the level of ongoing investment in R&D that allowed each OpCo to stay at the top of its industry. Such a constraint was needed because, like any other budget line item, the opportunities in R&D will always expand to fill the resources available. Allowing each OpCo to choose its level of R&D investment would permit relatively unfettered expansion and would necessarily take away from efforts in other areas, such as operational improvements, marketing, and so on.

The trade-off was that larger projects were strongly discriminated against for at least two reasons. First, large projects generally carried greater risk because of the greater resource commitment required. Second, because the R&D pie was limited, larger projects squeezed out the smaller ones, skewing the overall portfolio to larger, higher-risk undertakings. Consequently, each large R&D project not only increased risk but undermined the OpCo's ability to hedge that risk. Relaxing this resource constraint would allow the OpCos to manage their own strategic risk, but at the cost of diluting their focus on delivering current results.

Time In one respect, this entire book is about the way in which companies can effectively manage the trade-off between the present and the future. When facing up to this dilemma, the mechanism for managing current results has never been in question: it falls to operating management to deliver on the existing strategy. The degree to which they achieve that goal is relatively unambiguous, as their performance will be reflected in the current operating results of their divisions. But rewarding OpCo management for the future impact of current decisions was very difficult; the future, after all, is uncertain.

Consequently, at J&J, as at most every well-run company, operating managers' rewards were driven primarily by shorter-run measures of performance, connected either to current-year results or multiyear averages. This made perfect sense: operating management needed to attend first to operating results, if for no other reason than that no one else could. We live in a world of trade-offs, and it is appropriate that OpCo management focused its attentions on the near term. After all, someone had to.

Clearly, there needed to be a mechanism to manage long-term strategic risk, but making that the responsibility of OpCo managers would have limited their ability to deliver on the existing strategy. Recall the central finding of the research summarized in Chapter 3: operating companies that manage their own risk tend to do so by drifting to the middle of their industry's strategic space, trading performance for survival. The right kinds of limits on the time horizon over which an OpCo had to generate results, the resources it had at its disposal to meet its targets, and the way in which it could spend those resources made it very difficult for an OpCo inside J&J to fall victim to this kind of drift.[7]

8.1.2 Structural Constraints

Resource constraints determined what the OpCos could spend. Structural constraints limited *how* those resources could be spent.

Scope Within the context of a large and diversified company like J&J, each OpCo needed a clear sense of the industry it served and the opportunities that fell within its purview. Without these kinds of boundaries, J&J could easily have found itself with different OpCos pursuing nearly identical opportunities. Such duplication of effort would have been wasteful for shareholders and confusing for customers.

The downside of well-defined scope boundaries was that "white-space" opportunities could go unexplored, since inter-OpCo collaboration was difficult to initiate and sustain.

Scale The opportunities that an OpCo found attractive were determined in part by the size of the OpCo. An OpCo with $1 billion in sales had little interest in applying its capabilities to satisfying the needs of small markets. This was entirely appropriate: each OpCo was responsible for its own performance, and small opportunities do not meet the growth requirements of large organizations. Similarly, an OpCo with $25 million in sales would be unable to fund a $100 million opportunity. In other words, growth opportunities can be either too big or too small.

There are at least two downsides to constraints that drive scale-relevant growth. First, even if issues of scope could be overcome in the interests of a promising opportunity, the target market had to be more or less equally attractive to both parties, otherwise valuable synergies could go unexploited. In other words, scale got in the way of scope. Second, nothing big starts big, and tomorrow's whale is today's minnow. The problem is that most of today's minnows are tomorrow's meals, and knowing which is which remains a challenge. Relaxing the scale constraint, either in the interests of pursuing additional opportunities for scope or in order to pick up promising new ventures, would have reduced the strategic risk borne by each OpCo, but it would also have dispersed OpCo resources, undermining their performance.

In short, the scope constraints served to focus the OpCos' efforts on those industries where their knowledge was most relevant and their resources most valuable. Scale constraints demanded that these capabilities be applied against opportunities with the greatest near-term potential.[8] Together they focused OpCos on specific markets and specific profit targets.

8.1.3 Strategic Constraints

If resource constraints define how much to spend and structural constraints define how to spend it, strategic constraints define *whom* to spend it on.

Customers Unless a company can serve and continue to serve its current customers better than the competition can, it will fail. This requires a relentless focus on the kinds of innovations that consumers will pay for. This means dedicating the organization to pushing out the production possibility frontier at the point that defines an organization's existing strategy.

Without this relentless focus on existing customers, no company would have an ongoing business. The nature of markets is such that it usually takes your very best effort to come out ahead of the competition. Hoping that customers will settle for anything less than everything you have is not often a winning strategy.

The ubiquity of customer dependence is what lies at the heart of disruption theory (see Chapter 4's discussion of fast and slow change). What Clayton Christensen discovered is that new production possibility frontiers are often defined by firms that tackle a very different set of trade-offs in order to serve customers who are of no interest to established, successful firms. Over time, technological and process improvements eventually enable these new entrants to deliver performance/cost combinations that incumbents simply cannot match.

Unlike resource or structural constraints, which in a diversified company are choices for the corporate office to make, strategic constraints impinge upon all operating companies. Today's customers must be served today, and so operating companies are structurally unable to explore technologies that today are able to address only less demanding, less profitable markets even if those technologies might redefine their industry in the future. J&J's OpCos were no more exempt from this constraint than any other organization.

Risk Every operating company faces material strategic risk that increases with the intensity of its commitments. The possibility of mitigating this risk by creating real options was introduced in the Vivendi, BCE, and Microsoft case studies. These options are not free, however. Diverting resources to opportunities that are too expensive (money constraints), too long-term (time constraints), too far afield (scope constraints), or too big or too small (scale constraints) in order to create real options and mitigate strategic risk would have compromised an OpCo's ability to deliver results.

The costs of creating real options are not merely financial. Managing them effectively (something to be explored more deeply in Chapter 10) demands extensive top management attention. Real options can also create operational risk by confusing operating managers: should they focus on their business and their customers, or should they explore alternative business models and synergies with other parts of the organization?

Focusing the OpCos' energies on delivering against a specific strategy maximized the probability that they would achieve their objectives. However, the strategy paradox means those strategies were also the likeliest to fail. If OpCo-level strategic risks were left to OpCos to manage, the OpCos would likely have done what most autonomous businesses do: avoid extreme risk and make only those commitments required to clear the relevant performance hurdles. In other words, the OpCos would be in danger of not taking enough strategic risk.[9]

The risk constraint binding the OpCos, then, puts not so much an upper as a lower bound on the risks to be run. The combination of resource, structural, and strategic constraints serves to drive OpCos to riskier strategies than they would have been likely to pursue as stand-alone companies.

8.1.4 Breaking the Trade-off

Understanding the limits of OpCo-level action in terms of these constraints gave Holveck a much clearer way to assess the kinds of investments JJDC should not make. Anything that required a resource commitment within the financial reach of the OpCos, promised a payoff within the relevant time frame, addressed markets the OpCos sought to serve, and fell within their scale and scope boundaries should be left to the OpCos. And if the OpCos did not want to fund it, there was probably a good reason. Acting as a source of supplementary funding to the OpCos made JJDC a mechanism for circumventing the constraints that served to guide and focus the OpCos, thereby undermining their purpose.

However, as mechanisms simply for driving the OpCos to extreme strategies the constraints were incomplete; they offered no advantage to the OpCos or J&J. The OpCos were still subject to the strategy paradox, and a portfolio of high-risk, high-return OpCos was guaranteed only to increase the variance in the returns of J&J's portfolio of businesses, not necessarily the average.

What Holveck realized was that JJDC could add value by positioning itself as a mechanism for managing strategic uncertainty in ways that the OpCos necessarily could not. JJDC could explore the technologies, markets, and business models that were beyond OpCo constraints so that should the OpCos come to require those assets in order to compete, they would already be in place. JJDC could initiate the commitments needed to develop a new technology or a particular market presence in tentative, low-intensity ways that could then be dialed up as the OpCos came to recognize the need for a new complement of competitive weapons. In other words, JJDC could create the real options that the OpCos might eventually need. JJDC could resolve the strategy paradox!

Here is how.

8.2 TRANSCENDING CONSTRAINTS

Ethicon Endo-Surgery (EES), a J&J division in the Medical Devices and Diagnostics (MD&D) group, needed to find the next wave of innovation-driven growth. EES designed and manufactured surgical instruments, primarily laparoscopic devices for minimally invasive surgery and staplers for wound closure. These devices are used typically by abdominal and thoracic surgeons for both relatively routine procedures, such as a laparoscopic cholecystectomy (the removal of the gallbladder), and also in more exotic interventions, such as laparoscopic surgery to treat colon cancer or laparoscopic bariatric procedures (gastric bypass, or "stomach stapling") for the treatment of morbid obesity.

The use of laparoscopic devices requires small surgical incisions in order to gain access to the body cavity. These incisions typically require that patients be under a general anesthetic (GA), which shuts down much of a patient's autonomic nervous system. Under GA, patients will not breathe on their own and must be intubated. Drug dosages must be closely monitored and the patient's vital signs carefully watched in order to ensure that they do not regain consciousness during an operation but do regain consciousness when the operation is over. Anesthesiologists are therefore a critically important and highly valued member of any operating room team.

Once a patient is under GA, there are few limits to the nature and extent of the surgeries that can be performed laparoscopically. EES has succeeded in this sector of health care by improving the surgeon's access to tissue and ability to repair or remove that tissue through these small incisions. EES has built its franchise on making better tools for the most demanding laparoscopic surgeons in the world.

Endoscopic devices have very different functions. They are used to conduct investigations and minor treatments via natural orifices. Examples are colonoscopies, in which a gastroenterologist inserts a flexible scope through the rectum in order to examine the patient's colon, or an "upper GI," in which a scope is inserted via the esophagus in order to examine the patient's gastrointestinal tract. Beyond endoscopy lies natural orifice translumenal endoscopic surgery (NOTES), in which surgeries can be performed via these natural orifices without the need for a surgical incision.

Because of their less invasive nature, these sorts of procedures do not typically require an anesthesiologist and can be performed under "conscious sedation"—far beyond the local "freezing" you might get at the dentist, but far short of GA. In particular, conscious sedation does not require intubation because patients do not lose their spontaneous breathing reflex.

The most effective, fastest-acting anesthetics can be administered only by anesthesiologists, and their skills are valuable and so sometimes in short supply. Consequently, many endoscopic procedures have to be done without an anesthesiologist in attendance, and so drugs that can be administered by the surgeon, such as Demerol or Versed, must be used. Although effective, these solutions have their drawbacks: they take ten to fifteen minutes to reach peak effectiveness and they take one to two hours to clear a patient's system. They are difficult to titrate and often wear off during the procedure, requiring additional doses, which may further extend a patient's in-office recovery time. As a result, sedation can turn procedures that would otherwise take fifteen minutes or less into hours-long ordeals.

The good news for EES was that more effective drugs already existed. One of the most commonly used, Propofol, is very fast-acting and clears quickly, but its labeling states that it can only be administered by a person trained in the administration of anesthesia. And so EES had its opportunity: find a way to simplify the administration of more effective sedatives such as Propofol so that they can be used safely for procedure sedation by clinicians other than anesthesia professionals. In other words, advancements in endoscopy and NOTES turned far less on improvements in the devices than on pain management.

Now for the bad news. EES's potential breakthrough opportunity lay outside every one of EES's existing constraints:

Resources: Money and Time Since EES was starting from scratch, it was going to take money and time (and luck!) to simply create a product. Furthermore, developing a new device-drug combination product like this would require a level of testing and regulatory approval that went far beyond the time horizons required for improvements—even breakthrough improvements—to their existing product line. Conclusion: likely too expensive, likely would take too long.

Structure: Scope and Scale Assuming EES could create the right kind of product, it would not look like anything else in EES's existing product portfolio. Sure, it would be a device, but a device for administering drugs, not cutting and coagulating tissue. That was a drug maker's problem. But the opportunity was simply too small to matter to the large drug companies. They need billion-dollar blockbusters to get their pulses racing, and the best EES could offer was a slice of a comparatively small market where the competition (Demerol, etc.) was dirt cheap. Conclusion: beyond EES's scope, and too small to matter to the partners it needed.

Strategy: Customers and Risk Even if these problems could be overcome, EES would then have to sell its new Sedation Delivery System (SDS) to a whole new set of customers: gastroenterologists and NOTES surgeons—in short, just about anyone but the abdominal and thoracic surgeons it currently served. EES had a successful differentiation strategy in place for a particular product market. Entering the procedure-sedation market therefore constituted material strategic risk, since it was targeting unfamiliar customers with a very different value proposition.

To top it all off, EES shopped the sedation-technology idea to the business-development executives at the other J&J divisions to see if it would be a better fit with their priorities, but found no takers. In other words, this sedation opportunity not only fell outside of EES's constraints, it fell outside of everyone else's, too.

And so in 1998 EES turned to JJDC for help. EES told the JJDC team that it was on the hunt for an early-stage technology that would dramatically improve the effectiveness and efficiency of sedation for endoscopic procedures. It was clear that the kind of investment EES was after fell outside established constraints, but the merits of EES's analysis were evident. This was not the kind of "dog" proposal that was getting sent to JJDC because it was a bad idea; it was sent to JJDC because it was the right kind of good idea.

Brad Vail, a VP at JJDC, found just what EES had been looking for in Scott Labs, a small device company looking for seed money to fund clinical trials. JJDC made a $2 million investment for a 20 percent ownership stake, a seat on the board, and right of first refusal on commercialization rights. This created a viable "call option" on Scott Labs if the technology ultimately fit with EES's strategic vision. In addition, JJDC ensured that Scott Labs could continue to add to its own intellectual property so that if EES decided to pass on any follow-in investment the smaller company would still be a going concern. This gave EES a credible exit option: there is, after all, a market for start-ups, and if J&J were to develop a reputation for destroying everything it touched, it would become nearly impossible to tap this vitally important source of new technology.

The development of the technology over the next six years required tremendous courage and vision from EES's leaders. They had to fund the project and protect it from EES's constraints. Complementing EES senior management's efforts, Holveck and JJDC have been a strong voice for the development of the sedation project across J&J. The value of this support should not be underestimated. Holveck is a respected and experienced executive in the industry, and his personal endorsement is taken seriously because it is not given easily. His willingness to champion the sedation opportunity with J&J's executive team secured the tens of millions required to purchase global rights on the conscious-sedation technology.

Why would Holveck see such value here? What additional benefit could JJDC bring beyond the initial seed investment and deal structuring? As the sedation technology neared market launch, Holveck campaigned to get other divisions on board to find ways to leverage it in their businesses. For example, JJDC helped broker the funding of a compound development team inside Pharmaceutical Research & Development (PRD) in J&J's Pharmaceutical division to explore next-generation drugs for sedation. This was an opportunity that lay outside the scale and scope of PRD's constraints (conscious sedation is too small a market to align with PRD's existing strategic objectives), but this early-stage work created precisely the kind of option that manages J&J's overall strategic uncertainty in the pharmaceutical business: will the future continue to lie in blockbuster drugs, or will drug-device combinations be the key to tomorrow's success?

By developing what he calls an "internal syndicate" to explore the full range of possible applications, Holveck transformed JJDC, pulling it back from the brink of becoming an internal slush fund and instead making it a mechanism for creating a portfolio of real options on alternative strategies that the divisions would be unable to create for themselves. With JJDC managing strategic uncertainty for the OpCos, the overall corporation has a lower strategic-risk profile even as the individual operating divisions have sacrificed none of the focus required to compete in their individual markets.

In other words, the OpCos are likely no more adaptable than their stand-alone competitors because of their constraints; in fact, since their constraints push them out to extreme strategic positions, they might even be less adaptable than if they were stand-alone companies. Accepting this trade-off is what makes J&J's OpCos such formidable competitors in their markets. However, as a result of the OpCos' position within J&J, and the access this grants to the portfolio of real options JJDC is creating, the OpCos will be able to reconfigure their strategies far more effectively and rapidly than stand-alone entities ever could. That is, they will be able to transcend their constraints, achieving higher levels of performance at lower levels of risk.

8.3 CREATING STRATEGIC FLEXIBILITY

The case studies in Chapter 7 provide a window onto how a diversified corporation such as BCE or Microsoft can manage the strategic risk its operating companies face by creating real options on alternative strategies. BCE's portfolio of operating companies represented a suite of capabilities that could be recombined when and as required to cope with possible shifts in the telecommunications landscape. Similarly, Microsoft's investments in game consoles, new media, communications infrastructure, mobile technology, and consumer electronics provide opportunities to leverage or exploit the existing PC-based Windows franchise. Options on alternative strategies create *strategic* flexibility—that is, the ability to change strategy, something operating companies cannot typically do.

Comparing these two cases also reveals that it is very difficult to build strategic flexibility. The pressures on most companies to articulate a clear strategy and execute against it can be overwhelming, as BCE's Jean Monty discovered. In the context of a large, publicly traded company run by agent-managers, how does one determine which options to take, how much to pay for them, and how to realize their value? Perhaps more challenging still, how does one explain to shareholders and other constituencies why the corporation should have these options? For JJDC, Holveck needed an explicit approach to creating the strategic flexibility that erstwhile entrepreneurs like Bill Gates had the latitude to craft largely by intuition.

Strategic flexibility is very different from run-of-the-mill flexibility or adaptability. "Flexibility" means "change within existing constraints." Flexibility can be helpful, but *strategic* uncertainty demands *strategic* flexibility—

THE GROUP EXECUTIVE, REQUISITE UNCERTAINTY, AND WHO CREATES STRATEGIC FLEXIBILITY

Johnson & Johnson's hierarchy includes a layer common in large, diversified companies: the "group executive." Group executives typically oversee a cluster of businesses that are related to each other in some material way: they serve the same customers, rely on the same underlying technology, or have similar economics.

The function of the group executive is perhaps one of the least studied and poorly understood phenomena in large organizations. Nevertheless, the principles of organization discussed in Chapter 6 provide a way to think about the role.

In most companies, the group executive's vertical role is quite limited, and group heads are often largely a span-breaker, representing the CEO in control matters. The strategic importance of the group executive has typically focused on horizontal integration, ensuring that the group is able to capture synergies between related operating divisions.[10]

This is how the group level functions at J&J. The group chairman and the group operating committee, which consists of the heads of the OpCos in the group, work to ensure that the OpCos strategies are appropriate, and that any synergies that might enhance the effectiveness of those strategies are pursued effectively and efficiently.

As a result, the group level at J&J has a time horizon that is largely similar to that of the OpCos, and so the management of strategic uncertainty falls to the next level up in the hierarchy, the corporate office, which is where JJDC lives.

Other companies might use the group differently, focusing as much or more on the vertical dimension as the horizontal one. At General Electric, for example, the Healthcare division has created a bio-genetics business in a manner strongly redolent of Strategic Flexibility without the kind of corporate-level activity that features so prominently at J&J. This works because the group level has a time horizon that extends beyond that of the operating companies within GE's Healthcare division, and so the creation of Strategic Flexibility falls to group leadership.

The critical insight these differences suggest is that there is a choice to be made when it comes to the group level of the hierarchy: will it be primarily a horizontally integrating role, or a vertically differentiating role? Not being clear about the strategic purpose of the strategic group has been credited with much of the confusion and frustration experienced by companies with group structures and the group executives attempting to function within them.[11]

the ability to change strategies, which is something made largely impossible by the commitments required for success. Creating the real options required to implement new, different, effective, commitment-based strategies on a tempo defined by competitive markets can be done only in the spaces beyond constraints. Consequently, only the corporate office can devote resources to operating outside of the constraints that bind operating companies' actions. When referring to the ability of an operating company to change its strategy thanks to real options on alternative strategies, capitals will be used: Strategic Flexibility.

For Holveck to replicate the success of the conscious-sedation project and give the concept of the internal syndicate credibility, he would need to codify and formalize the way he saw JJDC managing the OpCos' strategic uncertainty. The framework that Holveck adopted has four basic components:

Anticipate The existence of strategic risk is a function of the unpredictability of the future. Consequently, managing strategic risk cannot hinge on improved prediction. However, it is possible to bound the range of possible futures that one might face. This is best done with scenarios. By creating a number of scenarios that define the "possibility space" over a relevant time horizon, one can create a framework for discussing the future without having to stake future success on guessing right.

Formulate With scenarios in place, it is possible to determine the strategies required to be successful under these different conditions. In other words, there is an *optimal strategy* for each scenario. Each optimal strategy can then be decomposed into its constituent *elements*—the technologies, capabilities, or other assets required to implement the strategy. Elements that are common to many of the optimal strategies are known as *core elements*, while those that are common to only a few optimal strategies or perhaps unique to one optimal strategy are called *contingent elements*.

Accumulate Core elements can be pursued without reservation, for there is no strategic risk associated with them; commitment is entirely appropriate, because there is very little chance of having "guessed wrong." It is the contingent elements that demand more creativity and require real options thinking.

Combining scenarios with optimal strategies places boundaries on the range of assets and capabilities an organization might need in order to be successful across a range of plausible futures. Accepting the unpredictability of the future does not imply a complete inability to place limits on what could conceivably happen.

Even with these limits in place, committing to all the resources required by every optimal strategy is generally not feasible. By investing in the contingent elements in an optionlike manner, a corporation can cover a far greater range of assets far more cost-effectively.

Operate   The *accumulate* phase results in a portfolio of options covering the contingent elements related to specific optimal strategies described in the *formulate* phase. These optimal strategies are in turn linked to the scenarios developed in the *anticipate* phase. The *operate* phase demands a close monitoring of the environment, which allows the corporation to determine:

- which of its scenarios most accurately captures the most important elements of the future that "arrives," which determines . . .
- which optimal strategy is most appropriate, which determines . . .
- which contingent elements are required, which determines . . .
- which options should be exercised and which should be abandoned.

Finally, since time's arrow has no tip, the set of scenarios used as the foundation for building a flexible strategy must be constantly reviewed and occasionally refreshed or renewed.

Consider JJDC's approach to each phase.

FIGURE 8-1 **STRATEGIC FLEXIBILITY**

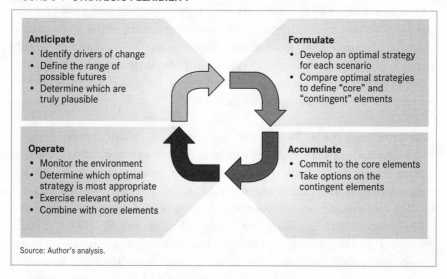

Source: Author's analysis.

8.3.1 Anticipate

The first question is the operating scope covered by the scenarios. JJDC chose to build a set of scenarios that addressed the health care industry at the highest level. It simply would not have made sense to build scenarios around the uncertainties facing, say, the surgery market, since that would limit JJDC's purview to the strategic risk faced by those divisions competing in surgery. The objective was to assess JJDC's current portfolio of investments and make new investments with an eye to J&J's position within the health care sector writ large.

The second key question is the time frame covered by JJDC's scenarios. Since the OpCos are typically concerned with five-year time horizons, JJDC felt it should look farther out. In keeping with Jaques's prescriptions, JJDC chose a ten-year horizon. Since the work described here was done in mid-2004, the end point the scenarios described was 2015.

There are a number of identifiable trends in the global health care industry. For example, in many nations, the average life expectancy has increased while the birth rate has declined. This implies an increase in the average age of the population. Additionally, obesity is on the rise almost worldwide. The confluence of age and weight problems implies a high likelihood of increased demand for treatments for osteoarthritis, heart disease, type II diabetes, Alzheimer's, and so on.

JJDC identified the following four dimensions of uncertainty within which these trends will play out:

The Economy The general level of economic activity and growth determines the money available for health care expenditures at the levels of government and individual consumers. This affects J&J's economic health, which in turn drives the capital available for investment in new treatments. The plausible bounds for economic activity for 2005–2015 were set at 0–4 percent compounded annual growth in GDP.

International Trade As a global company in an industry where national and even local market structures can have enormous ramifications, the prevailing international trade regime is very important. JJDC management concluded that, at its most restrictive, a series of relatively self-contained trading blocs might emerge. Motivated perhaps by security concerns, or a contracting global economy, or rising Chinese power, NAFTA could become a customs union or even expand to incorporate much of South America. For similar reasons, the EU could stop expanding while deepening the trade ties among member states. An ASEAN bloc of Asian nations might coalesce in response. At the other extreme, an ever more liberal global trading environment, precipitated by the removal of agricultural subsidies, the strengthening of patent and copyright laws, and a generally buoyant global economy, could emerge.

Technology Will proteomics fulfill the promise of decoding the genome, or will it prove an expensive disappointment? Will the communications infrastructure at last enable telemedicine? Will nanotechnology merge chemical and mechanical sciences to open entirely new treatment modalities? Or will the health care sector be forced to get by on incremental gains eked out of existing technologies? The pace and trajectory of technological improvements can be profoundly affected by efforts companies make to advance the state of the art, but luck invariably plays an enormous role. As a result, counting on either technological breakthroughs or stagnation is never a prudent course.

Market Structure Government plays a significant role in the health care industry in every nation. Beyond merely setting the rules for competition, governments determine the underlying structure of competition itself. Do private companies provide care? Who makes purchase decisions? Who pays? In almost every advanced economy there is an ongoing and often acrimonious debate about the level of government intervention that is appropriate. At one extreme, JJDC saw the ever-increasing share of GDP consumed by health care to be ultimately unsupportable. In response, they considered it entirely plausible that by 2015 a heavily socialized health care system might emerge in the United States, with governments mandating universal coverage and establishing in great detail the level of care to be provided and at what cost. Alternatively, perhaps an ever freer market for health care might emerge in response to those same pressures as political winds favored the deregulation of the health insurance sector so that consumers of health care might decide for themselves which health risks to accept and which to insure against.

Combining these four dimensions of uncertainty yielded four scenarios, each of which was a "corner solution" that captured the limits of what JJDC executives felt were believable combinations of these four variables.

8.3.2 Formulate

Developing a strategy designed to succeed under the conditions described by a specific scenario is generally straightforward. The existing machinery of competitive strategic analysis can be imported and applied with confi-

FIGURE 8-2   **JJDC'S SCENARIOS FOR 2015**

Scenario	Economic Growth	International Trade	Pace of Technological Innovation	Regulation	Summary
Who Wants to Be a Millionaire?	Strong	Liberal	Fast	Enlightened	• Patients able to pay • The innovation treadmill gets faster
The Dating Game	Strong	Liberal	Slow	Enlightened	• Brands under pressure • The rise of generics
Family Feud	Strong	Protectionist	Slow	Bureaucratic	• Employers and governments as payors • Regional trade blocs limit market sizes
Big Brother	Weak	Protectionist	Slow	Bureaucratic	• Governments as payors • Regional trade blocs limit market sizes • Severe margin squeeze and demand for lower costs

Dimensions of Uncertainty

Source: JJDC; author's analysis; data disguised.

dence. Industry structure and game theory provide powerful insights into competitive action and reaction.[12] Identifying core competencies and the threats and opportunities raised by market disruption can point the way toward successful execution.[13] By applying these frameworks in the context of a given scenario, it is possible to develop actionable strategies without first having to agree on a specific vision of the future.

For JJDC, the scenarios were only part of the job. In a company with more than 200 operating units, how could JJDC build four strategies (one for each scenario) for each of hundreds of different OpCos? Compounding the problem was that within each of those organizational units live sometimes hundreds of individual products, each of which competes in its own product market. How could JJDC be useful and comprehensive yet still complete its task within a time frame that would be relevant? Worse still, since J&J's existing organizational structure is designed to implement existing strategies, if JJDC were to build strategies for the divisions defined by the current structure, the team would be compromising, perhaps irretrievably, its ability to develop anything new and innovative. After all, JJDC is a mechanism for overcoming the constraints that define the ambit of the current organization. JJDC must therefore work outside of those constraints, not within them.

The answer was to look at the problem from the perspective of the end consumer. In every industry there is a complex, multiplayer chain of decision makers, distributors, and others who stand between the manufacturer and the end consumer. For J&J's health care businesses (as opposed to their consumer product division), this consists of purchasing departments in hospitals or hospital groups, public and private health insurance providers, doctors and other health care professionals, and caregivers (e.g., parents or other family members). Each of these groups influences which product or service is chosen to varying degrees and in different ways, but ultimately the goal is to alleviate suffering and restore health.

What matters to a consumer is whatever is compromising their health. Consequently, JJDC built strategies for addressing specific disease states, not for specific organizational units inside J&J. Taking disease state as the fundamental unit of analysis allowed JJDC to look across J&J's existing organizational boundaries (e.g., drugs and devices) and to not worry about the necessarily ever-changing organizational structure.

Like most of Western medicine, J&J has long emphasized the treatment of disease. But successful treatment is premised on accurate diagnosis, and both are obviated by effective prevention. So for each disease state the JJDC team mapped out J&J's existing portfolio of products by drug and device across these three modalities. Doing the same for JJDC's portfolio of investments revealed that JJDC was investing in ways that served largely to support J&J's existing strategy: in the main, JJDC's portfolio targeted the development of treatments for essentially the same disease states the OpCos were already targeting.

The overlap between JJDC's portfolio and J&J's products is neither good nor bad by itself. JJDC compensates for different types of constraints, and as long as its investments in those same disease state/modality combinations go beyond existing constraints in appropriate ways, then JJDC is fulfilling at least part of its mandate. For example, if JJDC is exploring technologies with a time horizon that goes beyond the limits that define the relevant OpCo, or if it is investing in potentially disruptive business models, then overlap at the level of disease state and modality is not a duplication of effort.

Some types of overlap, however, are cause for concern. Each scenario developed in the *Anticipate* phase has different implications for the relative influence of each of the various participants in the health care value chain. By looking at the interests and level of influence of each constituency under each scenario, the JJDC team determined the optimal allocation of resources to each of prevention, diagnosis, and treatment for each scenario.

For example, in the "Who Wants to Be a Millionaire?" scenario (so named for its generally buoyant complexion), patients not only pay their own way but are likely to be able to afford new treatments for whatever ails them. In other words, due to strong demand, the market will be supply-driven. Success will therefore turn on the ability of health care companies to create and market their new inventions.

Conversely, in the "Big Brother" scenario (so named because of the dominance of government as the key underwriter of medical treatment), prevention plays a key role because the benefits of effective prevention can be captured across large numbers of people.[14] Highly centralized purchasing and delivery of health care would also likely translate into the development and promulgation of standards and the slower adoption of new medical technologies, thus reducing the returns to certain types of innovation.

"The Dating Game" envisioned a world of supply-driven markets but with little new to supply as a result of technological and economic lethargy. With very little of substance upon which to differentiate products or services, health care companies are forced to reduce costs in order to seduce customers (the inspiration for the scenario's name) and become the preferred choice. Innovation is focused on delivery systems rather than underlying medical technology.

Finally, the "Family Feud" scenario saw employer-, HMO-, and insurer-driven health care that demanded highly customized solutions for the particular populations they served. With each of these powerful customer groups looking out for their own (hence "family feud"), companies such as J&J would not be able to focus on a particular modality or business model, but would need to have OpCos focused on each customer segment.

8.3.3 Accumulate

Identifying core and contingent elements for each disease state requires comparing the optimal strategies developed for each disease state in each scenario. Take, for example, stroke, the third-leading cause of death in the United States. Across the four scenarios there is always a market for a baseline level of commitment to treatment. However, the market's ability or willingness to pay for the more aggressive and expensive treatment modalities varies widely. Consequently, the more ambitious intracranial device or pharmaceutical approaches were deemed contingent: likely to be very successful under some scenarios, such as "Who Wants to Be a Millionaire?" but less successful under others, such as "Big Brother."

With stroke, a critical element of effective treatment is identifying its onset—a diagnosis problem. Part of the reason early diagnosis is very important is that the window for treatment at the onset of a stroke is very small: the most effective treatments must be administered within three hours of being stricken, while most stroke sufferers do not receive treatment until almost seven hours post-stroke. Yet few companies devote much attention to the development of definitive acute diagnostics—for instance, a device that people at higher risk of stroke might carry with them and use upon the onset of one or more of the warning signs.[15] Such diagnosis might allow for the timely administration of drugs, which could extend the treatment window.

There is evidence of increasing emphasis on stroke diagnosis in the medical community and in the population generally. For example, the American Stroke Association has launched a campaign to educate people on the signs of stroke so that they will seek treatment earlier. Leading indicators such as these persuaded JJDC to make some diagnostic initiatives core elements of the stroke strategy. Other diagnostic initiatives were not as clear-cut. For example, more precise longer-term predictors of stroke risk, such as genetic profiling, raise important ethical considerations, since they might affect people's employment prospects and what they pay for insurance. Consequently, these were seen as contingent, to be invested in accordingly.

Prevention activities include public education, which can take the form of advertising consumer products that can enable a lower-risk lifestyle. This includes weight management through, for example, sugar substitutes such as Splenda from J&J's McNeil Consumer Specialty Products division. McNeil's St. Joseph's Low-Dose Aspirin is also part of a prevention strategy, as it acts as a blood thinner in order to reduce the likelihood of suffering ischemic stroke. Both of these existing products could easily be positioned as part of an overall stroke-prevention effort, regardless of scenario. Consequently, each was deemed a core element of the stroke strategy. Contingent prevention initiatives included everything from services associated with reducing risk, such as smoking cessation, to aggressive surgical interventions, such as left atrial closure.

A 2×2 grid that captured existing and new development efforts, categorizing them by their core or contingent nature and connecting them to both their underlying modality (prevention, diagnosis, treatment) and J&J's high-level organization structure (consumer products, devices, pharmaceuticals), yielded an at-a-glance summary of J&J's strategic stance on stroke. This categorization allowed JJDC to assess how best to invest in existing and future initiatives.

This portfolio of core investments and contingent options constitutes the raw ingredients of a stroke strategy that can be optimized as competitive

FIGURE 8-3 **J&J'S STROKE STRATEGY**

		Make investments	Create options
	New	Acute diagnostics Risk assessment Consumer education "Nutraceuticals"	Neurostimulation Neuroregeneration Brain/machine interface Monitoring Caregiver support Rehabilitation services
Status of initiative			
		Nurture investments	Preserve options
	Existing	Atrial ablation St. Joseph's ASA Splenda	Left atrial closure Rehabilitation Carotid stents Immediate post-stroke drugs
		Core	Contingent
		Nature of Strategic Element	

Source: JJDC; author's analysis; data disguised; partial listing only.

conditions evolve. J&J avoided making a bold commitment to a particular approach, instead creating for itself true Strategic Flexibility. The various initiatives in the portfolio exist within established OpCos, and so each is a commitment from the perspective of operating management. But thanks to JJDC and the Stroke Management Group (SMG), a cross-divisional task force, J&J and its OpCos are positioned to reconfigure themselves as necessary to ensure that they have the right stroke strategy regardless of how the future turns out.

8.3.4 Operate

With the core and contingent elements identified, the next stage in the analysis is to determine which unit within J&J has responsibility for either implementing (in the case of core elements) or creating options on (in the case of contingent elements) each element. When an element falls within the constraints that define an existing business unit, it is up to that business's management to determine whether or not to pursue that element. When an element falls outside the bailiwick of all existing units, then it is JJDC's role either to fund the requisite investment from its own budget or to coordinate the appropriate joint activity by facilitating interunit cooperation.[16]

Since 2004, when this approach was developed and launched at JJDC, Holveck and his team have expanded its application to include the analysis of competitors. By mapping the full portfolio of their competition's products and announced research initiatives, JJDC is able to infer the bets they are placing. By integrating this analysis with a systematic collection of detailed internal data, JJDC has perhaps the most complete picture in the world of what disease states and modalities are being addressed by life sciences companies. With this in place, they can then readily identify the "white-space" opportunities where there is little or no activity. Sometimes the absence of activity makes sense: no one is investing there because it is a dry hole. On the other hand, armed with a set of scenarios and optimal strategies addressed to each, JJDC can see that some white space opportunities might have significant option value, and so scoop up valuable assets that others had dismissed.

Holveck now spends a good deal of his time communicating the new role of JJDC, a role that he sees becoming only more important over time. The operational uncertainty J&J faces today is no different from what it has always faced: healthcare is an exploratory business, and one never knows if the science will work until the exploration has been done. The strategic uncertainty that permeates the environment today, however, is a horse of a different color. The constraints that define the company's OpCos cannot be relaxed because the need to deliver results today is as acute as ever. But the need to find a way to go beyond those constraints *as a corporation* in order to manage strategic uncertainty—both mitigating risk and gaining exposure to valuable opportunities—has taken on new urgency and importance.

JJDC has come to fill this role by focusing on four activities:

Creating options When options on new capabilities or technologies are required in order to manage a particular strategic uncertainty that lies beyond the constraints of the OpCos, JJDC takes the lead by making the requisite investments in early-stage companies. COSAT complements this function by creating linkages to academic research facilities through grant money. Consequently, JJDC is a center of expertise backed up with hard dollars that can be invested to alter J&J's overall strategic risk and opportunity profile at comparatively little cost.

Preserving options Generalizing from the experience with Scott Labs and EES, JJDC makes it a point to manage its VC-like investment portfolio with an eye not merely to J&J's eventual benefit but also to the continued viability of the investment companies.

When a company JJDC has invested in for its strategic option value begins to pursue opportunities that are not aligned with the risks or opportunities that motivated J&J to invest in the first place, there is a decision to be made: does JJDC attempt to exercise some influence on the company to keep it aligned with J&J's key uncertainties, or does it let the company go its own way? Giving a small start-up too much strategic freedom could quickly undermine the option value and invalidate the original investment thesis. Too little could destroy the viability of the firm as a stand-alone entity, undermining J&J's ability to make similar future investments as well as foreclosing any meaningful exit strategy. After all, an option with no exit strategy is really just a commitment in disguise.

Exercising options As illustrated by the "internal syndicate" forming around EES's conscious-sedation technology and the SMG, JJDC plays a key role in providing resources and establishing strategic alignment among otherwise disparate parts of the organization in order to take advantage of the opportunities for scope created by J&J's diversity. In other words, without spending a dime on acquiring new technologies, J&J's existing portfolio of capabilities holds within it any number of options on collaborative opportunities. Identifying and capturing these synergies lie beyond the constraints of the OpCos, and so it falls to JJDC to determine when and how to exercise those options through internal venture formation or strategic integration programs.

Abandoning options Although often overlooked in many discussions of the more limited notion of corporate venture capital, the ability to abandon an option without suffering severe financial losses is critical to creating value by managing strategic uncertainty. JJDC therefore pays very close attention to its connections with the VC community at large in order to be able to spin off its investments on relatively attractive terms. What makes this possible is that JJDC has the discipline to sell off those investments that are financially attractive in their own right, *but no longer serve to manage strategic uncertainty for J&J*. Purely financial investors, like life sciences–focused VC funds, often find such investments very attractive, and that surplus often allows J&J to recover its investment or more, and so to manage strategic uncertainty at nominal direct financial cost.

This shift inside JJDC has culminated in a near-total revolution in the purpose of the organization. Whereas JJDC vice presidents—the people in charge of finding, making, and managing JJDC's investments—once saw their role as "making money," they now increasingly see it as "managing uncertainty." Sticking with this new mission is extraordinarily difficult. When your task is to turn a profit, success is relatively unambiguous. But when your objective is to "manage strategic uncertainty," how can you know when you have succeeded? After all, the need to manage uncertainty arises because the future is unpredictable. As a result, even options that do not pay off have value—in just the same way that fire insurance you never collect on because your house never burned down was nevertheless valuable.

How valuable? The inescapable fact is that we have no meaningful measures of future strategic uncertainty: we can no more measure uncertainty than we can measure future profitability. But as Einstein put it, "Not everything important can be measured, and not everything that can be measured is important." If there is a moral to this chapter, it is this: even if what JJDC does now is less measurable, it is almost certainly more important.

8.4 CAN THIS WORK FOR YOU?

J&J is to strategic frameworks what New York is to stage performers: if you can make it there, you can make it anywhere. The complexity of the issues J&J faces rivals that faced by any other industry or organization. It is the complexity of these challenges that demands such a carefully constructed and considered scaffolding of scenarios, strategies, strategic elements, and core and contingent classifications.

The four-phase framework for building Strategic Flexibility is proving to be a useful starting point for managing strategic uncertainty at J&J. It provides a coherent framework for identifying and addressing strategic risk within a context that connects the commitments a company must deliver on with the uncertainties that it invariably faces. There is, of course, a great deal more to say about precisely how to implement each phase:

Anticipate: how to build the scenarios and be sure that you have accounted for all the relevant uncertainties

Formulate: how to create optimal strategies and identify the core and contingent elements

Accumulate: how to create real options and ensure they remain valuable

Operate: how to "exercise" or "abandon" the real options you have created, and how to value them

These are the issues addressed in the next two chapters.

Johnson & Johnson's corporate venture capital arm, JJDC, has transformed itself into a mechanism for managing strategic

uncertainty. By creating and managing a portfolio of real options on alternative strategies, JJDC creates Strategic Flexibility *for J&J's OpCos. This allows focused divisions with high-risk, high-return strategies to change their strategic stance in ways they otherwise could not. The result is better overall corporate performance and lower overall corporate risk.*

---

1. J&J is by no means hesitant to start new operating companies, but JJDC often found technologies that were not yet commercializable, and so setting up their acquisitions as stand-alone OpCos was rarely a viable option. In addition, much of the value J&J could bring to these early-stage companies lay in leveraging new technologies within an existing J&J business, allowing it to reach new markets or compete in new effective ways.

2. Collins, James C., and Jerry I. Porras (1994), *Built to Last: Successful Habits of Visionary Companies,* New York: HarperBusiness.

3. See Hurstak, Johanna M., and Andrall Pearson (1992), "Johnson & Johnson: Hospital Services," Harvard Business School case study 9-392-050.

4. The literature on corporate venture capital is significant but not nearly as well developed as some of the other subjects used as building blocks in this book (e.g., organizational theory, strategy, randomness, etc.). For example, there remains some ambiguity in the definition of key terms such as "corporate venturing," "corporate venture capital," or "internal venture capital." For present purposes, "corporate venture capital" refers to early-stage equity investment by a corporation in a small start-up company. "Internal venture capital" refers to the mechanisms by which a corporation funds and launches new businesses that have been generated internally.

Many large companies have CVC functions, and there have been three noticeable waves in CVC activity that have coincided with booms in the venture capital (VC) industry: the late 1960s, the late 1970s, and the late 1990s. Each CVC expansion wave has been followed by significant retrenchment that typically exceeded the coincident pullback by VC investors. Corporate venture capital departments have an average life span of approximately three years.

The CVC research drawn on here includes:

Brody, Paul, and David Ehrlich (1998), "Can Big Companies Become Successful Venture Capitalists," *McKinsey Quarterly,* No. 2.

Burgelman, Robert A., and Liisa Välikangas (2005), "Managing Internal Corporate Venturing Cycles," *MITSloan Management Review,* Vol. 46, No. 4 (Summer).

Campbell, Andrew, Julian Birkinshaw, Andy Morrison, and Robert van Basten Batenburg (2003), "The Future of Corporate Venturing," *MITSloan Management Review,* Vol. 45, No. 1 (Fall).

Chesbrough, Henry W. (2002), "Making Sense of Corporate Venture Capital," *Harvard Business Review* (March).

Gompers, Paul A. (2002), "Corporations and the Financing of Innovation: The Corporate Venturing Experience," *Federal Reserve Bank of Atlanta Economic Review* (Fourth Quarter).

Markham, Stephen K., Stuart T. Gentry, David Hume, Ram Ramachandram, and Angus I. Kingon (2005), "Strategies and Tactics for External Corporate Venturing," *Research Technology Management* (March–April).

5. A possible third objective is to monetize assets that the company cannot commercialize. This, however, is more a way to use a corporate venture capital function to sell off assets for which there is not a well-functioning market. This objective has not been a documented source of material wealth creation.

6. Campbell, Andrew, and Robert Park (2005), *The Growth Gamble,* London: Nicholas Brealey International.

7. The time horizon dimension of strategic uncertainty is a useful benchmark but not a universal rule. In particular, in the pharmaceutical business the product-development time horizons can be measured in decades while the strategic uncertainties affecting the industry can evolve in shorter periods of time. In such instances, it is appropriate for the corporate office to deal with higher levels of strategic uncertainty even if their time horizon is shorter than that of operating managers as a result.

8. It is worth reminding ourselves that the terms qualifying time horizons ("short," "long," "near," "far") are relative. The near or short term for an OpCo at J&J can be five to seven years. The long-term strategic uncertainties might take two decades to play out. An OpCo leader at J&J can be responsible for a multibillion-dollar business and have a Requisite Uncertainty time horizon that exceeds the corporate-level time horizon in a different industry.

9. See Shiller, Robert J. (2003), *The New Financial Order: Risk in the 21st Century,* Princeton: Princeton University Press. Shiller explains how the absence of sufficiently powerful risk-management tools leads to a suboptimal level of risk taking. When risk is inappropriately distributed, the fact that we fear losses more than we regret foregone opportunity means that otherwise wealth-generating activity is avoided. Better risk management benefits everyone.

10. Stengrevics, John M. (1984), "Making Cluster Strategies Work," *Journal of Business Strategy,* Vol. 5, Iss. 2; (1984), "Managing the Group Executive's Job," *Organizational Dynamics,* Vol. 12, Iss. 3.

11. Oreal, Serge (1981), "The Role of Group Executives in the Strategic Management of Diversified Companies," *International Studies of Management & Organization,* Vol. 11, Iss. 2.

12. Porter, Michael E. (1980), *op. cit.,* for the "five forces" framework for industry analysis, and Brandenburger, Adam M., and Barry Nalebuff (1997), *Coopetition,* New York: Doubleday, for a helpful application of game theory to strategy development.

13. Hamel, Gary, and C. K. Prahalad, *op. cit.,* for more on core competence; and Christensen, Clayton M. (1997), *op. cit.,* for more on disruption.

14. Part of the explanation for this might lie in our general inability to think in terms of probabilities. We tend to think of ourselves as either having, say, diabetes or not—a binary state. Not having it means do nothing different. Having it means treating it. How aggressively to work to prevent it given a 5 percent chance vs. a 15 percent chance of developing the condition is not a question we tend to answer in ways that alter our long-term behaviors.

15. These are: (1) Sudden numbness or weakness of the face, arm, or leg, especially on one side of the body; (2) Sudden confusion, trouble speaking or understanding; (3) Sudden trouble seeing in one or both eyes; (4) Sudden trouble walking, dizziness, loss of balance or coordination; (5) Sudden, severe headache with no known cause. American Stroke Association (http://www.strokeassociation.org), accessed April 6, 2006.

16. It is important to note also that the technical risk associated with any given initiative must also be managed. Just because, for instance, an accurate, inexpensive, fast-acting, easy-to-use stroke diagnostic device would be successful doesn't mean it can be developed. Assessing and managing this technical uncertainty is a critical part of implementing this sort of strategy, but exploring this topic is beyond the scope of the present discussion.

CHAPTER NINE

WHAT IF . . . ?

A genuinely flexible strategy has two primary ingredients: scenarios and real options. This chapter addresses the first of these—specifically, how to build scenarios and how to use them as an input into the strategic planning process. Scenarios are most useful to the senior levels of the hierarchy where time horizons are long enough to contemplate strategic change. The differences among the generic levels of a hierarchy—corporate, operating division, and functional management—are explored in order to highlight the defining characteristics of decision making, as it relates to strategy, at each level.

To paraphrase Peter Drucker, for an idea to be of any use it must eventually degenerate into hard work.[1]

The Johnson & Johnson case study demonstrates that it is possible to manage strategic uncertainty using a formal and transparent process. However, there is still a good deal of conceptual unpacking required to lay bare the specifics of how to create Strategic Flexibility.

Strategic Flexibility consists of two fundamental constructs: scenario-based planning and real options. Scenarios allow one to take seriously the uncertainty of the future, while real options make it possible to act in a manner calibrated to that uncertainty. This chapter explores scenario-based planning and its implications on strategy making, planning, and decision making at each level of the hierarchy. The next chapter will focus on how to create and manage a portfolio of real options on alternative strategies, each one keyed to the competitive demands of a different scenario.

9.1 SCENARIOS: DON'T PREDICT, ANTICIPATE

We have an almost irresistible desire to know what the future will bring. That is why so much of this book has been devoted to examining the limits of forecasting. When it comes to making predictions for the purposes of strategic planning, we are pretty much wasting our time.

It would be a mistake, however, to conclude that we have no insight into the future, and that all we can do is throw up our hands in despair. After all, an obvious, but perhaps overlooked, implication of the fact that strategic uncertainty increases with one's time horizon is that strategic uncertainty can, well, increase. And if it can increase, then there can be more or less of it, and that necessarily implies that there are boundaries on what is possible and even plausible. Anyone who tells you that "anything is possible" is either speaking rhetorically or does not fully understand the meaning of "anything." There are limits to what can happen, no matter the time horizon under consideration. Scenario building is a tool for determining just what those limits are.

In some sense, scenario building has been around for as long as human beings have been able to imagine alternative futures and ask themselves "What if . . . ?" In the context of business planning, however, it has much more recent origins, growing out of military planning during World War Two and translated into the corporate sphere thanks largely to the efforts of the RAND Corporation.[2] Shell, the global oil company, is justly famous for having incorporated scenario-based planning into its strategy-development process as early as the 1960s.

Despite its provenance, scenario-based planning has had a very uneven and uninspiring history as a management tool. According to an annual survey of management practices, scenario building has typically languished, ranking below the mean in overall usage and satisfaction. On occasion, during periods when a confluence of adverse events precipitates a sense of foreboding about the future, scenario-based planning climbs the chart: in 2002, it rose to #9 on a list of twenty-five tools, up from #12 in 2001 and #16 in 2000. This was likely a consequence of the 9/11 attacks, the lead-up to the Iraq war, stock market turbulence in the wake of the dot-com meltdown, the onset of a recession of uncertain duration and severity, and a variety of other factors. Inevitably, however, it returns to its long-run equilibrium: by 2005, scenarios were back down to #16.[3]

A good deal of the dissatisfaction with scenario-based planning stems from the diversity of opinion surrounding what scenarios are for and how they are created. For example, are scenarios built around a specific decision or around general strategic issues? What time horizon is relevant? What factors should be included? What is a good scenario? How many scenarios are needed? And so on.

The answer to these and other related questions appears to be "it depends." And it depends on what one wants to use the scenarios for. Strategic Flexibility provides a context in which scenario-based planning is a starting point for the larger project of managing strategic uncertainty. As a result, the objective here is not to describe how scenario-based planning should be done, but rather to describe how it should be done *for this particular purpose*.

9.1.1   What Are Scenarios and What Are They For?

When grappling with strategic uncertainty the key is to avoid, on principle, reductionist point-predictions of the future. Anything that arbitrarily narrows the range of opinions considered will restrict management's ability to take seriously the full scope of future possibilities. It is critical, therefore, to find ways to preserve divergent points of view.

Scenario building makes this possible. In the context of managing strategic uncertainty, scenarios are best thought of as specific and full-blooded descriptions of different futures. They are not ranges for specific variables, such as interest rates, the price of oil, or the occurrence of a particular natural or human-made disaster. Rather, scenarios provide an efficient way to summarize and synthesize the interaction of all relevant variables into one coherent picture. Different scenarios capture different, and typically extreme, values for the full set of relevant variables, not slight changes "at the margin" for individual variables.

In any scenario there are likely to be a large number of relevant variables, too many to consider all at once. As a result, it is typically advisable to cluster these variables into specific dimensions of uncertainty.[4] So, for example, interest rates, exchange rates, the price of oil, the general level of economic activity, and so on might be variables that are reasonably clustered together into a single dimension of uncertainty such as "the economy." The more dimensions of uncertainty one considers, the more detailed each scenario will be. However, as will be illustrated below, the price of greater detail is an exponentially more difficult analytical challenge when using the scenarios as an input to strategic planning.

One way to make this trade-off is to think of each scenario as a "corner solution" in the "possibility space" of tomorrow. This space is defined by the intersection of the dimensions of uncertainty chosen, and scenarios mark out the limits of what is sufficiently plausible to warrant taking seriously. Each dimension of uncertainty is therefore an axis on a hyperplane, and the variables that go into that axis should be correlated, at least conceptually, with respect to their impact on strategic decision-making.

Scenario-based planning is often misused as a step in a forecasting process. Treating scenarios in this way betrays a persistent, inextinguishable, insatiable, and ultimately pathological desire for accurate forecasting. In fact, scenarios can no more represent what the future will hold than the lines of a tennis court tell you precisely where a serve will land. Descriptions of "interior" conditions—that is, "scenarios" that do not lie *on* the boundaries of the possibility space but instead *within* them—might be interesting, but they do not provide the information needed to determine the range of strategies an operating division might have to implement in order to succeed. An infinite number of interior scenarios can be imagined, and no organization can prepare itself for all of them. Using interior scenarios is therefore another manifestation of the prediction pathology. Scenarios can be used to create Strategic Flexibility when they provide a *ne plus ultra* for strategic planning, envisioning the extreme conditions for which a company must prepare.

Since scenarios must capture significant variation along a number of different dimensions, it is typically best to express each scenario as a single narrative—a story, if you will. There is quite literally no limit to the different rhetorical devices that can be employed to capture the relevant drivers in a compelling and memorable way.[5] The objective is to capture in high relief the relevant elements of a future in sufficient detail that one can imagine oneself actually living in that world. It must not be a caricature; it must be something you really believe could happen. Scenarios are not excuses to indulge a repressed urge to write science fiction or techno-thrillers. They must be credible, believable, fully dimensioned descriptions of a future state of affairs.

By using scenarios as a basis for strategic planning (hence the term "scenario-based planning"), an organization accepts that it cannot predict the relevant aspects of its future in a way that makes traditional strategic planning possible. Scenarios therefore crystallize and preserve a diversity of opinion among management team members.

Is this useful? Is not a shared vision of the future critically important to organizational success? How can a management team guide an organization's destiny if the members cannot agree on some basic assumptions about the competitive environment the company will face, and thereby determine what to do? Disagreements at the top will surely paralyze an organization.

Apparently not. A seminal 1985 study questioned the value of "top management team" (TMT) consensus and found that the level of disagreement among TMT members about key environmental variables and strategic goals is *positively* related to firm performance. This relationship held regardless of the "true" uncertainty, as approximated by the historical volatility of performance measures such as profitability and revenue.[6] Therefore, tools that allow the top team to recognize and preserve their disagreements about what the future will hold should actually improve results.

However, this may be true only at the most senior levels of an organization. More recent work has replicated the diversity/performance relationship when dealing with top management, but the lower down one goes in the hierarchy, or the more one addresses operational issues, the more consensus and agreement are associated with superior results.[7]

The value of consensus within a management team (referred to in the academic research as the "locus of consensus") seems to be driven by the need for coordinated action. The more a management team must coordinate its activities in order to achieve a specific goal, the more general agreement on the goal and how to achieve it is valuable. Operating division and functional management are faced with the challenge of making commitments to particular strategies or finding ways to achieve their designated objectives. Consequently, these levels of the hierarchy are well-served by high levels of strategic consensus because that is the best way to avoid incoherence or anarchy.

In contrast, Requisite Uncertainty (Chapter 6) implies that coordinated group action aimed at the attainment of specific goals is not something that is required of the senior management team. The corporate level should not be developing specific commitments, that is, strategy. Rather, its objective is to build a portfolio of real options—assets that provide the raw material for pursuing alternative strategies under different circumstances. In other words, the goal is to develop a set of investments that reflects *disagreement* about what the future holds.[8]

A set of scenarios consists of a number of individual stories, each carefully crafted and contextually complete, each based on a very different set of assumptions. For example, in the Johnson & Johnson case in the previous chapter, the scenarios were not variations on an underlying theme; they were radically different alternatives of how the most important factors affecting the health care industry might turn out. Formalizing these different views and making them the cornerstones of strategic planning makes it impossible to build consensus on a single set of internally consistent strategic initiatives. Instead, as intended, it provides a fundamentally different way of determining the portfolio of strategic initiatives required to create Strategic Flexibility.

A technique often conflated with scenario-based planning, contingency planning, is really very different and has a fundamentally different purpose. Functional management's responsibility is to implement a given strategy. Since the strategy cannot change (within the relevant time period), there is no point reflecting on whether a different strategy would be better. Critical strategic uncertainties might resolve themselves in ways that reveal the strategy is wrong, but for functional managers the task is to make the best of a bad situation. Under such circumstances, it makes sense only to question critical individual assumptions: will consumer demand materialize as expected? will competitors respond quickly or aggressively or not at all? will suppliers come through as expected? and so on. Each of these variations on an underlying strategic plan is not an alternative scenario, at least not as the term is being used here. Rather, this kind of planning helps put in place particular responses that preserve, insofar as possible, the viability of the larger strategic plan.

Contingency planning is less useful at the corporate level because it does not foster disagreement over strategy since it does not raise fundamentally strategic questions. Just because the strategy cannot be changed, however, does not mean that every supposition made regarding how best to *implement* that strategy will be correct. Contingency planning is therefore far more appropriate for functional managers because it allows them to consider those variables to which the organization can actually respond: launch the marketing campaign now or next quarter; implement a price change or not; expand hiring or implement layoffs; and so on.[9] Thinking through under what conditions functional managers will pull which levers is very valuable and a critical part of successful implementation. But tinkering with specific variables within a consistent set of underlying assumptions does not even come close to capturing the strategic uncertainty any organization faces over the long term. Scenario-based planning, on the other hand, avoids a single common set of assumptions and forces a management team to accept that it fundamentally has no idea what the future will bring and what sort of strategy is most appropriate.[10]

9.1.2 How Do You Create Scenarios?

Within the context of Requisite Uncertainty, the following five-step process has proved useful in building scenarios that a top management team can use as a foundation for building Strategic Flexibility. To illustrate the process, consider how Alliant Energy Corporation, a Wisconsin-based public utility holding company, addressed a key strategic question raised as a result of new opportunities in the electricity-generating market.[11]

1. Ask the Right Question Assessing strategic uncertainty does not mean examining one decision. Questions should not be framed in terms such as "Should we build a plant in China?" or "Does this acquisition make sense?" These are issues best dealt with using contingency planning, because they are only part of a particular strategy that an organization is seeking to implement effectively. Grappling with strategic uncertainty raises much more fundamental issues, such as: What are the underlying business models that will make sense? What will the balance of power be between the different stakeholders? How might this affect the viability of different ways of creating and capturing value?

Determining whether the uncertainties surrounding a given issue are self-contained or elements of strategic questions requiring a broader response by top management and the board is critical. The challenge is to assess the extent to which the relevant uncertainties can be addressed within the context of the existing strategy, or whether they signal potential challenges or opportunities that require fundamentally different strategic responses.

In Alliant Energy's case, the answer was relatively clear. The critical issue was whether or not to enter the merchant generation market, which was clearly a departure from the company's historical strategy as a largely regulated electricity services provider.

The market for merchant (i.e., non-rate-of-return regulated) electrical generating capacity experienced a strong boom in the late 1990s, and companies such as AES, NRG, Calpine, Mirant, Reliant Resources, and Enron enjoyed significant stock price runups in part as a result of their participation in this space. After a peak in the first quarter of 2001, a rapid collapse followed and many of these same companies suffered market capitalization reductions of greater than 50 percent from June 2001 to June 2002. This poor stock performance resulted in a credit crunch within the industry, limiting stock issues and tightening debt requirements. As a result, merchant generation companies had significant cash requirements, often resulting in forced asset sales.

Alliant Energy, which had fared better than many of its unregulated brethren, now had an opportunity to enter the more volatile unregulated generation business thanks to the availability of assets at seemingly attractive prices. This question could have been framed in terms of "Should we buy this or that plant?" Contingency analysis could then have been used to test the viability of a given asset at a given price. But with so many different investment opportunities to choose from, the analytical challenge would have been simply too much to handle. Which regions would have the greatest demand for electricity? How much capacity should be acquired? What kinds of technology made sense—for example, coal vs. natural gas? How might regulatory frameworks change? What might other competitors do? What kind of deal structure would make sense? A practically endless series of contingency analyses examining all the different combinations and permutations of possible asset acquisitions against the full range of possible outcomes associated with each relevant variable, even if calculable, would have been incomprehensible to merely human managers. Alliant Energy's top management recognized that they faced strategic uncertainty, something for which tools designed for tactical challenges were simply inadequate.

So Alliant Energy chose to ask a far more general, and consequently conceptually demanding but ultimately more practical, question: was this its chance to create valuable exposure to a new and compelling strategic opportunity? By looking at the issue through this lens, the question then-CEO Erroll Davis and his team were asking was no longer "Should we buy plant X for $Y?" but "Should we broaden our company's strategic scope and become in part a merchant generator?"

Defining the question often brings clarity to a related issue: what time horizon should a set of scenarios take into account? Standard prescriptions include rules of thumb such as "double the horizon of your longest-term strategic plan." Certainly, scenarios designed to capture strategic uncertainty will go beyond the horizon of traditional strategic plans, which tend to be premised on commitments, but there is no good reason to think that "double" is always the right number. Such advice is typically a heuristic designed to jump-start a conversation rather than a theoretically grounded principle.

Unfortunately, the best advice I can offer is decidedly circular. Since scenarios are intended to capture strategic uncertainty, the time horizon considered should be far enough out to capture strategic uncertainty. In some industries, this might be no more than five years; in others, it might be thirty years. In Alliant Energy's case, a ten-year horizon seemed sufficient to capture the uncertainties relevant to the investments under consideration.

2. Identify the Dimensions of Uncertainty With a strategic question and a time horizon in mind, the next step is to identify the dimensions of uncertainty that define the relevant possibility space. Often, this is done "bottom up," by clustering individual variables into dimensions. It can also be done "top down," decomposing overall strategic uncertainty into specific dimensions. In either case, a helpful heuristic is to ask what factors make it difficult to commit with certainty to a specific course of action. In other words, whatever it is you wish you knew is likely defining at least part of a relevant dimension of uncertainty. This last observation captures a critical point: a dimension of uncertainty will tend to be beyond your control. For example, whether or not a company enters a new market next year is not truly uncertain, at least to it, because that is something it decides.

Dimensions of uncertainty that crop up repeatedly in scenario-building exercises designed to capture strategic uncertainty are the macroeconomy, technology, and regulation.[12] Each of these is often the most tangible expression of a host of other uncertainties that are far more specific to individual organizations. In Johnson & Johnson's case, for example, regulation and the macroeconomy were captured in questions regarding international trade and the structure of the health care market in the United States. Each of these involved elements of political economy, and each was chosen because of its importance in shaping the particular strategic uncertainties J&J faced.

The number of dimensions of uncertainty to use is a judgment call, and considerations of practicality should inform that judgment. In a world with only one dimension of uncertainty, there is only a single axis. The end points of that axis constitute the range of uncertainties the organization must confront, and only two scenarios are required.[13] Each additional dimension of uncertainty—each additional axis—exponentially increases the number of scenarios needed to bound that possibility space (at least in theory; more on this below) according to the formula:

$$\text{Number of scenarios} = 2^{\text{Number of dimensions of uncertainty}}$$

. . . and so two dimensions demands four scenarios, while three dimensions demands eight and four requires sixteen scenarios to identify all the corners of possibility space.

The Alliant Energy team determined that there were five dimensions of uncertainty, each chosen for its significant impact on either the demand or supply of electricity. This implied 32 scenarios. Strategic Flexibility requires building complete strategies for the conditions described by each scenario, so this is not a practical number of scenarios to work with. But before examining how to collapse 32 scenarios into something more manageable, the next step is to determine the limits of uncertainty along each dimension.

3. Determine the Limits of Uncertainty Perhaps the most intellectually challenging element of scenario building is finding the appropriate boundary conditions on each individual dimension of uncertainty. How far might technology advance? How radically different could the sociopolitical landscape be? How robust or depressed might the overall level of economic activity be? Transcending preconceived notions and built-in limits that stunt the ability to imagine alternative futures—without descending into wild-eyed hand waving—is a delicate balancing act.

It is critical at this stage not to look for "consensus" forecasts; seek

FIGURE 9-1 **ALLIANT ENERGY'S DIMENSIONS OF UNCERTAINTY**

Dimension	Constituent Variables
Economy	GDP growth, amount of capital available to fund growth and investor perceptions, level of consumer spending, workforce demographic shifts that could influence consumer spending, and the level of political stability that could affect consumer and/or government spending.
Environment	Quality of air, water, weather intensity, public health, food supply, etc. Also includes policies to regulate environment, such as greenhouse gases, SOx, NOx, and other pollutants, etc.
Technology	Advances in energy and other sectors. This driver will be influenced by the level of research and development spending and incentives to develop new technologies. Includes consideration of demand-side, supply-side, and delivery technologies.
Policy	State/federal regulatory policies that influence level of competition, M&A policy, transmission policy, etc.
Public/ Customer Outlook	The public's attitude toward the environment, free markets, regulation, level of competition, acceptance of new technologies, and the economy, demographics, values, and risk tolerances of key constituencies.

Source: Alliant Energy; author's analysis; data disguised.

instead divergent opinions. Any given question will almost certainly have a conventional wisdom to appeal to, but the conventional wisdom is all but useless at this stage of scenario building. One must scan the environment for credible but outlying opinions with respect to what could happen over the time horizon of relevance and apply one's own judgment in determining which are credible. Once again, this is an art, not a science, and the only way to develop the appropriate intuition is to review previous work and get a feel for what useful scenarios look like.

As an example of how this can be done, consider the question of the global economy.[14] Many organizations are highly dependent on global trade either for critical inputs or for key markets. Many executives, government officials, and other decision makers around the world are building strategies based on the assumption that the trend toward globalization is irreversible. This conviction took hold during the 1990s when international integration accelerated dramatically. For example, in his 1999 bestseller *The Lexus and the Olive Tree, New York Times* columnist Thomas Friedman described globalization as "inexorable," likening globalization to the sunrise with the observation that "even if I didn't much care for the dawn, there isn't much I could do about it."[15]

On the other hand, it is possible that what lies ahead will be reminiscent of the early decades of the twentieth century, when business activities were constrained by protectionist walls and international conflict. Such views are increasingly credible given the problems plaguing global trade talks and geopolitical frictions with China. If the future brings still more international discord and disorder, the commercial impact could be enormous, raising the risks associated with popular corporate strategies ranging from cross-border buying and selling to acquisitions of foreign companies. International ventures would still be possible, and for some companies the new conditions would be advantageous, but it would be essential to observe new fault lines in the geopolitical landscape.

For each dimension of uncertainty, one must attend to many conflicting voices when considering the range of possible future states. The objective is to go beyond the general consensus but stop short of the merely imaginable. Somewhere between "entirely feasible" and "ludicrous" lies each organization's possibility space. Using this approach, Alliant Energy defined the limits of uncertainty along each dimension.

4. Determine the Final Scenario Set With five dimensions of uncertainty and two boundary conditions associated with each, Alliant Energy had a possibility space with 32 corner solutions ($2^5 = 32$). Developing optimal strategies for each and determining the core and contingent elements would be a monumental task. Thirty-two, or 16, or even 8 scenarios are generally too many. Luckily, the process of reducing this complexity to something more useful need not be arbitrary.

A scenario lies at the intersection of the extreme values of the dimensions of uncertainty. It is possible to identify all such intersections using a "truth table."[16] Such a table allowed the Alliant Energy team to look at each of the 32 scenarios and test it for internal consistency and overall plausibility. For example, in a governmental policy regime at the "Libertarian" extreme, it is highly unlikely that public opinion would have a pro-regulation bias, at least for any meaningful period of time; in the long run, the expectation is that U.S. government policy will reflect the overriding public appetite for a particular regulatory or legislative structure. Consequently, a scenario that posited those two conditions was internally inconsistent, and so not worth including in further analysis. In an exhaustive listing of all 32 scenarios, 8 included this combination, and so this single inconsistency between end points on two axes reduced the number of scenarios to be considered to 24.

OPPOSING VIEWS

How will global commerce evolve? You might think one way to find out is to confer with experts, but as any trial lawyer will tell you, there is a good-faith, *bone fide* expert supporting just about every point of view.

The Global Marketplace at Last	Trading Blocs and Balkanization
For the first time in history, every region of the world—and almost every nation—is tied into the same economy. —Peter Schwartz, Peter Leyden, and Joel Hyatt, futurists, in *The Long Boom* (1999)	*Despite the huge benefits of free trade and other aspects of the global economy, an open and integrated global economy is neither as extensive and inexorable nor as irreversible as many assume.* —Robert Gilpin, professor, Princeton University, in *The Challenge of Global Capitalism: The World Economy in the 21st Century* (2002)
Globalization has become, quite simply, the most important economic, political, and cultural phenomenon of our time. —John Micklethwait and Adrian Wooldridge, in *A Future Perfect: The Challenge and Hidden Promise of Globalization* (2000)	*As the new millennium dawns, the same seeds of global disorder, even anarchy, that grew into the years 1914–45 are being sown. Racialism and ethnic nationalism are already on the rampage on a small scale. Bigger powers show signs of going their own way. America is disengaging from Europe and vice versa, Germany and Japan are becoming more politically assertive, and China is rearming.* —Robert Harvey, *Global Disorder: America and the Threat of World Conflict* (2003)
The public sectors of most nations will drastically shrink . . . governments will see their role to be clearing the way for entrepreneurs to organize human resources, technology, and capital to create wealth for everyone. —Knight Kiplinger, *World Boom Ahead: Why Business and Consumers Will Prosper* (1998)	*A major war involving the West and the core states of other civilizations is not inevitable, but it could happen. . . . In the coming era, the avoidance of major intercivilizational wars requires core states to refrain from intervening in conflicts in other civilizations. This is a truth which some states, particularly the United States, will undoubtedly find difficult to accept.* —Samuel Huntington, *The Clash of Civilizations and the Remaking of the World Order* (1996)

FIGURE 9-2 **THE LIMITS OF UNCERTAINTY FOR ALLIANT ENERGY**

Dimension	Lower Bound	Upper Bound
Economy	*Stagnate* • 0% GDP growth for a decade • Japan-style deflation	*Robust Growth* • 5% GDP growth for a decade • Back to the 1990s
Environment	*Catastrophic* • Accelerated deterioration • Onerous regulation	*Benign* • Current pace of degradation • Policy "creep"
Technology	*Incremental* • Gradual advances • Limited disruption	*Radical* • Rapid advances • Some disruption
Policy	*Marxist* • Highly directive • Costly to comply	*Libertarian* • Regulatory roll-backs • Increasingly free markets
Public/ Customer Outlook	*Suspicious* • Pervasive pessimism • Antibusiness	*Trusting* • Confident in capitalism • Pro-market

Source: Alliant Energy; author's analysis; data disguised.

A similar process, detailed in Appendix B, along with summaries of the final scenarios used, allowed the team to eliminate all but six of the original 32. In addition, two scenarios—"Familiar Giants" and "Familiar Giants Part 2"—were differentiated only by the degree of economic activity. Although the economy is an important dimension of uncertainty, it is not necessarily definitive in every scenario. With every other determinant of underlying industry structure essentially unchanged, these two scenarios were collapsed into one, "Familiar Giants." The impact of economic uncertainties was captured in the context of other scenarios included in the final set.

5. Determine the Relative Probabilities Assessing the probability that the future an organization ultimately faces will most closely resemble a particular scenario is perhaps one of the most contentious issues in the scenario-based planning field. Ultimately, the purpose of building scenarios is to guide investments in real options on alternative strategies, and the value of those options is tied directly to the likelihood of a given option being exercised. Consequently, probabilities must be assigned to each scenario.

The scenario-building exercise will have failed if one or two scenarios dominate the management team's expectations for the future. Recall: scenarios serve to crystallize and preserve disagreement about the future. If a consensus emerges around one possible future when at first none existed, management will not have mitigated but instead exacerbated the problems associated with unjustified confidence about what lies ahead.

That is not to say that individual management team members might not have strong beliefs about which scenario most accurately captures their individual expectations for the future. It is only as a group that no one scenario should dominate. To sort out these differences, once the scenarios have been created it is helpful to have the team members vote, stating their beliefs about the probabilities associated with each scenario by secret ballot to avoid influencing each other's assessments. It is not uncommon for a team member to assign a probability of over 70 percent to one scenario in a set of four or five, implying a very strong belief that the future is going to turn out in a particular way. Collectively, however, the average probability for all team members tends to come out much closer to a uniform distribution, suggesting that the group has no shared view on what the future will bring.

Under these circumstances, the scenarios have done their job: every team member accepts that each scenario is plausible but has a strong belief about what the future will hold. This implies that everyone is considering the "tails" of their own probability distribution, but that the team as a whole is profoundly uncertain about the future.

9.2 STRATEGIES: DON'T COMMIT, FORMULATE

Requisite Uncertainty differentiates the levels of the hierarchy in terms of their relative emphasis on managing uncertainty and delivering on commitments. The different strategic balance at each level has important implications for each level's strategic objectives. To recapitulate and extend the argument made so far, it falls to the corporate level to create strategic flexibility by assembling a portfolio of real options on assets and capabilities that allows the operating divisions to change their strategies in ways they could not if left to their own devices. Individual operating divisions are left to implement a specific strategy but must still face up to material uncertainties that could derail their plans. They must therefore focus on *hedging* the strategy they have through careful contingency planning and, where possible, avoiding unacceptable risks. Finally, functional managers are responsible for *learning* how best to achieve the targets that have been set for them within the parameters set for them. Nevertheless, these different objectives imply material differences in how strategic planning influences decision making at each level.

FIGURE 9-3 **HIERARCHY, UNCERTAINTY, AND STRATEGIC OBJECTIVES**

Organizational Level	Strategic Balance	Strategic Question	Strategic Objective
Board	*Uncertainty*	What could threaten our survival?	Flexibility
Corporate		What could undermine our strategy?	Hedging
Business Unit			
Function	*Commitment*	What could derail our project?	Learning

Source: Author's analysis.

9.2.1 Board and Corporate: Build Flexibility

The Formulate phase of Strategic Flexibility requires the identification of the best, or optimal, strategy for each scenario. There is, of course, a well-developed toolkit for precisely this task, and a management team should use the strategic planning techniques that it finds most useful.

This analytical task is more challenging than traditional strategic planning because the management team must grapple with building strategies for multiple futures, and so must create several strategies—one for each scenario—rather than just one. At the same time, a different challenge is reduced, because no longer does strategic planning have to rest on a consensus regarding assumptions about future industry structure. Rather, the task is simply to determine the best response to the structure associated with a particular scenario.[17]

For example, when developing strategy, a critical element is the bargaining power of suppliers. Conventional strategic planning can tell you how to deal with suppliers with stronger or weaker bargaining positions, but it cannot tell you what the bargaining power of suppliers will be in the future. Often, much of the effort associated with building a strategy is tied to coming to some sort of actionable—but right only if you are lucky—assumption about what that bargaining power will be.[18] Working from a collectively agreed-upon set of scenarios obviates prediction, allowing the management team to proceed with the more straightforward, if by no means easy, task of determining how best to respond.

The level of detail required to determine the nature of these best responses will depend on what is needed to inform relevant action. In the Johnson & Johnson example, the appropriate responses were mapped out at the highest level, since the underlying decision was fairly high level: which scientific challenges should J&J tackle in the field of stroke (treatment, diagnosis, prevention; drugs, devices, biologics, consumer products, etc.). In Alliant Energy's case, the decision was whether and how to enter the merchant generation business. This required a far more detailed examination of the economic attractiveness of different generating capacities (measured in megawatts), generation technologies (roughly, different types of gas- or coal-fired generation plants), and plant locations in different parts of the United States.

Through a painstaking and laborious process, the team translated the parameters of each scenario into the inputs of an econometric model that captured, among other variables, the cost per megawatt of generation for each plant type, the demand for electricity by region, and the cost of carbon abatement. In addition, Alliant Energy's ability to invest in merchant capacity varied by scenario, for each scenario had different implications for the capital needs of the company's core regulated generation business. With the investment opportunities and Alliant Energy's investment constraints in place, it was possible to determine the optimal investment strategy for each scenario.

Additional analysis of these data revealed which combinations of capacity, generation technology, and region were "core"—that is, profitable, if to varying degrees—under all scenarios and those that were "contingent," or profitable only under some scenarios. For example, every generation technology was profitable—albeit in varying capacities—in one particular region under all scenarios, making such investments "no-regrets bets." Conversely, other combinations were profitable only under a particular scenario, making an option on that type of capacity in that region a better course of action. Such an option could be created through a joint venture or cogeneration agreement that would provide exposure to the opportunity while mitigating the risk. And finally, some regions yielded no attractive investment opportunities under any scenarios. Overall, what emerged was a way to think through the value of exposures to different capacities, generation technologies, and regions in a way that weighed the merits of each opportunity against its associated risk.

A critical feedback loop in this kind of economic modeling is assessing the profitability of investments with different deal structures but similar capacities and generation technologies. Specifically, committing today to any given large-scale project would result in lower generation costs than investing in a smaller project that could be expanded should future conditions warrant.

The profitability of an investment strategy can only be assessed accurately in light of the structure of the investments being contemplated.

We can generalize from this case to see how strategic planning plays out at the corporate level. Scenarios define different future competitive contexts, each one serving as the foundation for developing a distinct strategy. That strategy can then be decomposed into its constituent elements, where each element is a particular resource or capability. Those elements required across all scenarios are considered core, while those that are valuable only under one scenario are considered contingent. (This distinction is rarely binary, however, as most elements will have varying degrees of value across some subset of scenarios including more than one but fewer than all scenarios in the full set.) By committing to the core elements and taking options on the contingent ones, the corporate office can create the ability to implement the most appropriate strategy regardless of which anticipated future ultimately materializes.

Examples in business books are supposed to end with a flourish, recounting how management then made brilliant investment decisions that resulted in fantastic wealth creation. Alas, not this one. Instead, what this analysis revealed was that the kinds of investments Alliant Energy would need to make in order to achieve the risk/return profile acceptable to its board required more capital than the company was willing to commit to this opportunity. Despite the fact that there were any number of individual merchant generating investment opportunities that Alliant Energy could have signed up for, an analysis of the strategic uncertainty surrounding all of them revealed that none were advisable at that time.

Such an outcome is perfectly acceptable. Alliant Energy's inaction was motivated not by a timid avoidance of the unknown but by an informed assessment of what rewards were available at what levels of risk.

J&J's stroke strategy turned out differently. The company did not walk away from stroke research despite the risk. Instead, J&J was able to create a suite of core elements tied to specific types of stroke treatment and prevention. More aggressive treatments or broader-based prevention and diagnostic initiatives constituted a portfolio of real options on contingent elements, the ultimate value of which depends on the future structure of the health care industry. And Microsoft's corporate strategy appears to be based on core commitments to the personal computer operating system and an array of complementary contingent assets in mobile phones, consumer electronics, telecommunications, and entertainment.

In each of these two cases, the corporate office invested in ways that create options that collectively bequeath the operating units what they cannot create on their own: Strategic Flexibility.

9.2.2 Operating Division: Hedge the Downside

Managing strategic uncertainty demands that top management and the board structure their investments in ways that provide promising upside at acceptable risk. Recall, however, that as time horizons shorten, the latitude for strategic change is constrained. At the limit, managers dealing exclusively with questions of execution have essentially no strategic choices to make, and instead must focus their efforts on delivering on commitments. They might structure their actions in ways that allow them to learn how best to implement a given strategy, but changing the strategy they are charged with is typically not a possibility.

As suggested in Chapter 6, managers responsible for intermediate time horizons have a singularly difficult task. Understanding which corporate-level strategic options to create is of course difficult, but it is at least conceptually clean; the same can be said of the in-the-trenches functional managers who work at the other end of the uncertainty/commitment continuum. Managers working in the middle—typically leaders of operating divisions—still face material strategic uncertainty but lack the ability to respond strategically due to the inevitable mismatch between the pace of change in the environment and the adaptability of their unit. They can neither build flexible strategies nor put their heads down, roll up their sleeves, and get on with it. They must commit to a specific strategy yet find ways to hedge the downside.

The consumer division (Consumer) of SBC (now AT&T), the San Antonio, Texas–based telecommunications giant, faced just this challenge in the early 2000s as it squared off against the cable companies over voice, high-speed data, and video services. SBC's strategy, like the strategy of every capital-intensive industry, is necessarily slow to change: new network infrastructure can be deployed only so quickly, and it is network infrastructure more than anything else that defines where a telecommunications firm sits on its industry's production possibility frontier.

An optimal strategy that would definitively beat back the cable threat was readily identifiable but utterly unimplementable. SBC, like pretty much every other telecommunications service provider, had significant copper wire plant, especially along the "last mile"—really the last couple of hundred yards from the trunk lines into consumers' homes. Although in many cases these lines are largely a depreciated asset, it actually costs a great deal to keep this infrastructure working properly. However, replacing this with higher-capacity, lower-operating-cost fiber-optic cable is very expensive and time-consuming: trenching tens of thousands of miles of fiber in residential streets requires tens of billions of dollars and years of effort.

In contrast, cable companies, due largely to an accident of history, had higher-bandwidth, cheaper-to-operate infrastructure that lent itself quite easily to high-speed data, video, and voice. Consequently, cable companies enjoyed a structural advantage in the profitable provision of these services. In other words, they occupied a more attractive position on the communications industry's production profitability frontier. Due to the constraints of their infrastructure, phone companies were essentially unable to reach a similar or better position over a three- to five-year horizon. From the perspective of 2002, Consumer had to play the hand it was dealt. Within their planning horizon of five years, they were unable to change materially SBC's strategy. They had to execute the existing strategy as best they could. Nevertheless, significant uncertainties remained surrounding precisely how to achieve the best possible outcome and avoid material downside risk.

Operating division leadership faces a particularly difficult challenge, living in the middle ground between the management of uncertainty and delivering on commitments. The uncertainties these managers face are clearly strategic in nature, but the responses tend to be much more tactical. As a result, the toolkit is a mixture of strategic and operational approaches. To capture the strategic nature of the uncertainties they face, scenarios are invaluable, just as they are at the board and corporate levels. However, when it comes to responding to those uncertainties, an operating division does not have recourse to create options on alternative strategies, and instead must behave in a manner similar to line managers.

Consumer's management team began with a set of four scenarios that captured the relevant strategic uncertainties over a five-year horizon. Unlike Alliant Energy or Johnson & Johnson, Consumer did not have the luxury of considering the optimal strategy under each set of conditions. Rather, it had to model the most appropriate implementation of the strategy already in place. What combinations of price, rollout of new services, marketing agreements, cost cutting, and so on would best serve SBC's interests under each set of market conditions?

What this modeling exercise revealed was that under some conditions Consumer fared quite well, while different but equally plausible circumstances were nearly catastrophic. Had Consumer been able to pull strategic levers in response—for example, deploying new infrastructure, developing new capabilities, acquiring and integrating fundamentally new assets—it could have created acceptable outcomes no matter the conditions.[19] But because Consumer was an operating division working within an existing strategy, the range of possible responses was constrained.

An analysis of the economic impact of implementing its underlying strategy in different ways revealed that although two scenarios demanded quite different responses, they yielded nearly identical economic results. A third scenario, while not as attractive, was still much to be preferred over the fourth scenario in Consumer's set. This made it clear how Consumer should attempt to shape its future, where possible. For example, the choices Consumer made were likely to influence heavily its cable company rivals, and understanding the move/countermove dynamic might allow it to at least avoid the least attractive outcomes. The right pricing, service bundle, and distribution channel decisions would make it in cable's best interest to steer clear of a scenario that was especially debilitating for Consumer.

Consumer's top management decisions defined the objectives of functional managers working still closer to customers. For example, once Consumer's leaders had chosen pricing and other critical parameters in ways that steered the competitive battles away from particularly damaging scenarios, it then fell to those lower down in the hierarchy, working with still shorter time horizons, to make the best choices from the alternatives available to them within those parameters.

While that battle has been playing out over the last five years, the corporate level of what is now AT&T has not been idle. It has created new assets and capabilities that Consumer and the company's other operating divisions require to change their strategies in accordance with the demands of the competitive landscape that has emerged. For example, initiatives such as Project Light Speed have deployed significant fiber infrastructure, shifting AT&T's position on the industry's production possibility frontier. The acquisition of AT&T (which triggered the rebranding of SBC) created a much stronger enterprise operating division, while the acquisition of BellSouth provided additional scale in voice services and allowed much tighter wireline/wireless integration (in much the same manner as has been pursued by BCE; see Chapter 7).

Consumer's effective management of its strategic risk/return profile between 2002 and 2007 was critical to AT&T's ability to deliver on its commitments—commitments to a specific strategy that had been made, both deliberately and *de facto,* up to a decade, or more, prior. Hedging the risks attendant to that strategy was critical in allowing the corporate office to put in place the components needed to change not only Consumer's strategy but the other operating companies' strategies as well, in ways they otherwise could not.

9.2.3 Functional Management: Learning

Once the current strategy's risk has been hedged, there is, of course, still uncertainty to be managed, but not *strategic* uncertainty.[20] At this point, the questions are almost exclusively operational. What kind of advertising is the most effective, which distribution channels are working, and so on. In other words, Requisite Uncertainty prescribes that functional managers focus on learning how to make a strategy work, rather than hedging the downside of the strategy (the divisional leadership's job) or creating *bone fide* strategic options (the corporate office's job).

Take, for example, the implications of Bell Canada's convergence strategy on marketing and customer care. Recall from Chapter 7 that Bell, a division of BCE Inc., is the dominant local and long-distance telecommunications services provider in Canada. At the corporate level, BCE created an option on wireline/wireless integration with its partial equity stake in BCE Mobile in 1986, which was then exercised when BCE acquired full control, making Bell Mobility a division of Bell Canada, in 1999. Wireline/wireless integration had become a strategic commitment on which the operating division (Bell Canada) had to deliver. Implementing that strategy required an integrated customer service management capability. The strategic question relevant to functional management within Bell was therefore how best to develop that capability.

To answer this question, in 2001 Bell launched OneContact to deploy customized Siebel customer relationship management (CRM) software to specially trained customer service representatives (CSRs). This meant that inquiries relating to a variety of services could be addressed through a single customer service infrastructure. It would be foolish to roll out such an initiative all at once, thanks to the inevitable glitches attendant to integrating the two companies' customer databases. In addition, it was not clear what degree of operating flexibility an integrated customer service infrastructure would require: how frequently and how radically would product bundle or pricing options change? How quickly would they have to change? And so on.

To answer these questions, Bell began with a pilot project for C$10 million in order to demonstrate that Bell could "light up the screens" with a customized, cross-divisional CRM system that combined customer information from the two operating units. Rolled out to a carefully targeted group of 100,000 customers, the new capability was designed to provide valuable learning opportunities so that functional management could make subsequent rollout decisions based on more complete information. In fact, to the extent that organizations can be adaptable, it is at the functional level of the hierarchy that adaptability is most powerful and useful. When grappling with functional issues such as marketing, production schedules, and so on, it is likely that the pace of environmental change will most closely mirror the pace at which the organization can change.

This prudent and commonsense approach is not unique to Bell by any means. In the context of this discussion, however, it provides an archetype of how functional management's decisions have a fundamentally different strategic objective from that of operating divisions or the corporate office. Those managing Bell's CRM capabilities were learning how best to execute a strategy. That strategy—wireline/wireless integration—was chosen by Bell's senior leadership, a choice they could make only because BCE's corporate management had created the option. Different levels, different strategic balance, different approach to strategic planning, different relationship between strategy and action.

Scenarios capture the range of plausible future conditions within which an organization might have to operate. At the corporate level, the challenge is to build an optimal strategy for each of these possible outcomes and to analyze these strategies to determine the core and contingent elements. This creates the strategic foundation and strategic options necessary for operating divisions to have true Strategic Flexibility. Operating divisions should necessarily focus on choosing and implementing a particular strategy, one they created out of the core and contingent elements put in place by the corporate office. However, due to the uncertainties that impinge over an intermediate time horizon, business unit management must seek to hedge downside risk, accepting that their ability to substantively change strategy is severely limited. Finally, functional managers have no strategic latitude but can seek to learn how to deliver on the commitments already in place as efficiently and effectively as possible.

---

1. Drucker's comment was "Plans are only good intentions unless they immediately degenerate into hard work."

2. The works I have found most useful in understanding both the history and the state of the art in this field are:

Courtney, Hugh (2001), *20/20 Foresight: Crafting Strategy in an Uncertain World*, Boston: Harvard Business School Press.

Porter, Michael E. (1985), *op. cit.*

Ringland, Gill (1998), *Scenario Planning: Managing for the Future*, West Sussex: John Wiley & Sons.

Schoemaker, Paul J. H., with Robert E. Gunther (2002), *Profiting from Uncertainty: Strategies for Succeeding No Matter What the Future Brings*, New York: The Free Press.

Schwartz, Peter (1991), *The Art of the Long View: Planning for the Future in an Uncertain World*, New York: Doubleday.

Van der Heijden, Kees (1996), *Scenarios: The Art of Strategic Conversation*, West Sussex: John Wiley & Sons.

Of the books on this list, Courtney's and Schoemaker's bear the greatest similarities to the frameworks and concepts discussed here, in particular in their connection of scenarios with real options. Where I have borrowed from the ideas these authors have developed, additional endnotes explain how I hope to have extended their thinking. Other similarities are coincidental, as we have all been working in this field for some time, unfortunately often independently of each other.

3. See http://www.bain.com/management_tools/about_overview.asp?groupCode=1 (accessed March 12, 2006) for survey details.

4. There are a variety of nomenclatures and taxonomies used in the scenario-based planning literature. "Drivers," "dimensions," "themes," and many other terms are all used to capture different shades of meaning. Each framework is typically internally consistent, and I've not identified a compelling reason to prefer one to another. My advice is to use what works for you and not to be concerned about seeming discrepancies in labels or process. So long as you know what you want to use the scenarios for, any of the respected methods available will be up to the task of creating them.

5. See Fallows, James (2005), "Countdown to a Meltdown," *The Atlantic Monthly,* (July–August), for a particularly compelling scenario of 2016 in the form of a briefing memo to a newly elected president of the United States. Fallows, however, presents his scenario as a prediction predicated upon an extrapolation of current trends. Whatever his intent, it is a compelling scenario.

6. Bourgeois III, L. J. (1985), "Strategic Goals, Perceived Uncertainty, and Economic Performance in Volatile Environments," *Academy of Management Journal* (September).

7. Studies finding that consensus is positively related to performance include Homburg, C., H. Krohmer, and J. P. Workman, Jr. (1999), "Strategic Consensus and Performance: The Role of Strategy Type and Market-Related Dynamism," *Strategic Management Journal,* Vol. 20; and Dooley, R. S., F. E. Fryxell, and W. Q. Judge (2000), "Belaboring the Not-So-Obvious: Consensus, Commitment, and Strategy Implementation Speed and Success," *Journal of Management,* Vol. 26, Iss. 6. The case of discord was echoed in Enz, C. A. B., and C. R. B. Schwenk (1991), "The Performance Edge: Strategic Value Dissensus," *Employee Responsibilities and Rights Journal,* Vol. 4, Iss. 1. The contingent relationship between discord and performance was made in Kellermanns, F. W., J. Walter, C. Lechner, and S. W. Floyd (2005), "The Lack of Consensus About Strategic Consensus: Advancing Theory and Research," *Journal of Management* (October).

8. In keeping with the aphorism attributed to Cyrus the Great ("diversity in counsel, unity in command"), some argue that when options are being considered a great deal of disagreement is useful because it allows the team to consider all the possibilities. However, when a course of action is selected, consensus is highly valuable because it allows coordinated action.

In the same way that "horizon" thinking is helpful but shoehorns too much complexity into each level of hierarchy, this approach posits both the creation of options and the implementation of commitments at each level of decision making. Requisite Uncertainty admits of different levels of diversity and unity of opinion, but allocates these to different loci in the hierarchy depending on the strategic uncertainty faced—not the phase of "the decision," since the decisions being made at each locus are so different.

9. An example of the most relevant variables at different levels of analysis can be found in Schoemaker, Paul J. H. (1991), "When and How to Use Scenario Planning: A Heuristic Approach with an Illustration," *Journal of Forecasting,* Vol. 10, Iss. 6. Schoemaker identifies "macro-scenarios" that capture economic, political, social, and technological variables; "industry scenarios" that take in supplier, customers, competitors, and

substitutes; and "firm scenarios" that turn on issues of costs, demand, and prices, all funneling down to specific decisions.

Long time horizons, and the strategic uncertainty thereby engendered, might well require scenarios to incorporate variables from what are for Schoemaker different levels of analysis (e.g., the long-term emergence of new substitutes—an industry-level question—which might well hinge on how certain technologies evolve—a macro-scenario variable). I would therefore propose a slightly different take, one that relates scenario-based planning to the nature of the uncertainty being addressed. When the uncertainty is strategic in nature, scenarios are appropriate. As time horizons shorten, the latitude for strategic response shrinks and so the relevant uncertainties become more operational in nature. Under such circumstances, something closer to contingency planning is more useful—that is, the development of responses to specific possible future events. As with scenarios, however, the relevant variables could well cut across Schoemaker's levels of analysis; for example, some contingencies might have to do with the passage of key legislation that could require a radically different implementation of a given strategy.

In other words, recapitulating the arguments of Chapter 6, the relevant dimension of differentiation in a hierarchy is time horizon and strategic uncertainty, not complexity, relevant variables, budget, and so on.

10. Another way to sort out the conceptual furniture here might be to refer to "strategic scenarios" rather than the more "tactical scenarios" that I tend to think of as "contingency planning." The labels, in this case, aren't important; it is the distinction between coping with strategic vs. operational or financial uncertainty that is germane.

11. From the company's 2005 annual report: Alliant Energy Corporation is a public-utility holding company serving approximately one million electric and over 400,000 natural gas customers. Providing its customers in the Midwest with regulated electricity and natural gas service is the company's primary focus. Much of this discussion of Alliant Energy's use of scenarios is based upon consulting work I was involved with, which was summarized in Flaherty, Thomas J., Todd J. Jirovec, and Dwight L. Allen (2002), "No Surprises: Strategic Flexibility Can Help Companies Prevail in an Uncertain Future," *Electric Perspectives* (November–December).

12. In Mayo and Nohria, op. cit., six factors are identified that shape the competitive landscape in ways that CEO-level intervention is necessary: government, technology, global events, demography, social mores, and labor. The first two map directly onto factors identified in the main text. The rest certainly have an impact on the macroeconomy, but it would be an oversimplification to suggest an equivalence.

13. Those comfortable working in higher-dimensional space could of course imagine an axis that exists in its own hyperplane that requires more than two endpoints to bound it. In that case, the number of scenarios required is X^n, where X is the number of endpoints on each axis and n is the number of axes. Although I can describe this, I certainly can't imagine it, and you'd need Escher to draw it for you, so I don't recommend this approach. Our conceptual frameworks are always a trade-off between capturing the complexity of reality and respecting the limitations of our cognitive machinery.

14. See Allen, Dwight L., and Michael E. Raynor (2004), *Globalization at Risk: Why Your Corporate Strategy Should Allow for a Divided and Disorderly World*, Deloitte Research (www.deloitte.com/research).

15. Friedman, Thomas L. (1999), *The Lexus and the Olive Tree*, New York: Farrar, Straus and Giroux.

16. This approach is also known as the "Battelle method." See Brauers, Jutta, and Martin Weber (1988), "A New Method of Scenario Analysis for Strategic Planning," *Journal of Forecasting*, Vol. 7, Iss. 1.

17. Again, there are alternative approaches advocated by different scenario-building experts. Some suggest that the management team should build the different strategies together, while others advocate dividing the team into groups, each building a strategy for a given scenario. In my experience, the deciding factor is the size of the management team and the time and resources available for the effort. For a concise description of one effective approach, see Perrottet, Charles M. (1996), "Scenarios for the Future," *Management Review* (January).

18. That is not to say that powerful theories cannot provide meaningful guidance with respect to where the future might well lie. With respect to the issue of supplier bargaining power, see Christensen, Clayton M., Michael E. Raynor, and Matt Verlinden (2001), "Skate to Where the Money Will Be," *Harvard Business Review,* Vol. 79, Iss. 10. Whether or not material uncertainty limits the predictive power of a theory is an empirical question. For reasons given in Chapter 4, I tend to believe that the kind of strategic uncertainty to which this book is a response will always be a factor; but this, too, is uncertain.

19. At the limit, of course, one can imagine scenarios that entail genuinely inescapable misery, but these are likely to be such extreme conditions that questions of business success are of secondary importance—for example, large-scale nuclear war, global pandemics entailing tens of millions of deaths, and so on. When considering these kinds of issues, "success" is typically defined as simply "survival."

20. To repeat, that is not to say that no strategic uncertainty remains to be resolved in the short run, just that there is very little—indeed, perhaps nothing—that functional management can do to respond strategically to those strategic uncertainties. Hence, there is no strategic uncertainty to be *managed* at the level of functional management.

CHAPTER TEN

PREPARING FOR THE UNPREDICTABLE

Unless managers are willing to structure their investments in a manner that reflects the uncertainty revealed in the scenario-building phase, the company is not actively managing strategic uncertainty. Only by creating and managing a portfolio of real options on the contingent elements of alternative optimal strategies can companies defeat the strategy paradox.

Scenario building allows a company to formulate optimal strategies and identify core and contingent elements. What to do with the core elements is relatively straightforward: make the investment. Assets or capabilities that will be valuable no matter what can be committed to with a clear conscience.

What about the contingent elements? How can organizations make investments in what they "might" need in a manner that husbands capital yet allows the company to act when and as necessary?

Investing in contingent elements is so challenging that many organizations choose instead to build a "robust" strategy—that is, a strategy that is "good enough" under all possible scenarios. Identifying a robust strategy obviates strategic options on contingent elements, since only one strategy is required, and so every element of that strategy is a core element.

There is nothing intrinsically wrong with robust strategies. It is at least conceivable that some strategies are so powerful that they lead to optimal outcomes under all circumstances, making Strategic Flexibility irrelevant. But when contemplating the time horizons over which strategic choice is possible, the differences in competitive contexts are generally such that a one-size-dominates-all strategy will be hard to find. Robust strategies tend to result in mediocre, if acceptable, results under most circumstances and standout performance in none.

In other words, robust strategies are equivalent to the "stuck-in-the-middle" strategies discussed in Chapter 3. Companies that fear the mortality risk that comes with committing to extreme positions on their industry's production possibility frontier huddle in the middle, accepting lower returns in exchange for a better shot at long-term survival. Using scenario-based planning as a way to identify the most "in-the-middle," or robust, strategy is a perfectly legitimate application of the tool. Essentially, it allows you to deliberately position your company where many organizations end up drifting largely without realizing it.

Robust strategies accept, without so much as a whimper of protest, the trade-off between strategic risk and strategic return. In the financial world, "robust investing" would amount to accepting that some stocks are risky but offer high returns while some are more stable but offer lower returns—then simply choosing one or the other. A breakthrough in financial theory was the discovery of the "efficient frontier": that it is possible to achieve higher returns at lower risk (in expectation) with the right kind of diversification than by choosing any individual stock.[1] The science of asset allocation is based on the insight that investors can create the risk/return profile that best suits their preferences by diversifying their investments in a particular way.

Strategy can be described in similar terms. Committing to extreme strategies offers the promise of great reward but brings with it significant risk. Settling on a middle-of-the-road, or robust, strategy mitigates risk but at the cost of being able to generate significant returns. Only by creating options on the contingent elements needed to implement the strategy that is optimized for the future that ultimately emerges can a company reach the "efficient frontier" of strategic investment.[2]

So far this has been described only in outline. BCE's investments in BCE Mobile and CGI were options on contingent elements, each of which could be exercised or abandoned as the relevant competitive context emerged, or did not. The option on BCE Mobile was exercised, while that on CGI was abandoned. At Microsoft, in the late 1980s the firm maintained options on MS-DOS, OS/2, and Windows-based operating systems, as well as an option on WYSIWYG applications on the Apple platform. It pursued Windows, dropped MS-DOS and OS/2, and exercised an implicit option on integration between applications and the Windows OS. Today, the firm's portfolio of options is still more extensive, including consumer electronics, mobile phones, and telecommunications infrastructure. J&J's portfolio of options on contingent elements included opportunities to combine drugs and devices, an emphasis on prevention over treatment (or vice versa), and an ongoing search for opportunities to exploit synergies as appropriate.

These companies each created a portfolio of real options that has been actively managed to drive greater returns at lower risk. Examining how they have managed their portfolios reveals five stages to the process. First, a company must *Accumulate* (the third phase of Strategic Flexibility) the right portfolio of options (stage 1, *create*), then *Operate* (the fourth phase of Strategic Flexibility) that portfolio to best effect (stages 2–4, *preserve* and *exercise* or *abandon*). Maintaining an appropriately strategically flexible stance requires continuously *renewing* the cycle (stage five).

10.1   REAL OPTIONS: DON'T FOCUS, ACCUMULATE

Accumulating the real options needed to gain exposure to strategic opportunity or mitigate strategic risk begins with *creating* the portfolio of options.

10.1.1   Create

Scenario building and strategic planning (Chapter 9) allow a company to identify what options it needs. Actually creating those options can require some very careful and creative deal structures, but in general terms it is simple: invest in a manner that confers the right, but not the obligation, to make additional investments at some point in the future. This is what makes many of the investments at BCE, Microsoft, and J&J options on strategic elements rather than commitments to them.* BCE held partial stakes in companies that it could then either acquire outright or sell off as appropriate. Microsoft and J&J have similarly made a variety of toehold investments in different companies. In addition, each holds valuable options on integration between its various operating divisions: although the individual divisions are wholly owned, both companies have withheld the additional investment required to integrate those divisions pending the resolution of key competitive uncertainties.[3]

---

* In Chapter 9, I spoke of "options on alternative strategies," while here the somewhat more laborious "options on elements of alternative strategies" is used. The additional degree of precision has been introduced here to avoid creating unnecessary complexity too early in the exposition. The difference is that when an organization has full ownership of the elements required to implement an alternative strategy, it has an option on an alternative strategy that can be exercised by integrating those elements in the appropriate way. The option is on the alternative strategy, not on the elements required to implement it. When investments in the elements themselves are optionlike, then the option is on the elements required to implement the alternative strategy. So, for example, J&J's diversity creates options on alternative strategies involving the recombination and integration of its operating divisions, whereas partial stake investments by JJDC in companies exploring new technologies could be incorporated into the strategies of existing OpCos as options on elements of alternative strategies.

In every case, the key to creating a valuable option is knowing precisely what an option is being created *on*. This is something that, surprisingly, is often overlooked. The application of options thinking to strategies for growth is by no means new.[4] However, most explorations of the topic have had a financial perspective, seeking to apply techniques developed to value financial options to options on real assets (hence the term "real options"). As a result, the option value of any given investment has been conceptualized simply in terms of the uncertainty surrounding the future of that single initiative.

So, for example, a new-product launch might be subject to material uncertainty and have both significant downside risk and also big upside. Structuring the launch and rollout of that product in the form of an option, rather than a "big bang" commitment, would allow a company to cut its losses if circumstances turned out poorly, or ramp up its investment if success beckoned.[5] The "real option" in this case is on learning—the strategic objective of functional managers (see Chapter 9). Similarly, real options can be seen in terms of the additional applications of a particular technology or resource.[6] For example, Google has demonstrated that its search capability can be applied in a variety of ways: Web-based text and images, scholarly citations, books, maps, and so on, and that each of these applications can generate different income streams. As a result, the market has applied significant growth option value to the company.[7]

Thinking of real options in strategic terms has a similar conceptual structure but very different practical implications. When the real option is on a contingent element of a larger strategy, exercising the option consists not of ramping up or dialing back investment in a particular, self-contained initiative. Rather, exercising the option means recombining otherwise autonomous assets in a new configuration that shifts an organization's position along the industry's production possibility frontier. In other words, exercising a real option on a contingent element of a strategy is a mechanism for changing strategies.

The difference between a mere growth option and an option on a contingent element for an alternative strategy is subtle but enormously important. For instance, in the late 1980s, wireless telephony businesses had much better growth prospects than wireline telephony. An investment in a wireless telephony business therefore had much greater growth option value. By launching BCE Mobile, BCE created an option on that growth: it had the right but not the obligation to expand investment in that division as the growth potential became clear.

Wireline/wireless integration, however, is a strategy—a place on the telecommunications industry's production possibility frontier—that is unattainable by either a wireline or a wireless business independently. Because BCE had a wireline division in Bell Canada, launching BCE Mobile *also* created an option to pursue this very different strategy—something neither division would be able to do on its own. When BCE bought back the outstanding equity in BCE Mobile, creating Bell Mobility, it did not simply invest more in wireless in order to grow that business or capture a greater share of its profits: it invested in order to integrate the wireless division with its wireline operations, enabling those divisions to pursue a strategy otherwise unavailable to either one of them. BCE therefore exercised the *strategic* option inherent in its position in BCE Mobile, not simply the *growth* option. When discussing Strategic Flexibility, the options required are strategic options.

The U.S. financial services industry (FSI) provides a compelling example of how companies can create strategic options.[8] In 1999, with the passage of the Gramm-Leach-Bliley Act, financial holding companies were permitted to house banking, securities, and insurance products under one roof. In response, some financial services companies began to build scope through titanic cross-industry mergers, such as those uniting Chase Manhattan and J.P. Morgan, Citicorp and Travelers/Salomon, and Bank of America and Montgomery Securities. At the same time, some marquee names in investment banking, such as Merrill Lynch and Goldman Sachs, remain independent. The only safe conclusion is that the best way to respond to the changing relationship between investment banking and the other pillars of the financial services industry remains uncertain.

Technology is another key driver of uncertainty. For example, Web-based distribution has become a permanent element of banks' distribution channels. The Internet's impact has been even more significant in the American brokerage business. Consumers have moved online *en masse,* thanks to dramatic cuts in trading costs. However, these changes say little about what precisely will happen next. In brokerage, for example, did the Internet simply amplify the proclivity of Americans for trading equities? If so, then one might expect online trading to have little effect on the brokerage business elsewhere. Or did the Internet create an entirely new segment of stockholders who will spring up in other geographic regions as the technology and related services diffuse? Beyond brokerage, online mortgages have not taken off even in the United States despite significant efforts by incumbents and start-ups alike.

Deregulation and technology have combined to make the boundaries of the financial services industry increasingly permeable. Technology companies such as Microsoft and Intuit were among the first to act on the insight that the Internet could serve as a channel through which to provide financial services to consumers. Sony, too, has entered the Japanese financial services market through private-label offerings of various financial products, including credit cards and leasing. Extending its brand even further into financial services, it launched an Internet bank, Sony Bank, in partnership with J.P. Morgan Chase and Sumitomo Mitsui Banking Corp. In addition, wireless phone companies are threatening to siphon off retail banking by creating parallel payment infrastructures. How much of a challenge the financial services industry faces from this quarter remains unclear, but with unparalleled reach and consumer mind share, the telcos pose a threat—or create an opportunity—that deserves to be taken very seriously. Finally, online start-ups such as Autobytel and Realtor.com have added specific financial products, such as car loans and mortgages, respectively, that are complementary to their basic offering. In other words, in the course of mounting an Internet-based disruption of other industries (automotive sales and real estate brokerage, respectively), they are now competing against financial services incumbents and could disrupt them, as well.

This sort of turbulence was at its height in the late 1990s, and many financial services companies responded by investing outside of the financial sector using either acquisitions or joint ventures. The increasing diversity of their targets as levels of strategic uncertainty rose suggests strongly that companies sought to gain access to resources or capabilities that could be deployed as relevant opportunities either crystallized or evaporated. Three investment strategies were among the most popular: acquisitions, joint ventures, and partial ownership.

Acquisitions In the early part of the 1990s, between 25 and 30 percent of all mergers and acquisitions involved target firms in a different industry.[9] The first of five years that saw significant increases in the emphasis on non-FSI targets was 1996, and by 2000 more than 60 percent of all deals involved a target in an entirely different industry. This level has remained largely unchanged through 2005, but the number of different industries involved has continued to climb: in 2005, 146 different non-FSI industries were sources for acquisition targets, the highest ever. In other words, even if the percentage of total deals beyond the industry's boundaries is approaching some sort of natural limit, acquirers still feel compelled to range ever farther afield when choosing a target.

What does this mean? Acquisitions within the financial services industry will tend to be additional commitments to existing strategies: increasing the scale of the existing business to capture cost savings or opportunities to expand into new geographic regions. Such initiatives are subject to material operating risk, but the strategy itself is rarely in question.

In contrast, acquisitions beyond the boundaries of the established indus-

FIGURE 10-1 **TRENDS IN ACQUISITION TARGETS IN THE U.S. FINANCIAL SERVICES INDUSTRY: 1992–2005**

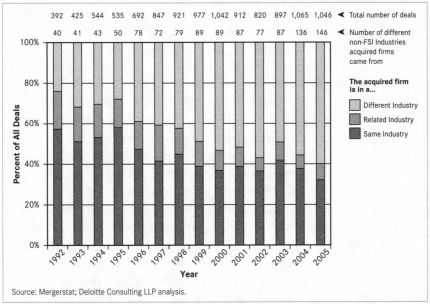

Source: Mergerstat; Deloitte Consulting LLP analysis.

The financial services industry is defined here as those companies with a primary SIC code between 6000 and 6499 inclusive. In keeping with the conventions of research in this field, a target company is in the same industry as the acquirer when the two companies have the same three-digit or four-digit SIC code. Related industries have the same two-digit SIC code. Different industries have only the first digit or no digits of their SIC in common. See, for example, Ramanujam, V., and P. Varadarajan (1989), "Research on Corporate Diversification: A Synthesis," *Strategic Management Journal,* Vol. 10, pp. 523–51.

try can be seen as a way to create options on an entirely different strategy. That option is exercised when the acquired firm is integrated into the operations of the mainstream business in a way that makes fundamental strategic repositioning possible.

When acquisitions are intended to create option value rather than extend the value of an existing strategy, there is necessarily a good deal of uncertainty attached to whether or not additional future value will be realized. It is precisely that uncertainty that justifies the acquisition in the first place. The implication, therefore, is that companies seeking to make acquisitions for option value should not be willing to pay the kinds of control premiums that acquirers often find themselves paying. Just as an option on a stock should cost much less than the stock itself, an acquisition that creates an option is not as valuable as an acquisition that solidifies an existing strategy (see section 10.3 for more on valuation).

Unfortunately, this can mean that it is often difficult to make an acquisition for option purposes, especially if another bidder sees the target as an essential part of an existing strategy: the firm that can justify a commitment will value the target firm more highly and will bid accordingly. Consequently, companies seeking to create options must often get creative.

Joint ventures Joint ventures (JVs) are created when two or more organizations create a new company, each partner typically investing a mix of cash and other resources. JVs have long been a topic of intense research interest, and they are an especially popular structure for investing in international expansion and research and development.[10] The benefits of joint venturing are access to critical resources—capital, knowledge, market access, and so on—that a firm could not afford to acquire on its own. A joint venture allows the partners to assemble just those bits of their organizations that are complementary into a new entity without one party having to acquire the other.[11]

Since JVs typically involve a lower level of commitment than outright acquisition, it is not surprising that they have historically been used as a vehicle for exploring new markets. Where just over 20 percent of all acquisitions in the FSI space were outside of FSI in 1992, well over 50 percent of JVs involving at least one FSI partner have been launched in industries other than FSI.

The benefit of joint ventures is that they reduce the cost because they are an option on an element of an alternative strategy, not an option on the strategy itself. The downside, however, is that they can set up highly competitive and potentially dysfunctional relationships between JV partners, which contributes to the notorious instability of JVs.[12] For example, suppose two firms wish to enter a given market that is subject to significant uncertainty. They establish a JV as a way to learn about this market as cost-effectively as possible. The first firm to learn what it needs to be able to compete in this new market on its own can then dissolve the JV agreement, launch its own operations, and strand its erstwhile partner.[13] Because of this observed dynamic, JVs have been positioned as "learning races," with each partner attempting to learn what it needs from the other, abandoning the JV as quickly as possible.[14]

One way to mitigate this problem is for the parties to a JV to establish explicit terms under which one or the other might expand its level of involvement or control, acquire the JV outright, or divest their interest if the option created by the JV does not come "into the money."[15] The problem with this approach is that when both partners in a JV see the JV as an option on a contingent element to a particular strategy, they are often motivated to exercise or abandon that option under similar circumstances. Imagine, for instance, a bank and a phone company creating a wireless-

FIGURE 10-2 **TRENDS IN THE TARGET INDUSTRY OF JOINT VENTURES INVOLVING U.S. FINANCIAL SERVICES INSTITUTIONS: 1992–2005**

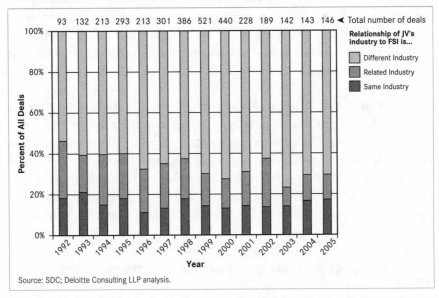

Source: SDC; Deloitte Consulting LLP analysis.

The same definitions of industry relatedness are applied in the analysis of joint ventures as in the analysis of acquisitions. However, since joint ventures can involve partners from different industries, the relatedness analysis reported here applies only to the financial services companies involved. The population of joint ventures analyzed consists of all joint ventures recorded by Securities Data Corporation (SDC) in which at least one partner was a U.S.-based financial services company. The relatedness of the new venture is an average of the venture's relatedness to all partners that are financial services companies, both U.S.- and non-U.S.-based.

payments JV. The new company would represent an option for each on a particular payments strategy. Should the relevant uncertainties be resolved in ways that make the new venture valuable, it will in all likelihood be valuable to both the bank and the telco. Then what?

To a large extent, the outcome is determined by the ownership structure of the JV. Barring explicit agreements that separate equity and control, anything other than a 50/50 structure amounts to a license for the majority owner to dictate the strategic direction and terms of dissolution.[16] Any party that enters into a JV for the option value will therefore likely insist on a 50/50 structure in order to secure the ability to exercise that option should circumstances warrant. But when both parties seek to exercise the option at the same time, under a best-case scenario a bidding war ensues and the victor walks away a victim of the winner's curse: when each party is willing to pay up to the full value of the asset, the winner necessarily pays more than the full value. Alternatively, one party is forced to acquire not only the JV but also its JV partner, which leaves unsatisfied the desire for capital efficiency that motivated the JV in the first place.[17] It is perhaps for reasons related to the difficulty of exercising or abandoning strategic options created through a JV that the number of such deals has fallen significantly from a late-1990s peak, whereas outright acquisitions of increasingly diverse targets have increased.

Partial ownership A third way to create options on contingent strategic elements, one that addresses directly both the desire to conserve capital and the need for control, is a partial equity stake. Unlike joint ventures, which typically involve a small number of investors (usually two and rarely more than four), purchasing a significant equity stake in an otherwise widely held company can create the requisite control with much lower levels of investment. Many of the examples discussed so far have taken just this form:

FIGURE 10-3 **TRENDS IN PARTIAL EQUITY OWNERSHIP IN THE UNITED STATES: 1995–2005**

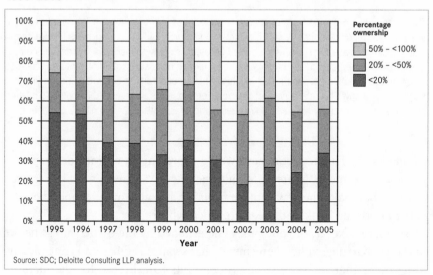

Source: SDC; Deloitte Consulting LLP analysis.

These data pick up equity ownership resulting from deals done in a particular year. For example, a company that acquires a 15% stake in 1995 and then increases that stake to 45% in 1999 and to 75% in 2004 is recorded three times and figures in the calculation of the distribution of equity ownership stakes in each of those years. In addition, because these data capture only individual deals, they do not necessarily represent the structure of the portfolios of partial equity stakes held by American companies. This chart suggests, however, an increasing willingness by American companies to hold equity positions in a theoretical "no-man's-land": greater than the 20% limit that allows companies to avoid consolidation, but less than the 100% control position that avoids any possibility of fiduciary conflict.

BCE, Microsoft, and J&J all have partial equity stakes in companies that afford the opportunity either to acquire full control (in order to exercise the option) or divest (in order to abandon the option) as the need to implement a given strategy either crystallizes or evaporates.

For JVs with option value, a 50/50 ownership structure is a default position. But when viewing partial ownership stakes as real options on future acquisitions, the question of "how much is enough" is not nearly as well studied.[18] One implication given significant attention is the reporting impact of owning more or less than that percentage of total equity that triggers balance-sheet and income-statement consolidation for reporting and tax purposes. In the United States, for example, owning 20 percent or more of another company requires this kind of consolidation. As a result, companies are often counseled to own less than this critical value.

However, of all partial equity stakes for which data are available, those in which the acquiring firm held less than 20 percent of the target firm's equity have fallen consistently: from over half of all deals in 1995 to fewer than one in five by 2002, rebounding by 2005 to about a third. What is most telling about these data is that there is no theoretical foundation for why a company would own more than 20 percent but less than 100 percent. What factors does a company consider when deciding whether to own 25 percent, 60 percent, 85 percent, or any other ownership stake?

Creating real options on the contingent elements of different strategies provides one way to think about how much one needs to own.[19] The objective, recall, is to establish an ownership stake that creates the right, but not the obligation, to invest further in order to serve particular strategic ends. An ownership position that does not achieve this creates no strategic option value. If an acquirer owns too little, it will be unable to exercise the option; if it owns too much, abandonment will be difficult. Determining how best to answer this question is the objective of the Operate phase.

10.2 IMPLEMENTATION: DON'T EXECUTE, OPERATE

Acquisition, joint venture, or partial equity stake are all reasonable ways to create options. Which mechanism is most appropriate for a given set of circumstances will depend on which one enables a firm to create the desired option value. Investments can have option value when they give an investor access to potentially valuable resources or capabilities. They *actually* have option value when the structure of the deal enables the investing firm to *Operate* its portfolio (phase 4 of Strategic Flexibility), which consists of an ability to *preserve* and *exercise* or *abandon* options as appropriate (stages 2–4 of managing a portfolio of real options).

10.2.1 Preserve

A financial option is valid for the period specified in the option contract, and the holder of the financial option need do nothing to maintain its validity during that time. Neither that level of detail nor that level of indifference in the interim is typically part of an investment in strategic options. Strategic options are usually much more open-ended, and their value usually must actively be preserved by those who hold them.

An investment made for its strategic option value will not be an integral part of ongoing operations; if it were, it would be a further commitment to the company's existing strategy, not an option on an element of a different strategy. When the focal company (the company holding the option) invests in a target company (the company that is the option), it will generally allow the target company to operate largely independently, primarily because to do otherwise would be to exercise the option.

The cost of the option can be more than simply the up-front investment. For example, the focal company might underwrite any losses incurred by a target company, increasing the cost of the option. With each additional infusion of cash, the option will have to be that much more valuable upon exercise to justify maintaining it today, while the desire to cut one's losses might precipitate either premature exercise or abandonment.

In contrast, if the target company can maintain at least break-even performance, the focal company can carry the option at nearly zero cost. Better still, if the target company is easily separable from the focal company, the focal company can abandon the option by selling its claims on the target company at or near what it paid, and so have enjoyed the benefits of holding the option for next to nothing.

Minimizing the cost of carrying and abandoning an option in this way has some straightforward implications for the relationship between the focal and target companies. Consistent with the prescriptions of proven management practice, since there are no meaningful synergies between target and focal company operations (if there were, it would be time to exercise the option), the focal company's corporate office should limit its interventions to setting objectives and monitoring performance against those objectives. In other words, the focal company should manage the target company as an "unrelated" division (see Appendix A for a more detailed discussion).

Unfortunately, the requirements of low carrying cost and painless abandonment cut against the needs of effectively *exercising* an option. Each option on a contingent element is necessarily only part of the full complement of assets needed to implement an alternative strategy, and so exercising a strategic option necessarily requires integrating that option with other elements, and typically with elements of the focal company's operations.

When two organizations that have little in common to begin with (recall: the focal company represents an option on resources or capabilities that are not needed now but might be needed later) are allowed autonomy in their respective markets, they will tend to drift ever farther apart. This can undermine the ability to integrate in the future. BCE provides another salutary example. In 1998, BCE merged Bell Emergis, a division that provided services allowing companies to take advantage of the Internet, with Mpact Immedia, a publicly traded company competing in the same industry, creating BCE Emergis (Emergis), in which BCE had a 65 percent equity stake. The strategic option value that Emergis created for BCE's Bell Canada division lay in the opportunity to create an e-commerce capability for Bell.

In order to minimize the cost of this option, BCE's CEO, Jean Monty, quite rightly expected Emergis to pursue a viable stand-alone strategy until such time as more formal and significant integration with Bell became advisable. In other words, Emergis had to stand on its own feet until it was time to exercise the option. Pursuing that success led Emergis to contemplate the acquisition of U.S.–based companies that served predominantly U.S. markets. During the late-1990s bubble, when these deals were on the table, Emergis's stock enjoyed a high multiple compared to BCE's, and so Emergis proposed using its equity to make these purchases. Had the more aggressive of these moves gone through, it would have served to dilute BCE's ownership position. In addition, because Bell's markets are exclusively in Canada, these deals would have diminished the strategic option value of Emergis for Bell.

As a result, in order to *preserve* the value of that option, BCE exercised the control it enjoyed over Emergis to redirect the company's growth strategy in ways that were economically comparable to U.S. expansion yet still strategically consistent with scenarios in which Bell and Emergis became more closely integrated.[20] This kind of control is a form of *strategic constraint* on the activities of a target company, imposed to preserve the value of the option.

In the end, BCE divested its stake in Emergis, and Emergis has continued to grow successfully on its own. The implication is that whatever strategic constraints BCE placed on Emergis did not undermine the company's long-term viability as a stand-alone entity. The message, then, is that when creating an option, the control structure must be such that the focal company can direct the target company's activities in ways that make future integration a possibility but not a necessity.

10.2.2 Exercise

Holding the right kinds of strategic options creates value indirectly—by mitigating strategic risk. Creating value directly, by exploiting strategic opportunities, requires *exercising* strategic options. This involves integrating the target company, or some subset of its resources and capabilities, with all or part of the focal company's operations in a manner that allows the focal company to pursue a new strategy. In other words, exercising a strategic option allows an operating division to change its strategy in a way that it otherwise could not.

The challenge of how best to reconfigure an organization's resources and capabilities has been tackled by a number of leading researchers. Concepts such as "modular corporate forms," "patching," "the Velcro organization," and "strategic integration" are part of a growing and diverse body of knowledge offering relevant insight.[21] Perhaps the most compelling consistency among these approaches is the importance each places on the ability to reconfigure resources as a response to environmental uncertainty. Each researcher concludes that strategic change demands reorganizing operating divisions' assets and capabilities so that they can offer the kinds of new products via the kinds of new business models demanded by a new competitive context.[22]

These researchers prescribe different processes for making the necessary changes. Recall the discussion from section 7.5: the debate is essentially between the merits of a top-down or bottom-up approach. What makes this back-and-forth all the more fascinating is that each camp (conveniently, but somewhat unfairly, polarizing the controversy) avers that its purported solution achieves the same ends: market orientation, speedy implementation, and efficient execution.

10.2.2.1 Bottom-up

The following example illustrates the merits of a bottom-up approach. The Book and Catalog divisions of a major printing company (identified only as PrintCo) had begun exploring digital printing technology more or less simultaneously.[23] Each division had an option on a contingent element—digital printing—that might be useful to their existing operations in the future. Neither division was able to achieve sufficient scale in digital printing to sustain a stand-alone digital printing unit. Each division's digital printing activities therefore had to be consolidated and reside in one of the two existing divisions.

Digital printing was most attractive for short, customized runs. Books tend to have long, standardized runs. The strategic uncertainty that the

Book division was hedging was the possibility of print-on-demand publishing and customized books—a longer-term concern. In contrast, the Catalog division saw immediate applications for digital printing technology in customized catalogs. In option terms, for the Book division, digital printing needed to be preserved, while for the Catalog division, it was time to exercise the option and commit. By "patching," or moving the digital printing activities in the Book division to the Catalog division, the initiative reached the scale needed to be of immediate commercial value, even as it maintained a window on digital printing for the Book division, which preserved the option it needed.

Patching, then, offers a way to think about bottom-up resource reconfigurations in the pursuit of new opportunities. In this example, the option was created by the business units themselves. One cannot always expect that. But provided the corporate level generally fulfills its responsibilities and creates a portfolio of resources that can be repatched in the appropriate ways, patching is a useful mechanism for exercising options on new strategies. Patching is fully consistent with the view that it falls to division-level management to choose the appropriate commitments from the menu of options created by the corporate office.

10.2.2.2 Top-down

An important qualification of this example, however, is that the digital printing opportunity fell within the resource, structural, and strategic constraints of the Catalog division. Their customers valued the new capability, the size of the opportunity was within their scale, and fairly routine interdivisional collaboration made the requisite patching possible. As a result, the lack of corporate office involvement is entirely understandable. What happens when exercising these options demands going beyond existing divisional constraints?

Under these circumstances, the merits of a strong, top-down approach to exercising options become clear. For example, News Corporation has long been led by a "heroic" CEO, Rupert Murdoch, who intervenes decisively and repeatedly in the competitive strategies of the corporation's operating divisions in order to overcome the limitations of divisional constraints.[24] Perhaps most famously, in 1987 Murdoch launched Fox Broadcasting in the face of enormous skepticism on the part of industry observers. With only a relatively few stations and affiliates, the new network had limited coverage and, thanks to its start-up status, could not afford much original content. No coverage and no content meant no viewers, no viewers meant no advertisers, and no advertisers meant no dice.

To the industry's general amazement, Murdoch pulled it off and Fox became profitable within five years. Its success was a result of Murdoch's willingness to direct the operations of the different divisions of News Corporation that were critical to the new venture's success. In particular, he directed the fledgling network to acquire six major market stations for $1.9 billion—a price that was generally agreed (by almost everyone except Murdoch) to be a gross overinvestment. He also redirected Twentieth Century Fox studios into television production: the studio provided over half of Fox Broadcasting's programming. All this was done on the strength of Murdoch's intuition and force of will. In the words of Jamie Kellner, the network's first president: "The most amazing thing to me . . . was they [Murdoch and Barry Diller, president of Twentieth Century Fox studios] had done no study whatsoever to see whether or not it was possible to build a fourth network. There was no business plan, no model, just guts."

Establishing Fox Broadcasting went beyond the resource, structural, and strategic constraints of all of News Corporation's operating divisions.[25] Even the repositioning of Twentieth Century Fox simply to support the new network exceeded the strategic mandate of the studio. Bottom-up patching could never have achieved Murdoch's results. Exercising the option that News Corporation's strategic diversification created seems to have been done almost entirely at the corporate level—in fact, by a very small group of especially driven and insightful individuals.

The necessary constraints on News Corporation's operating divisions made it impossible to cope with the uncertainty and commitment required to launch Fox Broadcasting at the operating division level. In other words, they were caught by the strategy paradox: they could not have made the commitments required to succeed, and as a result would have also avoided the risk of failure. This is not really all that surprising. Recall that in the cases of BCE and Microsoft, the successful and ongoing creation and management of a portfolio of real options worked best with a powerful CEO who was relatively insulated from capital market pressures.

10.2.2.3 Splitting the Difference

Do operating divisions *ever* really play a role in exercising options when doing so goes beyond their strategic constraints? And if exercising options is all about effecting strategic change, is it not up to corporate management not merely to create options but also to decide when and how to exercise them?

Some organizations might have to split the difference between these two extremes (bottom-up patching at PrintCo and CEO intervention at News Corporation). Divisional management can be critical when deciding when and how to exercise options, but corporate management may have to play an active role in loosening—but not breaking—the bonds of existing constraints. If the corporate level pushes too hard to have a particular option exercised, it might effect the necessary strategic change but the resulting organization will not be competitive ("the operation was a success, but the patient died"). Not enough pressure from corporate, and nothing at all happens.

The delicate balance between top-down and bottom-up can be seen in the integration of corporate and investment banking in Canada.[26] In 1988, a near-perfect natural experiment was set in motion. As a result of revisions to the Canada Bank Act in 1987, corporate and investment banking activities were permitted to combine under common corporate ownership.[27] Within a year, four of the five largest Canadian banks, controlling collectively almost two-thirds of the nation's banking assets, had acquired outright a leading securities dealer.

All of these deals were justified in press releases at the time in terms of synergies between lending (i.e., debt, or traditional corporate banking) and underwriting (i.e., equity, or securities dealing). None of the banks, however, undertook any immediate integration activities. From the vantage point of 1988, then, these acquisitions could be seen as options on integrating corporate and investment banking. The underwriting business was, after all, profitable in its own right, and so the cost of the option was simply any excess acquisition premium. The cost of exercising the option would be the additional investment required to actually integrate corporate and investment banking operations.

More than ten years later, however, only one bank, the Canadian Imperial Bank of Commerce (CIBC), had actively pursued integration. The three other acquiring banks—the Royal Bank of Canada (RBC), the Bank of Montreal (BMO), and the Bank of Nova Scotia (BNS)—grew their investment and corporate lending operations as essentially independent entities. The results were telling. Between 1991, when CIBC began pursuing integration aggressively, and 1997, the bank went from barely third in total corporate underwritings to a solid first. What is even more remarkable is that this first-place ranking was achieved solely through organic growth even as RBC *et al.* continued to make investment banking acquisitions.[28]

In strategic terms, what CIBC accomplished is very similar to what Murdoch did at News Corporation by creating Fox Broadcasting. Synthesizing corporate and investment banking to create a new suite of capabilities went far beyond the constraints of either operating division. Yet then-CEO John Hunkin would not have been mistaken for Rupert Murdoch: he threw no thunderbolts from Mount Olympus. The operating divisions affected were key drivers of the change, even as sizable constituencies within each resisted. So how did CIBC manage to exercise its option so successfully while the other banks, which in so many ways had identical starting points, were unable to realize similar value?[29]

The answer comes in two parts. First, Hunkin demonstrated the utility of integrated corporate and investment banking capabilities by sponsoring a number of carefully chosen experiments. In particular, the central premise of integration was to provide financing solutions to the bank's customers rather than trying to sell them "products": loans, securitized debt issues, equity flotations, foreign-exchange services, interest rate swaps, and so on. Doing this effectively meant creating "relationship managers," people in the bank who were able to understand a client's needs and bring to bear the relevant expertise. This was done by identifying those few individuals who already had the requisite abilities and proclivities for such a role, then explicitly sponsoring their efforts. This meant exempting them from established performance evaluation and career-management processes by, for example, deciding compensation and promotion questions based on a subjective assessment of each person's contributions to the larger strategic objective. This created a working prototype for what large-scale integration offered in a way that bottom-up patching could not, but still fell far short of the kind of large-scale intervention seen at News Corporation.

Second, as these preliminary efforts bore fruit, Hunkin and his management team began a slow and careful restructuring of existing systems, especially compensation, in order to encourage similar behaviors across the entire bank. Such changes were not straightforward, however. The market for talent in both corporate and investment banking is hotly contested, and in the densely networked Canadian banking community it is relatively easy for top performers to move from bank to bank. CIBC was attempting to make a significant strategic and cultural shift while the other banks were not. In the words of Pat Meredith, then the EVP of Corporate Strategy, "The investment bankers thought the corporate bankers were stupid and slow; the corporate bankers thought the investment bankers were sleezy and greedy." Those who valued the traditional approaches had viable alternatives elsewhere.

As a result, although Hunkin's *ad hoc* efforts could demonstrate that the option on integration created by the 1988 acquisition was in the money, actively committing on a large scale to exercising that option depended on widespread acceptance of the new strategy by those affected. By the mid-1990s, Hunkin's combination of vigorous persuasion and gentle coercion paid off: the new strategy began to take hold, and divisional management began to commit to a strategy of integration.

How to determine how much change an organization can absorb at what pace is not something for which it is at present possible to offer theoretically grounded advice. As Hunkin put it, "It's a balancing act, and you have to decide which sort of danger you're more willing to accept: the danger of moving too slowly or too quickly. It's almost impossible to get it just right." Whether or not Hunkin and the rest of CIBC's top management team did get it just right remains an open question. What is clear, however, is that they successfully integrated their corporate and investment banking operations, implementing a fundamentally different strategy and achieving significant competitive success as a result. CIBC's acquisition of a securities dealer in 1988 created the option. Exploring the competitive impact of integration with targeted experiments between 1990 and 1992 demonstrated that the option was "in the money." Exercising that option required demonstrating what integration looked like and why it was desirable, followed by process changes to trigger widespread change.

The archetype outlined in Chapter 6 had divisional management effecting strategic change by selecting new capabilities from a vending machine stocked with real options by a forward-looking corporate management. Reality, as ever, is far more complex. There is an unavoidable but ultimately useful tension between divisional management and the corporate office over the timing and nature of the exercise of options in the service of strategic change. That tension gives rise to an ongoing dialogue and even dialectic, and the mechanisms by which it is sorted out remains, unfortunately, difficult to describe and poorly understood.[30]

For now, a simplifying three-tier contingency will have to suffice. When exercising an option falls within the constraints of an existing division, exercising options can indeed be the sole prerogative of division management. When the magnitude of the change required goes beyond the constraints of any existing division, determining when and how to exercise a given option tends to rely much more on an activist corporate office and even heroic CEO. And when divisional assent is crucial to success, either due to corporate culture or the need for industry expertise and insight, then a capacity for collaboration between corporate and divisional management is crucial to determining when and how to exercise the relevant option.[31]

10.2.3 Abandon

Exercising an option is the process that transforms an option into a commitment. Curiously, the ability to exercise an option is not what creates option value; exercising the option creates commitment value. As noted above in the *preserve* discussion, it is the ability to abandon an option that makes it truly an option, and not merely a delayed commitment. If BCE had invested in CGI and as a result been *forced* to assume full control and integrate its IT consulting capabilities into Bell's operations, that initial stake would not have been an option. It was only BCE's ability to abandon the investment as circumstances required that allows us to say with certainty that BCE created an option.[32]

Yet, ironically, walking away from an investment is almost always seen as a sign of failure. Firms that divest their acquisitions or dispose of their partial equity stakes without realizing synergies are generally felt to have made bad initial choices.[33] Unfortunately, characterizing exit as failure creates a psychological barrier to abandoning options by exacerbating the negative impact of the "sunk-cost effect."[34]

The sunk-cost effect is the well-documented propensity of managers to assess the potential of a given project favorably, and hence continue to invest in it, if they have already made investments in it. As the expression goes, "in for a penny, in for a pound." In the context of investing in strategic options, if the initial investment required to create the option serves in reality to commit a company to subsequent investment, then the option is not an option at all. Companies that cannot abandon their "out-of-the-money" options have created for themselves the worst of all possible worlds: they have invested in projects based on option value that does not exist, and so can be expected to lose money.[35] The sunk-cost effect transforms options taken in the service of Strategic Flexibility into commitments that dissipate capital and management time, depressing returns without in any way deflecting strategic risk.

Abandoning options is far less ambiguous from a process perspective than exercising options. The corporate office—the level that creates the options—must also take responsibility for abandoning them. The reason is relatively straightforward. The process of capital allocation in most organizations is typically a form of competition among operating divisions for investment funds. Each puts the best face it can on its own prospects for growth and profitability. Division management's job, recall, is to make their division as successful as possible, and so "divest me" is rarely going to be the request. If, however, that division's value to the overall corporation lies largely in its option value, and that option falls sufficiently out of the money, then divestiture is the correct course of action, even if the division is successful on its own terms.

To return to the Microsoft case, although MSN is reasonably seen as a strategic option from the perspective of the corporate office, it should be seen exclusively as a commitment by the managers charged with MSN's success. Their careers (at least, their careers at Microsoft) depend on demonstrating the value of the operations they manage. If they are successful, they will deliver operating results that merit additional investment simply for the returns such investment would generate. Focused on their own performance,

THE PHONE COMPANY DIALS BACK

Another of the options on an alternative strategy that Jean Monty created at BCE was Bell Globemedia (BGM). A diversified media company in its own right, BGM's crown jewel assets are CTV, Canada's largest private television broadcaster, and the *Globe & Mail,* Canada's largest national daily newspaper. Other key divisions included Globe Interactive, an online information services company, and Sympatico, BCE's Internet services provider that had been launched by Bell in the late 1990s. Launched in January 2001, BCE owned 70.1 percent of BGM's equity, while The Thomson Corporation owned 20 percent and The Woodbridge Corporation (also controlled by the Thomson family) owned 9.9 percent.[36]

The explicit intent was that BGM would explore new opportunities that exploited the broad scope of BCE's capabilities, especially its core landline and wireline operations. BCE even set up a C$70 million fund to develop and launch convergence products and services.[37]

These initiatives bore little fruit, and when Monty resigned in 2002 and Michael Sabia acceded to the position of CEO, there was widespread expectation that, in addition to disposing of Teleglobe, BCE would quickly divest itself of BGM. Instead, Sabia expressed strong support for BGM, effectively preserving the option on media/telecoms convergence that Monty had created.[38] By late that year, however, Sabia said publicly that the hoped-for synergies were not materializing, and that media and telecommunications were "substantially different businesses."[39]

Backing out of a 70 percent stake in the largest media group in Canada is not something one does precipitously, however. It was not until 2006 that BCE brought in new investors in a manner that allowed it to reduce its ownership stake to 20 percent. Woodbridge increased its stake to 20 percent, while Ontario Teachers Pension Plan and Torstar Corporation each bought 20 percent stakes.[40] Woodbridge and Teachers were largely financial investors who likely saw the value of BGM primarily as a stand-alone media company. Torstar, however, is a large and diversified media company with a raft of publishing and television assets and may well have seen its stake in BGM as having option value on a different kind of media convergence than BCE once did.

Even as this seeming exit strategy played itself out, BCE continued to hold an option on media/telecoms convergence thanks to its still-important investment in BGM. Appropriately, as BCE's enthusiasm about the possibility of exercising those options—or its assessment of the likelihood of having to acquire control in order to realize those options—seems to have waned, its level of investment in BGM was similarly reduced.[41]

MSN's operating management cannot be expected to evaluate whether the option MSN represents for the corporation is perpetually out of the money.

Bank of Montreal's (BMO) options on its NAFTA-bank strategy provide a good example of prudent abandonment. In 1984, BMO acquired Harris-

Bank, the second-largest Chicagoland bank, giving BMO the most significant and enduring U.S. retail and investment banking presence among Canadian banks. With the passage of the North American Free Trade Agreement (NAFTA) in 1994, a "North American Bank"—one that could provide seamless cross-border services—became strategically viable.

Uniquely positioned among major banks because of its place on the commanding heights of the Canadian banking sector and strong regional presence in the United States, BMO sought to deepen its tentative ties with Bancomer, the second-largest Mexican bank. In the wake of the 1994 peso devaluation, the Mexican government permitted foreign investment in Mexican banks ahead of the schedule mandated by NAFTA. This regulatory change, coupled with the attractive asset prices as a result of the devaluation, led BMO to acquire a 16.2 percent equity stake controlling 20 percent of voting shares, along with eight seats on the Mexican bank's forty-four-seat board, in 1996.[42]

At the time, this investment was not described in particularly optionlike terms. "North America is fast becoming an integrated economy and our customers increasingly view North America as a single, unified marketplace. Expanded presence in Mexico is essential to meet their growing needs, and this alliance gives us added distribution channels that will benefit our clients," said then-CEO Matthew W. Barrett. "Having a partner such as Bancomer makes it particularly exciting for us."[43] Such language is hardly surprising, however. How much sense would it have made for Barrett to say, "We're investing in Bancomer to try out a few things, and if it doesn't work out, no harm done"?

Between 1996 and 2001, BMO and Bancomer pursued a number of collaborative initiatives, among them the development of specialized banking services for migrant workers of Mexican origin working in Canada's agricultural sector, with similar services targeted at the Hispanic population living in areas served by HarrisBank.[44] For the people charged with making such opportunities successful, cross-border services were a commitment, so they could not be expected to recommend their own disbandment.

Ultimately, however, the opportunities for significant synergies turned out to be limited, but not necessarily due to any operational failings on the part of those implementing them. Larger structural issues impeded successful integration. Consolidation pressures within the Mexican market were forcing ever-greater degrees of integration among Mexican banks, which limited the resources and attention Bancomer could devote to exploring cross-border linkages made possible by NAFTA. Finally, the Mexican government had instituted new capital requirements for its banks that would have necessitated significant additional investments by BMO if it were to maintain its stake. The result was that over a period of months, concluding in March of 2001, BMO disposed of its stake in GFB, selling to Banco Bilbao Vizcaya Argentaria (BBVA) of Spain. BBVA was the logical buyer, as it had been building a stake in Bancomer as an option on its own Latin American growth strategy.

Despite an after-tax gain of C$271 million on the sale, the business press was not kind to BMO.[45] The investment was variously referred to as a "disappointment" and signaled the "failure" of Barrett's "grand strategy."[46] This seems grossly unfair, and betrays our propensity to view any retreat as a sign of weakness rather than prudence. Through its investment in Bancomer, BMO had created exposure to a valuable strategic upside, the emergence of which was uncertain. At the relevant operating levels BMO and Bancomer explored the viability of that strategy, but the external circumstances that would have justified exercising the option on full integration never materialized. BMO therefore divested the holding. It is important to note that Bancomer still made sense as an investment simply in terms of its ability to generate returns, as evidenced by BBVA's willingness to pay an acquisition premium for BMO's minority stake. But it no longer had option value, and it was the option value on the larger NAFTA bank strategy that justified tying up BMO capital in Bancomer. When that option value evaporated, BMO had better things to do with the capital elsewhere.

BMO's Bancomer investment was a rational, considered, and capital-efficient way to create a strategic opportunity . . . that did not materialize. That is neither a failure nor a disappointment. The only way BMO could have managed the situation any better is to have predicted the future of cross-border banking integration in the face of an evolving trade regime and a highly turbulent Mexican financial services industry. And that, of course, was impossible.

10.3 VALUATION

Every example of strategic options discussed so far required someone, at some point, to spend real money. And although whether or not the option so acquired would ultimately be exercised or abandoned was uncertain, the amount of money spent to acquire that option was not. Having done all the analytical work required to identify which options are required, how does a manager decide how much that option is actually worth?

The value of a financial call option is essentially its expected value, which is a function of the probability of the price of the underlying asset, the stock, being at or above the strike price at some point in the future. A European call option is exercisable only at expiration, while an American call option can be exercised at any point up to expiration. The terms of the option contract specify the strike price and expiration. Either way the purchaser of the contract can estimate its worth by observing the price of the underlying asset and then estimating the distribution of possible future values for that stock.

For example, if the stock has a price today of $10, and an option is being offered with a strike price of $15, the critical estimate is the likelihood that the stock will be worth $15 or more sometime between now and the expiration of the option. This distribution of future values is typically estimated using historical price distributions. Stocks with historically wide distributions are felt to have much more unpredictable future values and so a greater probability of extreme future values. In other words, a stock that has moved 10 percent per month over the last year, even if the net gain has been 0 percent, is, all else equal, likelier to achieve a 50 percent gain over the next year than a stock that has achieved the same 0 percent annual return and has moved only 1 to 2 percent per month. Different historical volatilities lead to different estimates of the underlying distributions of possible future values.

The machinery of financial option valuation, including the widely promulgated Black-Scholes model, consists of different ways of estimating the probabilities of different future stock price values and the implications of those collective probabilities on the value of an option at different specific future prices. The field of real options valuation is firmly rooted in the same tradition. There is a well-established and highly elaborate body of work that uses the same tools and techniques created to value financial options to value real options.[47] The analogy between financial options and real options that allows these approaches to be applied is shown in Figure 10-4.

There are a number of conceptual and technical problems associated with applying this putative equivalence. The parameters required to value a financial call option are typically observable. The stock on which the option contract is written has a market price. The exercise price is stipulated in the option contract, as is the time to expiration. The risk-free rate is almost by definition the ninety-day Treasury bill interest rate, and the historical volatility of a stock provides a meaningful estimate of the range of future possible prices. The carrying cost is simply the opportunity cost of any dividends declared before the option is exercised, which can be estimated by observing the stock's historical dividend rate and payout schedule and mapping that to the time period over which the option runs. It is for this reason that sophisticated mathematical tools can provide useful estimates of value. If option valuation required primarily keen strategic insight, it is not clear what statistical simulation techniques would have to offer.[48]

In contrast, the real option analogs typically are not observable.[49] When

FIGURE 10-4 **MAPPING THE VALUATION PARAMETERS OF FINANCIAL CALL OPTIONS TO CHARACTERISTICS OF REAL OPTIONS ON CONTINGENT STRATEGIC ELEMENTS**

Financial Call Option	Real Option on an asset that is a contingent element of an alternative strategy
Stock price	Present value of the asset as a stand-alone enterprise
Exercise or strike price	Incremental investment required to incorporate the asset into the alternative strategy
Time to expiration	Time until the asset is no longer required to implement the alternative strategy, or scenario demanding the alternative strategy is no longer plausible
Risk-free rate	Risk-free rate
Carrying cost	Opportunity cost of strategic constraints required to preserve option value
Estimated range of stock's future price	Range of possible future values of the asset's contribution to the alternative strategy of which it is part

Source: Author's analysis.

making an acquisition, taking a partial equity stake, or investing in a JV, the price of the option is the premium paid above whatever the present value of the cash generated by that investment would be *if the option it represented were never exercised.* So when CIBC acquired Wood Gundy in 1988, Wood Gundy had a particular enterprise value. If CIBC paid anything beyond that enterprise value, that was the price paid for the option on integration with CIBC's corporate banking activities. Whether they actually did pay anything at all for the option depends on one's assessments of Wood Gundy's prospects absent such integration. In other words, whether CIBC overpaid for its option or paid anything at all is itself subject to considerable debate.

Neither can the strike price be observed. Exercising a real option can require some combination of acquiring additional equity or outright ownership plus the additional investment necessary to integrate a particular asset and implement a new strategy. In other words, exercising a real option is a form of postmerger integration challenge, something that is often fraught with difficulty and uncertainty.

The time to expiration and carrying costs are similarly unclear. The strategic option is valuable for as long as the alternative strategy requiring it remains viable within a scenario deemed sufficiently plausible. In other words, the option is valuable until it is no longer valuable, and who knows when that will be? Carrying costs amount to the cramp on profitability, if any, imposed by the strategic constraints required to preserve the option. Preserving option value, recall, means keeping the asset with option value "integratable" into the alternative strategy of which it is a part *and* keeping it viable as a stand-alone entity should the option need to be abandoned. This means that the carrying cost is the sum of any possible reductions in profits generated by the asset as a consequence of strategic constraints required to preserve the exercisability of the option *plus* reductions in the success of the strategy, should it be implemented, as a result of the autonomy maintained prior to exercising the option that was needed to preserve the ability to abandon the option. That was complicated to say. Imagine how tough it is to figure out.

But the task is difficult only if the comparison is the relative precision of financial option valuation. This comparison is entirely inappropriate. The purpose of real options, in the context of Strategic Flexibility, is to reduce strategic risk and increase exposure to strategic opportunity. These are outcomes that cannot be measured *ex ante*, and for which suitable proxies in the financial markets simply do not exist. After all, the strategic uncertainty that is relevant to scenarios, alternative optimal strategies, and strategic options plays out over years and possibly decades. Few markets for financial options have time horizons much beyond a year.

Strategic options create value by allowing subsequent investments to be based on better information. Unlike many of its industry brethren, BCE took an option on integration with IT consulting through its 42 percent equity stake in CGI. Some fraction of what BCE paid for that stake was the price of the option. (Since CGI had positive enterprise value, that 42 percent stake had stand-alone value.) Exercising that option would have required, in all likelihood, the outright acquisition of CGI at a cost much higher than the price paid for the option: BCE would have been purchasing full control in a market that recognized, as did BCE, the strategic value to Bell's much larger asset base. As it turned out, BCE walked away from those significant follow-on expenditures because the requisite strategic imperative failed to materialize.

This was an option because it had the right leverage structure. BCE paid much less to acquire the option than it would have paid to exercise it. Other phone companies that committed were unable either to exit as efficiently or avoid as thoroughly the pathologies of the sunk-cost effect because their initial investments were so much greater.

There are, of course, better and worse ways to bring some rigor to estimating the value of strategic options. Appendix C provides an example of how discounted cash flow and net present value stack up against more sophisticated, but still entirely tractable, option valuation techniques, and how the assessment of probabilities factors into that valuation. In the end, however, the value of strategic options is determined by the value the organization places on a particular risk/return profile. This is not something that can be priced with direct reference to close capital market proxies. The valuation of real options therefore necessarily relies more on common sense than on analytical rigor. The components of valuation are only conceptually the same for financial and real options, but this conceptual equivalence is helpful. It allows a senior team to build up the value to their organization of a given asset and trade off the contribution that asset makes to the management of strategic uncertainty against other uses of capital.

As a result, no valuation technique, no matter how sophisticated, will replace human judgment. Management must determine what kind of Strategic Flexibility can be created at what cost, while the board must determine what kind of Strategic Flexibility is worth having at that price.

10.4 RENEWAL

The future never gets here. That is why Strategic Flexibility is illustrated as a loop. Once an organization has gone through the process of building scenarios, developing optimal strategies, and identifying and acquiring the desired portfolio of strategic options, it is time to do it all over again. As events unfold, the relative probabilities attached to certain outcomes can be updated. Some options will be exercised, others preserved, still others abandoned. And as time's wheel turns, new scenarios will have to be created, which sets off another round of assessing the existing portfolio of options and, in all likelihood, the creation of new ones.

As a result, strategic planning built on Requisite Uncertainty and Strategic Flexibility is no longer driven by the calendar. Strategic planning should not begin with the fiscal year so that it can conclude twelve months later only to begin anew. Instead, a set of scenarios provides an evergreen context in which managers can evaluate the longer-term implications of current events. Each new piece of information now becomes a clue to where in the possibility space the future, defined by a particular time horizon, will fall. Once you start thinking in terms of scenarios and options, current events are no longer merely current; they become signposts for the future.

The cumulative weight of events over time eventually yields insights that allow each level of management to take the actions for which they are responsible: adjusting the scenario set and the portfolio of real options (corporate), making commitments and preparing for contingencies (operating division), or learning how best to deliver on promises already in place (function).

*The four phases of managing a portfolio of real options are cre-
ate, preserve, exercise, and abandon. Valuing real options in the
context of Strategic Flexibility is analogous to valuing financial
options, but the same analytical tools cannot be used without significant accommodation of the idiosyncrasies of real options.
Ultimately, real options are valuable in the management of strategic uncertainty. Consequently, determining what real options are
worth is a profoundly intuitive assessment based on the risk/
return profile that the board and top management feel is appropriate for the company.*

---

1. The seminal papers in the field of modern portfolio theory are Markowitz, Harry
M. (1952), "Portfolio Selection," *Journal of Finance,* Vol. 7, Iss. 1, pp. 77–91; Sharpe,
William F. (1964), "Capital Asset Prices: A Theory of Market Equilibrium Under Con-
ditions of Risk," *Journal of Finance,* Vol. 19, Iss. 3, pp. 425–42; Lintner, J. (1965), "The
Valuation of Risk Assets and the Selection of Risky Investments in Stock Portfolios and
Capital Budgets," *The Review of Economics and Statistics,* Vol. 47, Iss. 1, pp. 13–39;
and Tobin, James (1958), "Liquidity Preference as Behavior Towards Risk," *The Review
of Economic Studies,* Vol. 25, pp. 65–86.

2. See Schoemaker, P. J. H. "Disciplined Imagination: From Scenarios to Strategic
Options," in *International Studies of Management & Organization,* Vol. 27, No. 2,
Summer 1997, pp. 43–70 for a discussion of the links between scenarios and real options
in strategy.

3. Whether a given investment is an option or a commitment is of course a continuum. For expositional ease, I am willing to stipulate that a partial equity stake in a company with potentially valuable assets or capabilities is an option on an element of an
alternative strategy. In contrast, full ownership of that same company means that the
acquiring firm no longer has an option on the element, but is committed to it. However,
the option remains on the alternative strategy, which can only be implemented upon further investments in integration.

4. One of the first popular treatments of real options is Kester, W. Carl (1984),
"Today's Options for Tomorrow's Growth," *Harvard Business Review,* Vol. 62, No. 2.

5. Two articles by Timothy A. Luehrman are helpful in explaining how real options
are applied at the level of individual investment opportunities; see "Investment Opportunities as Real Options: Getting Started on the Numbers," *Harvard Business Review,*
Vol. 76, No. 4, and "Strategy as a Portfolio of Real Options," *Harvard Business Review,*
Vol. 76, No. 5.

6. Kim, Dong-Jae, and Bruce Kogut (1996), "Technological Platforms and Diversification," *Organization Science,* Vol. 7, No. 3.

7. Martin, Laura (2006), "What Is Google Worth," Soleil/Media Metrics, www.
soleilgroup.com.

8. For a fuller treatment of these issues, see Raynor, Michael E. (2002), *Strategic Flexibility in the Financial Services Sector,* Deloitte Research, www.deloitte.com/research/
strategicflexibility.

Given that megamergers in U.S. banking have continued apace, it would appear that

Banc One in fact had chosen the right strategy, but either leapt too soon or overestimated its abilities in implementation. In a very real sense, a material uncertainty about how best to create a national-scale bank perhaps was not given its due, and so a real options-based approach might have served the company well.

9. This might seem a fairly high number, but in fact might well have been an artifact of the SIC codes that occasionally classify as separate industries sectors of economic activity that share material similarities, and vice versa. The relevant observation is therefore not exclusively the absolute number of deals taking place in nominally different industries but the changes over time in the levels of activity within versus across putative industry boundaries.

10. Yu, Joseph, and Tang Ming-Je (1992), "International Joint Ventures: Theoretical Considerations," *Managerial and Decision Economics,* Vol. 13; Ouchi, W. G., and M. K. Bolton (1988), "The Logic of Joint Research and Development," *California Management Review,* Vol. 30, No. 3.

11. Katz, M. L. (1995), "Joint Ventures as a Means of Assembling Complementary Inputs," *Group Decision and Negotiation,* Vol. 4, pp. 383–400.

12. Gomes-Casseres, B. (1987), "Joint Venture Instability: Is It a Problem?" *Columbia Journal of World Business* (Summer), pp. 97–102; and Blodgett, L. L. (1990), "Factors in the Instability of International Joint Ventures: An Event History Analysis," *Strategic Management Journal,* Vol. 13, pp. 475–81.

13. Mohanram, P., and A. Nanda (1996), "Joint Ventures Among Potential Entrants," Harvard Business School working paper.

14. Hamel, Gary (1991), "Competition for Competence and Inter-Partner Learning Within International Strategic Alliances," *Strategic Management Journal,* Vol. 12, pp. 83–103; Inkpen, A. C., and M. M. Crosson (1995), "Believing Is Seeing: Joint Ventures and Organizational Learning," *Journal of Management Studies,* Vol. 32, No. 5. Some commentators have been especially critical of JVs when one party appears to be able to benefit in this way far more than the other. See, for example, Reich, R. B., and E. D. Mankin (1986), "Joint Ventures with Japan Give Away Our Future," *Harvard Business Review* (March–April), pp. 78–86.

15. Kogut, Bruce (1991), "Joint Ventures and the Option to Expand and Acquire," *Management Science,* Vol. 37, No. 1; Chi, T. (2000), "Option to Acquire or Divest a Joint Venture," *Strategic Management Journal,* Vol. 21, No. 6.

16. Collins, T. M., and T. L. Doorley (1991), *Teaming Up for the 90s: A Guide to International Joint Ventures and Strategic Alliances,* Homewood, IL: Business One Irwin.

17. An example of this is the 50/50 joint venture between BellSouth and SBC to create Cingular, the wireless services provider. To the extent that Cingular represented an option on wireline/wireless integration for both BellSouth and SBC, it was highly likely that each would be motivated to sell its share or acquire their partner's share under the same circumstances. Fortunately for SBC, it turned out that the acquisition of BellSouth made sense, so being able to acquire full control of Cingular only by acquiring BellSouth did not lead to the problems suggested in the main text.

18. There are distressingly few studies of any kind on the incidence of partial equity stakes and the strategic considerations relevant to making such investments. See Reynolds, R. J., and B. R. Snapp (1986), "The Competitive Effects of Partial Equity Interests and Joint Ventures," *International Journal of Industrial Organization,* Vol. 4, pp. 141–53; Dasgupta, Sudipto, and Zhigang Tao (2000), "Bargaining, Bonding, and Partial Ownership," *International Economic Review,* Vol. 41, No. 3 (August); and Kale, Prashant, and Phanish Puranam (2004), "Choosing Equity Stakes in Technology-Sourcing Relationship: An Integrative Framework," *California Management Review,* Vol. 46, No. 3 (Spring).

19. One rather esoteric ownership structure that got a lot of coverage in the late 1990s, but is relatively rarely used, is the "tracking stock," in which investors purchase the right to the value of a specific set of assets that are controlled by the same corporate management team. Tracking stocks essentially make it possible for a company to control a set of assets without owning them at all. It is, on the face of it, the perfect way to create precisely the kinds of options discussed here. See Raynor, Michael E. (2000), "Tracking Stocks and the Acquisition of Real Options," *Journal of Applied Corporate Finance,* Vol. 13, No. 2.

The governance issues surrounding tracking stocks are still more challenging than those associated with partial equity stakes (see following note). Their rarity suggests that these and other considerations make investors sufficiently uneasy that companies generally do not find tracking stocks a useful tool.

20. A critically important consideration when imposing this kind of strategic constraint is taking appropriate account of the interests of minority shareholders. If BCE were to redirect Emergis's strategy in ways that either destroyed value or simply failed to exploit significant opportunities, Emergis's equity value would suffer. This is akin to tolerating operating losses, and so would not only pose a very important governance question but also drive up the cost of BCE's option on Emergis.

21. Galunic, Charles D., and Kathleen M. Eisenhardt (2001), "Architectural Innovation and Modular Corporate Forms," *Academy of Management Journal,* Vol. 44, No. 6; Eisenhardt, Kathleen M., and Shona L. Brown (1999), "Patching: Restitching Business Portfolios in Dynamic Markets," *Harvard Business Review* (May–June); Bower, Joseph L. (2003), "Building the Velcro Organization: Creating Value Through Integration and Maintaining Organization-wide Efficiency," *Ivey Business Journal* (November–December); Burgelman, Robert A., and Yves L. Doz, "The Power of Strategic Integration," *MIT/Sloan Management Review* (Spring).

22. One useful categorization of the types of recombination required is *operational integration* versus *strategic integration* (Burgelman and Doz, *op. cit.*). Operational integration consists typically of economies of scope—for example, a shared sales force or manufacturing capacity. Strategic integration is the recombination of resources or assets from two or more operating divisions to create a new operating division—a kind of "internal joint venture."

This distinction seems to map nicely onto the "constraints" framework developed in Chapter 8. Operational integration falls within the constraints of established business units, while strategic integration falls beyond existing constraints. Where the constraints framework might prove more helpful is in determining under which circumstances corporate office involvement is required. Burgelman and Doz, and to a lesser extent Bower (*op. cit.*), tend to see strategic integration as necessarily requiring corporate office involvement. However, Johnson & Johnson has a history of creating new business units from parts of existing organizations without corporate office intervention *where the new businesses fall within the strategic constraints of the existing divisions.* This is because J&J has a culture and a history of internal entrepreneurship. What its units do not do, because they cannot, is integrate strategically in ways that go beyond those constraints.

Consequently, the distinction between strategic and operational integration does not, in my view, unambiguously define the nature of the appropriate processes. "Within" versus "beyond" the operating division constraints seems to be a more parsimonious framework.

23. Eisenhardt and Brown (1999), *op. cit.* These authors identify this example as a "typical" patching situation. It is especially instructive because it constitutes an instance of very-nearly strategic integration that was effected without the intervention of the corporate office.

24. Eisenmann, Thomas R., and Joseph L. Bower (2000), "The Entrepreneurial M-Form: Strategic Integration in Global Media Firms," *Organization Science,* Vol. 11, No. 3. The summary of the News Corp. example and the Kellner quotation are taken from this article.

25. Eisenmann and Bower (2000), *op. cit.,* explain that individual divisions did not control the necessary budget and could not invest over the requisite time horizon (resource constraints), lacked the organizational authority to marshal the requisite resources from across the corporation (structural constraints), and were too risk-averse to make the necessary investments (strategic constraints). Consequently, the need for some form of extra-divisional intervention is entirely understandable.

To be sure, this is an example of strategic integration, but it is not the strategic integration itself that defines the need for corporate-level involvement; it is the fact that it is an instance of strategic integration that goes beyond divisional constraints.

26. See Raynor, Michael E. (1999), CIBC Corporate and Investment Banking (A), (B), and (C), Harvard Business School cases #9-300-041, #9-300-042, and #9-399-165, respectively.

27. In Canada, as in the United States, corporate lending and securities underwriting were separated by law based on the belief that during the Great Depression banks had inappropriately extended loans to companies whose securities they had floated in an attempt to bolster their value, or misrepresented the value of securities in order to protect the solvency of firms to which they had extended loans. This took the form of the Glass-Steagal Act in the United States, and the Bank Act in Canada, both passed in the aftermath of the Great Depression, and significantly modified in both jurisdictions in the 1980s and 1990s.

28. CIBC remains the leading equity underwriter in Canada but has suffered a series of setbacks as a result of large commitments to growth in the U.S. markets. The firm bought and then sold Oppenheimer Securities, a U.S. broker. Through the aggressive pursuit of tier 1 investment banking status in the United States, CIBC secured a prominent role in Enron's financing, a Pyrrhic victory, as the bank ended up paying more than $2 billion in settlements to U.S. regulators in the wake of Enron's collapse.

29. The corporate headquarters of all four banks are within one city block of each other in Toronto's financial district. BMO, BNS, and CIBC are on the northwest, northeast, and southeast corners of King and Bay Streets, and RBC is one block south on the northwest corner of Bay and Front Streets. This is without question one of the more homogeneous industry settings one might study.

30. Professor Robert Burgelman of the Stanford Business School notes that "strategic context determination processes"—that is, how the boundaries within which operating managers develop substantive strategies—"may be among the most elusive, volatile, and precarious decision processes in organizations." See Burgelman, Robert (1992), "Intraorganizational Ecology of Strategy Making and Organizational Adaptation: Theory and Field Research," *Organization Science*, Vol. 2, pp. 239–62.

31. Johnson & Johnson Development Corporation (JJDC), Johnson & Johnson's corporate venture capital group, is a process-based solution that is, as at CIBC, a subtle mix of top-down and bottom-up initiatives. As an organ of the corporate office with its own investment budget and mandate, it has a "top-down" flavor reminiscent of the strategic integration efforts of heroic CEOs in the media sector. Yet much of JJDC's activity is dedicated to illustrating the merits of recombining operating company (OpCo) resources to create new capabilities and even entirely new OpCos. Support from OpCo leadership is critical to exercising specific options, suggesting a more bottom-up approach in many ways consistent with notions of "patching." Finally, the repeated nature of these activities, and the structured way in which JJDC goes about its role,

implies that it is possible to set up processes that can enable and facilitate the necessary action.

32. Ironically, we cannot say with certainty that options that get exercised were truly options. Without actually walking away from further investment, we do not know that an organization could have actually walked away. We can make educated guesses based on the structure of the initial deal and the organization's behavior under similar circumstances. So BCE's having walked away from exercising the CGI and Emergis options suggests strongly that it could also have walked away from exercising the BCE Mobile option as well, implying that BCE Mobile was in fact an option and not merely a commitment delayed.

33. Steiner, Thomas Lorenz (1997), "The Corporate Sell-off Decision of Diversified Firms," *The Journal of Financial Research,* Vol. 20, No. 2. The decision to sell is seen as motivated exclusively by bad performance on the part of the division sold off or a corporate need for extra cash elsewhere. See also Porter, Michael E. (1987), "From Competitive Advantage to Corporate Strategy," *Harvard Business Review,* Vol. 65, No. 3. Porter adduces the high incidence of asset disposals by diversified corporations as *prima facie* evidence that "the corporate strategies of most companies have dissipated instead of created shareholder value." Given his sample, Porter is almost certainly correct, but in a world where investments create option value, such disposals would be critical to demonstrating prudent management rather than rash and ultimately unsuccessful commitments.

34. Garland, Howard (1990), "Throwing Good Money After Bad: The Effect of Sunk Costs on the Decision to Escalate Commitment to an Ongoing Project," *Journal of Applied Psychology,* Vol. 75, No. 6. For an exploration of the sunk-cost effect in a very different, but compelling, context, see Staw, Barry M., and Ha Hoang (1995), "Sunk Costs in the NBA: Why Draft Order Affects Playing Time and Survival in Professional Basketball," *Administrative Science Quarterly,* Vol. 40, pp. 474–94.

35. Fink, Ronald (2001), "Reality Check: Look Closely at Real Options, and a Basic Assumption Begins to Quiver," *CFO* (September).

36. *Canada NewsWire,* January 9, 2001.

37. *Vancouver Sun,* April 4, 2001, p. D7.

38. *Montreal Gazette,* April 26, 2002, p. C9.

39. *National Post,* December 19, 2002, p. FP1.

40. *Globe & Mail,* August 7, 2006, p. B5.

41. In late 2006, just as this book was going to press, BCE announced that it would structure itself as an income trust. This creates a much stronger obligation for BCE to make prespecified "disbursements" than mere dividend payments on equity.

This restructuring came in a series of steps. First, in 2005, BCE created Bell Nordique, a company that contained those local phone lines in northern and rural Ontario and Quebec that faced relatively little competition from alternative providers such as cable companies. As a result of their relatively stable competitive contexts, the burden of disbursements is relatively easily borne. Similarly, in July of 2006, BCE's lines in eastern Canada that faced comparatively lower levels of competition and hence strategic uncertainty were combined in an income trust, Bell Alliant, and Bell Nordique was folded into it.

A short time later, Telus, one of BCE's main telecommunications competitors, became an income trust. Due to the tax treatment of income trust units over equity shares, this provided Telus with perhaps a lower cost of capital, which could have important implications for the competitive balance between the two companies. Since the Canadian government was rumored to be ready to change the tax treatment of income trust units in a way that eliminated this advantage—but "grandfathered" the trusts already in place—BCE faced the possibility of a permanent and structural disadvantage to a major competitor in a key factor market.

What remains unanswered is whether BCE's decision will significantly undermine the company's ability to manage effectively strategy uncertainty through the creation of the requisite strategic options. BCE's senior management has professed a desire to establish two income trusts: one for BCE, which faces material strategic uncertainty, and the Bell Alliant income trust, which faces less strategic uncertainty. Such a move would allow investors in each trust to price the units according to their beliefs on the magnitude and reliability of the disbursements. In my view, those who argue for a single trust believe either that BCE does not face any material strategic uncertainty, or that if it does, it should simply accept that risk in exchange for a richer cash payout in the shorter term.

In the wake of BCE's announcement, the Canadian federal government announced its intention to change the tax treatment of income trusts, resulting in widespread speculation that BCE would abandon the proposed conversion.

42. Waldie, Paul (1996), "B of M Closes Deal to Buy 16% of Mexican Bank," *The Globe & Mail,* March 30.

43. "Bank of Montreal to Acquire 16% Stake in Grupo Financiero Bancomer and Enter Into Strategic Alliance," PR Newswire, February 15, 1996.

44. Van Hasselt, Caroline (1999), "B of M to Expand in U.S. Midwest, Sun Belt Comper Says Part of Push Will Include Targeting Chicago Area's Hispanic Residents," *The Globe & Mail,* August 18; Craig, Susanne (1999), "Bank of Montreal Offers Specialized Banking Service to Mexican Migrants," *The Globe & Mail,* September 18.

45. "Bank of Montreal Sells Remaining Shares of Grupo Financiero BBVA Bancomer to BBVA," Canada NewsWire, May 3, 2001.

46. Olive, David (1999), "Bank of Montreal's Mexican Investment Hasn't Yet Fulfilled Barrett's Bold Plans," *Financial Post,* December 11.

47. A good place to start is Copeland, Tom, and Vladimir Antikarov (2001), *Real Options: A Practitioner's Guide,* New York: Texere.

48. Of course, the price of an option is not perfectly predicted by mathematical techniques. The range over which a stock price will vary in the future is only estimated by historical ranges and volatility. In fact, one could instead attempt to infer the future range of stock prices from the volatility implied by the option price. That is, instead of solving for the price of the option, one could observe the price of the option in the market and solve for the future volatility expected by investors. Unfortunately, if you are trying to determine if an option is fairly priced, this is not much help.

49. Amram, Martha, and Nalin Kulatilaka (2000), "Strategy and Shareholder Value Creation: The Real Options Frontier," *Journal of Applied Corporate Finance,* Vol. 13, No. 2. In particular, when it comes to creating estimates of the nonobservable elements of real options that can be observed, or at least estimated, when valuing financial options, the authors note that "when the value and exercise of investment [real] options cannot be linked to risks priced in the financial markets, the value of strategic [real] options is better captured by other frameworks." What some of those other frameworks might be is what I am suggesting in the main text.

CHAPTER ELEVEN

REINVENTING STRATEGY

Applying Requisite Uncertainty and Strategic Flexibility might have led Sony to make different decisions in its commercialization of Betamax and MiniDisc . These approaches have implications for how the company might address its current challenges. This thought experiment reveals that resolving the strategy paradox requires an organization to pursue both "deliberate" and "emergent" strategy formulation simultaneously. Ultimately, making the right kinds of commitments in an unpredictable world demands that strategic planning be based on an acceptance of our limitations and a willingness not merely to admit, but to embrace, what we do not know.

This book is about the challenge of thinking clearly about a future that we cannot see clearly. The key to doing this well is to remember that planning for the future does not mean imagining what choices we will make later. There are only ever the decisions one makes today, and in the context of strategic planning, what distinguishes those decisions is the time horizon one takes into account when making them.

Since hierarchical levels are similarly defined by the time horizons to be considered when making decisions, thinking about the future is necessarily the responsibility of senior management. And since the future is unavoidably uncertain, senior management's role is to manage uncertainty. Requisite Uncertainty and Strategic Flexibility provide the theoretical foundation and practical toolkit required to fulfill that responsibility. Adopting these prescriptions has profound implications for managers at every level of the hierarchy. In this concluding chapter I hope to show that taking uncertainty seriously requires a reinvention of our conventional approaches to strategy.

11.1 SONY REVISITED

Chapter 2 portrayed Sony as a victim of the strategy paradox, a firm that designed and implemented strategies that had every chance of success, yet failed due to unforeseen—and unforeseeable—events that ultimately favored competitors who made different choices. It is time to deliver on the promise made in Chapter 2, for although we can never know for sure if Requisite Uncertainty and Strategic Flexibility would have helped, it is worth at least exploring what sorts of actions would have been consistent with the concepts offered here and how that might have changed the outcomes.

11.1.1 Looking Back

Some of the difficulties Sony experienced with the Betamax might have been a consequence of a lack of differentiation in the strategic conversation within the company.[1] Betamax was designed and launched at a time when key product and marketing decisions were still being made by Sony's CEO, Akio Morita, and a close circle of about five associates. Collectively, this small group was able repeatedly to assess correctly the ways in which customers would use electronic devices, many of which were entirely new to the market.[2] As a result, it is completely possible that some or all of this key top team was heavily involved in formulating the strategy for Betamax.

Given this group's uncanny insight, this is not by itself a bad thing; after all, why not take advantage of whatever genius is available? The constraint is that no one can think about everything, and if the senior team was occupied with product features and strategic positioning—that is, choosing which strategic *commitments* to make—who was thinking about the strategic *uncertainties* that the Betamax might face?

Requisite Uncertainty might have helped Sony's corporate office by institutionalizing that level's responsibility to address longer-term strategic uncertainties and to devote resources to creating the relevant options. In the case of Betamax, the critical strategic uncertainty was how the device would fit into the entertainment industry. CTI had attempted to introduce its Cartrivision VCR as primarily a movie-viewing device but had difficulties securing titles from studios and was hampered by a particularly inconvenient retail distribution channel. Although there were fewer impediments to Sony's emphasis on TV time-shifting, the studios that provided much of television's content were hoping to have the device declared illegal, so this tack was hardly a sure thing, either.

Call these two scenarios "Prime Time-Shifting" and "Hooray for Hollywood." In the first scenario, the optimal strategy is relatively straightforward, and it is essentially what Sony did: fight the lawsuit and make your product the best TV-recording device around. Some negotiated settlement with the studios might have resulted in paying a royalty of some sort, but provisions could easily be made for that.

If movie viewing were to become critical to the success of the VCR, however, the optimal strategy would require a well-developed ecosystem that included both studios and distributors. Would movies be purchased or rented? Would they be "first run" or B-list? Would studios support this new market or fight it? A corporate office more obviously attuned to the management of strategic uncertainty might have looked into creating options that could have facilitated a shift into this application. For example, Sony might have collaborated with mail-order book clubs and documentary film makers to create a new market for movies that had difficulty getting distribution in theaters. This would have required a relatively small investment and circumvented the difficulties of securing retail distribution. Pioneering a model based on movie sales, rather than rentals, might also have appealed to the studios, and in any case would have put Sony in the forefront of this use of VCR technology. Such efforts would have likely violated the constraints of the operating division responsible for Betamax's launch, and so creating these options would have fallen to the corporate office.

At the division level, Betamax's bet was on product differentiation. The downside of this commitment was that the market would come to prefer less expensive products, rather than products that performed better. Hedging this downside could have been done by investing in a cut-down version of Betamax that was easier to manufacture, and then licensing that alternative technology widely. Sony would then have reserved the leading-edge product for its own manufacturing capacity, but would also have put in play a group of manufacturers competing on cost efficiencies with slightly inferior products. This would have allowed Betamax to cover a broader swath of the production possibility frontier without diluting Sony's focus on a product-differentiation strategy. As an additional hedge, if it turned out that in fact a lower-cost device was coming to dominate the market, Sony could have sold its licenses with buyback provisions. Each additional hedge would have cost something, and whether suitable terms could have been struck remains an open question. The point is merely that at the division level there were strategic hedges available that Sony did not take and perhaps did not even consider.

Requisite Uncertainty and Strategic Flexibility might have allowed Sony to create a nested series of options based on ever-longer time horizons. In the very short term, the various functional organizations were working diligently to ensure that Betamax had the features required to be a successful high-end TV-recording device. The division could have launched alternative product configurations via licensees with as little commitment as possible, and in a way that allowed Sony to take back either the profitability of these different products or to terminate them if licensees began to undermine a high-end approach that was proving highly successful. And the corporate office would have created options on entirely different strategies that would emerge over longer periods of time in ways that would have provided Sony with a window on that part of the industry that, in the event, proved decisive.

The MiniDisc case is perhaps less complex. Hoping to avoid the "chicken-or-the-egg" fate that befell DAT, Sony had invested in a record label, then attempted to capture synergies between that investment and their existing electronics business. This is, after all, what corporate strategy is all about, right?

Wrong, of course. The role of the corporate office is only in part to facilitate the capture of synergies; it also bears primary responsibility for managing strategic uncertainties. Rather than commit Sony to a strategy of device-content integration, the corporate office could have contented itself with simply having created the option on such a strategy through the acquisition of a record label. Whether or not subsequent integration would be required in order to advance the interests of either the device or content divisions was a question that had yet to be resolved.

Upon MiniDisc's launch in the early 1990s, seeding the market for the device by making Sony Music CDs available in MiniDisc format was a relatively costless form of integration. It was intended simply to make it easier for the MiniDisc to get over the initial hump of market acceptance: the availability of music was a necessary but not sufficient condition of success.

Unfortunately, by managing its presence in the music business for immediate synergy, rather than as an option on future synergy, Sony allowed the interests of its music business to constrain actions of its electronics business *in ways it would not have otherwise been constrained*. For example, the MiniDisc was explicitly an attempt to replicate the functionality of the compact audiocassette (CAC) in disc format. That should have meant easy copying between CD and MiniDisc formats, but the MiniDisc deliberately did not have the kinds of features that would have allowed it to compete more effectively with MP3 players that were compatible with file-sharing services.

Sony entered the music business believing that content and devices were complementary businesses. They are . . . sometimes. And sometimes they are highly antagonistic. By committing to a strategy of integration and synergy, Sony precluded itself from success under those circumstances when each division was better off left alone. Whereas with Betamax the successful management of uncertainty required doing more, in the case of the MiniDisc managing uncertainty required doing much less.

11.1.2 Looking Forward

For all its successes, today Sony is, by many accounts, a company going through an identity crisis. Especially in Japan, but in many other regions as well, Sony has diversified into a wide variety of businesses, everything from financial services (where it is a low-end player; see Chapter 10) to skin-care products (that are purportedly used by Japan's Crown Princess Masako). This has diluted the company's image and undermined Sony's ability to charge higher prices for some of its products.[3]

Even when the company seems to be creating options in the interests of managing uncertainty, it cannot escape criticism.[4] In anticipation of "networked entertainment," Sony morphed the PlayStation into a connected multimedia entertainment console while hedging the possibility that the TV might remain the key terminal device by taking partial equity stakes in set-top box maker General Instruments, DIRECTV (a satellite TV services provider), WebTV (which sought to Internet-enable the television), and Spyglass and Aperios, makers of application and operating system software for television-based systems.

If not the game console or the television, perhaps the PC might dominate, and so Sony's Vaio PC division built the most advanced multimedia capabilities into its products. And if not PCs? Sony hedged here, too, with its Sony-Ericsson joint venture to manufacture mobile phones. Finally, beyond devices, Sony invested in home networking technology and explored alternative business models in music and movie distribution with Pressplay and Movielink, online music and movie businesses, respectively. All this strategic insurance was very expensive, and many analysts said Sony was stretched too thin.

Empirical studies of the economic impact of Sony's ever-expanding diversification drive suggest that the company has not created value through synergies between its divisions.[5] Capital markets appeared to agree, as the company's share price has fallen from highs above $150/share at the height of the dot-com mania to under $40/share in 2005, when the decade-long tenure of Chairman and CEO Nobuyuki Idei came to an end.

Perhaps part of the problem was that Idei was convinced that synergies among the outposts of Sony's far-flung empire were the key to success, and he committed the company to that specific strategic course.[6] Viewing Sony's investments as options on different strategies that could be exercised when competitive conditions warranted and internal conditions permitted might have avoided an unnecessarily expensive and so-far fruitless quest for integration.[7]

Sony's troubles, however, are symptomatic of an industry-wide phenomenon. Many of the large media conglomerates that have been created over the last ten or more years have failed to deliver on their promises (either explicitly or implicitly made), and the whole idea of "big media" is being revisited.[8] As a result, some of these titans have either been dismantled or are under siege, and the results either way have not been promising.

For example, Viacom broke itself in two, creating Viacom Inc. and CBS Corp., corresponding roughly to "new media" and "old media." The view seemed to be that synergies were not materializing, and so focus must clearly have been the right response. Unfortunately, there is little reason to believe that the move has released, let alone created, any significant value.[9]

Meanwhile, TimeWarner has been under intense pressure to improve its operating performance in the wake of a persistent Carl Icahn, whose primary enthusiasm for the company seems to lie in his belief that it can be profitably dismembered. As a result, TimeWarner management is forced to attend to short-run turnaround efforts and at least be seen to be committed to a synergy-based strategy, much as was Jean Monty at BCE in the late 1990s.[10]

When neither splitting companies up nor leaving them whole satisfies the capital markets, surely it is time to consider another possibility: that the competitive future these firms face is profoundly uncertain and that demanding of corporate leadership a bold commitment to a surefire strategy is madness. How much better would it be if media executives—and executives at any company grappling with unpredictable and potentially turbulent environments—could discuss rationally and logically how they will deal with what they do not know instead of being forced to present a façade of prescience and unwavering dedication to a chosen path?

11.2 BOTH DELIBERATE AND EMERGENT BE

There is a long-running debate in the strategy field regarding the relative merits of "planning" versus "learning," or alternatively, "deliberate" versus "emergent" strategy-formulation processes. The fundamental distinction is between strategies that are based on commitments premised on accurate plans and those that emerge in near real time from flashes of insight in response to events.[11] The "planning," or "deliberate," school holds that strategy demands careful coordination and commitment, and that this can only be accomplished through foresight and advance preparation. The "learning," or "emergent," camp responds that the future is uncertain, and that in fact much of the strategy actually crystallizes as a result of the accumulation of many small decisions made in response to immediate concerns.

Subsequent researchers have qualified this debate, suggesting that the alleged dichotomy between deliberate and emergent approaches to strategy is a false one. Instead, each approach is appropriate under different circumstances: a deliberate approach makes sense when the future is clear (or clear enough), while an emergent approach is superior when dealing with material uncertainties. At the limit, a deliberate strategy sets an organization on a path, and while traveling that path, the "enacted" strategy emerges in response to the inevitable surprises and vagaries along the way.[12]

Requisite Uncertainty builds upon this contingent view. When it comes to strategic uncertainties, the far future is always less certain than the near future. Consequently, an emergent strategy process makes sense when thinking about the long term. And since the long term is the preserve of senior management, emergent strategy processes are most appropriate at that level of the hierarchy. In contrast, the shorter time horizons attached to divisional and functional management imply more deliberate strategies, since there are concomitantly fewer strategic uncertainties to account for.

With each level of the hierarchy thinking about and acting along its own time horizon, the organization as a whole will have deliberate and emergent strategy processes at work simultaneously. Senior management, pursuing a more emergent approach, creates options on alternative strategies; divisional management takes a more deliberate approach because it must make specific commitments and exploit options created by the corporate level at some point in the past. This deliberate bent is tempered by the need to seek hedges against future bad luck in the pursuit of the chosen strategy; and functional management is the most deliberate of all, seeking only to execute the chosen strategy as effectively as possible, operating more or less in a perpetual present.

This model is potentially quite different from many people's intuitions about strategy formulation. Rather than a master plan crafted on high, which is then implemented by an adaptive, responsive organization, we see instead senior management creating options in keeping with the prescriptions of Strategic Flexibility while lower echelons enjoy progressively less strategic latitude.

Devoting the CEO and the board to questions of strategic uncertainty is a significant shift in emphasis for many organizations. Often overwhelmed by their fiduciary responsibilities to fulfill the control function, boards and senior managers often lose sight of their very different responsibilities associated with strategy. And when it comes to strategy and the long term, uncertainty is the only constant, and choosing options over commitment is the most reasonable response to that uncertainty.

11.3 THE STRATEGY OF HUMILITY

In tragedy, the hero's downfall is often a consequence of hubris: the exaggerated pride or self-confidence that leads one to believe that extreme success is preordained, inevitable, and deserved. Strategic tragedies are often attributable to the same flaw. The willingness to stake one's success on the ability to make commitments today that will not pay off until years into the future is either evidence of a high tolerance for risk or the height of arrogance. The Ancients teach the only defense against hubris is humility: the recognition that, whatever our strengths, the realm of what we cannot foresee or control far exceeds our grasp.

If strategy, and those who craft it, are to avoid the pitfalls of hubris, then here, too, must humility take center stage. Strategy, to be more useful, must begin with a clear identification of uncertainty and how that undermines our ability to commit. In other words, strategy should begin with what we do not know rather than with what we do, for successful strategies must be built *upon* uncertainty, not in *spite* of it. And the need humbly to identify the limits of our knowledge and admit our ignorance is most acute where uncertainty is greatest: at the highest levels of the hierarchy.

Traditional strategic planning is not blind to uncertainty, but it treats it as an afterthought: commit first and ask questions later. The prescriptions of industry analysis, core competence theory, and disruptive innovation are all tremendously powerful, but they should come *after* an assessment of critical uncertainties, not before. For although we know it, our hubris often prevents us from admitting and submitting to the unfortunate fact that we cannot foresee everything that matters, control all that we would like to, or always create the outcomes we desire.

Bowing to the limits of our station need not imply that we aim lower: a Macbeth or an Oedipus who accedes to the vagaries of fate can still be king, but he rules the kingdom very differently. Similarly, a strategy built on humility can still succeed; it just looks very different from a strategy built on hubris. This book has explored those differences and argued that a strategy of humility is a better and nobler way to think about the future of your company.

1. I have no inside information about Sony's decision-making processes, and I am unaware of any careful studies on the topic. As a result, my inferences must be seen as tentative.

2. Christensen, Clayton M., and Michael E. Raynor (2003), *The Innovator's Solution: Creating and Sustaining Successful Growth,* Boston: Harvard Business School Press, Chapter 3, note 10. This assessment of Sony's decision making was offered in an interview Christensen had with Mickey Schulhoff, who worked for more than twenty years as the CEO of Sony America and for much of this time as a member of Sony Corporation's board of directors.

3. Fackler, Martin (2006), "Cutting Sony, a Corporate Octopus, Back to a Rational Size," *New York Times,* May 29.

4. Chakravorti, Bhaskar (2004), "Whether to Bet, Reserve Options, or Insure: Making Certain Choices in an Uncertain World," *Ivey Business Journal* (January–February).

5. Inoue, Yasuhiro (2003), "Hard and Soft Mega-Media Conglomeration: Has Sony's Strategy Created Synergies," *Keio Communication Review,* No. 25.

6. Belson, Ken (2005), "Curse of a Visionary: The Undoing of Idei at Sony, a Departing Chief Executive Failed to Get the Company to Live Up to Expectations," *New York Times,* March 9.

7. *The Economist* (2005), "Bad Strategy, or Bad Management?" March 12.

8. Fabrikant, Geraldine, and Richard Siklos (2005), "Big Media a Tough Sell to Jittery Investors," *New York Times,* November 3.

9. Farrell, Mike (2006), "Split-Up's a Rocky Road for Viacom Sibs," *Multichannel Newswire,* July 24.

10. Siklos, Richard (2006), "Time Warner's Anxious Autumn," *New York Times,* September 3.

11. Perhaps the most explicit expression of this debate is a series of articles that appeared in 1990–1991. See Mintzberg, H. (1990), "The Design School: Reconsidering the Basic Premises of Strategic Management," *Strategic Management Journal,* Vol. 11, pp. 171–95; Ansoff, H. Igor (1991), "Critique of Henry Mintzberg's 'The Design School: Reconsidering the Basic Premises of Strategic Management,'" *Strategic Management Journal,* Vol. 12, pp. 449–61.

12. Christensen, Clayton M., and Tara Donovan (2000), "The Process of Strategy Development and Implementation," Harvard Business School working paper.

HOW DIVERSIFICATION CAN CREATE VALUE

Firms operate in markets for critical inputs, including capital, resources of various types, and a wide variety of products and services. All the markets in which these goods are traded are subject to failure: firms might not always be able to acquire what they need at prices vendors are willing to sell them at.

Using the concept of market failure, economists and management scholars have sought to explain the existence of different types of diversified firms.[1] Different diversification strategies are responses to the failure of different markets, and each diversification strategy requires a different administrative system to realize its value-creating potential. Specifically, the failure of *capital* markets results in *unrelated* diversification, which is best managed using *competitive* systems in order to capture *governance* economies. *Vertical integration* is a response to the failure of *product* or *information* markets and requires *constraining* systems to capture *coordination* economies. *Related* diversification compensates for the failure of *resource* markets and functions best under *cooperative* systems to capture *scope* economies.[2]

UNRELATED DIVERSIFICATION

In an unrelated diversifier, the operating divisions are not related in any meaningful way. Were the business units in an unrelated diversifier (or any other diversified firm) stand-alone entities, they would have direct contact with capital markets via their own boards of directors. The challenge is to detail the benefits and costs of interposing the corporate layer between the operating units and the capital markets and to describe the conditions under which the benefits will exceed the costs.

The theoretical defense of unrelated diversification is based on alleged failures in the capital markets to cope effectively with the inevitable agency costs of employing managers (i.e., agents) as stewards of firm resources. Due to their privileged access to and understanding of company information, managers can knowingly and willingly misrepresent the facts of any given investment proposal in order to further their own personal gains. This is known as *managerial opportunism* made possible through *information impactedness*. Your mother would call it "lying."

Whether or not individual managers are virtuous or vicious is irrelevant. Information impactedness makes the *possibility* of managerial opportunism inescapable. Consequently, investors demand a higher rate of return than they would if they were certain that managers were always truthful. This serves effectively to increase the cost of capital to the firm, which results in positive net present value opportunities going unfunded. This is arguably a failure of the *capital* markets.

Oliver Williamson, in his 1975 book *Markets and Hierarchies,* makes the case that the corporate office can monitor divisional management more effectively than can shareholders and the market for corporate control. First, the corporate office can gather information on divisional performance and behavior through internal audits that are not subject to information sensitivity concerns. External investors typically must rely on blunter measures, and so will typically detect malfeasance much later than a corporate office might. Also, because corporate managers will have access to otherwise privileged information, they are less likely to be exploited by misrepresentations of fact by potentially opportunistic divisional managers than are external investors. Finally, when investors need to intervene in order to correct managerial misbehavior, they must do so through expensive and typically ineffective board proxy fights or even more expensive battles for corporate control. In contrast, corporate-level managers can intervene directly in divisional operations or simply replace divisional management, which is a much finer-grained and less expensive means of course correction. In other words, corporate management can detect problems sooner, correct problems more effectively, and act faster and less expensively than can shareholders.

A critical problem with this defense of unrelated diversification is that whatever level of managerial opportunism is created by information impactedness at the level of the operating units surely also exists between the corporate office and shareholders. In other words, the Trasymachian question remains: who will watch the watchers? There is no answer to this objection: managers (agents) are stewards of shareholders' (principals') resources. Charging another agent to steward the behavior of the first still demands a mechanism for monitoring this new layer of agency. Consequently, Williamson's argument for unrelated diversification turns on a *reduction* in monitoring costs, not their elimination:

. . . I do not mean to suggest that opportunities to express managerial preferences in ways that conflict with the preferences of the stockholders have been extinguished as a result of the conglomerate form. [Read: Managers can still lie.] The continuing tension between management and stockholder interests is reflected in numerous efforts that incumbent managements have taken to protect target firms against takeover [cites omitted]. *Changes in internal organization have nevertheless relieved managerial discretion concerns* [emphasis added].[3]

In other words, an unrelated diversifier makes sense so long as the sum of the costs incurred by the corporate center in monitoring the divisions and the costs incurred by shareholders in monitoring the corporate office are less than the costs to shareholders of monitoring each division individually. Since the benefits of the corporate structure in an unrelated portfolio stem from improved governance, successful unrelated diversifiers are said to capture *governance* economies.

Capturing governance economies depends on the ability of the diversified firm to mete out capital to its highest-yield use more efficiently than external capital markets can. In essence, the goal for the corporate office in diversified firms seeking governance economies is to replicate the relationship between freestanding firms and the external capital market and then exploit its hierarchical relationship with divisions to overcome managerial opportunism.

To achieve this, the corporate office must evaluate divisions' proposals for future investment. Once projects have been selected, the corporate office must monitor these investments in order to detect managerial misconduct or incompetence and effect corrective action in a timely manner. Both of these factors require that the corporate office be able to measure precisely and compare divisional economic performance. This in turn implies that divisional performance be measured by objective, and hence typically quantitative, metrics such as return on investment (ROI).

Keeping divisional management focused on divisional performance typically means explicitly linking the compensation of divisional managers with divisional performance. Consequently, divisions within the diversified corporation often view each other no differently than independent firms might. Although divisions might not compete for customers, they compete for the capital the corporation has available to invest, which in turn translates into opportunities for divisional managers to earn rewards and advance their careers. Since divisions are competing, even if only for capital, the managerial structures required to capture governance economies are referred to as *competitive* systems.

VERTICAL INTEGRATION

A firm is vertically integrated when it consists of multiple business units that have material customer relationships with other units in the firm. In other words, vertical integration involves internalizing transactions in goods or services that are outputs of one division and inputs to others.

During the late nineteenth and early twentieth centuries, many American firms were compelled to diversify by vertically integrating by expanding their activities downstream from production into distribution. The reason for this diversification was to compensate for the absence of firms providing the services needed to develop and serve a mass market on a continental scale. Companies could not work with focused firms that, say, distributed their goods west of the Mississippi because there *were* no distribution companies operating west of the Mississippi. This constituted the limiting case of failures in the product markets: utterly "missing markets" for critical products and services. Consequently, many firms had no choice but to diversify through vertical integration, providing for themselves what no one else could provide for them.[4]

There are today few missing product or service markets, yet vertical integration persists. There are two reasons, each related, but in very different ways, to failures in the market for information that lead to incomplete contracts: *opportunism* or *unspecifiability*.

In the case of opportunism, two parties transacting in a market might require mutual investment in highly specific assets. Once these investments have been made, one party, deliberately or not, will be in a position to "hold up" the other, depending on the relative value at stake. The classic example is the case of Fisher Auto Body and General Motors in the early part of the last century. Fisher invested in die casts for GM's auto bodies and was the sole supplier to GM. Faced with higher costs than expected, Fisher was able to "hold up" GM and extract higher prices to cover the overrun. GM was therefore the victim of a market failure, yet because Fisher was an independent company, GM had no managerial mechanisms to remedy the situation. Consequently, GM acquired Fisher, vertically integrating in order to eliminate the possibility of any future opportunism by Fisher.[5]

Unspecifiability arises when two parties attempt to contract for products or services the precise parameters of which remain, due to technological immaturity, poorly understood and comparatively vague. For example, between 1999 and 2003 attempts to create legal online music services such as Pressplay, Rhapsody, MusicNet, and MusicNow generally failed. There were at least two reasons: first, their relative inability to create an economic model that appealed to all the relevant parties; and second, their relative inability to create a service that customers found easy to use. For example, most of these services required monthly fees even if you never downloaded a single song. In addition, the piracy protection was seen by many as intrusive, and managing the music across your computer, your MP3 player, and any CD you might want to burn was clunky, at best.

In contrast, Apple's iTunes music store, launched in 2003, has been a huge hit, and in 2006 enjoyed more than 80 percent of all legal music downloads. A big part of the reason is that Apple integrated the critical elements of what was, in 2003, an immature technology. By creating both the online service and the music-playing device, Apple was spared the burden of capturing value with just its online service; it could compensate for whatever reluctance consumers might have to paying "fair value" for online music through increased sales of its iPod music player. In addition, because Apple made the software for both the service and the device, the user experience was far superior, and Apple could also keep the piracy protection effective but largely invisible.

The organizational difference was that Apple was vertically integrated while its erstwhile competitors were not. Pressplay and others had to struggle with creating a value chain across multiple participants using legally binding contracts applied to messy, ill-understood, and constantly changing technologies and economic models. Apple's vertical integration allowed it to create and capture value along a much broader swath of the value chain. As a result, Apple created the far more successful online music service.[6]

Whether arising from opportunism or unspecifiability, vertical integration's advantages arise through a superior coordination of activities. Achieving this coordination requires the corporate office to intervene in divisional activities more than the corporate office of an unrelated diversifier might: competition between divisions that need to collaborate is potentially destructive.

At the same time, divisions can be expected to enjoy considerable autonomy with respect to how they seek to coordinate their actions. Divisions in a vertically integrated firm are likely to operate largely as independent firms transacting in a market, but enjoying the added benefit of easier and more complete communication. Occasionally, they also operate under restrictions with respect to whether or not they can use outside suppliers. Consequently, capturing *coordination* economies is best done under a *constraining* administrative system.

RELATED DIVERSIFICATION

Edith Penrose argued in her 1959 book, *The Theory of the Growth of the Firm,* that in order to prosecute successfully a given line of business, a firm must acquire two kinds of resources: physical resources (tangible things, such as plant, equipment, land, raw materials, etc.) and human resources (labor, clerical, technical, or managerial staff, etc.). More recent work has extended this list to include intangible or invisible assets, such as brand, patents, and intellectual property.[7]

Resources are defined as static bundles of potential services. In other words, a given resource can be employed in a variety of ways, and it is the way in which a resource is employed, not the resource itself, that determines its value in use. So, for example, a steel mill is potentially a dance hall or a place to make steel. The building, the furnaces and so on, are all simply resources, and their value depends on what you do with them.

A firm that has assembled the complement of resources necessary to compete successfully in a given product market is likely to find that at least some of its resources are not fully employed. For example, a firm might require a product research and development capability, which implies the hiring of engineers, the construction of laboratories and testing facilities, and so on. These resources come in fairly discrete units and so are not infinitely divisible. Consequently, firms are likely to find it difficult to balance precisely their research and development capability with, for example, their marketing and distribution function.

One possible outcome of this imbalance is that a firm's research and development function might well be able to undertake the development of more products than the firm's marketing function can cope with. In order to exploit fully the productive capacity of the resources devoted to research and development, the firm is motivated to expand its marketing and distribution to cope with additional products. But expanding the marketing and distribution capability is in turn likely to create an imbalance, requiring an expansion of, for example, the firm's production capacity. This "growth spiral," and its concomitant *de facto* product market diversification, is a particularly salient manifestation of the more prosaic observation that hot dogs come in packs of twelve and hot dog buns come in packs of eight. If you do not want to have anything left over, you need to keep buying packages of each until everything balances out.

Diversification motivated by the desire to exhaust fully the productive opportunities available to all of a firm's resources is likely to spiral outward from the "epicenter" of the firm's original complement of resources. Driven by a desire to acquire as few additional resources as possible in order to operate at capacity, firms will acquire additional resources that are "related" to their existing complement. For example, a company that creates computer graphics for movies might branch out into computer games in order to take fuller advantage of some of its programming resources. Firm diversification that is resource based is *related* diversification.

The only theoretical justification for allowing an excess of any one resource to drive diversification is the inability of the firm to sell this excess in the resource markets. For example, why could our graphics firm not simply sell the "leftover" time that its programmers have on their hands? The answer is that it is very difficult to create the kinds of contracts required to do this effectively. There is material uncertainty surrounding how much time will be available, and for how long. Many resources are simply not sufficiently divisible and specifiable to be bought and sold in sufficiently small increments.

Similarly, consider intangible assets such as brands, copyrights, or patents. A pharmaceutical company might hold a patent on a particular molecular formulation that it feels might have additional applications in, for example, veterinary science. It might lack the research capacity to explore this opportunity, and so could seek to sell the rights for veterinary applications to another pharmaceutical firm. For this additional application to be commercially viable, however, the selling firm might have to make available additional information that could compromise other product development opportunities. For example, there might be important drug interactions explored in order to enable human use that one needs to understand to sell the drug for veterinary use but that do not make sense to research simply for the veterinary application. Revealing the full science behind these interactions could undermine valuable competitive advantage. In these sorts of cases, companies cannot realize the full value of their resources because of a failure in the *resource* markets. Because the related diversification required to overcome this sort of market failure increases the operating *scope* of the firm, related diversifiers are said to capture *scope economies*.

Capturing scope economies requires a high degree of cooperation among operating divisions. Each division must be allowed and indeed rewarded for contributing to the success of the others, and the value of the contributions made can be difficult to assess. Recall: as with vertical integration, it is the failure of the market for key inputs that makes related diversification necessary. Consequently, "marking to market" the value of a given instance of cooperation is essentially impossible. As a result, one often sees more subjective evaluation systems, with a greater degree of compensation tied to the performance of the organization as a whole, rather than to the performance of individual divisions. In short, failures in the resource markets demand related diversification to capture scope economies through *cooperative* administrative systems.

STRATEGIC DIVERSIFICATION

Section 7.4 explores how diversification that creates real options on alternative strategies can create hedge risk in ways that investors cannot replicate. Does this show up in the performance of firms that diversify in this way?

Examining the performance implications of diversification is a tricky business at the best of times; the notes to Chapter 7 provide some references framing that debate. Attempting to capture the performance impact of strategic diversification presents an entirely new level of difficulty.

Strategic diversifiers might typically have a group of related or vertically integrated divisions and one or more unrelated divisions. The argument is that a division that represents a real option on a synergy is neither related nor vertically integrated with any divisions right now; if it were, its value would not lie in the *option* it creates on synergies but in the synergies it makes possible *now*. Consequently, a strategic diversifier will have at least some divisions in its portfolio that are unrelated to all the others, even though it is not seeking to capture the kinds of governance economies that traditional unrelated diversifiers seek. However, firms willing to seek future synergies (from either related or vertical connections) are likely to have some experience capturing similar synergies in the past, so they are less likely to have a completely unrelated portfolio. The archetypal strategic diversifier therefore has an unrelated division and a group of either vertically integrated or related divisions.

The research into strategic diversifiers was motivated by an implication of established corporate contingency theory. Specifically, if each "pure" diversification strategy (unrelated, vertically integrated, related) requires a particular administrative system to be most successful (competitive, constraining, and cooperative, respectively), then a portfolio that mixes diversification strategies will have to mix administrative structures. This promises to be difficult for two reasons. First, the defining characteristics of each administrative archetype are mutually exclusive. For example, divisional managers' compensation cannot both be predominantly tied to divisional performance (competitive systems to capture governance economies in an unrelated diversifier) and predominantly tied to overall firm performance (cooperative systems in a related diversifier to capture scope economies). Second, if a strategic diversifier were to employ a group structure to separate the unrelated from the related or vertically integrated divisions in order to implement the appropriate administrative structure on each group of similarly connected divisions, this would impose additional costs on the corporation without creating any additional benefits (recall: established corporate contingency theory cannot appeal to option value). Consequently, strategic diversifiers should suffer a performance penalty.

An analysis of the performance profile of dynamic diversifiers is consistent with these expectations. As measured by return on assets (ROA), dynamic diversifiers perform on a par with traditional diversifiers. That is, they gain nothing in the present. However, expectations of future performance, as measured by Tobin's q-value, tend to be materially higher for dynamic diversifiers than for unrelated, vertically integrated, or related diversified firms. Most intriguingly of all, these increased expectations are most visible when the overall level of volatility in the stock market is high, suggesting increased uncertainty surrounding prospects for the economy as a whole.[8]

In other words, strategic diversifiers enjoy operating performance that is equal to that of pure diversifiers, but their Tobin's q-values are higher, implying that investors expect hybrids to perform better than pure diversifiers in the future.[9] Strategic diversifiers are the most likely to create an exercisable option by acquiring an unrelated division that has the possibility of being transformed into a division that generates synergies similar to those captured by an existing integrated group in the corporate portfolio, resulting in an opportunity to capture additional synergies without having to master a new administrative structure.[10]

Strategic diversification can be summarized in much the same way as the three other established diversification profiles. Strategic diversification compensates for failures in the risk markets and creates *option* economies. Capturing this option value requires the relationships between the operating divisions and the corporate office to change over time, as discussed in section 7.4. Consequently, rather than crafting an administrative structure optimized for the needs of a given portfolio structure, a strategic diversifier must have a *dynamic* administrative structure.

FIGURE A-1 **MARKET FAILURE, DIVERSIFICATION STRATEGY, ADMINISTRATIVE SYSTEM, AND CORPORATE VALUE ADDED**

Market Failure	Diversification Strategy	Administrative System	Corporate Value Added
Capital markets	Unrelated	Competitive	Governance economies
Resource markets	Related	Cooperative	Scope economies
Product markets Information markets	Vertical	Constraining	Coordination economies
Risk markets	Strategic	Dynamic	Option economies

Source: Author's analysis.

1. Dundas, K. N. M., and P. R. Richardson (1980), "Corporate Strategy and the Concept of Market Failure," *Strategic Management Journal*, pp. 177–88.

2. Easily the most impressive body of work on diversification by a single group of researchers is the series of articles by Hill, Hitt, and Hoskisson during the 1990s. Through careful theoretical development and large-scale survey research, they establish "corporate contingency theory," in which the relationships between market failure, diversification strategy, corporate value added, and administrative systems are established. The only element of corporate diversification not explored explicitly in their scholarly work is the "strategic" diversification resulting from a real options-based corporate strategy. The principles they develop, however, are very useful in exploring this phenomenon. The list below is not exhaustive but should provide a sense of the depth of their research.

Hill, C. W. (1994), "Diversification and Economic Performance: Bringing Structure and Corporate Management Back Into the Picture," *Fundamental Issues in Strategy: A Research Agenda*. R. P. Rumelt, D. E. Schendel, and D. J. Teece. Boston, MA: Harvard Business School Press, pp. 297–322.

Hill, C. W., and R. E. Hoskisson (1987), "Strategy and Structure in the Multiproduct Firm," *Academy of Management Review*, Vol. 12, Iss. 2, pp. 331–41.

Hill, C. W. L. (1988), "Internal Capital Market Controls and Financial Performance in Multidivisional Firms," *The Journal of Industrial Economics*, Vol. 37, pp. 67–83.

Hill, C. W. L., M. A. Hitt, et al. (1992), "Cooperative Versus Competitive Structures in Related and Unrelated Diversified Firms," *Organizational Science*, Vol. 3, Iss. 4, pp. 501–21.

Hitt, M. A., R. E. Hoskisson, et al. (1997), "International Diversification: Effects on Innovation and Firm Performance in Product-Diversified Firms," *Academy of Management Journal*, Vol. 40, Iss. 4, pp. 767–98.

Hoskisson, R., C. Hill, et al. (1993), "The Multidivisional Structure: Organizational Fossil or Source of Value?" *Journal of Management*, Vol. 19, Iss. 2, pp. 269–98.

Hoskisson, R. E. (1987), "Multidivisional Structure and Performance: The Contingency of Diversification Strategy," *Academy of Management Journal*, Vol. 30, Iss. 4, pp. 625–44.

Hoskisson, R. E., J. S. Harrison, et al. (1991), "Capital Market Evaluation of M-Form Implementation and Diversification Strategy," *Strategic Management Journal*, Vol. 12, Iss. 4, pp. 271–79.

Hoskisson, R. E., and M. A. Hitt (1990), "Antecedents and Performance Outcomes of Diversification: A Review and Critique of Theoretical Perspectives," *Journal of Management*, Vol. 16, Iss. 2, pp. 461–509.

Hoskisson, R. E., M. A. Hitt, et al. (1993), "Construct Validity of an Objective (Entropy) Categorical Measure of Diversification Strategy," *Strategic Management Journal*, Vol. 14, Iss. 3, pp. 215–35.

3. Williamson, O. E. (1975), *Markets and Hierarchies*, New York: Free Press. See also Williamson, O. E. (1985), *The Economic Institutions of Capitalism*, New York: Free Press.

4. Chandler, A. D. (1977), *The Visible Hand: The Managerial Revolution in American Business*, Cambridge, MA: Harvard University Press. See also Livesay, H. C., and P. G. Porter (1969), "Vertical Integration in American Manufacturing, 1899–1948," *Journal of Economic History*, Vol. 29, Iss. 3, pp. 494–500.

5. Klein, B., R. G. Crawford, et al. (1978), "Vertical Integration, Appropriable Rents, and the Competitive Contracting Process," *Journal of Law and Economics* 21: 297–326; Harrigan, K. R. (1985), "Vertical Integration and Corporate Strategy," *Academy of Management Journal,* Vol. 28, Iss. 2, pp. 397–425.

6. Pogue, David (2003), "What Price Musical Glory," *New York Times* "Circuits" Column. Pogue's article is a practical and concrete discussion of more general issues explored at greater length in Christensen, Clayton M., M. E. Raynor, and Matt Verlinden (2001), "Skate to Where the Money Will Be," *Harvard Business Review* (November).

7. There is a broad literature in this space. Perhaps the seminal work is Itami, Hiroyuki (1987), *Mobilizing Invisible Assets,* Cambridge: Harvard University Press.

8. In what is only charitably described as a suggestive finding, an entirely subjective classification of industries into high, medium, and low levels of strategic uncertainty reveals that strategic diversification is most prevalent in industries characterized by high levels of strategic uncertainty, and that strategic diversifiers enjoy the most generous expectations premium in those same industries. High-strategic-uncertainty industries include the TMT industries mentioned in Chapter 7, as well as pharmaceuticals and health care. Medium-strategic-uncertainty industries include aerospace, automotive, and high-tech manufacturing. Low-strategic-uncertainty industries include airlines, agriculture, and oil and gas. In these industries, strategic diversification is rare and strategic diversifiers appear to suffer an expectations penalty.

9. Raynor, Michael E. (2000), "Hidden in Plain Sight: Hybrid Diversification, Economic Performance, and 'Real Options' in Corporate Strategy," in *Winning Strategy in a Deconstructing World* by R. Bresser, D. Heubal, M. Hitt, and R. Nixon, London: John Wiley & Sons, Chapter 4. When I did this research, I conceptualized what I have come to call "strategic" diversifiers as "hybrid" diversifiers in virtue of their deviation from "pure" unrelated, related, and vertical diversification strategies.

10. This is, admittedly, an approximation. Assessing a firm's diversification strategy as part of a large-scale, longitudinal empirical analysis requires the use of distressingly blunt instruments: the SIC codes of divisions as defined for reporting purposes in U.S. equity markets. Thankfully, whatever its shortcomings in any particular case, this approach has a long and respected tradition and when dealing with large populations of firms has tended to square with informed managerial intuitions and business practices.

For an assessment of the various diversification measurement methods and the overall usefulness of a SIC-based approach, see Lubatkin, M., H. Merchant, et al. (1993), "Construct Validity of Some Unweighted Product-Count Diversification Measures," *Strategic Management Journal,* Vol. 14, pp. 433–49; Hall, E. H., and C. H. St. John (1994), "A Methodological Note on Diversity Measurement," *Strategic Management Journal,* Vol. 15, pp. 153–68; Montgomery, C. (1982), "The Measurement of Firm Diversification: Some New Empirical Evidence," *Academy of Management Journal,* Vol. 25, Iss. 2, pp. 299–307; Hoskisson, R. E., M. A. Hitt, et al. (1993), "Construct Validity of an Objective (Entropy) Categorical Measure of Diversification Strategy," *Strategic Management Journal,* Vol. 14, Iss. 3, pp. 215–35.

SCENARIOS AT ALLIANT ENERGY

Boiling down all the possible combinations of states of drivers of uncertainty into a manageable number of scenarios can be daunting, but the process outlined below can make it tractable. Listing all the possible combinations can quickly reveal many scenarios that are implausible due to internal contradictions. For example, due to the inconsistency between "libertarian" policy and "suspicious" public opinion, all the possible scenarios that combine the states of these two drivers are eliminated. In addition, "robust" economic growth and "catastrophic" environmental conditions are unlikely, eliminating still more scenarios from detailed analysis.

Shaded boxes indicate a combination of states of drivers that appeared to be unlikely enough to render the scenario of which they were a part sufficiently implausible to dismiss from further consideration. The boxes capture combinations of states of drivers that described scenarios that were worth further consideration. The set of six captured here was further reduced to five by collapsing "Familiar Giants" and "Familiar Giants Pt. 2," for reasons explained in the main text.

The final scenarios are summarized in the second table in this appendix.

TABLE B-1 **DETERMINING THE FINAL SCENARIO SET**

		Drivers of Uncertainty			
Economy	Technology	Environment	Policy	Public Opinion	Scenario Name
Robust	Incremental	Benign	Libertarian	Trusting	Familiar Giants
Robust	Incremental	Benign	Libertarian	Suspicious	
Robust	Incremental	Benign	Marxist	Trusting	
Robust	Incremental	Benign	Marxist	Suspicious	Public Outcry
Robust	Incremental	Catastrophic	Libertarian	Trusting	
Robust	Incremental	Catastrophic	Libertarian	Suspicious	
Robust	Incremental	Catastrophic	Marxist	Trusting	
Robust	Incremental	Catastrophic	Marxist	Suspicious	
Robust	Radical	Benign	Libertarian	Trusting	Techno-World
Robust	Radical	Benign	Libertarian	Suspicious	
Robust	Radical	Benign	Marxist	Trusting	
Robust	Radical	Benign	Marxist	Suspicious	
Robust	Radical	Catastrophic	Libertarian	Trusting	
Robust	Radical	Catastrophic	Libertarian	Suspicious	
Robust	Radical	Catastrophic	Marxist	Trusting	
Robust	Radical	Catastrophic	Marxist	Suspicious	

Drivers of Uncertainty

Economy	Technology	Environment	Policy	Public Opinion	Scenario Name
Stagnate	Incremental	Benign	Libertarian	Trusting	Familiar Giants Pt. 2
Stagnate	Incremental	Benign	Libertarian	Suspicious	
Stagnate	Incremental	Benign	Marxist	Trusting	
Stagnate	Incremental	Benign	Marxist	Suspicious	Sustained Recession
Stagnate	Incremental	Catastrophic	Libertarian	Trusting	
Stagnate	Incremental	Catastrophic	Libertarian	Suspicious	
Stagnate	Incremental	Catastrophic	Marxist	Trusting	
Stagnate	Incremental	Catastrophic	Marxist	Suspicious	Enviro-Meltdown
Stagnate	Radical	Benign	Libertarian	Trusting	
Stagnate	Radical	Benign	Libertarian	Suspicious	
Stagnate	Radical	Benign	Marxist	Trusting	
Stagnate	Radical	Benign	Marxist	Suspicious	
Stagnate	Radical	Catastrophic	Libertarian	Trusting	
Stagnate	Radical	Catastrophic	Libertarian	Suspicious	
Stagnate	Radical	Catastrophic	Marxist	Trusting	
Stagnate	Radical	Catastrophic	Marxist	Suspicious	

Source: Alliant Energy; author's analysis; data disguised.

TABLE B-2 **SCENARIO SUMMARIES**

Scenario Name	Summary
Familiar Giants	With the downfall of energy merchants with limited assets such as Enron, public opinion supports the traditional purveyors of power—IOUs that have substantial asset bases and are unlikely to default on their obligations. In general, market regulation encourages competition among numerous participants. However, a number of legal and regulatory hurdles, which were designed to ensure that energy contracts will not be defaulted upon, inhibit the ability of smaller companies (or companies with limited assets) to compete. Larger IOUs, including a number of foreign competitors, are seen as bringing stability (and credibility) to volatile energy markets. Additionally, a number of Oil & Gas majors have begun to acquire generation assets and energy-trading organizations. Significant industry consolidation takes place as regulatory approval policy reflects the public perception that "bigger is better."
Public Outcry	Although the general economy is experiencing moderate—if somewhat uneven—growth, the energy industry is still struggling with the backlash of events from early in the decade. The results of early efforts to deregulate energy markets have convinced energy consumers that deregulation cannot possibly benefit them in any way. In fact, previous failures to identify and implement a market structure that works have left customers feeling that they are bearing the brunt of those failures through significantly higher energy prices. Customers are actively calling for strict regulation of all aspects of the energy industry. This call to end experiments with free energy markets and for the strict reregulation of the industry is taking somewhat extreme forms in many areas of the country. Some opponents are calling for full "federalization" of the system; however, this subset of consumers is generally considered radical. This idea is being carried out to some extent through the increasing municipalization of utility infrastructure. Municipal ownership and operation of utility systems is viewed as the best way of eliminating the risk that many now view as having run rampant under deregulation experiments. Similarly, failed deregulation experiments have left investors with a negative perception of the industry. Even with calls for reregulation, they are wary of as-yet-unidentified ways for energy companies to "game the system" and exert market power. Other sectors of the economy are beginning to demonstrate increased growth over that experienced early in the decade and are viewed as much less risky than energy. Industry participants are, therefore, finding themselves struggling to raise the capital needed to meet their proposed expenditures and available capital tends to be deployed to meet infrastructure upgrade requirements and for incremental technological improvements. No breakthroughs are made that materially advance the way that customer requirements are supplied.

Scenario Name	Summary
	The environment continues to be a concern as scientific evidence of global warming continues to mount. And, although no catastrophic phenomena have occurred to cause environmental issues to be the highest priority, public opinion is influencing policy makers to implement increasingly stringent environmental controls. Among these controls are strict requirements for siting of new energy infrastructure—for example, generating plants and transmission lines.
Techno-World	After several decades of incremental technological improvements, a number of significant breakthroughs begin to take place. Distributed generation and most renewable energy sources are still more expensive than centrally generated fossil fuels, but the cost gap is quickly decreasing. At the same time, demand for these technologies has increased exponentially, fueled by a heightened awareness that long-term substitutes must be found for fossil fuels and a renewed emphasis be put upon energy quality and reliability (e.g., high-tech manufacturing). Technological breakthroughs are not limited to the energy industry—significant technological advances have been made in many areas, and these advances are driving productivity growth and significant economic expansion. Skepticism over the California energy crisis and Enron has faded into the background as some jurisdictions are seeing positive results from deregulation.
Sustained Recession	Under this scenario, the U.S. economy is experiencing a period of sustained repression that is much like that witnessed in Japan over the past decade. The U.S. economy is hampered by continued lack of growth, with small gains in GDP growth found to be unsustainable and quickly reversed. Traditional monetary policy measures (e.g., control of interest rates and monetary supply) are not able to stabilize the economy, and the general consensus is that extreme measures will be required to "shock" the economy back into growth mode. The sustained repression has led to actual price deflation through continued use of discounts in an attempt to boost consumer spending. As a result, consumer confidence is badly shaken and consumer spending has been reduced to bare essentials. Similarly, investors have exited the capital markets and are looking to preserve what liquidity they have. Corporate capital spending, like consumer spending, has been squeezed to minimal levels as well. All of these events combine to create a self-perpetuating cycle. Scientific evidence of global warming continues to point to significant environmental deterioration. However, because of economic woes, the strict measures that might otherwise be called for are put off until more prosperous times and current policies are enhanced incrementally in an effort to stave off disaster. Energy customers and investors alike have called for reregulation of the industry. The energy-price volatility experienced under

Scenario Name	Summary
	deregulated markets earlier in the decade is viewed as being a significant contributor to the current economic stagnation. Investors are bitter from the losses they incurred when many unregulated energy players failed spectacularly, and the customers, who were left to pay for these failures through price increases, are fervent about the need for strict regulation of the industry. As a result of this overwhelmingly negative attitude, capital availability is even more restrictive for energy companies and every decision made and action taken is heavily reviewed by multiple regulators.
Enviro-Meltdown	A number of highly publicized environmental catastrophes, including several public-health epidemics linked to environmental contamination by power providers, focus public attention on the environment. There is a renewed public interest in taking immediate action to reverse negative environmental effects, even if such action will result in more expensive electricity. Global institutions push for environmental reforms and global minimal environmental standards, requiring wealthier nations to subsidize environmental efforts of developing nations. Domestically, federal and state governments react by enacting legislation that further protects the environment through emission restrictions, as well as through subsidies of renewable energy sources.

Source: Alliant Energy; author's analysis; data disguised.

REAL OPTION VALUATION

Discounted cash flow (DCF) valuation techniques, such as net present value (NPV) analysis, are well-understood and widely used tools for comparing investment opportunities. Using these tools requires predicting the cash flows associated with a given project and then discounting the associated cash flows into present-day currency using an appropriate risk-adjusted rate. For example, building a new manufacturing plant might have negative cash flows in early periods as a result of the costs of building the plant, followed by positive cash flows as a result of selling the plant's production. A terminal value is ascribed to the project at the limit of one's confidence in the cash-flow projections. If the discounted cash flows have a value of 0 or more, then the project is said to clear its hurdle rate and is a profitable investment. This approach is illustrated below.

Highly uncertain investment environments reveal the many weaknesses of this approach. For example, a common practice is to increase the discount rate applied to highly uncertain cash flows, thereby reducing their value. However, uncertainty raises the possibility of pleasant surprises as

FIGURE C-1 **A TRADITIONAL NPV PROJECTION**

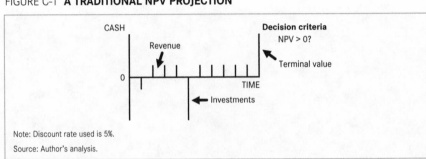

Note: Discount rate used is 5%.

Source: Author's analysis.

well as downside risk. Consequently, arbitrarily increasing the discount rate serves only to penalize uncertainty when, in fact, as with financial options, higher levels of uncertainty surrounding an investment's outcome might actually make that investment more attractive.

To try and cope with this fact, more sophisticated NPV approaches include the use of expected NPV (eNPV). Most often, this takes the form of estimating a high, medium, and low outcome to a project. Probabilities are assigned to each outcome, and the eNPV of the project is the weighted average of the three NPV calculations.

When projects are all or nothing in nature, this is an appropriate response. However, many projects have naturally occurring stages, or can be made to have stages, which implies that the full investment required to implement a given project is not made all at once. Rather, an organization can invest some money to learn something about how best to pursue an opportunity in order to maximize both the probability and the magnitude of a favorable outcome. In such instances, even eNPV approaches are inadequate, because they penalize potentially valuable flexibility in implementation.

To see why, consider two possible cash flows associated with launching a new product. In the first instance, the product is launched at a cost of $175. The eNPV of this launch is $1.19.

Implementing a preliminary market test, at a cost of $15, allows the firm to update its assessment of the probability of the high, medium, or low outcomes. In eNPV terms, however, the test serves only to increase the negative cash flows at the outset (due to the cost of the test) and delay the positive future cash flows by one period. As a result, a market test serves to depress the eNPV of the product launch to –$13.87. The test would appear to be a bad idea.

FIGURE C-2 **A TRADITIONAL EXPECTED VALUE CALCULATION**

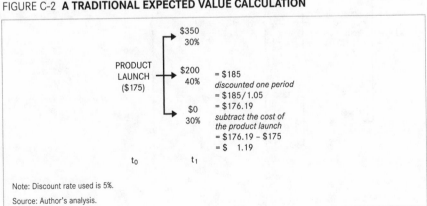

Note: Discount rate used is 5%.

Source: Author's analysis.

What this approach ignores is that managers can respond to the information that the test gives them. Specifically, if the test has an unfavorable outcome, the NPV of a product launch is significantly negative: –$139.89. Consequently, the product would not be launched at all if the test were negative. If the test results are uncertain or positive, the NPV of a launch is above $0—at $8.33 and $127.38, respectively—then a launch makes sense.

The test, in other words, can be seen as an option on the launch: it purchased for the company the right, but not the obligation, to make further investments—namely, the $175 required to launch the product. At a cost of $15, the test yields a present value to the overall project of $34.30, since the expected negative present value of launching in the face of a negative test result is avoided, and the eNPVs are simply the probability-weighted outcomes of results with positive eNPVs. The result is a net option value (NOV) for the project of $19.30—more than ten times the eNPV of the product launch with no test, while an eNPV approach to valuing the test yielded a negative NPV.

Finally, it is important to note that flexibility is not always worth the cost. In this instance, if the market test had cost more than $34.30, the most

FIGURE C-3 **COMPARING EXPECTED VALUE WITH NET OPTION VALUE**

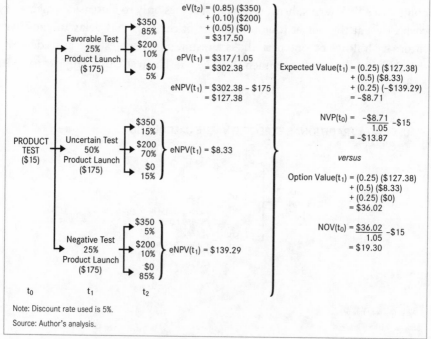

Note: Discount rate used is 5%.

Source: Author's analysis.

appropriate response would be simply to launch the product, since the eNPV of the launch is positive. A systematic approach to determining the NOV of flexibility provides the information needed to decide when it is worth the investment.

Of course, this approach is but the simplest of those available. Real option valuation techniques can be enormously sophisticated. Occasionally, however, that sophistication can get in the way of providing useful decision-making support, largely because the inputs required to apply the more powerful and subtle approaches are often unavailable. As a result, I have found it useful to use valuation techniques that facilitate a strategic discussion and keep all the assumptions very close to the surface. After all, much of what is being discussed are subjective judgments about what the future might hold, and highly precise computations based on necessarily imprecise assumptions are of limited value.

This exerpt is adapted with permission from the 2001 Deloitte research study "Strategic Flexibility in the Financial Services Sector: Creating Competitive Advantage Out of Competitive Turbulence" by Michael E. Raynor. The original study can be found at www.deloitte.com/research.

INDEX

ABOUT THE AUTHOR

Michael E. Raynor is a consultant with Deloitte Consulting LLP and a Deloitte Research Distinguished Fellow. He works with senior executives in the world's leading corporations across a wide range of industries, including telecommunications, media and entertainment, pharmaceuticals, medical devices, energy, and manufacturing. He lectures around the world to audiences of all sizes on corporate and competitive strategy.

In his client work and research, Michael explores the challenges of corporate strategy and innovation. His first book, *The Innovator's Solution*, coauthored with Professor Clayton M. Christensen, has been on the *Wall Street Journal* and *New York Times* bestseller lists and won several "best book of the year" awards in 2003.

In addition, Dr. Raynor has published extensively in managerial and academic journals and teaches in the MBA and Executive Education programs at the Richard Ivey School of Business at the University of Western Ontario in London, Canada.

Dr. Raynor holds an undergraduate degree in philosophy from Harvard University, where he was a John Harvard Scholar; an MBA from Ivey, where he was awarded the Nelson M. Davis Memorial Scholarship; and a DBA from the Harvard Business School, where he was awarded the George S. Dively award for research excellence. He lives in Mississauga, Canada.